Black Soldiers of the Queen

The Natal Native Contingent in the Anglo-Zulu War

P. S. THOMPSON

THE UNIVERSITY OF ALABAMA PRESS
Tuscaloosa

The University of Alabama Press
Tuscaloosa, Alabama 35487-0380

Library of Congress Cataloging-in-Publication Data

Thompson, P. S. (Paul Singer)
Black soldiers of the queen : the Natal native contingent in the Anglo-Zulu War / P.S. Thompson.— Rev. ed.
p. cm.
Includes bibliographical references.
ISBN-13: 978-0-8173-5368-1 (pbk. : alk. paper)
ISBN-10: 0-8173-5368-2
1. Zulu War, 1879. 2. Zulu War, 1879—Regimental histories. 3. Great Britain. Army—Colonial forces—South Africa—History—19th century.
I. Title.
DT1875.T45 2006
968.4'045—dc22
2006000238

THE NATAL NATIVE CONTINGENT IN THE ANGLO-ZULU WAR 1879

P. S. Thompson

ISBN 0-620-30298-4
Revised Edition, 2003

The author wishes to express his appreciation to the University of Natal Research Fund for its financial assistance in the preparation of this work, especially the cartography. The opinions expressed and the conclusions reached in this work are the author's and not those of the University or Fund.

The financial assistance of the Centre for Science Development towards the publication of this work is hereby acknowledged. Opinions expressed in this publication and conclusions arrived at are those of the author and are not necessarily to be attributed to the Centre for Science Development.

CONTENTS

LIST OF MAPS

ABBREVIATIONS USED IN NOTES

AJLC	A.J. Lucking, private collection
BGV	Bergville, magistrate's records (NAD)
C	Command (British parliamentary paper)
CFP	Carl Faye Papers (NAD)
CP	Chelmsford Papers (NAM; microfilm in NAD)
CSO	Colonial Secretary's Office, records (NAD)
GH	Government House, i.e. records of the Governor (NAD)
GN	Government Notice
GO	Government Orders
GTN	Greytown, magistrate's records (NAD)
KCAL	Killie Campbell Africana Library (Durban)
DCM	Killie Campbell Africana Library (Durban)
NA	*Natal Advertizer*
NAD	Natal Archives Depôt
NAM	National Army Museum (London)
NC	*Natal Colonist*
NGG	*Natal Government Gazette*
NM	*Natal Mercury*
NW	*Natal Witness*
PMB	Pietermaritzburg, magistrate's records (NAD)
RM	Resident Magistrate
RMD	Richmond, magistrate's records (NAD)
SNA	Secretary for Native Affairs, records (NAD)
SP	Shepstone Papers (NAD)
TN	*Times of Natal*
VLM	Verulam, magistrate's records (NAD)
WC	Evelyn Wood papers (NAD)
WO	War Office, records (Public Records Office, Kew)

PREFACE TO THE AMERICAN EDITION

In 1964 the release of the film *Zulu*, starring Stanley Baker and Michael Caine, and in 1965 the publication of the book *The Washing of the Spears*, written by Donald Morris, generated a popular interest in the Anglo-Zulu War which has endured to the present day. Numerous books and television documentaries have appeared, and at the time of the centenary another movie, *Zulu Dawn*. By this time the Anglo-Zulu War is probably the best known of Queen Victoria's small wars of empire. *Zulu* has attained iconic status. The *Journal* of the Anglo-Zulu War Historical Society is in its seventeenth year.

Why is this so?

Apart from the real dramatic appeal in the events of the war, some of them vividly if not always accurately captured in the books and films, there are certain intrinsic factors underpinning the popular interest. The war was short – just eight months long – and the course of it was simple: British invasion, defeat, invasion again, victory (and the reverse, of course, for the Zulu). There were half a dozen short, pitched battles, and a dozen or so attractive or intriguing personalities to reckon with. It was a case of imperialism (or colonialism) against an indigenous people defending their independence, Europe against Africa, white against black. The average reader easily grasps the outline and main features and then fits in the dramatic details.

Yet in all the literature on the war simplification has resulted in an omission. The war was not simply one of white against black, colonial against native. Over half of the fighting men in the invading British army were blacks from the Colony of Natal, and they served the Queen willingly. They have not fared well at the hands of popular or scholarly writers.

This book tells the story of the Natal Native Contingent, those Africans in the imperial service. It arose out of research on the Colony of Natal in the war and a desire to develop fully the role of the black soldiers of the Queen. It was written for a local readership, with the intention of providing a comprehensive narrative in painstaking detail, for it seemed unlikely any other would appear, given the prejudices of the day. I hope that it has served the memory of these soldiers well, and am pleased that their deeds may become known to foreign readers as well.

FOREWORD

The Broken Statue

In the Court Gardens across the street from the City Hall in Pietermaritzburg, the capital of the colony and then the province of Natal, are the monuments in memory of those who served and fell in the Anglo-Zulu, South African and World Wars. During the evening of Wednesday, April 13, 1994, one of the four statues on the base of the Anglo-Zulu war monument was dislodged and fell on the pavement. The local newspaper showed a photograph of the statue. Evidently it had been pulled off or thrown down from the plinth. The head, arms and legs were broken off, as were many small pieces, as a result of the fall and perhaps an afterthought of destruction. The press report referred to it as the statue of a "colonist" and a "civilian settler". It was removed for restoration without further comment.

The following day a friend asked if I saw any significance in the destruction. The statue in fact represented an African soldier of the Natal Native Contingent. Its visage and dress differentiated it from the statues representing the European soldiers and sailor. Was breaking it an act of vandalism or a political statement? We considered. The monument was surmounted by the female figure of Victory, quite out of reach. Each of the four statues below stood on a corner of the plinth, within easy reach, but a person would have to look rather carefully to distinguish which represented whom of Her Majesty's loyal subjects. The one that had been broken was at the back of the monument, facing the garden and less noticeable from the street.

Position rather than politics made it particularly vulnerable. We frankly doubted that those who pulled it down either knew or cared that it represented an African soldier.

Doubt in this instance arose from the fact that so little has been said or written about the African soldier in the Anglo-Zulu war that he is virtually its unknown soldier. About half of the British army which invaded Zululand in 1879 consisted of African soldiers, yet the ample literature on the war contains very little about them. And the reason for this is partly political, partly cultural. In the heyday of empire the European had no time to glorify the feats of indigenes, unless they were the reflective ones of a foe. In the wake of empire the African had no desire to glorify them, unless they were feats of resistance. In popular historical perspective the Natal Native Contingent, as the Africans in the imperial service were collectively called, represented collaboration in colonial rule, egregiously incorrect politically and best forgot. It is fairly safe to say the new history textbooks for South Africa are hardly likely to mention the contingent at all.

The cultural reason for the obscurity is racialistic. The literature of the war has a predominantly European readership, and this readership has evinced practically no interest in what non-Europeans, except for the enemy, did in the war. The potential African readership probably will be pre-empted by the political considerations just mentioned. It would suit broad African and narrow Zulu nationalist aspirations alike to portray the war as a black-white struggle.

Then why write the history of the Natal Native Contingent? Is it not better the African soldier of the Queen remains unknown. Let the broken statue be of a "colonist". To raise his ghost might add another element to internecine strife in the province.

One reason for this work is that the history of the war, military and political, as embodied in the ample literature, is still incomplete, and a full understanding of it cannot be had until the important part in it played by the majority of the people of Natal is told. The Natal Native Contingent constituted much of that military and political contribution.

Another reason is that the prejudice in favour of seeing a conflict between African and European, between black and white, denies many brave men their meed of praise and distorts our appreciation of the past, just when a composition of old animosities is very much needed.

On March 20, 1996 the statue of the African soldier, restored with great care, returned to the Court Gardens. The local newspaper carried a photograph and a report, which now referred to the "soldier". If only what he represents were better known and what is long forgot were recalled. After all the monument was erected in 1883 "in memory of Honour and in hope of Peace".

Chapter 1

THE COMING OF THE WAR

Peace and war

'A curious phenomenon occurred 7th January,' a Christian missionary in the Upper Umkomanzi Division wrote in 1878. 'A bright star appeared near the moon at noonday, the sun shining brightly – *Omen* – The natives from this foretold the coming war with the Amazulu'.[1]

A year later the British and Zulu fought that war. The British, enjoying superior organization, technology and communications, brought the force of empire to bear and defeated and destroyed the Zulu kingdom. British motives in provoking the war ranged from political aggrandizement to economic exploitation, as was the case in most imperialist wars of the nineteenth century, but there was a defensive motive as well. The Zulu kingdom had emerged as a warfare state and as such posed a threat to the stability of southeastern Africa. That threat had to be removed.

The war lasted nine months and had four phases. First, the British army invaded the Zulu country but retreated after a disastrous defeat at Isandlwana. Second, the British stood on the defensive. The imperial forces regrouped and were reinforced. The Zulu state gained no advantage from its temporary ascendancy. Third, the imperial army invaded the Zulu country again, and inflicted a severe defeat on the Zulu at Ulundi. Finally, the British pacified the country and captured the Zulu King, exiled him and broke up his kingdom into thirteen chiefdoms.

The British launched their attacks on the Zulu kingdom from the colony of Natal, which bordered the Zulu country on the south and west. When the war began, Her Majesty's subjects were all involved in it, however close by or distant from the actual fighting. The population of the Colony was estimated at that time to be 361 587, of whom only 26 654 were Europeans and some 16 999 were Indians. The great majority of people – 319 935 – were Africans.[2] Why should Africans support Europeans against other Africans? Why should African chiefs support the Great Queen faraway against the Zulu King near by?

For support the colonial power they did. They owed much to the British and little to the Zulu. The British had brought peace to a land ravaged by warfare, the source of which had been Zulu expansion. The British had introduced order to a land where there had been anarchy. The British did not kill people and steal their cattle, but the Zulu and their client peoples had done so.[3] The Zulu people regarded themselves as superior to all others.[4] So perhaps did the British, but they did not translate their superiority so directly into oppression.

The British had established the Colony of Natal as an offshoot of the Cape Colony, that is, the more developed and extensive territory which formed the hinterland of their base at Cape Town, at the southern tip of Africa. British traders had been active on a small scale at Port Natal, but it was the intrusion of Dutch farmers into Natal that had obliged the British government to intervene in the region. These Dutch farmers had left the Cape and with it, they supposed, British rule. They had obtained from the Zulu King the cession of most of the land which Natal later encompassed. The Zulu King had distrusted them and sent his army to rout them out, but they had recovered from the blow and in turn defeated the Zulu. Then they had allied with and elevated a pretender to the Zulu throne, and claimed more land in compensation.

The Dutch farmers laid claim to extensive tracts of land, but their government was largely nominal. It wielded little power after the wars of conquest. There was peace with the Zulu. The cessation of Zulu raids and of destructive marches of fugitive chiefdoms to escape the Zulu made the Dutch republic a haven. People who had lived there before or who saw advantage in doing so now came to settle. The Dutch feared they were being swamped – or would be swamped – by unwanted hordes. It was not a stable situation, irrespective of the peace. Moreover the Dutch were still British subjects, notwithstanding their putative secession from the empire. So the British government intervened in 1843, liquidated the Dutch republic of Natalia, and established the Colony of Natal in 1845.[5]

British rule was not followed by a massive immigration of Britons. In the first seven years less than five thousand came. The relatively small groups brought to settle did not do well at farming and many gathered in the towns – Port Natal, renamed

Durban, and Pietermaritzburg, the former Dutch and now the British seat of government – and in small villages. Most of the Dutch farmers left the Colony. Speculators bought up many of the farms and as absentee landlords charged modest rents. The rest of the land belonged to the British Crown, by virtue of its paramountcy and by default of any European claimant. The people who lived on the land did not understand what Europeans meant by property in land. They considered it within a chief's power to assign its use to homesteads.[6]

The life of the people in fact was little changed by British rule, at least early on. The British Supreme Chief and his head men, *viz.* the Lieutenant Governor and the Secretary for Native Affairs, Resident Magistrates and Administrators of Native Law, interfered as little as possible with their way of life. Of course, they demanded service and tribute from time to time, and in unaccustomed ways, such as work on roads and money from homesteads. Otherwise what changes occurred were largely the result of increased trade and communications, which offered new merchandise and opportunities to make money, a new medium of exchange. These were consequences of the British coming, but they did not appear to be part of a British plan to overhaul the existing way of life.[7]

A chief remained leader of his people. Chieftaincy was hereditary, a selected son of the Great Wife succeeding his father. Where the chiefdom had many people or was far-flung the chiefs' head men were responsible for the government and administration of the sections. The chief had the power to distribute land for use in the area in which his people lived. It was at his great place that the leading men gathered with him to hear complaints about abuses and violations of custom, and what they decided had the force of law.

The largest chiefdoms also had military organization. Youths at a certain age would be called up for service, no longer for fighting, but rather for special work at the chief's place and to celebrate the annual Feast of the First Fruits. This age set, the *ibutho*, enjoyed a life-time with its members, whether it was embodied for the chief's purposes or dispersed to their homes in the long intervals between.[8]

For a generation family life retained its orderly, predictable existence. The head of the homestead was chief of his family – wives, to whatever number he preferred, could afford and attract, and his children, as well as elderly and collateral members who depended upon him for sustenance and protection. Within the family unit everyone had a place and life was measured out in relationships, duties and rites from birth to death.[9] The spirits of ancestors lived in and around the homestead, and sometimes intervened in its affairs in the form of animals or in dreams. If they were unhappy, untoward things happened. They must be honoured and appeased.[10]

If things went seriously wrong then some baleful force was at work. It was not for the head or the elders to sort out. Rather, a diviner, especially inspired and skilled to such tasks, should be summoned, and would ferret out the malefactor. The wrongdoer must be punished and the wrongdoing must be offset by certain observances and medications.[11] Thus the harmony of communal life would be preserved.

Wives and daughters had there duties. These included keeping the hut and its furnishings tidy, cooking the food and maintaining the utensils, and hoeing and planting the patches outside the circular enclosure of the homestead. Husbands and sons looked after the cattle, which were the wealth of the family, the most acceptable medium of exchange. They did the heavy work of building and the hunting;[12] however, game was becoming scarce in these times, with ever more people and settled ways.[13]

Corn and milk were the staples of the diet, eked out by vegetables and fruits, and such meat as could be had – cattle were slaughtered only for special occasions. One usually ate well in the wet summer, unless there was some pestilence or exceptional drought, and ate much less in the dry winter, as stores became depleted. None the less the diet was generally balanced and even Europeans commented favourably on the fine physique and good health of the people.[14]

In good seasons life could be easy. There were celebrations, those that marked the rites of passage and the first fruits of the harvest. They afforded time for talk and song. Chance encounters and visits meant cheerful conversation, and opportunity to dip snuff and perhaps smoke cannabis.[15] People were generally of a complaisant disposition. They did things together and their complaisancy made for greater harmony.[16]

All this was possible because there was peace in the land. The British held the Zulu at bay. The inroads of the Zulu or their clients' armies were no more. The troubles which the Zulu Kings Shaka and Dingane had apparently unleashed upon the country were at an end. Fugitive chiefdoms on the move no longer moved back and forth, eating up the people and being eaten up by each other. Among the wanderers and sufferers were the amaHlubi and the amaNgwane, who came to rest beneath the mountains upcountry, the amaChunu and the aba-

Thembu, who settled along the middle Thukela, and the amaQwabe, at the coast. All would furnish levies to the Natal Native Contingent. All had once lived in what was now Zululand and had left or been driven out in the time of troubles.[17]

The colonial government later conjectured that the number of people living in what was to be Natal at the end of the troubles amounted to no more than 13–14 000.[18] Peace meant security. Refugees began to flow in. There had been relatively few people in Natal in the early 1840s – under Dutch rule. Estimates vary between 20 000 and 42 000. With British rule many more people came to Natal. By the mid to late 1840s the population was estimated at between 75 and 100 000. Refugees from elsewhere, especially Zululand itself, continued to flow into the Colony.[19] With natural increase the African population grew to about 320 000 in 1879.

Peace and stability thus brought problems. There probably was land enough for all, but it was distributed unevenly.[20] The chiefdoms which existed at the time or came into Natal soon after had been greatly concerned with security and occupied rugged fastnesses which were less tillable.[21] The white settlers, though few in number, practised a different form of agriculture and bought and sold tracts of land. Very early on they claimed much of the arable land, even though they could not cultivate or graze it all.[22]

What need had a man for a large piece of land? The homestead grew what it needed, to consume and to lay by until the next harvest, and more was plenty, surplus for the chief. Of course, more people meant more homesteads and more cattle required more land for grazing. Yet there was more land for grazing – empty land which the Crown and Europeans said was theirs but which they did not occupy or use. The Crown did not charge rental. Absentee landlords sometimes charged and sometimes did not. The charges were not oppressive.[23]

It was only on white farmers' land that there was much friction. Some white farmers charged rental, but more often they demanded work of their tenants. If one did not comply, he ran the risk of fines – or more insulting, flogging – and even eviction. If evicted he might have to go back to the Location, that is, the place which the colonial government had set aside exclusively for occupation by his chiefdom.[24] By the late 1870s some of the Locations were becoming crowded, in that poor land no longer subsisted many people except in poverty.[25]

The British government had anticipated such problems. It had had a very chequered career with colonies all around the world for over two hundred years, and experience foretold that there would be competition here for resources between white and black settlers, and that it must regulate it to prevent hostility and violence. There was land for all. It should be allocated according to how many people there were and how they would use it.[26]

The result had been that in 1847 a government commission had set aside about two million acres or one sixth the land area of the Colony as 'Locations' for chiefdoms. Much of the land was on the periphery of the Colony. Between 1846 and 1849 seven Locations were established. By 1864 there were forty-two Locations, but most of the new ones were small and situated in the southwest.[27] Perhaps two-fifths of the African population lived in the Locations in 1879. The majority of the African people lived on Crown lands and European farm lands.[28]

There had been plans to set up schools in the Locations and to instruct people in European crafts, but these had not materialized for want of money and personnel. Most people were not interested in European education. Christian missionaries offered some basic schooling of the European kind, but to what good? The white settlers said the education spoilt people for work. It certainly unfitted them for settled life in the homestead.[29]

Christianity was the religion of Europe, not of Africa. Initially the missions took in displaced persons and deviants of one sort or another. Conversion practically alienated them from the great majority of people. The so-called converts were likely to backslide under pressure or from disillusionment. Only at a few places did the converts establish communities on the European model. Stations such as Edendale and Driefontein (Methodist), Mvoti (Congregationalist), New Germany (Lutheran), Springvale (Anglican), were outstanding examples.[30] They pointed a way to the future perhaps, but it was a future without the established African values.

The missionaries – a variety of sectarians, devoted and often skilled – battled to instil the tenets of the Christian faith.[31] They had spoken of the Great One – Nkulunkulu, or Mvelinqangi, the first deity in existence but now remote – and likened him to their Christian God; but most people had never thought much of Nkulunkulu, or confused him with other aboriginal deities. Their immediate concern was with the spirits of their ancestors. Indeed, there had been some people who did not remember a great one at all.[32]

Worse, missionaries attacked the very cornerstone of society, marriage, by forbidding Christians to have more than one wife and treating the bride's joining the groom and the transfer of cattle from a groom's to the bride's father's homesteads to cement the union as though it were an exchange of chattels. In their eyes the man bought the woman and she became his slave. It was absurd. What wife could hold up her head in the homestead without the customary transfer of cattle? She would not respect herself, nor could she expect the respect of others. The missionaries would rend society asunder. No chief encouraged them. Some positively opposed them. The British government knew their shortcomings. White farmers despised them as much as black settlers did.[33]

The missionaries made little progress. Apart from the exceptions mentioned, their efforts to convert people were a failure. Only between three and four per cent of Africans were Christians.[34]

More threatening to the ordered life of chiefdom and homestead was the lure of towns and villages and the influence of European ways. In town or village, especially young people, would earn money for themselves and lose the habits of respect and discipline which characterized homestead life. It was true that money would be used to buy cattle, which were still the real basis of wealth and the means to marriage, but the established way of life had become vitiated. Elders increasingly complained of the insubordinate behaviour of young people, both male and female, especially those who knew town life.[35]

There was no denying the markets of the towns, where homesteaders sold corn and other produce to feed Europeans and to buy hoes and pots and cloth and beads and other manufactures for their own use. Chiefs might keep a check on this trade and restrict profits by limiting land needed to produce for sale. And apart from the iron plough and hoe, and the wagon, there was no point in imitating the white farmer's techniques, certainly not in the Locations. A man could not break away from his chief to become an independent producer. A man could not apply innovation in cultivation without arousing suspicion of sorcery.[36]

The British recognized and sustained chiefs and chiefdoms. Fifty-three chiefs had claimed hereditary status when the British had established the Colony.[37] Where there had been peoples without chiefs, because of the destruction and anarchy wrought by the troubles, the government had grouped such peoples together and appointed chiefs.[38] There were ninety-nine recognized hereditary chiefs thirty-five years later. There were also forty-six appointed chiefs and head men,[39] although they did not, of course, enjoy the reputation of hereditary ones. The point is the government left no room for loose persons, at least not legally. Every man had his chief, every chief had his people. Ideally they would be living together in one place, though in practice they might live in several places.[40]

A man might switch his allegiance. A succession to rule might be disputed and lead to a division of the chiefdom. The government tolerated and sometimes even connived at these divisions, but within limits.[41] On occasion it would intervene to punish or to depose a defiant chief. In 1857 it had dissolved the hereditary Hlangwini and Sithole chiefdoms, because of the recalcitrance of their chiefs. In 1873 it had dissolved the hereditary chiefdom of the amaHlubi, because of the rebellion of its chief Langalibalele. Dissolution was a shock. It broke with tradition. The Zulu Kings Shaka and Dingane had broken up chiefdoms, but they had acted arbitrarily. Would the Supreme Chief, and the Great Queen he represented, become a despot as well?[42]

The government also worked to circumscribe the power of chiefs in the exercise of customary law. It left them the power to assign land (except that belonging to white farmers) for homesteads, but it had deprived them of power in major criminal cases. In 1875 they had lost ultimate jurisdiction over minor criminal cases, and were required to make timely reports of civil cases to an Administrator of Native Law. A chief could not summon the *amabutho* for the Feast of the First Fruits without the Supreme Chief's permission. Yet he was made responsible for the collection of the hut tax, which was a major source of colonial revenue. There was also a tax on dogs, ostensibly to check their number and so protect the white farmers' sheep.[43]

The government almost overstepped the mark. A marriage law in 1869 had set a schedule for the transfer of cattle for brides according to their status. It prohibited a marriage without the bride's consent. The government also made divorce easier for women, and unwanted wives took advantage of the dispensation, which aroused the resentment of men. A £5 marriage registration fee was regarded as a move to get more young men to work for settlers. It was also regarded as a move to curb the increasing number of heads of homesteads who used their monopoly of cattle from taking more wives, while young men, for whose marriages they might have allocated cattle, found it harder to obtain sufficient to marry and to establish homesteads. For marriage marked a person's majority. In 1875 the government repealed the marriage fee, but doubled the hut tax. Polygamy remained, but expansion meant greater expense: more wives meant more huts. Young men thus found less competition from elders when they wished to marry.[44]

If the government had a great fault it was in doing too much to preserve the forms of established life. In 1875 a Native High Court had been set up to try major criminal cases and to hear appeals against the decisions of white magistrates. In 1878 the government had introduced the first code of 'native' law.[45] Yet there was no *general* law. There were customs and practices. Law, like religion, varied from people to people. There might be similarities, but there were discrepancies as well. The government wanted to consolidate the so-called law, yet its magistrates for the most part lacked sure knowledge of the various customs and practices. There were complaints about faulty decisions.[46] The administration of justice was not always disinterested. It was not always fair. It was often slow. Those who administered justice in the first instance – chiefs and head men – usually took bribes.[47]

The order and stability which the British had brought thus led to prosperity and increase and these ushered in problems of change. In short, time had not stood still. The white settlers were encroaching and demanding. Fortunately, the Supreme Chief checked their extravagance and pretensions. A man could still live his life away from them without being troubled by them. The government sought to protect the old and true. Above all the British kept the peace.

Peace for how long? In 1877 the British had annexed the Dutch settler state of the Transvaal, which bordered Natal and the Zulu country. The British government wanted to confederate the British and Dutch territories in southern Africa. The Zulu kingdom stood in the way. The Zulu kingdom was the most formidable opponent the British had to face on the subcontinent. It had developed the customary age sets of young men, the *amabutho*, into highly disciplined and motivated military formations. They were trained to offensive warfare, and there was a real danger that the Zulu King would send them against the Dutch of the Transvaal or the Swazi kingdom to the north. The Zulu King, Cetshwayo kaMpande, respected British power. His policy towards Natal was pacific. His policy towards the Transvaal was not, because Zulu and Dutch disputed the boundary between them. The British became a party to the dispute when they annexed Transvaal. Therefore the British government must eliminate the Zulu threat to secure the stability in the region. Some settlers and speculators might have economic motives, but the British government's motive was political. The warfare state of the Zulu must be terminated.

Seizing on the boundary dispute and sundry small incidents, and then formulating an impossible ultimatum, which aimed to dissolve the bases of the kingdom itself, the British High Commissioner in South Africa worked to bring on a war in which Britain, with its superior army, would quickly defeat the Zulu. The brightest star of African resistance would be dimmed and added to the British constellation. War was not wicked, it was necessary. The warfare state of the Zulu was an anachronism. It had outlived its time. Britain represented civilization and progress. The Zulu state, if it could be called that, represented barbarism and backwardness. A short war would bring a long peace. At least, this is the way the pro-war British rationalized their action.[48]

Would the people of Natal support Britain in its aggression? Would the chiefs heed the call to war of the Supreme Chief?

There were doubts among the white settlers that they would. We do not know what the chiefs thought about the impending war. Public opinion, as we know it, did not exist. The same missionary in the Upper Umkomanzi Division wrote:[49]

> ... In our neighbourhood (fifty miles south of Maritzburg) it was quite a common thing for the natives to chaff the white men, and to threaten them with Ketchwayo [the Zulu king], saying that the day was coming when 'all the white men would be driven into the sea'. This sort of talk arose, not so much from the disaffection of Natal natives as from the knowledge they had of what was brewing in the land whence they had fled for refuge in Natal.

Conception of the Contingent

The Colony of Natal was like the Zulu kingdom in that the great majority of people recognized a single person as their supreme leader. Indeed, what putative overlordship the Zulu King had once had south of the Thukela now belonged to the British Crown; but even without it the chiefly system implied a hierarchy and an ultimate authority. The Colony's first Secretary for Native Affairs had built a polity on the 'tribe' – the term generally used to describe a chiefdom with a historic common lineage or, less often, as in the case of an artificial chiefdom or a Christian mission, a community which was given a new identity.

Chiefs of 'tribes' and head men of sections of 'tribes', hereditary or appointed, must be recognized by the Supreme Chief. From 1866 they received a nominal stipend from the government for the public, i.e. 'tribal' duties they performed.[50] They owed allegiance to the Queen, and historic claims to authority notwithstanding, they retained their power at the pleasure of the Queen. The Queen was represented in the person of the Supreme Chief, the Lieutenant

Governor of the Colony, and his agent, the Secretary for Native Affairs.

Every chief had the prerogative to call upon his people to perform certain duties. At the prospect of war against the Zulu kingdom the Supreme Chief, Sir Henry Bulwer, exercised his prerogative to call on Her Majesty's loyal subjects for military service. He was prompted and largely guided in his action by the Lieutenant General commanding Her Majesty's forces in southern Africa.[51]

The Lieutenant General, the Honourable Frederic Augustus Thesiger, after October Lord Chelmsford, arrived in Natal in August of 1878, fresh from victory against the Gaika and Gcaleka chiefs in the eastern part of the Cape Colony.[52] He had been favourably impressed by the performance of local levies in the Cape Colony. The Mfengu people, who were believed to be earlier refugees from the Zulu borderlands and had become clients of the Crown, had had grievances against the Xhosa peoples who had taken them in and then exploited them. They had turned to the British for help and been given that and land.[53] Their soldiers' performance had varied according to where and whom they were fighting, but generally they had acquitted themselves well.

They had served under colonial officers in the war just ended. They had practically armed and uniformed themselves. The only way of identifying the motley crowd was by having each man tie a red cloth around his forehead or one of his arms. Perhaps the general's attention was drawn to an analogous situation in Natal, where erstwhile clients of the Zulu King, among others, had found security under the Crown.

The Supreme Chief did not want a war. He was loath to do anything which might cause alarm in the Colony or to provoke the Zulu King.[54] There was also a small war of African resistance in the recently annexed Transvaal, and it was not going favourably for the Dutch and British. The military arrangements for a Zulu war languished, until the High Commissioner, Sir Bartle Frere, arrived in Natal at the end of September.[55] The Queen's chief emissary, he was superior to Lieutenant General and Lieutenant Governor. He pressed boundary dispute, border incidents and impossible demands, until by the end of November there was little doubt about the result, although the fiction of a peaceful settlement was entertained some time longer.

In the event of war the British regular army forces available obviously would not suffice, so colonial forces would have to be used in conjunction with them. This necessity was recognized by all who had a hand in the strategy,[56] but the Lieutenant General and the Supreme Chief had very different ideas about how the colonial forces should be used.

The Lieutenant General had been in Pietermaritzburg scarcely a week when he received a memorandum (dated August 17th) on the raising of 5500 men among the chiefs of the Colony for military service. The author of the memorandum was Lieutenant Colonel Anthony Durnford, Royal Engineers, whose long service in Natal and close acquaintance with its people made him something of an expert on the subject.

Colonel Durnford proposed a Native Contingent of five regiments of infantry and five troops of cavalry, officered by colonists of substance and a degree of acquaintance with their men. The men would be partially uniformed in European clothing and would be issued rifles and knives. They would be supplied meal and slaughter oxen for their rations. (Youths would accompany them and carry their camp equipment and reserve ammunition). The Colonel dealt with all these matters in detail, and estimated that it would cost £28 667 to field the Native Contingent for a year. He even specified the 'clans' from which he wanted the contingent recruited.

The Lieutenant General read and annotated the memorandum, especially with regard to the availability of officers and rifles.[57] Then he submitted a memorandum of his own to the Natal government, on August 24th. It described five columns invading Zululand from Natal and the Transvaal, the Natal three having attached Native Corps of 5000 men each. Every available man should be enrolled in the Native Contingent. In that way the government's and settlers' anxiety about the loyalty of the population would be allayed. A rising, which some settlers feared, would be forestalled by mixing up the African young blood with the British soldiery in the column.[58]

Nothing happened. After a time the Lieutenant General began to prod, and in September the reluctant government asked the Resident Magistrates (who represented the Crown in the counties and divisions into which the Colony was divided for administration) to report on the various 'tribes' and their numbers.[59] A sense of urgency was imparted to the Supreme Chief by the High Commissioner, after he arrived in Pietermaritzburg on September 26th.[60]

That same day the Lieutenant General despatched another memorandum, in which he proposed organizing the men available in battalions of 1000 each, subdivided into companies of 100 and sections of 10 each. Firearms would only be given to some, because there were not enough for all. Men who had officered the Mfengu levies in the late Cape war would be invited to take charge of the Natal ones because there apparently were not enough Natal colonists to do so.[61] Another memorandum, two days later, specified 6000 men be attached to the three invading columns in equal portions. It stressed an organization based on units of ten men, and limited the guns to one man in ten.[62]

The Supreme Chief was distressed by these proposals, which did not conform to his ideas of facilitating the military's demands, and which transferred control of the levies from him to the military. Of course, he had to consider the objections of colonists, although these were neither so vigorous or sustained as might be expected. There was an objection to giving firearms to men who heretofore had been deliberately prevented from getting them by a very restrictive system of licences. There was also the objection to unfamiliar Cape officers, who would not understand the language or the customs of the men.[63]

Most important was the objection to the form of organization. The Supreme Chief believed that the men called out should keep their traditional organization, rather than be forced into a European mould, which was what the Lieutenant General proposed.[64] The Acting Secretary for Native Affairs, John Wesley Shepstone, was adamant for the 'traditional' organization, although he conceded a limited use of firearms and the need of white officers:[65]

> The natives of this Colony are quite sufficiently organized to engage in any active operations against people of their own race and colour; they should in my opinion be taken as they are and with the weapons they use and to which they have been accustomed. Guns could be given to those who know how to use them.
>
> To introduce a new system or mode of warfare among them at present would tend to destroy the confidence they naturally possess in the system which they have all along been exercised [in] [and it] would necessar[il]y cause much delay in case of emergency.

The Acting Secretary expressed his belief that almost every 'tribe' in the Colony retained the 'Zulu' military system, having been subject to Zulu rule. Thus the men were organized by age or other criteria in *amabutho*, with their special names and sometimes distinctive shields. The *amabutho* assembled for the Feast of the First Fruits, where they practised movements and sang songs but they rarely assembled otherwise. Both the government and the peace had sapped their vigour, and their men were conscious of their inferiority to their counterparts of Zulu army.[66]

What the Lieutenant General called for was a 'regimental' organization, an innovation based on the British military system. The Lieutenant General and Colonel Durnford were determined to have their way in organization. The Colonel's experience, in the Langalibalele rebellion of 1873, convinced him that the 'traditional' organization was useless.[67]

The military was not indifferent to settler fears. Guns would be issued to only ten per cent of the men – those who presumably knew something about using them. European officers and non-commissioned officers would be in control. Denied officers and guns to replicate the regimental organization after the war was over, the veterans would not be a future threat to the peace.[68]

The Lieutenant General became impatient with what appeared to be paperwork obstructionism by the civil authority. The High Commissioner urged the military and civil authorities to compose their differences. The pressure of necessity resulted in the organization of the Natal Native Contingent in accord with the military's wishes. African soldiers would be fitted into the European military mould.

Colonel Durnford seems to have expected that he would be appointed commandant of all the Native Contingent. This would have been impractical and the Lieutenant General's staff opposed it. The Colonel was assigned to command the part of the Native Contingent which made up the No. 2 Column. Then he was unhappy that the government did not assign to him the men of particular chiefdoms which he had named in his memorandum. The Lieutenant General prevailed again: the men were assigned, in addition to those the government had already provided, thus making the regiment of the Native Contingent which formed the No. 2 Column the largest (3000 men) of the three formed. The Colonel also wanted to make exceptions in the organization of his command. What these changes were to be is not clear. The Lieutenant General resisted them on the grounds the regimental system should be applied uniformly.[69]

It remained to inform the chiefs of the arrangements. In the first week of November Durnford went to the upper divisions of Weenen County to interview the chiefs of the 'clans' whose services he specially wanted.[70] Acting Secretary Shepstone, accompanied by two members of the general's staff, went on a long circuit through Umvoti and Victoria Counties to interview the chiefs who would furnish men to the No. 1 and No. 2 columns.[71] Meanwhile, the Supreme Chief circularized the Resident Magistrates on November 20th about the purpose and

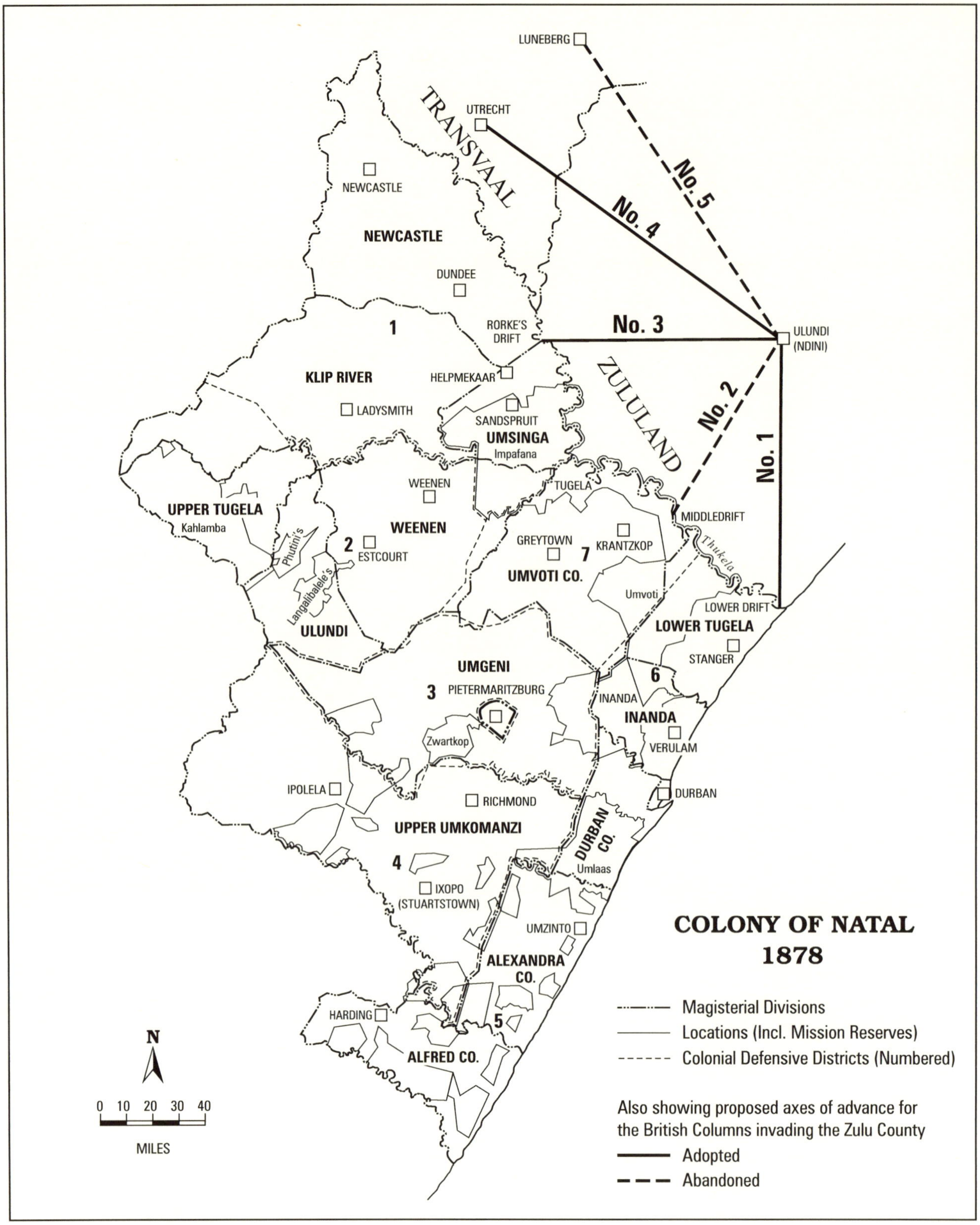

form of the 'special Native Contingent',[72] and the Lieutenant General issued a general order on the 23rd, setting out the regulations for the contingent. They were a refinement of Durnford's memorandum,[73] and will be described in the following chapter.

Finally, the Lieutenant General was determined that African soldiers organized on the European model should conduct themselves towards the enemy according to prevailing European norms in warfare. On the eve of the invasion of the Zulu country, he sent a memorandum to column commanders, instructing them to explain to the members of the Natal Native Contingent that they should not willfully kill a woman or child or wounded man; nor should they burn any huts except by the specific orders of the column commander himself. Those who violated these orders were liable to a punishment of hanging and flogging, respectively.[74]

Call to arms: A variety of responses

'The Anglo-Zulu War was to prove the high-water mark of colonial/chiefly collaboration'.[75] This is the considered opinion of the most recent historian of the relations between the Great Queen and her chiefs. We have little information about the way in which chiefs and people responded to the call to war. Different ones responded in different ways. Consider the following examples.

At the coast: the amaQadi

The amaQadi had good reason to hate the Zulu. They had been loyal to Shaka, founder of the kingdom and been well treated by him, but his brother and successor, Dingane, had suspected them because of it. He had massacred all he could find and the remnant had escaped into the bush south of the Thukela, from which they had emerged only after another brother, Mpande, overthrew Dingane. Under British rule the amaQadi had gathered round the chief Mqawe to live in peace by the Nanda hill.[76]

Mqawe received the order from the Supreme Chief to call out five hundred of his men for military service. The amaQadi lived in the Inanda Location, which had been set aside by the government for them and other tribes some thirty years before. The order was not unexpected. Mqawe and several other chiefs had been summoned by the Resident Magistrate of the division to a meeting at Verulam, the seat of the magistracy, in early November. Misjaan, as the Acting Secretary of Native Affairs was known, the Supreme Chief's agent, had explained to them that the troubled state of affairs in the Zulu kingdom was such that the government considered it necessary to take steps to defend the Colony. The government would act only on the defensive. If it became necessary, chiefs would be required to call out certain numbers and assemble armed men. The steps to be taken were to be purely defensive in character.[77]

Towards the end of November there was another order. Chiefs should hold their men ready to assemble in about ten days time. Then there was another interval. There was uncertainty about when they would be called up, also about what they would be called up to do. The Resident Magistrate, Mr. Barter, was silent. Some men, who wished to avoid service, had time to get out of the way.

Mqawe had told the Acting Secretary that he might get ten or even twenty men, but not five hundred. Deliwayo, the young chief of the amaNyuswa, who also lived in the Inanda Location, was required to raise two hundred. He had spoken likewise. Misjaan had replied sharply. They were not *independent* chiefs from whom the government was begging assistance. They should understand that he was there to give them the word of the Supreme Chief. They knew well what that meant. The two chiefs had replied in turn that they were not objecting to what they were being ordered to do.

Then came the order calling the men up. It was dated December 18th. The Lieutenant General wanted the men to assemble at the Nonoti River between the coast road and the sea, and in just three days time. They would be organized into companies and battalions. They would be part of the 2nd Regiment, Natal Native Contingent. The commander would be a British army officer, Major Graves. Until recently he had been Protector of Immigrants at Durban.

Mqawe ordered out every available man in his chiefdom, not only those in the Inanda Division over which Barter presided, but those who lived in smaller settlements near by, in the Lower Tugela Division, which borders Zululand, and inland, in the Umgeni Division, around Pietermaritzburg. He announced that his young men would not go alone. He would go with them. There was a quick response. They did not all go at once, of course; nor was it possible for them all to get to the Nonoti by the 21st, but 404 did arrive at the camp between the 21st and 23rd, and 101 arrived in various small groups within the next few weeks. There had been some question among the white people about Mqawe's loyalty.[78] His action vouched for it.

In the foothills of the mountains: the amaNgwane

Ncwadi had succeeded recently to the chieftainship of the Ngwane people, who lived in the foothills of the Kahlamba, in the Upper Tugela Division of the Colony. His father, Zikhali, had died in 1863, and Ncwadi had grown up under the regency of an uncle. He was deemed too young to lead his people in war.

He was willing to fight. His people had reason to oppose the Zulu. Their earlier home was in the Zulu country. They had been driven from it by the Ndwandwe chief about sixty years before and they had settled in approximately this same region.

Under their chief Mathiwane they had made war upon their neighbours and obtained a certain ascendancy over them. Then they had been driven into what was now Basutoland and beyond it, to the west, by the Zulu under Shaka. They had fought their way into the Cape Colony, but the people there had been called on by the British to defeat and eject them. Shaka's successor, Dingane, had allowed them to return. Then he had murdered Mathiwane. The Dutch had come and had supported a revolt against Dingane. The new chief Zikhali had cast his lot with them. He had moved with his people into the Dutch republic and settled on the upper reaches of the Thukela. The Dutch republic gave way to the British colony. A Location had been demarcated and confirmed to them. They numbered perhaps 1800 huts. Most of them were in Zikhali's Location, but there were a few also on the farms of colonists.

The amaNgwane early on had armed their *amabutho* with short stabbing spears, such as the Zulu had.[79] Their martial spirit had been bruised by misfortune, but a tradition survived, despite the British peace. Zikhali had recognized and named six *amabutho*. Under Ncwadi there were four more.[80] These the government might call upon in the event of war with the Zulu kingdom.

Early in November Colonel Durnford arrived at the Upper Tugela magistracy. In 1873 he had led an expedition against the rebel chief Langalibalele, who had lived in that area. The experience had acquainted him with the peoples there. He had got the government's permission to raise part of the Native Contingent among them. He would lead them personally. It was arranged that they should provide three hundred men on foot and one hundred men on horseback. The Colonel had conferred with the Resident Magistrate, Mr. Allison. It was arranged that the men in the division would parade at the magistracy. On parade they would be inspected and the fit ones chosen for service. Also, it would be seen who had guns and could use them. Allison assembled the men, and as a result many of the amaNgwane were called upon for service.

The amaNgwane thus prepared for war. The chosen men were told to hold themselves in readiness. Then came the fateful calls – first for the mounted men, then for the foot. On December 24th those on horseback mustered at the magistracy. The horses were small to medium size by English standards, but hardy and very useful. Under the magistrate's son the mounted men rode in a body to Pietermaritzburg, where they reported to Colonel Durnford at Fort Napier three days later. There they were issued Swinburne Henry carbines. There were 157 of them, more than half again the number required. There were at least five head men amongst them. They were led by Nyanda, Zikhali's brother, and henceforth they were known as Zikhali's Horse.

The foot soldiers gathered at Ngoba, the place of Ncwadi, where they performed the rites which tradition required before war. Mr. Allison, with a background in Christian mission work, did not like this 'doctoring', but the Colonel had agreed to it because the people thought it was essential. It was nine days, not the four which Allison expected, before they finally marched. At daylight of the second day of the new year they set out from his office for Greytown, to join the 1st Regiment of the contingent. His son accompanied them, as he had the mounted men. The magistrate provided fifteen cattle for rations on the march, rather than the niggardly three or four the government had suggested. In the event the ration was excessive, for the number of foot soldiers had been diminished by the surplus of mounted ones. They ate well on the march. 243 reported to Colonel Durnford on January 6th and 7th.[81]

On the border: the amaChunu

In the thorn country along the middle Thukela lived the amaChunu. Their chief Phakade was an old man, also very fat. Because of his infirmity his eldest son and heir, Gabangaye, exercised the chiefly power. There were rumours among the white people that Phakade was disaffected and would not obey the government's orders.[82]

There were strong links between the Chunu and Zulu peoples and, of course, they lived just across the Thukela from each other. Fugitives from Zululand sought out the Chunu Location. Their customs were the same. There were also historic animosities. There had been bad blood between Shaka, the Zulu King, and Macingwane, the Chunu chief. Macingwane had fled with his people before Shaka could strike, into the thorn country south of the Thukela and the Mzinyathi. They had raided and destroyed other peoples as far south as the Mzimkhulu. They had tried to settle down, but the Zulu power had found them out and eaten them up. Macingwane himself had become a wanderer until, it was said, he had been eaten by Bhele cannibals.

According to one account, most of the survivors had sought the protection of one of Shaka's trusted lieutenants, but Dingane had murdered him. They had joined in the pretender Mpande's revolt. Finally Phakade had led them from the Zulu country to the Thorns again. He had refused to return. Mpande harried him and the Dutch gave no help. According to another account, the survivors had sought the protection of Shaka himself, who had given it but then killed Macingwane's heir. Phakade, son of a lesser wife and hitherto not considered in the succession, had preserved himself somehow. He had dissembled until Dingane's time, when he had crossed the Mzinyathi into the Msinga and later moved to the Thorns. Mpande, now the Zulu King, had, with leave of the Dutch, sent an expedition to punish the amaChunu for stealing cattle and women.[83]

With the British there was peace at last. The Chunu Location was demarcated in the lower division of Weenen County, but the people were so many that some lived in the adjacent counties as well. Phakade ruled well and attracted adherents. The number of his huts now exceeded three thousand.[84]

There was a rugged grandeur about the thorn country in which the amaChunu lived. It was broken into high mountains and narrow valleys. It was also forbidding to cultivation. Natal had recently experienced a long drought. It was most severe in the thorn country, which in the best of times is dry. Starvation was a real danger in places, and men were scattered elsewhere in search of livelihood, chiefly to white settlers' farms and especially up-country, where the drought was less severe. There was some question whether or not the chiefs in the thorn country could get all of the men together in the time the government required.[85]

Phakade was ordered to furnish six hundred men for the 3rd Regiment of the Native Contingent, which formed part of the No. 3 Column that would invade Zululand from the west. Gabangaye, also advanced in years, was described as somewhat stupid and stubborn, but he was not disloyal. Ultimately he furnished more men than actually required. Perhaps the prospect of regular rations and pay appealed to the men as much as the prospect of adventure.

Muster day, December 14th, brought the levies of Phakade and his neighbour, the chief Mganu, to the Weenen town lands. The only people more numerous than the amaChunu in the Colony were the abaThembu of Mganu, but the two chiefs' levies were about equal in size. Both were fully armed for war, with spears, sticks, shields. Both had preserved the *ibutho* system, but Phakade's military organization was superior to Mganu's. Long peace had reduced the formidability of the *amabutho*. They had assembled only for important occasions, such as the Feast of the First Fruits every spring. Some men did not even have the traditional weapons any longer.[86]

While the Chunu levy was being enrolled, some young men went down to the river to drink. They came back by a path where some men of the Thembu levy were sitting, and one of them stepped on a Thembu shield. The owner sprang to his feet and struck the man who had insulted him. Young men from both groups now joined battle with sticks and stones, but, fortunately, not spears. The row brought the magistrate and his clerks out of the office. They and some of the head men on both sides broke up the fight in a few minutes. There were minor flesh wounds, nothing more serious.

The magistrate marched the abaThembu across the river and pointed to a place at some distance. He told them to go and to stay there until he ordered them to leave. Then he returned to complete the Chunu roll. When he finished, he marched the levy about two miles in a direction opposite to the abaThembu. He gave it similar instructions: if they left without orders they would be dealt with strictly. He also sent for the Natal Mounted Police detachment at Estcourt, the county seat, to come at once in case there was another fracas. The police – all seven of them – arrived in the evening. There was no more fighting. Next morning the levies of the isiGqoza and the amaBhele arrived to be enrolled. The magistrate not only placed them well apart but put police between them.

On the 16th the four levies marched off to the front – one at a time, with intervals of 300 yards between them. A policeman was at the head of each levy with orders to keep the distance, both in marching and camping. Before they left, the magistrate told the men of each levy why they were called out. He also said that fighting or quarrelling among them would be severely punished.[87]

The Christian village: Edendale

Six miles to the west of Pietermaritzburg was the village of Edendale, founded as a Wesleyan mission in 1851. The inhabitants numbered about a thousand. They lived on the mission land or on land just beyond its boundary. About a third of the mission's 6000 acres was commonage. Most of the remainder was divided into smallholdings purchased and cultivated by the members themselves. In their habits, in their dress, and even in their dwellings the people followed the model of England. They had higher and lower schools. Many could read and write English. Some spoke it well. Most of them professed to be Christians. Between three and four hundred were church members, and a larger number were on probation. Many were amaSwazi, some were baSotho. Few had roots in Natal.

They had no chief. The community's affairs were in the charge of a Board of Trust, consisting of the General Superintendent of Wesleyan Missions, the Secretary for Native Affairs, and the Surveyor General of the Colony. They met as need arose.[88] Immediate management was the responsibility of three leaders chosen from the community itself.[89] Timothy Gule was the head man at this time.[90]

It would be hard to find a less warlike people in Natal, but in war government has its uses. The High Commissioner visited Edendale twice, the Lieutenant Governor thrice, once on a Sunday, when he prayed with the congregation.[91] On November 23rd Colonel Durnford asked the Government for permission to raise fifty mounted men among them for the Native Contingent.[92] Christians they might be, but they were still subject to Native Law and must obey the call of the Supreme Chief. The Government's message was conveyed to the leader of the community. Could it raise a troop of mounted men for immediate service in the event of war?

A meeting of men was held to consider the matter. One of the leaders, Daniel Msimang, put the question. He put it in a way which could not be denied:

> We have sat under the shadow of the Great White Queen for many years in security and peace. We have greatly prospered, and some have grown rich. We enjoy great religious privileges, and have brought up our sons and daughters to honour God, and to walk in his ways. Our schools have provided a good education for our children, to fit them for a useful life in this land, and now their children are enjoying a like blessing. Under God and the Missionary Society we owe it all to the Government of the Great White Queen. We are her children, and in this time of great peril she sends to us to help her against our common foe. We all know the cruelty and the power of the Zulu King, and if he should subdue the Queen's soldiers and overrun this land he will wipe out all the native people who have dwelt so long in safety under the shadow of the Great White Queen. Shall we not gladly obey her, when she calls for the services of her dark children?
>
> They answered: 'We will'.

Young men volunteered for service. Fathers decided who would go and undertook to get horses and saddles.[93] Some sixty volunteered immediately, but only fifty four were allowed to go.[94] Among those chosen most were church members. Several were class leaders and local preachers. Many were already married, with families.[95]

Timothy Gule appointed John Zulu Mtimkulu the head man of the unit. He was an older man, not one of the larger landowners as were Gule and Msimang. Evidently he was chosen to be the leader in the spiritual sense. In a military sense the leader was Simeon Kambule,[96] the son of the late Elijah Kambule, the second largest landholder in the community. Elijah Kambule had served Colonel Durnford as interpreter in the expedition against the rebel chief Langalibalele in 1873 and had been killed in action.[97]

Colonel Durnford asked the government for the mounted men on December 16th. General orders were issued on the 18th. Two days later fifty-five men were ready to go, all handsomely mounted. A service was held in the church and they were commended to the care of Almighty God. Farewells followed, and were made in silence. In silence, too, the men departed from the village. The Reverend Allsopp and the senior members of the church's Leaders Meeting went at the head of the troop. About three miles down the road they all halted. They uncovered their heads and listened while the Reverend Allsopp prayed. The Leaders moved to a side of the road, and Simeon Kambule took charge of the troop. The young troopers saluted the older men, and rode on without them to Pietermaritzburg.[98]

At the magistracy they were enrolled and directed to report at Fort Napier. There they were issued the rest of the kit and tents, which they must carry. They also received Martini-Henry rifles, the firearms of the British army. A young settler, with some experience in warfare in the Cape, Henry Davies, was assigned to be their officer. Colonel Durnford appointed Simeon Kambule Sergeant Major, though John Zulu Mtimkulu retained a nominal headship of the unit. There was scarcely time to drill. On December 23rd they left for Greytown where they would join the No. 2 Column.[99]

NOTES

1 Thomas B. Jenkinson, *Amazulu. The Zulus, Their Past History, Manners, Customs and Language* (London, Allen, 1882), p. 6.

2 *Blue Book for the Colony of Natal,* 1879 (Pietermaritzburg, Vause, Slatter, 1879), Section V, 4 and 5.

3 The distinction between the Zulu and their client chiefdoms in this respect is made in John Wright, The dynamics of power and conflict in the Thukela-Mzimkhulu region in the late 18th and early 19th centuries: a critical reconstruction (University of the Witwatersrand, Ph. D., 1989), chapters 5 and 6, but especially pp. 232, 239, 252, 259, 262–264, 269, 278, 285–188 and 293–194. Of course, those who were attacked probably did not make fine distinctions. Recent historiographical considerations touching on the region in this period are covered in Carolyn Hamilton and John Wright, Making precolonial histories: past trends and present debates (a paper presented to the Southern African Historical Society at its conference, July 2–5, 1995). Their work is also included in *The Mfecane Aftermath: Reconstructive Debates in Southern African History* (edited by Carolyn Hamilton; Johannesburg. Witwatersrand University Press, and Pietermaritzburg, University of Natal Press, 1995), particularly chapters 5–7.

4 Wright, Dynamics of power, pp. 310–318. John Wright and Carolyn Hamilton, 'Traditions and transformations: The Phongolo-Mzimkhulu region in the late eighteenth and early nineteenth centuries,' in *Natal and Zululand from earliest times to 1910: A new history* (edited by Andrew Duminy and Bill Guest; Pietermaritzburg. University of Natal Press and Shuter and Shooter, 1989), pp. 72–73.

5 Charles Ballard, 'Traders, Trekkers and Colonists,' in *Natal and Zululand from earliest times*, pp. 121–125. Peter Colenbrander, 'The Zulu kingdom, 1828–1879,' in *ibid*, p. 97. Edgar H. Brookes and Colin de B. Webb, *A History of Natal* (Pietermaritzburg, University of Natal Press, 1965), pp. 29–28, 49–50. John Lambert, *Betrayed Trust: Africans and the State in Colonial Natal* (Pietermaritzburg, University of Natal Press, 1995), pp. 7–8. See also *Proceedings and Report of the Commission appointed to inquire into the past and present state of the Kafirs in the district of Natal ... 1852–1853* (Pietermaritzburg [n.p. 1852]), p. 8.

6 Ballard, 'Traders, Trekkers and colonists,' pp. 126–129. Brookes and Webb, *History of Natal*, pp. 61–66. Lambert, *Betrayed Trust*, pp. 8–9, 15–16, 72. Jenkinson, *Amazulu*, p. 11–12. Lewis Grant, *Zulu-Land; or Life among the Zulu Kafirs of Natal and Zululand, South Africa* (London, Trübner [1863], p. 96. G.H. Mason, *Life with the Zulus of Natal[,] South Africa* (London, Longman, Brown, Green and Longmans, 1855), p. 184. *Report of the Natal Native Commission, 1881–2* (Pietermaritzburg, Vause, Slatter, 1882), p. 2.

7 *Report of the Natal Native Commission*, pp. 3, 11, 15, 16, 25. Lambert, *Betrayed Trust*, pp. 18–20, 23, 29–31, 45, 47–48. See and *cf. Proceedings and Report,* pp. 19–20, 22–23, 27, 44. *Cf.* Norman Etherington, 'The "Shepstone system" in the Colony of Natal and beyond the borders,' in *Natal and Zululand from earliest times*, pp. 174–175.

8 *Proceedings and Report*, pp. 21, 34, 39. *Report of the Natal Native Commission*, p. 6. Lambert, *Betrayed Trust*, p. 24, 26, 28–29, 33. Jenkinson, *Amazulu*, p. 25. Mason, *Life with the Zulus*, p. 184. Joseph Shooter, *The Kafirs of Natal and the Zulu Country* (London, Stanford, 1857), pp. 106–107.

9 *The Colony of Natal. An Account of the Characteristics and Capabilities of this British Dependency* (compiled and edited by Robert James Mann; London, Jarrold [1859]), pp. 34–35. *Proceedings and Report*, pp. 39–40. 'Evidence of Henry Francis Fynn before the Native Commission, 1852,' in *The Annals of Natal* (edited by John Bird; Cape Town, Maskew Miller [192-], I, 115–116. Shooter, *The Kafirs of Natal*, pp. 105–106. Lambert, *Betrayed Trust*, pp. 39–40, 52. The description of life which follows telescopes accounts written between the 1840s and the 1870s on the assumption that, apart from changes externally forced, the way of life remained much the same. It will be noted that accounts concerned with the Zulu, *i.e.* the people living in Zululand, and with others outside Natal, such as William C. Holden's *The Past and Future of the Kaffir Races* (London, Nichols, [1866]), are omitted. The historic differences between the peoples of Natal and Zululand seem sufficient to warrant their omission. This discrimination among sources takes into account and attempts to avoid as much as possible the great difficulty cited by Eileen Krige in her comprehensive work, *The Social System of the Zulus* (London, Longman Green, 1936), p. vi: 'Firstly, and unfortunately in most of the published accounts, no indication is given as to particular locality or section of the Zulus referred to. The omission is serious, because, though most of the tribes in Natal and Zululand call themselves Zulus, many differences of custom occur, particularly as between the people of Natal and those of Zululand proper.'

10 'Evidence of Henry Francis Fynn,' p. 106. Grout, *Zulu-Land*, p. 135–136. Mason, *Life with the Zulus*, pp. 93–97. Shooter, *The Kafirs of Natal*, pp. 163–166. *The Natal Diaries of Dr. W.H.I. Bleek, 1855–1856* (translated by O.H. Spohr; Cape Town, Balkema, 1965), p. 37. *Journal of the Rev. George Champion[,] American Missionary in Zululand 1835–9* (edited by Alan R. Booth; Cape Town, Struik, 1967), p. 82. William Ireland, *Historical Sketch of the Zulu Mission, in South Africa ...* (Boston, American Board of Commissioners for Foreign Missions [n.d.]), p. 11. Josiah Tyler, *Forty Years Among the Zulus* (Boston, Congregational Sunday School & Publishing Society, 1890), p. 46. For a general analysis and description, see H. Callaway, *The Religious System of the Amazulu. Izinyanga Zikubala; or Divination as existing among the Amazulu, in Their Own Words ...* (Springvale, John A. Blair, 1870), pp. 127–256.

11 'Evidence of Henry Francis Fynn,' pp. 107–111. Grout, *Zulu-Land*, pp. 119, 149–158. Ireland, *Historical Sketch*, pp. 10–11. Jenkinson, *Amazulu*, pp. 27–30. Mason, *Life with the Zulus*, p. 99 *et seq.* and 197 *et seq.* Shooter, *The Kafirs of Natal*, pp. 141–150. *The Colony of Natal*, p. 37. Lady Barker, *A Year's Housekeeping in South Africa* (London, Macmillan, 1886), pp. 160–190 *passim.* Henrietta Robertson, *Mission Life among the Zulu-Kafirs* (edited by Anne Mackenzie; Cambridge, Deighton, Bell, 1866), p. 21. For a general description and analysis, see Callaway, *The Religious System of the Zulu*, pp. 257–448. See also Natal Native Commission, 1881–2, *Evidence taken by the Sub-Committee for Umvoti County* (Pietermaritzburg, Vause, Slatter, 1882), pp. 17, 22, 25, 28, 31, 48, 52, 58, 60.

12 *The Colony of Natal*, pp. 34–35. 'Evidence of Henry Francis Fynn,' p. 121. Grout, *Zulu-Land*, pp. 99–100. Ireland, *Historical Sketch*, pp. 6–7. Jenkinson, *Amazulu*, pp. 9–10. Shooter, *The Kafirs of Natal*, p. 17. For remarks on the hard lot of women see also Charles Barter, *The Dorp and the Veld; or Six Months in Natal* (London, Orr, 1852), pp. 219–220.

13 For the early period of the Colony see Adulphe Delegorgue, *Travels in Southern Africa*, I (translated by Fleur Webb; Pietermaritzburg, University of Natal Press, 1990), chapters

6, 7, 11, 12, 13 *et passim*; Mason, *Life with the Zulus*, pp. 73–80 *passim*; Shooter, *The Kafirs of Natal*, pp. 40–42; Tyler, *Forty Years*, pp. 35, 39; John William Colenso, *Ten Weeks in Natal. A Journey of a First Tour of Visitation Among the Colonists and Zulu Kafirs of Natal* (Cambridge, Macmillan, 1855), p. 251; and Allen, F. Gardiner, *Narrative of a Journey to the Zoolu Country, in South Africa* (London, Crofts, 1836), p. 16. *The Natal Diaries of Dr. W.H.I. Bleek* indicates (p. 4) the disappearing of large animals, and Jenkinson, *Amazulu*, remarks (pp. 8–9) on their scarcity.

14 Colenso, *Ten Weeks in Natal*, pp. 33–34. *The Colony of Natal*, pp. 33, 35–36. Grout, *Zulu-Land*, p. 95. Ireland, *Historical Sketch*, pp. 5, 7. Jenkinson, *Amazulu*, p. 9. Shooter, *The Kafirs of Natal*, pp. 16, 28. Tyler, *Forty Years*, pp. 43–44. Also see Mason, *Life with the Zulus*, chapter 22, and *cf.* Lambert, *Betrayed Trust*, p. 42.

15 Barker, *A Year's Housekeeping in South Africa*, p. 254. Barter, *The Dorp and the Veld*, pp. 208–209, 219. *The Natal Diaries of Dr. W.H.I. Bleek*, p. 15. Colenso, *Ten Weeks in Natal*, pp. 125–126, 256. *The Colony of Natal*, p. 36. Gardiner, *Narrative of a Journey*, p. 96. Grout, *Zulu-Land*, pp. 16, 108–110. Ireland, *Historical Sketch*, p. 8. Jenkinson, *Amazulu*, p. 53. Mason, *Life with the Zulus*, chapter 23 and especially, pp. 62, 121–123, 226–228. Shooter, *The Kafirs of Natal*, pp. 9, 25–27, 221, 232–236. See also Magema, M. Fuze, *The Black People and Whence They Came. A Zulu View* (translated by H.C. Lugg and edited by A.T. Cope, Pietermaritzburg, University of Natal Press, 1979), chapter 16.

16 Barker, *A Year's Housekeeping in South Africa*, pp. 119, 121, 164. *The Colony of Natal*, pp. 38–40. Grout, *Zulu-Land*, pp. 181–182.

17 See Wright, Dynamics of power, pp. 272–273 and 305–306, and especially for the amaNgwane and amaHlubi, pp. 210–222, 283–284; the amaChunu, pp. 223–230, 247, 283–285; the abaThembu, pp. 239–246; and the amaQwabe, pp. 373–375.

18 *Report of the Natal Native Commission*, p. 32. See *Proceedings and Report*, p. 31 and *cf.* p. 15, which suggests 25 000.

19 *Report of the Natal Native Commission*, pp. 14, 32. *Proceedings and Report*, pp. 6, 8, 13, 15, 31, 33. Barter, *The Dorp and the Veld*, pp. 195–206 *passim*. Colenso, *Ten Weeks in Natal*, pp. xxvi, 16. See Colenbrander, 'The Zulu Kingdom,' pp. 97–107 *passim* for Zulu groups entering Natal, and see also Lambert, *Betrayed Trust*, p. 10, and *cf.* p. 32.

20 *Cf. Report of the Natal Native Commission,* pp. 7–8, and Lambert, *Betrayed Trust*, pp. 11, 29–30, 33, 71.

21 See Lambert, *Betrayed Trust*, pp. 8–9, 71–72.

22 *Proceedings and Report*, p. 17.

23 See and *cf. ibid.*, pp. 10, 12, 15–16, and 30 and 72–74 *passim*. *Report of the Natal Native Commission*, pp. 10, 35.

24 See Lambert, *Betrayed Trust*, pp. 13–15, 18–19; his comments on the postwar period seem applicable to the late prewar as well. *Report of the Natal Native Commisison*, p. 10. *Proceedings and Report*, p. 14.

25 See *Report of the Natal Native Commission*, pp. 7–8, 33–35, and *Evidence taken by the Sub-Commission for Umvoti County*, pp. 3, 20, 53–54. Lambert, *Betrayed Trust*, pp. 11–12, 71–72. Jenkinson, *Amazulu*, p. 13. *Cf. Proceedings and Report*, p. 18.

26 *Proceedings and Report*, pp. 12–15.

27 *Ibid.*, pp. 14, 17. Lambert, *Betrayed Trust*, p. 10. *Cf.* Brookes and Webb, *History of Natal*, p. 60.

28 *Report of the Natal Native Commission* estimates (p. 35) 169 800 in the Locations, 162 600 on private lands and 42 600 on Crown Lands at the end of 1881.

29 *Ibid.*, p. 11. *Evidence taken by the Sub-Committee for Umvoti County*, p. 4, 13, 15, 21, 29, 34, 36, 39, 42, 55. Lambert, *Betrayed Trust*, pp. 11, 51–52. Norman Etherington, 'Christianity and African society in nineteenth-century Natal,' in *Natal and Zululand from earliest times*, pp. 282, 285–286, 289.

30 Etherington, 'Christianity and African Society,' pp. 280–283, 287, 292–294. *Cf.* Lambert, *Betrayed Trust*, p. 51.

31 Etherington, 'Christianity and African Society,' pp. 277, 28–282, 286, 294–295.

32 Callaway delineates the creator and his work in *The Religious System of the Amazulu*, pp. 3–126. Colenso, *Ten Weeks in Natal*, pp. 134, 142. Gardiner, *Narrative of a Journey*, pp. 152, 314. Grout, *Zulu-Land*, p. 136. Ireland, *Historical Sketch*, p. 12. Mason, *Life with the Zulus*, pp. 63–64. Shooter, *The Kafirs of Natal*, pp. 159–160. David Leslie, *Among the Zulus and the Amatongas: With Sketches of the Natives, Their Language and Customs; and the Country, Products, Climate, Wild Animals, &c*, (edited by W.H. Drummond; Glasgow, private publication, 1875), p. 207. *Cf. Proceedings and Report*, p. 26.

33 Etherington, 'Christianity and African Society,' pp. 281–282. Lambert, *Betrayed Trust*, pp. 35, 51. Ireland, *Historical Sketch*, p. 7. Mason, *Life with the Zulus*, p. 118. *Proceedings and Report*, p. 38. *Cf. Report of the Natal Native Commission*, pp. 12–13, and see *Evidence taken by the Sub-Commission for Umvoti County*, pp. 8, 11, 15, 21, 27, 36, 38, 41, 46, 49, 50, 54, 59.

34 Etherington, 'Christianity and African Society,' p. 282–286. Lambert, *Betrayed Trust*, pp. 16, 18, 52. See and *cf.* population and congregation statistics in the *Blue Book for The Colony of Natal.* 1879, Sections H and V, 4 and 5.

35 Lambert, *Betrayed Trust*, p. 18. *Evidence taken by the Sub-Commission for Umvoti County*, pp. 4, 5, 12, 13, 16, 21, 27, 31, 39, 42, 46, 50, 55, 59.

36 Lambert, *Betrayed Trust*, pp. 34–35, 43–50 *passim*. *Report of the Natal Native Commission*, pp. 8, 15. *Evidence taken by the Sub-Commission for Umvoti County*, pp. 3, 13, 20, 39, 54. See also, Jenkinson, *Amazulu*, pp. 9–10, and Shooter, *The Kafirs of Natal*, p. 17.

37 *Proceedings and Report*, pp. 35–36. They represented forty-six different 'tribes'. Thirty-four chiefs of twenty-one tribes claimed to be 'aboriginal' to the Colony (*ibid.*, p. 32). *Report of the Natal Native Commission* states (pp. 37–39) that there were ninety-four tribes living in the area of the Colony in 1812 and forty-two of these lived there in 1837, when altogether sixty-four tribes inhabited the Colony.

38 *Proceedings and Report*, p. 22. Etherington, 'The "Shepstone system",' p. 178. Lambert, *Betrayed Trust*, states (p. 24) that the then Secretary for Native Affairs, Theophilus Shepstone acknowledged the authority of fifty-six chiefs and appointed nine new ones.

39 *Report of the Natal Native Commission*, pp. 33, 40, 44, 45. The hereditary chiefs ruled over sixty-three tribes with 63 979 huts; the appointed chiefs and head men ruled over sixteen with 24 727. There were twenty-three appointed head men who had 'charge of portions of tribes or collections of people (remnants of tribes)' (p. 33), which numbered twenty-three but had only 3 087 huts (p. 46); they included Christians in mission reserves (see pp. 43–44).

40 *Ibid*, pp. 41–46 (Appendix G, Schedule 3A). Lambert, *Betrayed Trust*, pp. 27–28, 33–34; also see, p. 62.

41 Lambert, *Betrayed Trust*, p. 24–25, 36. David Welsh, *The Roots of Segregation in Natal 1845–1910* (Cape Town, Oxford University Press, 1971), pp. 115–116.

42 Lambert, *Betrayed Trust*, pp. 26, 31–32. Welsh, *Roots of Segregation*, pp. 120–122. Etherington, 'The "Shepstone system",' pp. 179, 183, 185. Bill Guest, 'Colonists, confederation and constitutional charge,' in *Natal and Zululand from Earliest Times*, pp. 151–152. See also *Proceedings and Report*, p. 29.

43 Lambert, *Betrayed Trust*, pp. 19, 23, 29, 30. Welsh, *Roots of Segregation*, pp. 116, 150–155. Etherington, 'The "Shepstone System",', p. 175. *Report of the Natal Native Commission*, p. 15.

44 Lambert, *Betrayed Trust*, pp. 37, 46, 52 Welsh, *Roots of Segregation*, pp. 83–84, 85, 91, 94. *Report of the Natal Native Commission*, p. 5. *Evidence taken by the Sub-Commission for Umvoti County*, pp. 11, 15, 16, 33, 36.

45 Welsh, *Roots of Segregation*, pp. 155–156, 164–166.

46 Lambert, *Betrayed Trust*, p. 61. Etherington, 'The "Shepstone system",' p. 173.

47 *Report of the Natal Native Commission*, pp. 3–4. *Evidence taken by the Sub-Commission for Umvoti County*, pp. 2, 9, 12, 14, 19, 20, 37, 41, 45, 52, 53, 56, 60.

48 See and *cf.* Brookes and Webb, *History of Natal*, pp. 124–135 *passim*; Etherington, 'The "Shepstone system",' pp. 185–189; Guest, 'Colonists, confederation and constitutional change,' pp. 161–162; *The Anglo-Zulu War: New Perspectives* (edited by Andrew Duminy and Charles Ballard, Pietermaritzburg, University of Natal Press, 1989), pp. 1–77 *passim*; C.F. Goodfellow, *Great Britain and South African Confederation 1870–1881* (Cape Town, Oxford University Press, 1966), pp. 111–167 *passim*; and Graham Dominy, Awarding a 'retrospective white hat'? A reconsideration of the geopolitics of 'Frere's War' of 1879 (a paper presented to the Natal History Workshop at the University of Natal (in Pietermaritzburg), October 24–25, 1984.

49 Jenkinson, *Amazulu*, p. v.

50 Lambert, *Betrayed Trust*, p. 23.

51 Intelligence Branch of the Quartermaster-General's Department, Horse Guards, War Office, *Narrative of the Field Operations connected with the Zulu War of 1879* (London, Her Majesty's Stationery Office, 1881), p. 15. GH 1411, p. 206, and 1412: 4550/1878. CSO 1926: 3990/1878.

52 *Narrative*, pp. 8, 17.

53 See Philip Gon, *The Road to Isandlwana: The Years of an Imperial Battalion* (Johannesburg, Donker, 1979), pp. 123, 139, 158; John Ayliff and Joseph Whiteside, *History of the Abambo generally known as Fingoes* (Butterworth, privately printed, 1972), pp. 63–69. The most recent account of the Cape Wars is Noël Mostert, *Frontiers: The Epic of South Africa's Creation and the Tragedy of the Xhosa People* (London, Cape, 1992), which gives only a summary account, pp. 1249–1254, of the last one. The provenance of the amaFengu has been questioned recently – see Alan C. Webster, Land expropriation and labour extraction under Cape colonial rule: the war of 1835 and the 'emancipation' of the Fingo (Rhodes University, M.A., 1991).

54 C. 2220, p. 232. *Cf.* GH 1412: 4550/1878 and H.H. Parr, *A Sketch of the Kafir and Zulu Wars* (London, Kegal Paul, 1880), p. 153.

55 GH 1411, pp 107–110. TN, September 27, 1878: 'Arrival of Sir Bartle Frere in the City.'

56 *Narrative*, p. 15. See also NW, November 7, 1878: leader.

57 Durnford's memorandum (August 17, 1878) in CP 26–20. *Cf. A Soldier's Life and Work in South Africa 1872–1879. A Memoir of the Late Col. A.W. Durnford, R.E.* (edited by E. Durnford, London, Sampson Low, Marston, Searle & Rivington, 1882), pp. 333–339.

58 See GH 1424, pp. 145–146, 151–152. The complete memorandum also appears in *Lord Chelmsford's Zululand Campaign 1878–1879* (edited by John P.C. Laband; Stroud, Army Records Society, 1994), pp. 8–9.

59 Gerald French, *Lord Chelmsford and the Zulu War* (London, Lane, 1939) pp. 46–47.

60 See 1/VLM: 3/2/1: circular, J. Bird to Resident Magistrate, Inanda Division, September --, 1878.

61 GH 500: 3780/1878.

62 C 2220, pp. 284–286; also see GH 512, pp. 96–105.

63 See Bulwer's memoranda in GH 1411, pp. 81–105; 1411, pp. 194–241; 1421, pp. 65–85; 1422, pp. 3–13; 1424, pp. 168–170. French, *Lord Chelmsford and the Zulu War*, p. 85. See and *cf.* leaders in NW, August 27 and November 17, 1878; TN, October 9 and December 30, 1878; NM, December 10, 1878; NA, January 16, 1879; and letters and comments in NW, November 2, 1878; NM, November 23, 1878, and February 7, 1870; TN, December 20, 1878; NC, January 2, 1879; and the memorial (November, 1878) in CSO 672: 4734/1878.

64 See Bulwer's memoranda, cited in n. 63.

65 SNA 1/1/32, no. 151. GH 500, pp. 146–149.

66 GH 1423, pp. 140–146; *cf.* GH 1422, pp. 3–13. SNA 1/1/32, no. 188. See *Report of the Natal Native Commission*, pp. 6–7, and *Evidence taken by the Sub-Commission for Umvoti County*, pp. 3, 22, 55. On the putative inferiority of Natal to Zulu fighting men, see SNA 1/1/32, no. 188; Parr, *Sketch of the Kafir and Zulu Wars, pp. 154–155; H.M. Bengough, Memories of a Soldier's Life* (London, Arnold, 1913), p. 127; and Sonia Clarke, *Zululand at War 1879 (Houghton, Brenthurst, 1984), p. 121.*

67 *A Soldier's Life and Work*, pp. 201–202. Frances E. Colenso, *History of the Zulu War and Its Origin* (London, Chapman & Hall, 1880), pp. 250–251. See also C2220, p. 285, and Charles L. Norris Newman, *In Zululand with the British throughout the War of 1879* (London, Allen, 1880), p. 20.

68 *Narrative*, p. 15. GH. 1424, pp. 145 *et passim*. C 2234, p. 40. NW, August 27, 1878; leader.

69 GH 1326, pp. 184–185; 1411, p. 232; 1421, p. 81; 1424, pp. 168–172: *A Soldier's Life*, p. 202. TN, November 2, 1878: GO 209. *Lord Chelmsford's Zululand Campaign*, pp. 30 and 33. Also, *cf. Narrative*, p. 15.

70 GH 1411, pp. 161–163.

71 See SNA 1/7/11, unnumbered, for Shepstone's report, November 3, 1878. SNA 1/1/32, no. 118. SP 34: Chelmsford to Shepstone, November 2, 1878.

72 GH 1412: 4550/1878.

73 NA and NM, November 28, 1878: GO 205.

74 *Lord Chelmsford's Zululand Campaign*, p. 51.

75 Lambert, *Betrayed Trust*, p. 35

76 A.T. Bryant, *Olden Times in Zululand and Natal* (London, Longmans, Green, 1929), pp. 493–496.

77 SNA 1/1/32, no. 118.

78 *Ibid.* and 1/1/33, nos. 21 and [65]; 1/6/11, no. 17. 1 VLM, 3/1/1/8, p. 381. NM, December 12, 1878, and January 7, 1879. 'The Native Contingent.' NM, January 18, 1879: leader.

79 Shepstone's history, in SP 90, pp. 67–68. N.J. van Warmelo, *History of Matiwane and the Amangwane Tribe and told by Msebenzi to his kinsman Albert Hlongwane* (Pretoria, Government Printer, 1938), pp. 5–6, 169 and 170 n. Bryant, *Olden Times*, pp. 136–146 *passim*. Shooter, *The Kafirs of Natal*, p. 377. Ayliff and Whiteside, *History of the Abambo*, pp. 5–17 *passim*. CSO 1925: UT 220.1878. See *Report of the Natal Native Contingent*, p. 41; SNA 1/1/34, no. 160; and 1/BGV, IV, 270 and 273.

80 Warmelo, *History of Matiwane*, p. 223.

81 1/BGV, IV, 271, 272, 272–273, 278, and 336–337. CSO 673: 4807/1878 and 1925: C133/1878. UT 305/1878. SNA 1/6/11, no. 12, and 1/6/12, nos. 1 and 39. 1/BGV, IV, 280 and 326. *Lord Chelmsford's Zululand Campaign*, p. 84. TN, December 20, 1878: GO 228.

82 NM, December 16, 1878: 'Pakade Loyal.' See also NW, November 30, 1878, report.

83 Statement of Magidigidi KaNobebe in *The James Stuart Archive of recorded oral evidence relating to the history of the Zulu and neighbouring peoples* (4 vols., edited and translated by C. de B. Webb and J.B. Wright; Pietermaritzburg, University of Natal Press, 1976–1986), II, 87. SP, 90, pp. 65, 76, 78. Bryant, *Olden Times*, pp. 267–272.

84 *Report of the Natal Native Commission*, p. 43.

85 CSO 1925: C737/1878. SNA 1/6/11, no. 21. NM, December 16, 1878: leader. TN, December 27, 1878: 'On the Road to Helpmakaar.'

86 CSO 673: 4889/1878, SNA 1/1/33, no. 1 and 1/6/11, no. 20. See Paterson's and Mganu's statements to the Native Commission, in *Evidence taken before the Natal Native Commission, 1881* (Pietermaritzburg, Vause, Slatter, 1882), pp. 346 and 350, respectively, as well as Magidigidi's statement, in the *Stuart Archive*, II, 86; and *Report of the Natal Native Commission*, p. 43 *et passim*. NM, December 16, 1878: 'Pakade Loyal.' NM, December 19, 1878: 'The Native Contingent.' NW, December 17, 1878: 'The Gathering of the Clans,' and December 24, 1878: 'The Recent Affray near Estcourt.'

87 CSO 673: 4889/1878. NM, December 19, 1878: 'The Native Contingent.' NW, December 17: 'The Gathering of the Clans,' and December 24, 1878: 'The Recent Affray near Estcourt.'

88 See the Reverend J. Allsopp's answers to questions, in *Evidence taken before the Natal Native Commission*, pp. 20–21.

89 Owen Watkins, 'They Fought for the Great White Queen,' in *The Zulu War and The Colony of Natal* (edited by G.A. Chadwick and E.G. Hobson; Mandini, Qualitas, 1979), p. 153.

90 SNA, 1/1/225: 1165/1896.

91 S.M. Meintjes, Edendale 1850–1906: a case study of rural transformation and class formation in an African mission in Natal (University of London, School or Oriental and African Studies, Ph. D. 1988), p. 370.

92 CSO 1925: 4370/1878

93 Watkins, 'They Fought for the Great White Queen,' pp. 153–154.

94 Meintjes, Edendale, p. 372.

95 Watkins, 'They Fought for the Great White Queen,' pp. 153–154. Watkins is very vague with dates and may be telescoping events. He also states that a hundred mounted men were raised. It is presumed here that Msimang spoke from a prepared statement. *Cf.* Meintjes, Edendale, pp. 371–372.

96 See SNA 1/1/225: 1165/1896; also, the lists of landowners in Meintjes, Edendale, pp. 413–416.

97 See the short biography by R.C.A. Samuelson, in SNA 1/1/316: 4/1903; and Meintjes' lists.

98 CSO 673: 4807/1878. SNA 1/6/11, no. 12. TN, December 20, 1878: GO 228. Watkins, 'They Fought for the Great White Queen,' pp. 154–155. TN, August 15, 1879: 'Welcome to the Edendale Men.' *Cf.* Meintjes, Edendale, p. 372, and F. Reginald Statham, *Blacks, Boers & British: A Three Cornered Problem* (London, Macmillan, 1881, p. 179).

99 TN, December 30, 1878: 'Notes by the Way.' 1/PMB: 3/3/1/1, p. 685. SNA 1/1/225: 1165/1896. Norris Newman, *In Zululand with the British*, p. 27.

Chapter 2

MOBILIZATION – THE FIRST REGIMENT, PIONEERS AND MOUNTED TROOPS

The call-up and organization of the Contingent

The High Commissioner was determined to remove the threat of the war-like Zulu in order to secure a confederation of settler colonies under the aegis of Britain. Disputes and incidents served to produce a crisis. By the late spring of 1878 the prospect of war was very real. In early November the Lieutenant General got from the Supreme Chief the authority to raise the Natal Native Contingent on a regimental basis.[1] The Contingent was planned in detail, called into service, and prepared for battle within the next two months. It had a vital role to play as scouts and skirmishers when the imperial columns invaded the Zulu country.

General Orders giving the regulations for the Native Contingent were issued on November 23rd. Further orders, on November 28th, designated three regiments of infantry and their commanders.[2] The Lieutenant General wrote to the Secretary of State for War that when the contingent was mobilized he would be ready to invade Zululand.[3]

Colonel Durnford superintended the arrangements for raising and organizing the contingent. An officer from Britain with staff experience was specially assigned to help him.[4] Placards were put up[5] and notices were placed in the newspapers,[6] inviting colonists to apply to be officers and non-commissioned officers. The Lieutenant General would select and the Lieutenant Governor and High Commissioner would approve the candidates.[7]

Equipping the contingent stimulated the economy of Pietermaritzburg. Several businesses worked round the clock, with extra help, to fulfil contracts for belts, cartridge boxes and other items. One firm had a large order for harnesses and belts, another for water tins and powder flasks, yet another for tents – for the officers, not the men.[8]

On December 11th the High Commissioner's ultimatum to the Zulu King was delivered. Rejection was expected, war would follow in due course; however, the Zulu King was given until the end of the month to make a definite reply and until January 10th to comply with its terms.[9] The climate of war descended upon Natal. British troops arrived and took position on the various lines of advance.[10]

Delays with tents held up mobilization of the contingent, then delays getting officers and non-commissioned officers,[11] but finally the preparations were complete.

The first General Orders calling the Native Contingent into service were issued on December 11th.[12] The government estimated there were 64 794 able bodied men suitable for military service in the Colony.[13] Of these only 7550 were to form the Natal Native Contingent – 7000 infantry, 250 cavalry, 300 pioneers.[14] The Supreme Chief gave them to the Lieutenant General for service with the British army. Thus they entered the imperial service and left the service of the Colony. They would be paid and paid for by the British government. They would serve for as long as it required.[15]

Would the chiefs respond positively? Would the men come forward willingly? There was some doubt. The government did not want any coercion, yet there were reports of it in the Lower Tugela and Umgeni divisions.[16] As we have seen, the misgivings of the Europeans were unfounded. The chiefs were loyal and the men came forth willingly.

A sharp distinction was made between the foot soldiers on the one hand and the mounted men and the pioneers on the other. The infantry man remained as naked as he came, except that he was to be issued a blanket – blue for 1st Battalion, grey for 2nd Battalion, green for 3rd Battalion, in each regiment. One man in every ten would be issued a muzzle-loading rifle.[17]

Some European settlers regarded firearms in natives' hands as more dangerous to them than to the Zulu and the authorities doubted that many would know how to use them. They issued them largely to raise morale, for the enemy was known to have guns in quantity. One rifle for every tenth man did not seem dangerous.[18]

In addition to the firearms and spears there were tools – a hundred pick-axes, shovels, and cane knives for each Battalion, which also came to one-in-ten; and fifty hand axes and bill hooks, which in a desperate situation could be used as weapons.

A twenty-two pound cooking pot was provided for every ten men, and the daily ration per man was a pound of maize meal, a pound and a half of fresh meat, and two ounces of salt. It would be a spartan life, but a man could look forward to regular meals and pay – twenty shillings a month. This was at least an improvement on living conditions in the Thorns. And if soldiering took a man away from family and security, it recompensed him with camaraderie and adventure.

The mounted men fared better. They were paid thirty shillings a month and were issued with carbines or rifles. The uniform consisted of a coat and trousers, a pair of boots, a blanket and a haversack, plus the hat with a scarlet puggaree, the strip of cloth which became the badge of the contingent. Each man rode his own horse (and the army would pay no more than £10 for loss of it).[19]

The Edendale men – yiDeni, some heathen would call them – considered themselves a cut above the rest. The Reverend Allsopp asked the government to raise their pay so they could cover the expenses of their horses and saddles. The military authorities raised it to £3 a month. The Edendale men also disdained heathens' rations. Simeon Kambule, now sergeant major, asked for beef, bread, coffee and sugar. These were refused. Kambule vowed they would provide rations at their own expense.[20]

In addition to the mounted and foot soldiers, the contingent contained pioneers, men who would do the engineering work. The colonial government regularly called on chiefs to provide men for work, chiefly on the roads. Durnford had formed a special force from the amaNgwe to do such work and block the passes to Basutoland after Langalibalele's rebellion.

There was a need of special units for engineering work. The Supreme Chief suggested and both the Lieutenant General and Durnford called for these units. The colonial government raised and equipped the pioneers and turned them over to the military. The Supreme Chief did not like the militarization of labour units, but conceded that it might be necessary to make an otherwise unpopular duty attractive. The Acting Secretary for Native Affairs selected three chiefs who would furnish the men, and it was arranged that these would be organized in three companies under officers (one captain and two to four lieutenants) of the Royal Engineers. The pioneers received the same pay, arms and rations as the other men on foot, but they were clothed in red jackets and white trousers.[21]

The levies of pioneers were ordered to report to Fort Napier early in December. The first to arrive, on December 23rd, were from the Inanda Division, near the coast. They were Mbozana's men, amaNgangoma, who lived around Verulam, and Hlokolo's amaNgcolosi. They had responded promptly to the call-up and seemed quite keen. They marched through Pietermaritzburg singing a lively war song. They were put in the engineer's yard near the city gaol and given an ox, which they killed, cooked and ate. This was to be the daily fare. For the next week they were drilled by Captain W. J. Nolan, R.E. Red coats and white trousers were issued, and some guns, but in what proportion and to whom is not clear. The High Commissioner and Lieutenant General inspected them on the 6th and were greeted warmly with cheers.[22]

Mbozana's men, designated No. 1 Company, marched out of town on the 11th to join the No. 3 Column at Helpmekaar.[23] Hlokolo's men made up half of No. 3 Company. The complement was provided by the chief Mahoyiza. The company, under Captain William Allen, left to join the No. 2 Column at Kranskop on January 3rd or 4th.[24] No. 2 Company, under Captain G. Beddoes, also composed of Mahoyiza's men, left on December 30th to join the No. 1 Column at the coast. They, too, were dressed in red jackets and white trousers. They sported forage caps with a yellow band. One in five carried guns. Every man carried a tool – spade, pick or axe. At the lower Thukela they were placed under the direct supervision of an officer of the Royal Engineers with the column.[25]

No. 2 and 3 Companies took longer to form because Mahoyiza, a chief in the Umgeni Division, could not get three of his five head men to send the men requested. Part of the problem was that Mahoyiza was not popular with his people, the amaQanya. Some men called up did not want to serve, and two headmen resorted to fines of cattle. Also, the Resident Magistrate found out that one of the settlers did not want to lose labour and had interfered with one of the head men to thwart the Supreme Chief's will (yet it was the head man and not the colonist who was brought to court for this). Delays in getting the men led the Resident Magistrate to call on other chiefs, but while waiting for them, most of Mahoyiza's levy came in.[26]

The military authorities were optimistic in supposing levies would arrive at the column's assembly points in three days. In fact, it would take much longer than that just to communicate the information to the chiefs and then for the men to get under way. The drought was breaking and wet weather made it difficult to cross streams.

Many chiefs had people in several parts of the colony and the Resident Magistrates had not been told whether they should enrol all of the chiefs' men required or just those who lived in their divisions.[27]

The Acting Secretary for Native Affairs, chafing at the military's overriding of his preference for traditional organization, gave coastal magistrates the impression in November that the military was entirely responsible for whatever happened. The Resident Magistrate of Inanda sent messages to chiefs and left them to get their men together and find their way to the 2nd Regiment's assembly point. He did not know how many went. They arrived late, and some were hungry, having had no food for the march.[28] The Supreme Chief wanted to know why. The Acting Secretary replied that he had told the chiefs what was expected of them and the magistrates had only to let them do it. The Supreme Chief retorted: 'I do not think that Barter [the Resident Magistrate] has understood, or perhaps it is that [the] SNA [Shepstone] has omitted to inform him, that he, as Magistrate of his Division, had to take care that the number of men ordered out from his division was duly provided'.[29] The magistrate then referred to the Acting Secretary: 'When you came down and communicated certain orders to the Chiefs of this Division from the Supreme Chief, I understood from you that I was in no way to interfere in the matter ... I have *religiously* abstained from doing so in any way whatever... .'[30]

The Acting Secretary of Native Affairs obviously had his shortcomings. He also was in competition with other authorities he had earlier scorned. Thus the Resident Magistrate of Weenen, when he explained the fracas between Phakade's and Mganu's levies to the Acting Secretary, added: 'it is somewhat confusing to me, to have no less than three different departments all giving me orders or instructions respecting the raising and mustering of natives in my division – vizt the Colonial Secretary, yourself and Colonel Durnford ... .'[31]

It is hardly surprising that the Acting Secretary was ill by the end of December. Early in the new year had to ask for a week's leave. He did not fully recover until the end of February.[32]

The Natal Native Contingent was almost complete when the ultimatum expired and a state of war commenced on January 10, 1879. A few men had still to come in, but the great majority had assembled. They had been divided into battalions and companies and had begun training on British lines. Already the respective infantry regiments and mounted troops had different characteristics. Their careers also would be quite different.

The First Regiment and Mounted Troops – No. 2 Column

Officers and non-commissioned officers, with details of the 1st Regiment and the mounted troops of the No. 2 Column, left Pietermaritzburg for the assembly areas near Greytown on December 23rd.[33] The long drought ended in cold, wet days alternating with hot dry ones punctuated by electrical storms – weather typical of summer in Natal. Freshets and mud slowed the movement of troops to the front. The road to Greytown was uphill much of the way and wagons stuck repeatedly, spinning out a march of about thirty-five miles over four days. The first levies of foot soldiers arrived on the 28th and the column began to take shape.[34]

The No. 2 Column consisted of the 1st Regiment, the mounted troops, and a rocket battery, which was made up of British regulars.[35] Colonel Durnford had been put in command of the column as well as the regiment on December 9th,[36] and the call-up of men had begun just over a week later.[37]

The mounted men had been first off the mark, the Edendale Horse reporting at Fort Napier on the 23rd[38] and Zikhali's Horse reporting on the 27th.[39] Two other troops arrived in the meantime – Jantze's Horse from the Ipolela Division,[40] in the southwest of the colony, and Hlubi's Horse from the Ulundi Division,[41] below the Kahlamba.

Jantze was the preferred name of the Chief Mqundana. He was an appointed, not a hereditary chief. His people were the amaXimba, an artificial 'tribe' made up in the earlier days of the Colony out of fragments from the time of troubles. He had fought with the Dutch settlers against the Zulu King Dingane and been a loyal, if rather impulsive and sometimes careless, supporter of the British overlord. He had served with Durnford in the Langalibalele expedition. Durnford considered Jantze courageous as well as useful, and had specifically asked for his service now. He responded so promptly to the Supreme Chief's call that he seems to have anticipated it.[42]

Hlubi and his people were baSotho. Their forebears had lived on the east bank of the Mzinyathi, before being driven beyond the Kahlamba by the Zulu. They had regrouped and prospered beyond the mountains, until the people quarrelled among themselves and fought one another. One part, under Hlubi's father, had allied with the amaHlubi of Langalibalele, hence Hlubi's name. They had crossed over the mountains and entered the British colony in 1867. There they were called Tlokwa (in Sotho) or Hlongwane (in Zulu). Later they became enemies of Langalibelele, and under Hlubi, then a young chief, served under Durnford in the 1873 expedition. At Bushman's River pass, when others had lost their nerve, the young chief and his men remained steady. Durnford had not forgotten. He became their patron. He called on them for guides in 1877, when Britain seemed to need military backup in Natal following annexation of the Transvaal. Hlubi was in his mid forties, mature and dependable. He would say later, when he had repossessed the lands of his people, that the war was between Knowledge, which was represented by England, and Ignorance, which was the Zulu kingdom.[43] The reputation of the mounted baSotho was such that Britons and many colonists used the term 'Basutos' for mounted levies in imperial service, even though historically and linguistically Hlubi's people had little in common with their mounted fellows, the amaNgwane and the Christians.

The 1st Regiment had three battalions – on paper.[44] The 1st Battalion consisted for the most part of those good fighting men whom Durnford had especially asked for and the government consented to call – the amaNgwane, the amaNgwe and the amaBaso.[45] The Ngwane people have been described. The amaBaso were some of Langalibalele's people, who had been scattered and given to live on colonists' farms following the 'rebellion'. Durnford and others, including Bishop Colenso, had criticized the severity of their punishment and obtained a partial reconstitution of the chiefdom, but not restitution of their land. Their head man was Faku.[46] The amaNgwe (also called Phutili) were their neighbours, who had been implicated in the rebellion for taking care of the fleeing rebels' cattle and thus brought punishment on themselves as accessories. This, too, had been mitigated thanks largely to Durnford. The people were governed a regent, Mazikali, the great wife of the late chief Manzezulu.[47] Thus Durnford had a special relationship with the highlanders involved in the Langalibalele affair, and they were the core of his column.

The rest of the 1st Battalion was made up of amaNyuswa from the Umvoti Location and of abaseMbo from the Upper Umkomanzi Division. Each contributed enough men for about a company, and thus were a minority in the battalion.[48] The Acting Secretary had selected the former, while the battalion commandant, Captain Montgomery, had asked for the latter, because they lived in the same area as he – he knew them and they knew him, and thus, rather like Durnford, he supposed they would provide a loyal nucleus for his command.[49]

The 2nd Battalion consisted almost entirely of men from Locations in Umvoti County, selected by the Acting Secretary. There were two separate levies of the amaBomvu, one each of the amaChunu and abaThembu, and a smaller one of the amaZondi, also known as abaseNgome.[50] The 3rd Battalion was supposed to consist of two levies of considerable strength, but thanks to chopping and cutting of the list following the changes proposed by Durnford and because of the Acting Secretary's miscalculations, it was made up instead of four levies very much under strength.[51]

Durnford's column was to have 3 050 men, according to the revised schedule. Of these 2 750 were to be foot and 300 to be mounted.[52] Men for the 1st and 2nd Battalions and the mounted squadrons had been called up in the third week of December.[53] The infantry had been ordered to assemble at Greytown a few days after Christmas.[54] The cadres and mounted men reached the point of assembly on the 28th,[55] and about a thousand of the infantry came in just afterward, on the 28th and 29th.[56] They were organized into companies – five for the 1st Battalion and four for the 2nd Battalion.[57] On January 6th Durnford reported only 927 men in both Battalions.[58] Then the amaNgwane from Upper Tugela and the abaseMbo from Upper Umkomanzi arrived for the 1st Battalion, as well as the complement of the 2nd Battalion. Durnford's report on January 8th indicates that the 2nd Battalion was at full strength and the 1st Battalion short only one company (of amaNyuswa).[59]

The 3rd Battalion was just forming. The men had been called up on December 31st, and the battalion was expected to number just over 800 by February 8th. It never obtained this strength – on January 30th it numbered 176. The Acting Secretary had intended originally that Bomvu and Zondi levies from Umvoti should comprise the Battalion, but then the Bomvu levies for the 2nd Battalion had fallen short, and he had to shift. The 2nd Battalion got its strength, but not the 3rd Battalion, which drew instead from the amaZondi and other small chiefdoms in the county, the amaCele and amaThuli.[60]

The shortfall in numbers was due also to colonists who wanted to keep farm labour. The two Bomvu chiefs Homoyi and Sobuza, handed over 507 men. Shepstone had put them down for 1 100. Sobuza stated that he could only produce 250 instead of 600 because the farmers placed difficulties in their way.

Umvoti County farmers complained about the loss of 'servants'. The magistrate was willing to exempt those actually working on farms, but found many idle men were kept back by the landowners. The magistrate of the Upper Tugela Division exempted men who lived on owner-occupied farmers.[61] The principal casualty of the shortfall ultimately was the

3rd Battalion, which thus finally numbered between 185 and 275 men.[62]

The No. 2 Column was unique among the five columns in that it consisted almost entirely of colonial levies. A few mounted units of white settlers were allocated to the column, but were transferred to the coast on January 4th.[63] The only British regulars in Umvoti County (apart from the officer and ten men of the Rocket Battery) were the companies garrisoning Greytown.[64]

The Lieutenant General had planned for the five columns to advance simultaneously on Ulundi, but by December, he had reduced the number to three – the No. 1 Column advancing from the coast, the No. 3 Column advancing from northern Natal, and the No. 4 column advancing from the Transvaal. The relegation of the No. 2 Column reflected logistical considerations – the terrain between the Middle Drift of the Thukela and the Zulu King's great place of Ulundi consisted of difficult ridges and streams mostly athwart the lines of advance. The Lieutenant General no longer deemed it practicable for transport. He retained the column as a strategic block to a Zulu raid into the heart of Natal. Eventually it would cross at the Lower Thukela sometime after the No. 1 Column and to the left of it and open communication with the No. 3 Column.[65]

The partly formed column halted near Greytown on December 28th. Durnford, detained in Pietermaritzburg until he relinquished his engineering responsibilities on the 26th, soon joined it, and on 31st it moved to a camp at d'Almaine's farm near Kranskop.[66] The 1st and 3rd Battalions would be based there for the rest of the war. The setting was the gently rolling grassland of the Umvoti plateau, where the Dutch had staked out generous farms for themselves. The beauty of the place was not at first noticeable to the men, for it rained the better part of three days. Durnford sent two companies of the 2nd Battalion to Kranskop on January 2nd to make a road down to the Middle Drift. He received a report that the enemy was in force across the river and brought up the whole regiment next day. The report proved false. The column returned to camp, leaving a company on outpost at the kop.[67]

There was little time before hostilities began in which to inculcate the essential skills of British soldiering. Montgomery had started by drilling his officers at Fort Napier. The 1st Battalion had its first parade on the morning of December 15th. The officers of the 2nd Battalion mustered the following day. When the non-commissioned officers arrived, there was sufficient cadre for battalion drills.[68] They had two weeks to practice before leaving for the front.

The men had no training at all for war, their martial experience having been limited to mock combats before their chiefs at the Feast of the First Fruits.[69] One young officer later remembered that the men of his company – amaNgwane – 'had, from want of practice, lost the art of using an assegai' [as the British called the stabbing spear] and were totally without discipline'. None the less the men of the column seemed very warlike and eager to fight. When the column halted at d'Almaine's they rehearsed an encounter with an imaginary enemy some fifty yards in front; they postured in attack and then closed on their opponents, spearing with gusto.[70] Their mime recalled the historic tactics of the people who lived in Natal and Zululand. Only among the Zulu people were they still practised with purpose.

Zulu *amabutho* were trained to attack rather than to defend. They advanced in extended order, the centre of their line engaging the enemy in front and the wings swiftly enveloping his flanks. This was the well known 'chest and horns' formation. Success depended on dash and discipline as well as surprise and numbers, for a wary opponent could either evade contact in rough terrain, as the amaSwazi did, or make an all-round defence and use firearms to repel the attack, as the Dutch did. Zulu conservatism prevented further tactical innovation. Zulu leaders recognized that firearms were advantageous, and they imported rifles of all kinds, but they did not change their tactics to make good use of them. Nor were their soldiers trained in marksmanship. The best the Zulu army could do with its thousands of guns was lay down a harassing fire and delegate individuals to snipe. The people of Natal did not see this ossification of Zulu tactics. They had more confidence in the Zulu *amabutho* than their own, notwithstanding a general willingness to fight for the British Queen who had brought peace and stability to the land against the Zulu King who represented war and destruction.[71]

There seems to have been no comprehension among the Natal chiefs of the system which the British military wished to impose on their levies, whatever the Acting Secretary for Native Affairs and the Lieutenant General's staff officers may have told them about it in November. Would the levies be round pegs for the military's square holes, as the Supreme Chief and Acting Secretary expected? The civil authorities regarded the military's experiment as a mistake, but would it also be a failure?

The main camp was established, the levies filled up the battalions, and Durnford introduced the regimen of a modern European army. 'Alert Parade' was held at three every morning and the men stood in formation, weapons in hand, until daybreak.

Then they drilled for a couple of hours, Durnford often taking charge of the mounted troops. Rations were served out at six. There was a parade at seven, then breakfast. There were parades at eleven and two. Bed was usually at seven.[72] Health was good. What sickness there was was blamed on the generous meat ration rather than the wet weather.[73]

Drill occupied much of the time. The levies were divided into companies and put through simple column movements, such as marching in review, to the flank (by fives), and present arms. Commands were given in English. The movements at first were not quite what the officers expected – but the men were quick to learn, though some considered the drill harassing.[74] The chief and head men of the amaNgwane later complained that they had had no time to learn the military organization. The new military formations confused them. The mounted men had a sham fight and target practice with their rifles, and the Edendale men did very well in the shooting.[75]

The Lieutenant General visited and observed of Durnford's contingent, on New Year's Day: 'The officers speak very confidently about their men, and a very good feeling seemed already to have been established amongst them'.[76] Durnford informed him a week later that 'an excellent spirit pervaded his native battalions'.[77]

It was axiomatic for Durnford and the Lieutenant General that quality of officers determined quality of force. The ideal British officer was a gentleman of good character who got on well and was professionally competent. Durnford had planned that officers of the contingent would be raised from all classes of colonists in Natal, but especially farmers' sons speaking Zulu, who had grown up with and knew the men they would lead; however, he also allowed for traders and hunters familiar with the Zulu country, as well as 'men who had served Her Majesty as officers, soldiers or seamen'.[78]

The Lieutenant General doubted that the Colony of Natal had sufficient men for the purpose, and made arrangements for others, who had led auxiliaries in the late Cape war, to come to Natal to officer the 2nd and 3rd Regiments. British army officers 'on special service' – usually men on leave or seconded from regiments at home in order to get combat or professional experience abroad – would furnish some leaders. The agreement between the military and civil authorities was that the Lieutenant General would nominate men for the approval of the Supreme Chief and High Commissioner.[79]

In effect the 1st Regiment and the mounted troops – the No. 2 Column – did draw most of their officers from Natal. Advertisements were placed in newspapers for applications from November 9th. From November 21st General Orders named the new officers, and the command structure of the first two battalions of the regiment was practically complete within a month. Most of the appointments to the 3rd Battalion were made in late December and early January.[80] A special effort to recruit non-commissioned officers was made from November 25th, but probably because of their low rank and number the military made the appointments without reference to the civil authorities or mention in General Orders.[81]

Doubtless motives varied among the applicants. Young men probably looked forward to adventure and rationalized it as patriotic duty. Pay was good: thirty shillings a day and forage for two horses for a commandant, fifteen shillings and forage for one horse for a captain, and eleven shillings and forage for one horse for a lieutenant. Officers would have to provide their own uniforms and horses, of course, although it was fairly easy to get the latter on good terms from the army's remount depot.[82] A sergeant major's pay was nine shillings a day, a sergeant's seven and a corporal's six. Non-commissioned officers would be provided uniforms and did not ride horses.

Each Battalion was to have ten captains and twenty lieutenants, thirty sergeants and thirty corporals. Service was for six months. Both officers and non-commissioned officers were issued rifles and ammunition, bayonets and belts, and the red puggarees.[83] Durnford described himself thus in a letter to his mother:

> I wonder whether you would admire my appearance for the field? Boots, spurs, dark cord-breeches, serge patrol-jacket, broad belt over the shoulders, and one around the waist – to the former a revolver, and to the latter a hunting-knife and ammunition pouch. A wide-awake soft felt hat with a wide brim, one side turned up, and a crimson turban (puggaree) wound round the hat – very like a stage brigand.[84]

With his long drooping moustache it is easy to understand why. He was probably one of the best dressed officers. Their uniform consisted essentially of the same sporting dress. There were no red coats.

The four commandants were experienced officers. Durnford himself had a career of thirty-three years in the Royal Engineers, although his combat experience was limited to the expedition in 1873. He had had several postings in the British Isles and had served in Ceylon, where he had met his wife, from whom he was now separated. This was his eighth year in Natal. He was well known if not so well liked in the Colony. He balanced between the hard and soft schools of colonists when it came to 'native affairs', although his public concern for the injured parties of the 1873 rebellion made his sympathies plain. For all that he remained thoroughly professional. So was his staff. Captain Brunker, 26th Regiment, initially assigned to organize the contingent, had left to serve in a mounted colonial unit, but in his place as staff officer came Captain Geoffry Barton, 7th Foot. Captain William Francis Dundonald Cochrane, 32nd Foot, was orderly officer. Both were officers on special service. George Shepstone, a son of Theophilus Shepstone, the Colony's former Secretary for Native Affairs, was Durnford's Political Assistant.[85]

The commandant of the 1st Battalion was Alexander Montgomery, Esquire.[86] Formerly captain in the 7th Fusiliers, he had come to the Colony with a typically large Victorian family and taken up a farm near Mid-Illovo, which he named 'Ismont'. He was a member of the local gentry, a Justice of the Peace, and dabbled in politics. He was a capable officer. The dark side of his character only became apparent later.

Major Harcourt Bengough of the 77th Regiment was commandant of the 2nd Battalion. He had begun his military career in the Crimea just as the war there ended, and had spent most of it since in India. He was a thinking officer. He liked tiger-hunting, but he also learnt Russian, Persian, Arabic and Burmese. On the ship from England to South Africa he studied a Zulu grammar and dictionary and compiled a military phrase book for the use of his officers in Natal. It was printed and offered for sale in the Colony, with a good puff in General Orders and in the local press, but it was not officially required.[87]

The commandant of the 3rd Battalion was Captain Charles E. Le M. Cherry, 32nd Foot. He was genial if colourless, of middle age, and his health was failing.[88]

Among the subordinate officers were a few with some military background, but the great majority were young men without military pretensions.[89] Perhaps they had been cadets at school, if they had secondary education; they may have had target practice with the local rifle association; and a handful might have been in the army or the militia; however, men in the Colony's active militia units were not allowed to take service with the Native Contingent.

Durnford was responsible for vetting applications for officers. The Lieutenant General's military secretary referred the applications to him indiscriminately. Thus an appreciable number had to be weeded out – those men who were unfit because of defects of personality and background.[90] For instance, one young man told Durnford that he had served in the Cape Colony and the way to make natives fight was to get behind them with a whip. Durnford told him that if that was his attitude, then he should make his will beforehand: if one of his men stabbed him he would deserve it.[91] It is not surprising, given his care, that Durnford soon drained the pool of talent. A Durban newspaper judged the officers as a pretty mixed lot:

> ... Among very many names that could not be improved upon, there are a few which suggest doubt as to the existence of that tact, experience, and discretion, which are so indispensable in the effective control of armed bodies of natives. We are glad, however, to see that positions of superior responsibility have been found for many colonists, of varying ages, whose names are in themselves a guarantee of efficiency for their posts.[92]

Some men who were suitable did not come forward because of their domestic condition or business affairs or prior commitment in the militia. Others were simply prudent to a degree. There was no forgetting the day at Bushman's River pass when Durnford's little expedition had confronted a mass of fleeing rebels: he had declined to open fire because the Lieutenant Governor had expressly forbidden it, yet the rebels had crowded forward aggressively, opened fire themselves, and forced the expedition to retire in inglorious disorder. Durnford lost five men to the rebels' fire, one of them the son of the Colonial Secretary.[93] A member of the Legislative Council, learning now that one of his sons wanted to join the Native Contingent, stopped him. 'I knew that Colonel Durnford who was to command the native force was brave to rashness, and I did not therefore think my son should join it'.[94]

Durnford wanted local men, whose circumstances made them familiar with the customs and language of the people. He himself did not speak Zulu, nor did all of his officers, and the regulations for the contingent accordingly provided for an interpreter for each Battalion.[95] Some of the amaNgwane still found it difficult to get on with officers who could not speak Zulu or spoke it so imperfectly that they could not be understood.[96]

A booklet, entitled 'General instructions for the management of natives for the guidance of officers appointed to the Natal Native Contingent, and others who may have natives placed under them', was distributed by order of the Lieutenant General. It was a primer in what we would call race relations. In sentiment it was Durnford, but not its rather patronizing style. Montgomery later claimed that he had written out suggestions which the Lieutenant General then had had drafted into the formal instructions. A likely author would be the

Honourable W. Drummond, intelligence officer on Lord Chelmsford's staff.

The instructions numbered eighteen. They began: 'The Natal Zulu may be looked upon as an intelligent, precocious boy, with the physical strength of a man'. The gist of what followed was treat-him-well-and-he-will-serve-you-well.

Maintain a superior stance in all dealings with him. Avoid racialist tactlessness: 'Never use epithets of contempt such as niggers, Kafirs, &c. Call them "abantu" (people) "amadoda" (men) or "amabuti" (soldiers)'. Care and patience would make soldiers of them: 'A quiet, firm tone is the one to adopt. An intimation that they are behaving like common kafirs (amakafula), and not like royal soldiers (amabato wenkosi) is certain to produce an effect'.[97]

'[A] commission in the N.N.C. is anything but a sinecure,' reported an officer who described Durnford's rigorous programme for a local newspaper.[98] Durnford was strict and did not tolerate shirking. One morning Montgomery was on the sick list. The senior captain of the 1st Battalion, Charles Hay, was persuaded by other officers to scamp parade. They formed up without their horses, which was contrary to orders. Durnford apparently left the mounted troops to attend the infantry. Where were the horses? Hay told him they were on the sick list, too! The humour palled as Durnford took charge of drill: 'Now, gentlemen, I think we will do a little skirmishing'. It was done at double quick. The officers, fully accoutred but unmounted, struggled to keep up with their lightly accoutred and barefoot men. At the end of a few hours they were exhausted. As he left them, Durnford expressed to Hay the hope that his horse would be fit to work the next morning.[99]

The instructions mentioned punishments for the men without specifying them. Corporal punishment did not apply to officers (and Durnford disliked it for the men). The only man flogged in the regiment was a disobedient non-commissioned officer: Bengough ordered the punishment summarily, but had it carried out in a secluded spot, out of sight of the men.[100]

The Lieutenant General soon changed his mind about having the No. 2 Column act in conjunction with the No. 1 Column, out of concern for the safety of the Natal border in the Umsinga Division. The Msinga was occupied by various peoples, many of whom had furnished men to the 1st and 3rd Regiments of the Contingent. Although it was rough country, a Zulu raid might penetrate it and go deep into Natal, threatening the line of communication north of Pietermaritzburg as well as creating popular commotion. Although a Native Border Guard was organized to prevent this, the Lieutenant General decided that something more was needed: a force 'under so energetic a commander as Lieutenant-Colonel Durnford will, I feel sure, entirely remove any apprehension that may now exist in the Umsinga district regarding a hostile raid ... .'

On January 8th he ordered Durnford to move his two strongest battalions of infantry and five troops of mounted men to the Sand Spruit valley, near the Umsinga magistracy. At that position he could protect the border, and the Border Guard there would be under his control. Durnford was even permitted to counter-raid if it served the purpose of defence. The No. 3 Column would cooperate in clearing the border of dangerous enemy forces when it entered the Zulu country, at which time Durnford would receive further orders to move.[101]

It was not until the war began, on January 10th, that Durnford started with five of the mounted troops and the rocket battery, escorted by two companies of Ngwane foot, to Burrups', a well known way station on the road north from Greytown. Next day he rode on to meet the Lieutenant General, who had changed his mind again. Durnford was instructed to bring the detachment at Burrups' and one battalion of infantry to Rorke's Drift as soon as the No. 3 Column cleared it and moved on.[102] Chelmsford directed Durnford to join the No. 3 Column with his mounted men and rocket battery, and have the battalion watch 'the gates of Natal,' that is the border between Rorke's Drift and the Msinga mountain, and in due course cross the river there. The two battalions remaining at d'Almaine's farm were to cross at the Middle Drift as soon as the No. 1 Column reached Eshowe.

The main body of the No. 2 Column remained near Kranskop. The officers and men, unaware of the Lieutenant General's changes of plan, still expected to invade Zululand by way of the Middle Drift. Spirits rose when they were ordered to move down to the crossing at daybreak on the January 14th. In fact, Durnford was disobeying the Lieutenant General's instructions. He had told the Lieutenant General that the Zulu forces opposite had left the border, but then the missionary at the station near Kranskop had informed him that they had returned in strength and were threatening to invade Natal. The missionary had contacts in the Zulu country and a good telescope. The information seemed credible even though the river was too high for crossing on the 13th and few enemy were seen.[103] The Lieutenant-General did not see any threat, He wrote sharply:

Dear Durnford

Unless you carry out the instructions I give you, it will be my unpleasant duty to remove you from your command ... When a column is acting separately in an enemy's country I am quite ready to give its commander every latitude, and would certainly expect him to disobey any orders ... if information which he obtained, showed that it would be injurious to the interests of the column under his command – Your neglecting to obey my instructions in this present instance has no excuse, you have simply received information in a letter from Bishop Schroeder [sic], which may or may not be true and which you have no means of verifying ... .[104]

Durnford was about to descend into the valley of the Thukela when an orderly delivered the dispatch. He read it with a look of disgust and ordered the force to return to camp.[105]

The No. 3 Column was preparing to move forward to a new camp in Zululand, under Isandlwana hill. Durnford put that portion of his column at Burrups' on short notice to move, and on the 17th began an arduous march through the thorn country into the Msinga. Durnford liked vigorous exercise – long rides in changing weather were a tonic.[106] Now he was in his element. He wrote to his mother:

You would have been pleased at seeing us in the night, marching, dark night, 'watercourse' roads, self leading, with an orderly and lantern, then cavalry, each man leading his own horse, rocket battery next then infantry, the waggon train straggling over some five miles of road. Crossing rivers in large boats in the night, horses swimming, then cattle killing, cooking on the red embers, horses feeding, men eating and sleeping, etc. All the sights and sounds of camp life which I love.[107]

The mounted men reached Sand Spruit in the afternoon. The infantry came up later, but Durnford was off again with the mounted troops, rocket battery and its small infantry escort, to Vermaak's, above Rorke's Drift. On the 19th the Lieutenant General ordered him to cross the Mzinyathi with this vanguard in the wake of the No. 3 Column. Bengough, with the 2nd Battalion at Sand Spruit, should prepare to cross the river further down, off the right flank of the column, in three days time.[108]

On the 21st George Shepstone rode to the Lieutenant General's headquarters to report Durnford's progress, and returned with directions that Durnford should hurry on, along with the pioneers at the crossing, and join the No. 3 Column.[109]

NOTES

1 *Narrative*, p. 15.

2 TN, November 2, 1878: GO 209.

3 French, *Lord Chelmsford and the Zulu War*, p. 150.

4 TN, November 15 and 18, 1878: GO 195 and 197, respectively.

5 NW, November 23, 1878: 'Natal Native Contingent'. NC, November 26, 1878: report.

6 See, e.g. TN, November 11 and 13; NC, November 14 and 16; NA, November 28, 1878.

7 CSO 666: 4113/1878.

8 TN, November 21, 1878: 'Native Levies.' NW, November 21, 1878; NC, November 23, 1878: reports.

9 *Narrative*, pp. 15–17. TN, November 20, 1878. See NM, November 28, 1878: GO 205.

10 *Narrative*, pp. 18–20. GH 1412: 4550/1878.

11 WC II/2/2: Chelmsford to Wood, December 4 and 10, 1878. See also *A Soldier's Life*, p. 201.

12 TN, December 20, 1878: GO 227 and 228, and Extra, December 13, 1878: GO 220. NW, December 5, 1878: 'The Situation'. CSO 672: 4760/1878, 670: 4556/1878, and 673: 4807/1878. SNA 1/6/11, no. 17. Curiously, there is ample documentation for the mounted troops and the 2nd and 3rd Regiments, but not for the 1st Regiment and the pioneers.

13 GH 1412: 4550/1878.

14 *Ibid.* gives the number as 7400, but it was later revised.

15 NM, November 28, 1878: GO 205.

16 Clarke, *Zululand at War 1879*, p. 67. SNA 1/6/11, no. 19 and 1/1/33, no. [65]. *Cf.* 1/VLM: 3/2/1: 261/1879, and 1/BGV, IV, 278.

17 NM, November 28, 1878: GO 205.

18 NW, November 2, 1878: 'Arming the Natives.' NM Supplement, November 23, 1878: 'The Defence Question.' NM, December 1, leader, and December 12, 1878: 'The Native Contingent.' NC, January 2, 1879, report. GH 500, pp. 146–147; 512, pp. 109–111; 1412: 4550/1878; 1423, p. 45–48. CSO 672: 4707/1878; 2621, p. 358, SNA 1.1.32, no. 151 and 1/1/33, no. [65]. 1/VLM 3/2/1: C82/1878. *Narrative*, p. 15. French, *Lord Chelmsford and the Zulu War*, p. 85.

19 NM, November 23, 1878: GO 205. Apropos billhooks as weapons, see *The Zulu War Journal of Colonel Henry Harford, CB* (edited by Daphne Child; Pietemaritzburg, Shuter and Shooter, 1978), p. 12.

20 CSO 678: 3 and 5/1879. TN, January 8, 1879: GO 4. Watkins, 'They Fought for the Great White Queen,' p. 155. CFP 8/16: statement of Luguba Mbata.

21 GH 500, pp. 164–168; 1411, pp. 242–261. SNA 1/1/31, no. 59. TN, December 20, 1878: GO 227, and Extra, December 13, 1878: GO 220. C2234, p. 39. Colenso, *History of the Zulu War*, p. 253. Initially the Lieutenant General envisaged that a detachment comprising two companies of Royal Engineers would accompany each invading column (*Lord Chelmsford's Zululand Campaign*, p. 10).

22 GH 1411, p. 253. CSO 1972, p. 71. SNA 1/1/31, no. 62, and 1/6/11, no. 23. TN, November 27: 'Military Notes;' December 9, 1878: 'The Engineer Contingent.' NA, December 5, 1878; 'Maritzburg.' NW, December 5: 'The Situation;' December 12, 1878: 'Military Movements.'

23 *Narrative*, p. 19. NW, December 12, 1878: 'Military Movements.' TN Extra, December 13, 1878: GO 220.

24 See the list in SNA 1/1/31, no. 59, and the reports in 1/6/14, no. 12, and 1/6/15, nos. 20 and 46. TN, January 15, 1879: GO 9. 1/GTN: 3/2/1: 648/1878. CSO 1872, p. 209. *Cf.* CSO 1972, p. 201, and NC, December 31, 1878, report.

25 *Narrative*, p. 19. TN, January 1: GO 235, and January 3, 1879, report. NC, December 31, 1878, report. Ian Castle and Ian Knight, *Fearful Hard Times: The Siege and Relief of Eshowe 1879* (London, Greenhill, 1994), p. 42.

26 SNA 1/1/31, no. 62; 1/1/33, nos. 27 and 50; 1/6/11, no. 18; 1/6/15, nos. 20 and 46. CSO 677: 4737/1878. 1/PMB: 3/3/1/1, pp. 712–713.

27 SNA 1/1/31. no. 70; 1/1/33, nos. 1 and [65]; 1/6/11, no. 20. CSO 1925: C160/1878. 1/VLM 3/2/1: 847I/1878.

28 SNA 1/1/33, no. [65]; 1/6/11, no. 23. 1/VLM: 3/2/1: 847I/1878; 3/1/1/8, p. 381.

29 1/VLM: 3/2/1: 847I/1878.

30 1/VLM: 3/1/1/8, p. 381.

31 SNA 1/1/31, no. 60.

32 GH 1423, p. 140. SNA 1/1/31, no. 67; 1/1/33, nos. 22, 33, 39, 55; 1/6/11, no. 19.

33 *A Soldier's Life*, p. 210. NW, December 24, 1878: 'Military.' *Cf. Irish Times*, May 5, 1879: 'A Survivor of Isandula,' which states they left on the 22nd.

34 Norris-Newman, *In Zululand with the British*, p. 27. TN, December 30, 1878: 'Notes by the Way.' NM, December 28, 1878: 'The Native Contingent,' and January 6, 1879: 'With the Native Contingent.'

35 TN, December 11, 1878: GO 218. *Cf. Narrative*, p. 142. CSO 681: 393/1879. NM, January 13, 1879: 'With the Native Contingent.'

36 TN, December 2 and 11, 1878: GO 209 and 218, respectively.

37 SNA 1/6/11, nos. 12 and 13. CSO 1972, p. 150.

38 SNA 1/1/31, no. 64. *Cf.* 1/PMB: 3/3/1/1, p. 85. TN, August 15, 1879: 'Welcome to the Edendale Men.'

39 SNA 1/1/33, no. 12.

40 CSO 666: 4194/1878.

41 Weenen Add. 1, p. 345.

42 CSO 666: 4194/1878. SNA 1/6/11, no. 14, and 1/7/12, pp. 43–44. *Report of the Natal Native Commission*, p. 44.

43 See and *cf.* returns in GH 1412: 4550/1878, CSO 1928: 4417/1878 and W65/1879; and SNA 1/6/11, no. 20. *A Soldier's Life*, pp. 320–321. Colenso, *Ten Weeks in Natal*, pp. 78–79, 172, 180, 210–211. Jenkinson, *Amazulu*, pp. 94–95, 148. P.L. Brentz, 'Hlubi,' in *Dictionary of South African Biography*, 111, 395. S. Bourquin, 'The N.N.C. and Associated Units during the Zulu War of 1879,' in *The*

Zulu War and The Colony of Natal, pp. 112–113. R.W.F. Drooglever, *The Road to Isandhlwana: Colonel Anthony Durnford in Natal and Zululand 1873–1879* (London, Greenhill, 1992), pp. 49–55 *passim*.

44 TN, December 2, 1878: GO 209.

45 *A Soldier's Life*, pp. 339–340. CSO 1925: C133/1878.

46 Drooglever, *The Road to Isandhlwana*, pp. 79, 83, 84.

47 *Ibid.*, pp. 75–85 *passim*. See C. Boast to the Acting Secretary of Native Affairs, May 5, 1880, in Weenen Add. 2/2, no page given, and April 29, 1881, in Weenen Add. 1, pp. 383–385; and his report (March, 1880), in Weenen Add 1, pp. 366–367.

48 *Cf.* CSO 1925: 4370/1878. SNA 1/6/14, no. 4.

49 CSO 668: 4334/1878.

50 CSO 1925: 4370/1878. SNA 1/6/11, no. 20. *Report of the Natal Native Commission*, p. 42.

51 GH 1326, p. 185; 1424: 453/1878 and C127/1878. CSO 1925: 4370/1878. SNA 1/6/14, no. 4.

52 SNA 1/1/31, no. 59.

53 *Cf.* CSO 673: 4807/1878; 1925: 4370/1878; 1972, p. 150; and *A Soldier's Life*, p. 191.

54 CSO 1972, p. 150.

55 NM, January 6, 1879: 'With the Native Contingent'.

56 *Ibid.*

57 Bengough, *Memories of a Soldier's Life*, p. 111. NC, January 11, 1879: 'With Colonel Durnford's Column.'

58 CSO 681: 393/1879.

59 *Cf.* SNA 1/1/31, no. 67; 1/1/33, nos. 5 and 12; 1/6/11, nos. 20, 55 and 56.

60 CSO 1925: 4370/1878, and 1972, pp. 201, 271. SNA 1/6/11, nos. 20 and 55, and 1/6/14, no. 4.

61 SNA 1/1/34, no. 82, and 1/6/11, nos. 18 and 20. I/BGV, IV, 264, 276. TN, January 6, 1879: 'Umvoti County.'

62 SNA 1/6/11, no. 20, and 1/6/14, no. 4.

63 NM, January 11, 1879, telegram dated January 10th.

64 J.P.C. Laband and P.S. Thompson, *War Comes to Umvoti: The Natal–Zululand Border 1878-79* (Durban, University of Natal Department of History, 1980), pp. 31 and 36.

65 *Narrative*, p. 17, *Lord Chelmsford's Zululand Campaign*, pp. 20–21, 42, 106. French, *Lord Chelmsford and the Zulu War*, p. 261. C2234, p. 41. C2242, pp. 18–19. Chelmsford to Pearson, December 31, 1878, CP 27–5.

66 NM, January 6, 1879: 'With the Native Contingent.' NC, January 11, 1878: 'With Colonel Durnford's Column.' Bengough, *Memories of A Soldier's Life*, p. 111. *A Soldier's Life*, pp. 199, 201. *Cf. Irish Times*, 5 May, 1879: 'A Survivor of Isandula,' which gives the 29th.

67 *A Soldier's Life*, p. 206. Bengough, *Memories of a Soldier's Life*, pp. 111–112. NC, January 11, 1879: 'With Colonel Durnford's Column.' NW, January 16, 1879: 'With Col. Durnford's Column.'

68 TN, December 6, 1878, 'Military and Volunteer Notes.'

69 GH 1421, pp. 69–70, and 1423, pp. 140–146, 154–157. SNA 1/1/32, no. 118. *Evidence taken before the Natal Native Commission*, p. 346.

70 NW, January 16, 1879: 'With Col. Durnford's Column.' NW, January 19, 1929: reminiscence by T.M.C. Nourse.

71 J.P.C. Laband and P.S. Thompson, *Field Guide to the War in Zululand and the Defence of Natal 1879* (2d rev. ed. Pietermaritzburg, University of Natal Press, 1983), pp. 3–7. Clarke, *Zululand at War*, pp. 48, 121. *Evidence taken before the Natal Native Commission*, p. 347. Bengough, *Memories of a Soldier's Life*, pp. 80–81. W.H. Stafford, 'Stirring Days of Old Times. A story of Isandlwana,' p. 4. SNA 1/1/32, no. 118.

72 *Cf. A Soldier's Life*, pp. 205 and 210, and NC, January 18, 1879, citing a NW report.

73 NM, January 13, 1879: 'With the Native Contingent.'

74 Bengough, *Memories of a Soldier's Life*, pp. 106 and 111. NW, January 6, 1879: 'With the Native Contingent.' NC, January 11, 1879: 'With Colonel Durnford's Column.' 1/BGV: IV, 344. 1/GTN: 3/2/1: G91/1879.

75 Bengough, *Memories of a Soldier's Life*, p. 111. 'Personal History [of the Disaster of the Battle of Isandlwana 22nd January 1879] dictated by Captain Walter H. Stafford, January 1928,' p. 2. NC, January 11, 1879: 'With Colonel Durnford's Column.' NM, January 13, 1879: 'With the Native Contingent.'

76 *Lord Chelmsford's Zululand Campaign*, p. 52.

77 C 2242, p. 18.

78 CP 26–20: Durnford's proposal, August 17, 1878. *A Soldier's Life*, pp. 333–334.

79 GH 500, p. 139, and 111, p. 230. CSO 666: 4113/1878. C2234, p. 39. TN, October 23: 'Native Levies;' and December 16, 1878: GO 223. Colenso, *History of the Zulu War*, pp. 252–253.

80 See reports in TN, November 11 and 13, 1878, and NC, November 14 and 16, 1878: and GO in CP 26–13 and TN, December 2, 1878 – January 22, 1879 *passim*.

81 GH 1422, pp. 11–12. See reports in NW, November 23, 1878; NC, November 26, 1878; NA, November 28, 1878.

82 NM, November 28, 1878: GO 205. TN, December 6, 1878: GO 213.

83 NM, November 28, 1878: GO 205.

84 *A Soldier's Life*, pp. 199–200.

85 *Ibid.*, p. 201. Drooglever, *The Road to Isandhlwana*, pp. 141, 158 *et passim*. TN, December 20, 1878: GO 228, and Extra, December 13, 1878: GO 219. *The South African Campaign, 1879* (compiled by J.P. Mackinnon and Sydney Shadbolt; London, Hayward, 1882), pp. 308, 310.

86 On Montgomery see *Natal Who's Who* (Durban, Natal Who's Who, 1906), p. 140, and Laband and Thompson, *War Comes to Umvoti*, p. 111. Durnford first asked W.D. Wheelwright, Resident Magistrate of Umvoti County, to be commandant of the battalion, but the government refused to release him (CS0 1972, p. 67).

87 Bengough, *Memories of a Soldier's Life*, pp. 103–104, and see ch. 1–7 *passim*. TN, January 8, 1879: GO 4.

88 On Cherry see Laband and Thompson, *War Comes to Umvoti*, p. 109.

89 On the youthfulness of the 2nd Battalion's officers, see NW, April 19, 1879: 'Harry's Complaints (Continued).'

90 *A Soldier's Life*, p. 253. Colenso, *History of the Zulu War*, p. 253. TN, November 15, 1878: 'Native Levies.' NC, November 16, 1878: 'Native Levies.'

91 *A Soldier's Life*, p. 254.

92 NM, December 19, 1878: leader.

93 Drooglever, *The Road to Isandhlwana*, pp. 49–54.

94 *The South African Journal of Sir Garnet Wolseley 1879–1880* (edited by Adrian Preston; Cape Town, Balkema, 1973), p. 239.

95 NM, November 28, 1878: GO 205. TN, December 6, 1878: GO 214.

96 CSO 1926: 953/1879. 1 BGV: IV, 244.

97 See the pamphlet in CP 26–11, also TN, December 9, 1878: 'The Native Contingent,' and similar reports, December 10th, in NC, NM, NW. Jabez Molife, one of the baSotho who served with him in 1873 and was with him now as an interpreter, wrote after Durnford's death: 'We are black, but we don't wish to be "niggers",' the last term being an insult. Durnford told him: 'Never mind, Jabez, our blood is all the same colour, and before God all men are equally good who do their duty rightly.' This spirit of fair play Durnford imposed on his officers. After the war Molife said that the baSotho were very pleased at how they were treated by the army, the 'amatroops' never insulted them. (*A Soldier's Life*, pp. 323–324).

98 NC, January 18, 1879: report.

99 *A Soldier's Life*, p. 205.

100 *Ibid.* Bengough, *Memories of a Soldier's Life*, pp. 109–110. Instructions (pamphlet in CP 26–11). See also Montgomery's letter in TN, January 22, 1879.

101 C 2242, pp. 27–28.

102 *Cf.* reports in TN, TM, NW, January 15, and NM, January 17, 1879. *Narrative*, p. 32. French, *Lord Chelmsford and the Zulu War*, p. 72. C 2242, p. 47.

103 *A Soldier's Life*, p. 212. French, *Lord Chelmsford and the Zulu War*, pp. 72, 77. Laband and Thompson, *War Comes to Umvoti*, p. 30. CSO 1925: 250 and 279/1879.

104 CP 27–39: Chelmsford to Durnford, January 14, 1879. French, *Lord Chelmsford and the Zulu War*, p. 79.

105 *A Soldier's Life*, p. 212.

106 *Ibid.*, pp. 212, 214. Drooglever, *The Road to Isandhlwana*, p. 18. TN, January 22, 1879: report. NM, January 27, 1879: 'With the Natal Mounted Native Contingent.'

107 *A Soldier's Life*, pp. 214–215.

108 *Ibid.*, pp. 213–214. CP 27–52: Chelmsford to Durnford, January 19, 1879. French, *Lord Chelmsford and the Zulu War*, p. 81. NM, January 27, 1879: 'With the Natal Mounted Native Contingent.'

109 NW, January 25, 1913: H.F. Fynn, 'My Recollections of a Famous Campaign and a Great Disaster.'

Chapter 3

MOBILIZATION (continued) – THE SECOND AND THIRD REGIMENTS

The Second Regiment – No. 1 Column

The No. 1 Column was to advance from the lower Thukela towards the Zulu 'capital' of Ulundi. The 2nd Regiment was attached to it and accounted for 2 000 of its 3 800 men.[1]

According to General Orders on December 18th the 2nd Regiment was to assemble in three days time at the Nonoti River.[2] It took three weeks instead of three days to complete the regiment.[3] On the 21st, the appointed time, only 101 of Mqawe's men from the Inanda Division had arrived at the camp. Captain Hart, 31st Foot, the regiment's staff officer, arrived at the camp on the 22nd with 140 of Deliwayo's men, whom he had collected at Stanger. (He was particularly struck by the men's various and striking hair dressings.)

There was no enthusiasm for war and there was a real fear of the Zulu power among the coastal people; but there was no denying their duty to the Supreme Chief. The Resident Magistrate of the Lower Tugela Division was sure coercion had been used, but his counterpart in the Inanda Division was sure it had not.[4]

The Acting Secretary for Native Affairs had reckoned on the chiefs Deliwayo, Macebo, Musi and Ziphuku furnishing 200, 200, 500 and 100 men, respectively, to make 1 000 for the 1st Battalion, and on the chiefs Mqawe, Sotondose and Dikwayo furnishing 500, 400 and 100, for the 2nd Battalion. Mqawe, Dikwayo and Deliwayo and Ziphuku made up their allocations, but Musi could get only two--thirds, Macebo half, and Sotondose less than half their allocations. Perhaps Sotondose's difficulty owed to many of his people living on white settlers' farms. In any case, four other chiefs (Gudu, Kamanga, Manaba, and Mlungwana) were ordered to send men to the 2nd Battalion to make up for the shortfall. To cover Macebo's and Musi's shortfalls the chiefs Mgcangca and Tatalambu were ordered to send men to the 1st Battalion. By the end of the year the regiment had 1 106 men. By January 10th 1 975. On the 16th, as the column prepared to advance into Zululand, the regiment numbered 2 022, actually exceeding the paper strength assigned to it.[5]

The camp was on a hill in a loop of the Nonoti, surrounded by some thick but scattered bush. Here the men became acquainted with the British military regimen. They were issued with red puggarees and blue and grey blankets. The men of the 1st Battalion wore the puggarees over the right shoulder and under the left arm; those of the 2nd wore them round the head. The blue blankets were for the 1st, the grey for the 2nd Battalion. They also got enough to eat. One in ten men received a rifle, but the rifles were old muzzle-loaders and many of them had weak mainsprings. There was some rifle practice, but it was hampered by a lack of ammunition. Every morning they learned how to change front and to wheel. In the afternoon, when the battalions paraded, they practised the same movements on a larger scale. They also did some entrenching. It was not really difficult. Captain Hart wrote home on New Year's Eve: 'They are the most intellegent blacks, and best black soldiers – so far as I can tell without yet having seen them fight – I have ever seen.' He complimented them on their quickness in drill and attack, but, as he observed, after all the Native Contingent would be on the flanks of the attacking British and would follow up their success by a charge and pursuit to turn the enemy retreat into a rout.[6]

The Lieutenant General inspected the Nonoti camp on December 29th. The 1st Battalion was drawn up along the road to the camp to receive him when his carriage arrived just after 7 a.m. He alighted and walked between the lines, accompanied by several staff officers and Major Graves, commandant of the regiment. After he had passed the men formed in twos and followed him to camp, singing a war song. At the top of the hill he addressed the officers and non-commissioned officers, urging them particularly to keep the men from committing acts of cruelty, burning huts and attacking women and children. Then he inspected the 2nd Battalion. He returned to his carriage and continued on to column headquarters at Fort Pearson, on the lower Thukela.[7]

The 2nd Regiment differed from the 1st Regiment in several important respects. First of all, it did not bear the impress of Durnford, with his intimate acquaintance with the chiefs and men of his unit. The commandant was Major Shapland Graves, 2nd Foot. An uninspiring leader, he had just been seconded to the colonial government as Protector of Immigrants. As such he was responsible for looking after the well being of Indians who had been indented to work the sugar plantations. The Lieutenant General had wanted a Commandant Von Linsingen, from the Cape frontier, to lead the regiment, but he could not come; therefore he appointed Graves, who by that time had already been seconded to command a colonial defensive district. Colonel Pearson, the column commander, had known Graves for twenty-two years and considered him a reliable officer.[8]

Second, the regiment's levies were selected by the Acting Secretary for Native Affairs, who, as we have seen, made several errors in the calculation of manpower. The coastal chiefs had been unenthusiastic about fighting, and the regiment had no core of 'good fighting men' such as Durnford had chosen for the 1st Regiment.

Third, the regiment was officered by adventurers from the Cape Colony, a major departure from Durnford's plan but one which Lord Chelmsford considered necessary because he did not believe there would be enough Natalians for the task.[9] The officers and non-commissioned officers were raised chiefly from among those who had served with levies in the Cape frontier wars. Indeed, they were recruited by their former commandant, William John Nettleton, and they expected him to command the regiment. Instead they got Major Graves, who had no combat experience and a brusque manner, but Nettleton persuaded them to accept his subordination. He was appointed commandant of the 2nd Battalion, while Graves commanded the 1st Battalion as well as the regiment. These Cape men were a proud lot. Many wore medals and grumbled about fatigue work – they had enlisted to fight not work. The non-commissioned officers were a motley collection of youths and middle-aged men. One of them wrote a poem 'Nettleton's Black Watch' which would appear in a Durban newspaper. They had had a good send-off at the Cape, but did not receive a hearty reception in Durban. They were quartered indifferently for a few weeks in hotels, on the flats outside town, and even in the prison, while they were outfitted. They left town on December 19th.[10]

Most of them were ignorant of the language and customs of the men they were to command, even to the point that they could not convey orders. There were fifteen who spoke neither English nor Zulu, only German.[11] One of the officers described the levies as 'a likely set of men' and another remarked that most were 'healthy men in the prime of life', but another complained of their 'incessant howling' and wrote that they were inferior in physique to the Gaika and Gcaleka of the Cape and lacking 'the noble bearing of the Old Colony Kafir'.[12] No wonder the editor of a Durban news- paper regretted that more Natal colonists had not been found instead of the Cape mercenaries – only twenty Natalians were recruited to serve with regiment in Durban.[13] Colonel Pearson regarded the regiment's officers as ineffectual.[14]

For their part the men were confused by officers and non-commissioned officers who could not speak their language and gave orders in English (or broken English) accompanied by many oaths. Men who saw their erstwhile employers in the white settlers' mounted corps wondered why they were not put in command of them.[15] Many little incidents occurred, which did not augur well for the unit. Graves was to opine that many of his officers would have to be whipped before they learned their duties, but the contingent was not under the British Mutiny Act (as was the regular army) and all he could do was dismiss, fine or reduce an officer in rank.[16]

The No. 1 Column could not ford the lower Thukela now that the rainy season had begun. From the 6th to the 10th of January a Naval Brigade worked to set up steel wire hawsers across the 300 yards of stream for a pont. Meanwhile the 2nd Regiment moved camp to the right bank of the river, in proximity to the rest of the troops of the column. Before daylight on the 12th the crossing started. The 'pont', a square, clumsy boat, began carrying the Naval Brigade across at dawn. When they were across, No. 2 Pioneer Company was ferried over. Then went some of the British infantry. The men of the regiment, waiting to cross, watched with great interest and anxiety. There was excitement at the drift, where men of all units intermingled. The enemy did not appear, and so the crossing continued uninterrupted. The men of the 2nd Battalion seemed especially anxious as their turn to cross approached. They were kept out of the pont with some difficulty until their turn came.[17]

The pont could carry 80-100 men or a heavy wagon or span of oxen at a time. It took two days to get most of the troops across and several days more to move equipment and provisions. The steel ropes were worked by men of the Native Contingent. The 1st Battalion remained at Fort Pearson on fatigue duty. A new fort, Tenedos, was erected on the left bank to protect the pont.[18]

The enemy still had not shown himself, but Zulu homesteads in the neighbourhood were demolished. Some pioneers had tried to loot these on the first day and had been seized and punished for it, but now, for greater security, some of the 2nd Battalion were put to this work, and frequently groups of them were seen carrying the straw crowns of huts down to their camp, as though they were large umbrellas.[19] On the 15th the 1st Battalion crossed the river, leaving oxen to give motive power to the pont.[20] The column was encamped on the spur of a low ridge running parallel to the river. The camp of the 1st Battalion was on the left and that of the 2nd Battalion was on the right of the others.[21]

On the 17th Fort Tenedos was completed. On the 18th the column began its advance into Zululand.[22] Two companies of the 1st Battalion, B and G, were left as a garrison for the fort. B company consisted of Deliwayo's amaNyuswa and they refused to be left behind unless A company, also Deliwayo's men, stayed. Consequently A was ordered to stay and G to go. The officers of G company had not packed to go, so it was arranged that they stay with A company and A's officers go with G. The men of A company indignantly formed on parade and vehemently refused to go back without their own officers, whom they said they understood and liked! So G Company marched under its own officers. A and B Companies were still unhappy. They claimed they had been the first men to join the battalion, and it was unfair for them to be held back while all the others were going to fight.[23]

The Third Regiment – No. 3 Column

The No. 3 Column was to invade Zululand at Rorke's Drift. A pont would be launched in the Mzinyathi, similar to the one on the lower Thukela. The column assembled at some distance from the river. The British regulars and white settler militia assembled around Helpmekaar, on the high land overlooking the river valley.[24] The 3rd Regiment of the Natal Native Contingent assembled at Sand Spruit, near the magistracy of the Umsinga Division.[25] The site of the camp was both grassy and stony.[26] The country was open, trees growing only in ravines and alongside streams. There were also innumerable ant hills. Grey lizards lodged in holes, and snakes were common. The bird life included a range of local varieties from crane and bustard to lark and partridge.[27] The regiment encamped on a flat, and it was exposed to the heat of the sun during the day and to violent thunderstorms which followed in the evening. The nights were cold and there was mist in the mornings.[28]

General Orders, issued December 17th, named four chiefs who were to provide men of the 3rd Regiment. They were to assemble at Sand Spruit the following day to be organized into companies and battalions.[29] In fact, the mobilization of levies was well underway before then. The officers of the regiment had left Pietermaritzburg for Sand Spruit on the 7th, and the Resident Magistrate of Weenen County, where the chiefs and most of their people lived, had been ordered to start the process of mobilization on the 5th. His assistant turned over 1 452 men at the camp on the 18th.[30]

The two battalions were divided between two camps. On December 20th the Resident Magistrate of the Umsinga Division, who was fluent in Zulu, addressed the levies and various camp followers. He praised the regiment's commandant and officers and described their services in the recent Cape frontier war. He told them what to expect in the forthcoming war and appealed to them to help bring it quickly to an end. The audience listened attentively and only interrupted to express approval.[31]

Afterwards the men were issued cooking pots, belts and blankets – blue ones for the 1st Battalion, grey for the 2nd, and red puggarees. Otherwise they were dressed like the enemy – with a few animal skins.[32] One in ten received rifles: about 300 Martini-Henrys, the standard British weapon, and 205 Enfields, old but still serviceable muzzle loaders. The latter were divided equally between battalions, but the 2nd Battalion seems to have received most of the Martini-Henrys. There seems to have been little if any practice. Ignorance of the weapons led a captain in the 1st Battalion to speculate that the Martini-Henrys in the hands of his men were more dangerous to friend than foe. He did not worry about the muzzle-loading Enfields – the men usually forgot to tear off the end of the paper cartridge or put the cartridge ball into the muzzle first, so the rifle would not fire.[33]

We have already met the amaChunu and abaThembu as they mustered at Weenen, and observed that the amaBhele and isiGqoza followed them as they marched off to the front. The latter two were unlike the amaChunu and abaThembu, who had hereditary chiefs and an historical character. The amaBhele had had more than half a dozen chiefs when they had been driven from their historic lands by the amaNgwane (themselves escaping from Zulu attacks). Most of them had fled southwards and become servants of chiefs on the Cape frontier. After a frontier war in 1834-1835 they had been emancipated, and subsequently many had been able to return to their old lands. The amaBhele in Weenen County now numbered close to a thousand huts.[34] Their chief Ndomba was appointed by the government.[35]

In contrast, the isiGqoza were Zulu. They had been followers of Mpande's son Mbulazi. Mbulazi had contested the succession with his half brother Cetshwayo, whose faction was known as the Usuthu, at the battle of Ndondakusaka in 1856. Cetshwayo had defeated and destroyed Mbulazi and thousands of his followers. Mkhungo and Sikhota, also sons of Mpande and half brothers, had fled with survivors into Natal in 1857. They had been settled on vacant land near Weenen. Mkhungo was widely regarded as pretender to the Zulu throne, in opposition to Cetshwayo. The Colony had been caught up briefly in a war scare in 1861, when it was rumoured Cetshwayo was going to send a force to seize the fifteen-year old pretender and his half-brother at a mission station near Pietermaritzburg, where they were being educated by the Bishop of Natal. The scare had blown over, but Mkhungo remained a potential rival to the Zulu King. His following had grown over time. The original land given to him had become insufficient and many of the people now lived on Crown lands and white settlers' farms.[36] Mkhungo was now too old and fat to lead his men to war. That honour fell to Sikhota, although one of Mkhungo's sons represented him in the levy.[37]

Mkhungo was required to furnish three hundred fighting men. 358 turned out. It was not because many were starving – the drought having affected their lands severely – but because they wanted to fight. They went to war with a burning martial ardour, not simply to serve the Queen, but to avenge themselves against the Zulu King.[38] Included in the number were 100 men from a later group of refugees from Zululand, whose allegiance Mkhungo and Ndomba had disputed and the Natal government had assigned to Ndomba. They paid taxes under Ndomba, but considered Mkhungo their chief. The men of this group left the Bhele levy and joined the isiGqoza when they arrived at Sand Spruit.[39]

Sikhota presented himself to Commandant Lonsdale. He was a handsome man, with a commanding presence, and he was attached to the staff. He asked Lonsdale for one of his shirts to wear as a mark of his favour. Lonsdale gave him one and Sikhota immediately put it on. This was not easy, and required the assistance of his head man, for he was tall and fat and Lonsdale was not, but once he had the shirt on he wore it around the camp for days.[40] Meanwhile the isiGqoza drew themselves apart and would have nothing to do with the other levies.[41]

The Acting Secretary for Native Affairs had again miscalculated numbers available. Phakade was to supply 600, Mganu 600, Ndomba 500 and Mkhungo 300; however, the levies which arrived at Sand Spruit on the 18th numbered 732, 560, 270 and 273, respectively. Ndomba fell so far short of his quota because most of the amaBhele lived on white settlers' farms and were subject to labour controls. Some also lived on the Weenen Town lands and a few in the nearby location, but the drought had hurt everyone, and many men had sought work elsewhere in the Colony, and some as far away as the Diamond Fields of the Cape. There were also delays because some of Phakade's and Mganu's people lived outside the Weenen Division and other Resident Magistrates had to call them out.

The Resident Magistrate of Weenen did not have the authority or the personnel to impress the men in private service and suggested that Ndomba's allocation be reduced and the shortfall be made up by other chiefs. He tried to get more men from those who had supplied them, but they reported that there were no more able bodied men left at home.[42] The government ordered the Resident Magistrate of the adjacent Klip River Division to raise 330 men from six small chiefdoms. 294 men from them were turned over to the military on January 10th, and more continued to flow in from various quarters until the number reached 450.[43] Ultimately the 3rd Regiment was over strength by some 300 men, whom the Lieutenant General proposed to leave at Rorke's Drift for road work and other duties while the column advanced into Zululand.[44]

Early on the morning of December 21st, the officers began sorting men into companies and giving companies names. At 10:30 bugles sounded parade call. Commandant Lonsdale, in charge of the 1st Battalion, and Commandant Cooper, in charge of the 2nd, had to blow the bugles because there were no buglers (which a General Order had lately corrected, but not soon enough in this case). There was great confusion, but gradually the companies were ranged on the plain below the camp for inspection. Some officers found their companies had too many men, others found theirs had none, and a reapportionment had to be made.[45]

The amaChunu, abaThembu, and isiGqoza had preserved the *ibutho* system[46] and there was some resentment against the breaking up of traditional formations.[47] Phakade's men objected strongly to being mixed up in new formations; however, Lonsdale prevailed and the Chunu levy was arranged in six companies in the 2nd Battalion. Some allowance was made for feelings. The *ibutho* system included the naming of units, and this was carried over to the companies. Thus among the Chunu companies were 'The Skies', 'Strangers' and 'Lions'.[48]

The isiGqoza was organized in three companies in the 1st Battalion, which also included four companies of abaThembu and one company of amaBhele.[49] Presumably the remaining five companies (one in the 1st Battalion and four in the 2nd) were made up of latecomers to the initial levies and the men from Klip River.[50]

After the companies were formed they were drilled. The first drill lasted till lunch and the second began in mid afternoon and lasted three hours. Lonsdale and his officers worked hard at drill. The men did not like but learnt the new movements. It was difficult for them to form and keep a line. The work was eased by substituting a two-hour drill before breakfast for the one before lunch, because of the mid-day heat.[51] To facilitate the movements, small flags were introduced for each company. The number of the battalion was painted on each, as well as some device. When possible the latter was an image of whatever the company was named after. A pig, a young bull, and the like. The men were quite pleased with these flags. They were also the source of amusement and many jokes.[52]

By the end of the first week in January Lonsdale was sanguine about his regiment, telling the Lieutenant General that 'his Zulus' were superior in every way to the amaMfengu he had commanded in the Eastern Cape. He was ready to 'go in' with them and believed they could be depended upon entirely.[53]

The commandant of the 3rd Regiment, Rupert LaTrobe Lonsdale, was a former lieutenant in the 74th Regiment ('Black Watch'). He had been the leader of Mfengu levies in the late Cape war and a special magistrate in the Mfengu district. He was also commandant of the 1st Battalion,[54] a dual arrangement similar to Graves' in the 2nd Regiment. E.R. Cooper, another frontier war veteran, had served in the 96th Regiment and was commandant of the 2nd Battalion.[55]

The Lieutenant General had asked Lonsdale to recruit officers and men in the Eastern Cape when it became apparent that Natal would not provide enough. Some 60 officers and 120 non-commissioned officers had enrolled at Kingwilliamstown in 'The Royal Swazi Levy', evidently under the impression that they were going to the Transvaal rather than Natal. They had left Kingwilliamstown by train on November 20th, amid farewells and good wishes of family, friends and spectators. The local newspaper called them as fine a body of men as ever left the town. A short sea voyage brought them to Durban on the 25th, and next day they marched to Pietermaritzburg. There they were detained some time waiting for uniforms and firearms. On December 7th they were paid. Many got drunk in the local canteens and some got into fights. Three days later they marched for Sand Spruit. At Mooi River some of them pilfered the local hostelry.[56]

It was observed in Durban that Lonsdale's group seemed to be 'highly respectable and well disciplined',[57] and in Pietermaritzburg that they were 'a mixed lot ... just the stuff for a rough life'.[58] The adjutant of the regiment, Lieutenant Henry Harford, 99th Foot, would reminisce: 'All were adventurers, and all the very best of fellows, ready to do anything and go anywhere.'[59] George Hamilton-Browne, a captain in the 1st Battalion, would write later: 'The officers were chiefly a smart lot of young Colonials, most of whom spoke Zulu, all of them good shots and fine horsemen.' Each company had three officers and six non-commissioned officers. He could not flatter the non-commissioned officers:[60]

> The non-coms were a motley crowd, a few of them old soldiers and ex-clerks, the majority of them runaway sailors, ex-marines, and East London boatmen. They were an awful tough crowd, but they looked a hard-fighting lot and though their language was strong, and they were evidently very rough, they looked also very ready, and I afterwards found that most of them did not belie their looks.

Thus Durnford's injunction about quality of leadership was disregarded, though one might argue it was out of necessity. The interaction between the officers and non-commissioned officers and the men of the levies was marked by friction, notwithstanding Lonsdale's making it quite clear that officers should allow the head men to give orders and otherwise not to interfere with the men. Indeed, he regarded the officers rather as escorts to levies, believing that was what the Lieutenant General desired.[61]

Not all of the officers whom Browne supposed spoke Zulu did in fact; many of them spoke the Mpondo dialect of Xhosa, and many others did not speak a local language at all.[62] There were no battalion interpreters at first, and Lonsdale urged that some be provided. He himself relied on his Political Assistant, Samuel Grant.[63] Fortunately, young Lieutenant Harford had been raised in Natal and knew Zulu well. Every morning disgruntled men squatted in rows or semicircles in front of his tent in order to make complaints. Most of these complaints concerned food, especially about who would get the heads of the cattle killed that day.[64] Also, men did not like it when the innards were sold by the butchers on private account and not given to them. They considered a ration of one quarter of a beast per company and a pannikin of meal for each man too little. And some found the drill unduly painful, it went on and on and the old men become tired. Orders could not be understood, and when men spoke up and said so the officers said they were impertinent. When they made mistakes the officers hit them. Many men were flogged six to twenty lashes, for washing in certain streams and urinating in certain areas, but they knew of no orders which stated they were not to do these things.[65]

The regiment left Sand Spruit on January 2nd to go to Rorke's Drift, where the entire column was massing. An enemy presence of several thousand was also reported near the drift.[66]

The Lieutenant General was very keen to impress on the members of the Native Contingent the standards of 'civilized' warfare and instructed commandants especially on this matter. He persuaded the government that Durnford, Graves and Lonsdale should be made Justices of the Peace, the better to enforce discipline. He determined to speak to the

3rd Regiment, as he had the 2nd Regiment. It was arranged that he would inspect and address the regiment on the 9th. Lonsdale was informed in advance, but failed to tell his adjutant, and then forgot himself, perhaps because he had a sun stroke the previous day.[67]

Indeed, the administration of the regiment left something to be desired, Lonsdale's optimism notwithstanding. There seemed to be no long roll, at least for the 1st Battalion. There were no regular returns for it. Men kept coming and going, without leave, and the officers were unable to get to know the men personally. Harford learnt about the impending inspection on a chance visit to headquarters a few hours before and rode to camp directly. He found Lonsdale sitting in his tent, looking over his Masonic paraphernalia, and reminded him of it. In great haste Lonsdale dispatched men to the units at drill, some miles distant. He told Harford to go one way and he would go the other to get things ready. He leapt on his horse, which threw him off, and he lay unconscious on the ground. Harford called the surgeon before galloping off.

Cooper and Hamilton-Browne got the battalions together in time. The companies executed the simple movements they had learnt very well. The Lieutenant General delivered his address to one battalion then to the other. He told the men that they were associated with Her Majesty's troops and must behave like them. They were not to harm the enemy's women and children or wounded men, who should be made prisoners of war. He told them that they should not burn the enemy's homesteads unless he gave them the order.[68] The Lieutenant General made a memorable impression. One of the Chunu headmen remembered long afterwards that the General 'had a very prominent nose, and a rumbling rasping voice. Whenever he passed, someone would shout "Ten Shun" and soldiers and we had to stand and stiffen our bodies'.[69]

Lonsdale was unconscious all the while, and when he regained his senses much later he still could not assume command. Major Black of 24th Regiment, a tough old regular officer, was eventually assigned to command of the regiment during Lonsdale's recovery. Hamilton-Browne was promoted to command of the 1st Battalion.[70]

On January 11th the No. 3 Column crossed into Zululand. The 24th Regiment and other troops crossed the river at the pont, while the Native Contingent crossed on either side, the 1st Battalion about 300 yards below, at the drift, and the 2nd Battalion at a ford about 600 yards above it. It was still dark when the men rose, and as they moved to the river, a thick mist formed which obscured everything.

The 3rd Regiment was the first unit to cross. The 1st Battalion went over where the current was strong and the river rather deep. (One of the officers saved a mounted infantryman who lost his horse and would have drowned). The men, wearing their feathers and carrying their shields, sticks, blankets and other equipment, descended into the cold stream, which rose up to their waists. They did not shout, as they usually did in movements, but made a low whistling noise as the water rose over their bodies. At some places the water came up to men's necks.[71]

The 2nd Battalion crossed where there was a hard bed. The leading company formed a double chain across the river, between which the others crossed. (Lieutenant Harford thought that this arrangement was to ward off crocodiles). The first men to enter the water hummed a war chant which those who followed took up. The sound reminded Harford of the buzzing of a great swarm of bees. On the other side, the officers formed up companies, and an elderly diviner named Ngabangi was allowed to address them. He trotted back and forth along the line, speaking eloquently for almost an hour, giving an account of the Zulu nation. Presumably it was an account favourable to the British cause – the men applauded by rattling their spears against their shields and exclaiming 'Gee!'. The address was broken off when the order came to move. The 24th had been contacted, and the battalion moved forward about a thousand yards to support it.

As soon as all the infantry was across, it advanced up the hill. In the centre two battalions of British regulars put out several companies in skirmish line. On the left the 1st Battalion threw out four companies in skirmish order, anchoring the flank on a bend of the river and connecting with the regulars, while the remaining companies remained in reserve. On the right the 2nd Battalion threw out five companies in an extended order, and the remaining companies formed a reserve on the extreme left flank. The entire force advanced several hundred yards and halted until the fog lifted.[72]

The mist dissolved under the rising sun, revealing the reserve units of the column formed in squares on the hills. Here they stayed, while tents and equipment were ferried across the pont. The mounted troops, who followed the 2nd Battalion over, passed through the ranks and scouted the Zulu country for several miles in advance. The men were exposed to the hot sun all day and had no food until evening, when they pitched camp where they stood and another thunderstorm broke. It rained all night.[73]

The column was strung out along the left bank of the river, but its vulnerability to an attack seems not to have concerned anyone at the time.

During its stay there, the 3rd Regiment continued to drill. On the 14th the levy from Klip River arrived, bringing the regiment to overstrength. An hundred were told off as a reserve to remain at the pont, and the rest, variously estimated at four to almost six hundred, were attached to the 2nd Battalion.[74]

The war had come. Three columns of imperial forces – units of the British regular army, the Native Natal Contingent, and white settler militia – were ready to invade the Zulu country. The contingent was indispensable to the enterprise. The regiments attached to each column would serve as light infantry – scouting out the enemy and skirmishing with him in battle. The mounted troops would provide a more mobile force for the same purpose. The regimental organization was new to the men, but they were learning the drill quickly. Unfortunately, they did not have sufficient time to learn it well enough. There were also problems with some of the European officers and non-commissioned officers. But all in all the Lieutenant General and his column commanders were optimistic. There was no reason to believe that the war would not be a short one and they would be victorious.

NOTES

1 *Narrative*, pp. 13, 17, 19, 145.

2 TN, December 20, 1878: GO 228.

3 SNA 1/1/33, no. [65]. See and *cf.* SNA 1/6/11, no. 21 [*sic*: no. 23]. *Letters of Major-General FitzRoy Hart-Synnot* (edited by B.M. Hart-Synnot; London, Edward Arnold, 1912), pp. 93–94.

4 SNA 1/1/33, no. [65], and 1/6/11, no. 21 [*sic*: no. 23]. 1/VLM, 3/2/1: 57I/1879. NM, January 7, 1879: 'The Native Contingent.' *Cf.* NW, December 14, 1878: 'The Native Contingent.' Also see NW, January 18, 1879: 'War with the Zulus.'

5 SNA 1/1/33, nos. 34 and [65]; 1/6/11, nos. 17 and 21 [*sic*: no. 23]. TN, December 20, 1878: GO 228.

6 *Letters of Major-General FitzRoy Hart-Synnot*, pp. 96–97. NM, January 3, 1879: 'Visit of Lord Chelmsford to the camp at Nonoti.' NC, January 16, 1879: 'News from the Native Contingent:' October 11, 1879: 'Libel Case. Graves v *The Natal Colonist*;' and October 21, 1879: 'A Protest.' H.F. Norbury, *The Naval Brigade in South Africa during the Years 1877–78–79* (London, Sampson Low, Marston, Searle & Rivington, 1880), p. 221.

7 NM, January 3, 1879: 'Visit of Lord Chelmsford to the Camp at Nonoti.' *Letters of Major-General FitzRoy Hart-Synnot*, p. 98.

8 NM, November 27: 'The Native Contingent;' December 10, 16, 1878, reports. NC, October 11, 1879: 'Libel case. Graves v. *The Natal Colonist*.' TN, December 2, 1878: GO 209. NGG, 736: GN 341 (November 4, 1878).

9 GH 500, p. 139. GH 1411, p. 230. C 2234, p. 39. TN, October 23, 1878: 'Native Levies.'

10 NM, November 27: 'The Native Contingent;' December 18: 'Commandants Nettleton and Lonsdale's Corps;' December 20, 1878: 'Departure of Cdt. Nettleton's Corps;' and January 3, 1879: 'Nettleton's Black Watch,' NC, October 11 and 14: 'Libel Case, Graves v *The Natal Colonist*; and October 21, 1879: 'A Protest.' TN, November 25 and December 20, 1878: GO 203 and 228, respectively.

11 NM, January 18: leader; January 21: 'The Native Contingent;' February 3, 1879: 'The Native Contingent.' NA, February 4, 1879; leader. NC, October 11, 1879: 'Libel case. Graves v. *The Natal Colonist*.' 1/VLM, 3/2/1: 1224/ 1879. WC II/2/2: Chelmsford to Wood, February 19, 1879. Hart noted (*Letters*, p. 86): 'You cannot imagine what a strange collection of men the Europeans of our regiment are: we have English, Irish, French, Germans, Danes, Swiss, Dutch, Norwegians, Swedes, Belgians, and besides the Europeans, America is represented. I expect there are some strange personal histories among these men.'

12 NM, January 3, 1879: 'Visit of Lord Chelmsford to the Camp at Nonoti.' NC, January 16: 'News from the Native Contingent;' and January 28, 1879: 'Natal Natives from a Kaffrarian Point of View.'

13 NM, January 18, 1879: leader.

14 C2260, p. 107. *Cf.* SNA 1/1/33, no. [65] and NM, January 21, 1879: 'The Native Contingent.'

15 SNA 1/1/33, no. [65]. NM, January 21, 1879: 'The Native Contingent.'

16 NA, February 4, 1879: leader. NC, October 11 and 16, 1879: 'Libel case. Graves v. *The Natal Colonist*.'

17 Norbury, *The Naval Brigade*, p. 219. *Letters of Major-General FitzRoy Hart-Synnot*, pp. 99–100. D. Stainbank diary, January 13 and 14, 1879. TN, January 17, 1879: 'The Passage of the Tugela.'

18 *Narrative*, p. 22. Norbury, *The Naval Brigade*, p. 219. TN, January 20, 1879: 'From the Lower Tugela.' NC, January 16, 1879: report.

19 TN, January 17, 1879: 'The Passage of the Tugela.' NW, January 18, 1879: 'With Col. Pearson's Column.'

20 See and *cf. Narrative*, p. 22 and Norbury, *The Naval Brigade*, pp. 219–221.

21 See the map of the camp (January 13, 1879) in CP 7–3. Evidently the 1st Battalion's camp was laid out before actually occupied.

22 *Narrative*, p. 22.

23 NM, January 29, 1879: 'Correction.'

24 *Narrative*, pp. 17, 19.

25 CSO 674: 4945/1878. TN, December 20, 1879: GO 227.

26 *Zulu War Journal of Colonel Henry Harford*, p. 12.

27 W.E. Montague, *Campaigning in South Africa: Reminiscences of an Officer in 1879* (London, Blackwood, 1880), pp. 86–87. *War and Peace in South Africa 1879–1881: The writings of Philip Anstruther and Edward Essex* (edited by Paul M. Butterfield; Melville, Strydom [1986], p. 16.

28 G. Hamilton-Browne, *A Lost Legionary in South Africa* (London, Laurie, [19–], p. 91. Norris Newman, *In Zululand with the British*, p. 20.

29 TN, December 20, 1878: GO 227.

30 CSO 670: 4566/1878; 671: 4631/1878; and 675: 4945/1878.

31 Norris Newman, *In Zululand with the British*, p. 22. TN, December 30, 1878: 'Notes by the Way.'

32 *Zulu War Journal of Colonel Henry Harford*, p. 12. H. Smith Dorrien, *Memoirs of Forty-Eight Years' Service* (London, Murray, 1925), p. 28. TN, December 30, 1878: 'Notes by the Way.'

33 Hamilton-Browne, *A Lost Legionary*, p. 103. *Zulu War Journal of Colonel Henry Harford*, p. 12. *Cf.* SNA 1/6/11, no. 50.

34 SP 89, p. 136. See also Shooter, *The Kafirs of Natal*, p. 377, and Ayliff and Whiteside, *History of the Abambo*, pp. 2, 8, 11, 16–17.

35 *Report of the Natal Native Commission*, p. 45.

36 G.B. Nourse, The Zulu invasion scare of 1861 (University of Natal, M.A., 1948), pp. 10–11, 27–28, 35–38, 40, 67–68. Mankanganu's statement in *Evidence taken before the Natal Native Commission 1881*, pp. 357–358. Norris-Newman, *In Zululand with the British*, pp. 21–22. *Cf.* Robert Russell, *Natal: The Land and its Story* (6th ed. Pietermaritzburg, Davis, 1899), pp. 201–203, and Colenbrander, 'The Zulu Kingdom,' pp. 103–107.

37 TN, December 30, 1878: 'Notes by the Way.' Norris Newman, *In Zululand with the British*, p. 21. *Cf. Zulu War Journal of Colonel Henry Harford*, pp. 12–13.

38 TN, December 30, 1878: 'Notes by the Way.' NM, December 16, 1878, leader. CSO 674: 4945/1878, and 1925: C737/1878. *Cf.* SNA 1/6/11, no. 20.

39 SNA 1/6/11, no. 20. *Cf.* Hamilton-Browne, *A Lost Legionary*, p. 106.

40 TN, December 30, 1878: 'Notes by the Way.'

41 CSO 674: 4945/1878. Hamilton-Browne, *A Lost Legionary*, p. 107.

42 CSO 674: 4945/1878. SNA 1/1/31, no. 59 and 70; 1/1/33, no. 1; and 1/6/11, nos. 20, 49 and 52. TN, December 20, 1878: GO 227.

43 SNA 1/1/31, no. 70; 1/6/11, no. 20; 1/6/12, no. 62.

44 CSO 1925: 494/1879. CP 27–45: Chelmsford to Frere, January 17, 1879; but the date is given as the 16th in *Lord Chelmsford's Zululand Campaign*, p. 20.

45 TN, December 30: 'Notes by the Way;' and December 6, 1878: GO 214.

46 See *Evidence taken before the Natal Native Commission, 1881*, pp. 346 and 350, and Stuart Archive, II, 86. It is assumed that the isiGqoza retained the Zulu military organization.

47 GH 1421, pp. 93–94.

48 CSO 674: 4945/1878.

49 *Ibid.* See Hamilton-Browne, *A Lost Legionary*, pp. 106–107.

50 *Cf.* CSO 674: 4945/1878 and SNA 1/6/12, no. 62.

51 GH 1421, p. 94. TN, December 30, 1878: 'Notes by the Way.' Hamilton-Browne, *A Lost Legionary*, pp. 97 and 105. *Zulu War Journal of Colonel Henry Harford*, p. 12.

52 *Zulu War Journal of Colonel Harford*, p. 15. See also SNA 1/1/33, no. 51.

53 *Lord Chelmsford's Zululand Campaign*, p. 55.

54 See Norris-Newman, *In Zululand with the British*, p. 21, and report in NW, November 21, 1878; also Gon, *The Road to Isandlwana*, p. 158. CP 26–13: GO 203 and 209. TN, December 11, 1878: GO 217.For Lonsdale's military career elsewhere, see Simon Bendall, 'A Minor Military Dynasty of the Eighteenth and Nineteenth Centuries, in *Journal of the Society for Army Historical Research*, LXXXIII, no. 334 (Summer 2005), pp.110–130, on the Lonsdales.

55 TN,November 25, 1878, GO 203. See and *cf.* Norris-Newman, *In Zululand with the British*, p. 21.

56 GH 1422, p. 54. C 2234, p. 39. NM, November 18: 'Native Forces:' and November 26, 1878: 'The Royal Swazi Levy.' NW, December 5, 1878: 'The Situation.' NA, December 7, 1878: 'Maritzburg.' TN, December 27, 1878: 'On the Road to Helpmakaar.'

57 NM, December 26, 1878: 'The Royal Swazi Levy'.

58 NA, December 7, 1878: 'Maritzburg.'

59 *Zulu War Journal of Colonel Henry Harford*, p. 11.

60 Hamilton-Browne, *A Lost Legioniary*, p. 99.

61 GH 1421, p. 116.

62 SNA 1/1/33, no. 51.

63 CSO 674: 4945/1878.

64 *Zulu War Journal of Colonel Henry Harford*, p. 13.

65 SNA 1/1/33, no. 51.

66 SNA 1/1/33, no. 1. See *Narrative*, p. 19, and Norris-Newman, *In Zululand with the British*, pp. 29, 31–32.

67 CSO 670: 4536/1878. CP 27–6 [Chelmsford] to Deputy Adjutant General, December 31, 1878. NC, January 18, 1879: report. NW, January 16, 1879: 'The Zulu War.' *Cf.* Hamilton-Browne, *A Lost Legionary*, p. 109.

68 Hamilton-Browne, *A Lost Legionary*, p. 101. *Zulu War Journal of Colonel Henry Harford*, pp. 13–14, although there apparently is some confusion about the time and place. NW, January 16 and 21, 1879: 'The Zulu War.' NC, January 18, 1879: report.

69 CFP 8/16: statement by Lugubu Mbata.

70 TN, January 13: GO 9, and January 22, 1879: GO 13. Hamilton-Browne, *A Lost Legionary*, p. 109.

71 *Narrative*, p. 26. The map following p. 44 in C2242 evidently is incorrect. NW, January 21, 1879: 'The Zulu War.' TN, January 20, 1879: 'The Zulu War.' *Whom the Gods Love ..... A Memoir of Lieutenant Neville Josiah Aylmer Coghill, The 24th Regiment 1852–1879* (compiled by Patrick Coghill; Halesworth, n.p., 1968), p. 102.

72 NW, January 16 and 21, 1879: 'The Zulu War.' TN, January 20, 1879: 'The Zulu War.' TN, January 22, 1879: GO 14. Frank Emery, *The Red Soldier: Letters from the Zulu War* (London, Hodder and Stoughton, 1977) p. 72.

73 *Zulu War Journal of Colonel Henry Harford*, pp. 16–18. TN, January 20, 1879: 'The Zulu War.' NW, January 21, 1879: 'The Zulu War.' *Cf.* Hamilton-Browne, *A Lost Legionary*, pp. 101–102.

74 Hamilton-Browne, *A Lost Legionary*, p. 116. Norris-Newman, *In Zululand with the British*, p. 32. NW, January 18 and 21, 1879: 'The Zulu War.'

Chapter 4

THE THIRD REGIMENT IN THE ZULU COUNTRY

Encounter at Batshe River

The British invasion of Zululand began when the Zulu King failed to comply with the ultimatum to demilitarize his kingdom and place it under British tutelage. Three columns crossed the border into Zululand, one at the coast, another from northern Natal, and the other from the Transvaal. The idea was for the columns to converge on Ulundi, the seat of the Zulu King, and in so doing to compel the enemy to attack them. Of course, the enemy would be repulsed and the Zulu King would be obliged to make peace on British terms. That was the presumption.

Each column consisted of infantry, artillery, and cavalry, along with service units. Infantry made up the great part of each column. It consisted of British infantry and the Natal Native Contingent in the coast and Natal columns. There were relatively few artillery and cavalry. Indeed, the shortage of the latter was crucial. Moreover the cavalry was not really cavalry in the true sense, but comprised some mounted infantry, a variety of militia units, and the Natal Native Mounted Contingent (which moved from Kranskop to join the column in northern Natal). Lord Chelmsford, the lieutenant general commanding forces, supposed that technology and training assured the superiority of these forces against the numerically superior Zulu army – however, the British knew very little about Zulu dispositions and intentions. Lack of cavalry aggravated the deficiency.

The No. 3 Column was the central one of the advance. Lord Chelmsford accompanied and thus commanded it. The column embarked on the campaign full of confidence. The crossing of the Mzinyathi was unopposed. No Zulu force of consequence was in the offing, which augured well. No one could have guessed that after a few victorious minor actions, the British would meet with defeat. The invasion culminated in the battle of Isandlwana on January 22nd. It was one of the greatest disasters ever experienced by British arms.

But let us not run ahead of the narrative; rather let us return to the No. 3 Column camped on the left bank of the Mzinyathi and follow them in their advance into Zululand.

The No. 3 Column had not had any contact with the enemy during the day it crossed into the Zulu country. Yet it was now in the region dominated by the powerful Zulu chief Sihayo. Some of his sons had crossed the river into Natal the previous year to seek out and kill errant wives. This killing had gone unpunished. One of the points in the British ultimatum was that the guilty men be turned over for justice. Of course, they were not turned over and Sihayo was regarded as one of the men responsible for the war.

The Lieutenant General ordered a reconnaissance in force on January 12th. The object was to explore the further route of the column, towards Siphezi hill, also to probe up the Batshe river, where Sihayo was known to have his main homesteads, and to see what enemy was there. The 1st Battalion of the 3rd Regiment was ordered out for the reconnaissance. Also included were four companies of British infantry and all the mounted troops, chiefly colonial militia.[1]

Reveille sounded just before daybreak. At five the reconnaissance got underway. The advance guard consisted of the mounted troops. The 1st Battalion, eight companies strong (two were left in camp), followed. Captain Browne was commandant of the battalion, but Major Black, the British officer in command of the regiment during Lonsdale's illness, accompanied the force and was the real commander. The force marched over a low ridge and descended into the valley of the Batshe. There were homesteads about, but they seemed to be unoccupied. In front and a little over a mile away, across the little river, was Ngedla hill. Its front was a steep cliff four hundred feet high. Among the rocks on the hillside Zulus were seen moving about. The track now turned up the valley, which narrowed just ahead to less than a mile wide. The reconnaissance force arrived at the river, and heard the lowing of cattle, also the war cries of the Zulu men guarding them. Mounted scouts reported that men were driving the cattle, evidently from the various homesteads, up towards the hill.

There was a halt, while the Lieutenant General and the column commander planned to capture the cattle. The mounted troops drew off and moved to the right, in order to pass round the hill and cut off the enemy. The 1st Battalion and most of the British infantry extended in skirmish order and wheeled to the right, facing the precipice and the place where the cattle presumably were.

The men moved into position. Browne's orders were to capture the cattle and not to use firearms unless the enemy did. The Lieutenant General also said that he would hold him personally responsible if his men harmed any women or children, then wished him good luck. Browne repeated this to his officers. The companies were in line, and he ordered them to advance. The companies moved forward steadily over rough and stony ground. The men leapt over and jumped about boulders and bushes, so that the line became very crooked. They sang war songs and some paused to sharpen their spears against stones.

Browne was determined to bring them to close quarters for a charge as soon as possible. He had no confidence in those who had rifles. He gave orders no one was to fire. They must trust to their spears. The battalion was closing on a draw in the hillside. Apparently the cattle were concealed there. If there was going to be a fight, it would be in narrow confines: enemy below penned in at the bottom, enemy above firing down on the attackers. Browne ordered his two flanking companies to move to the sides of the draw and to work their way from there. The rest of the men waited until the flanking companies were in position before advancing again.

The songs died away. Men began to hang back. The non-commissioned officers began to kick the ones who shrank, also strike them with the butts of their rifles. Browne realized that they must be led. He and his officers went to the front.

A voice from the rocks called out, asking by whose order the white army came and whether or not they were enemies. There was a halt and the query was translated. It is not clear what exactly was the response. A British newspaper reporter on the spot was certain there was none, but Browne later wrote that Captain Duncombe, one of his officers fluent in Zulu, replied that they were there 'by order of the Great White Queen'.

Browne ordered his men to advance again, and Black sent back to find out when they could open fire. The Lieutenant General replied that they could fire only after they were fired upon. A shot from behind a large boulder struck one of the men of the contingent. Other shots followed. Browne ordered his men to charge. The enemy let go a massed volley, and firing became general on both sides.

Browne, Duncombe and another captain charged forward. They were followed by a single company, No. 8, of the isiGqoza (of the three companies, the second had been left at camp and the third was moving on the flank). They locked in battle. It was Zulu against Zulu, fighting hand-to-hand. Shields clattered against each other. The isiGqoza plunged home their stabbing spears, hissing 'guzzie'. They were joined by the other officers and non-commissioned officers of the battalion. They drove the enemy from rock to rock into the draw. The defeated Zulus took refuge behind the cattle.

The other companies of the battalion, apart from those on the flanks, had fled. Their officers and non-commissioned officers had tried to stop them. They had hit them with the butts of their rifles, even their fists, and kicked them. Major Black ordered a part of the British infantry to fix bayonets, led them straight at the fugitives, and made them stop and turn around. They were driven towards the front, but they would not be driven into action. Their officers and non-commissioned officers tried to move them. Instead those who could started shooting, as fast as they could. Some of them jammed cartridges into their rifles so they could not fire. Those who did shoot aimed at nothing in particular.

The battle was suspended while the cattle were cleared out. Behind them were women and children. They were brought out, and none of them were harmed. While all this was being done, the Zulu men climbed up a narrow path to the top of the hill and rolled large stones down to block the way. From the top and from the cliffs the enemy continued to fire, but his aim was bad. The officers and non-commissioned officers of the battalion returned the fire.

The valley resounded with gunfire. The shots and their echoes made it difficult for the regulars in support to locate the sources of firing on the hill. The enemy concealed himself in caves in the cliffs. When an individual was observed he was subjected to concentrated fire.

Two companies of the battalion and some of the British infantry on the left flank worked around to the cliffs in front. Lieutenant Harford, the regimental adjutant, climbed up and at great personal risk entered one of the main caves, where he persuaded the surviving defenders to surrender. Meanwhile the mounted troops reached the top of Ngedla from the rear. A number of the 1st Battalion as well as the British infantry managed to get to the top through the draw. Some of those who no longer had their red head bands were almost shot by the mounted men.

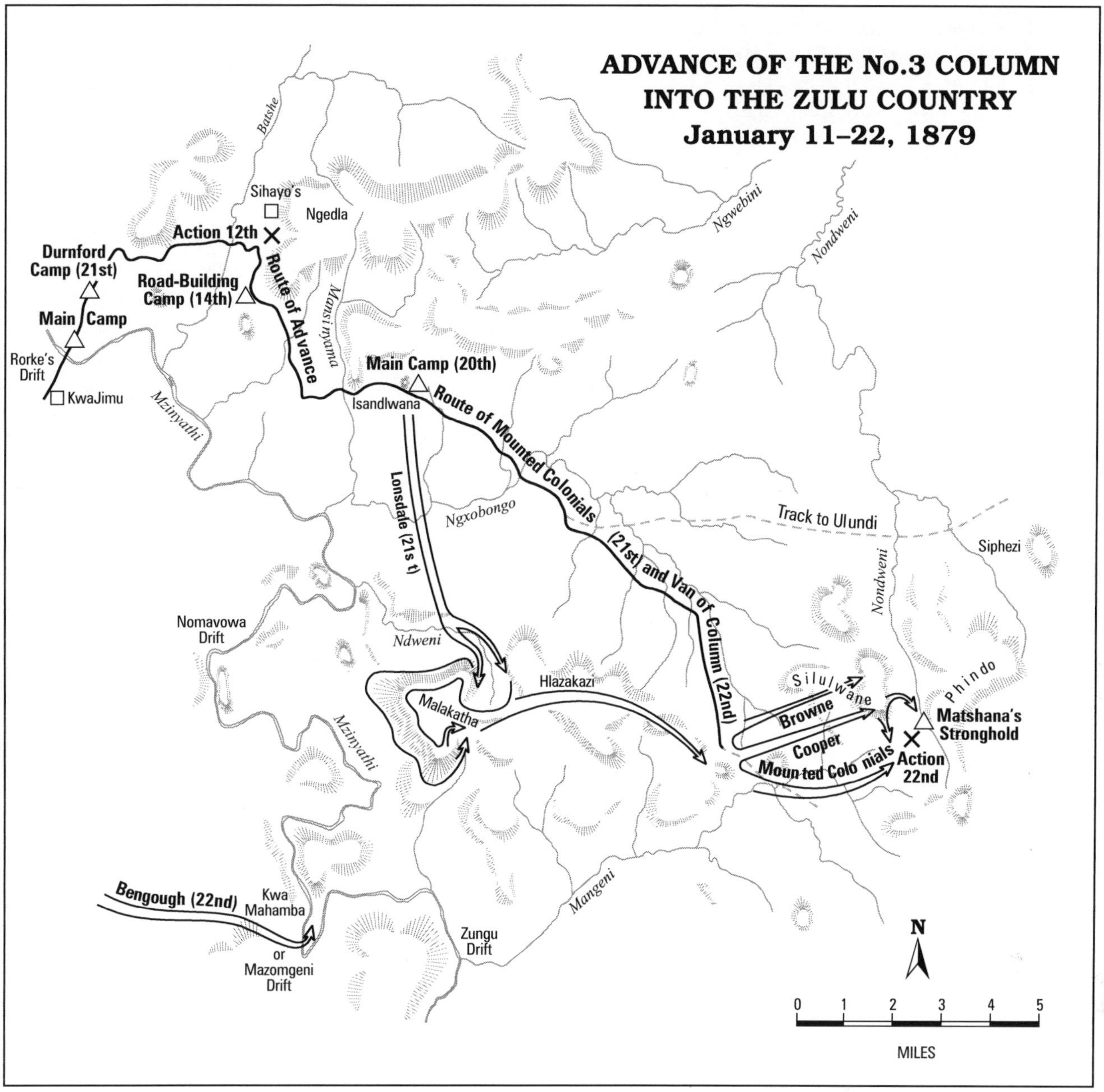

Ngedla is one of those flat-toped hills which are a familiar feature in Natal and Zululand. On top there is a gradual slope to a narrow crest. The last of the enemy could be seen retiring behind this crest, almost a mile away. To the north, beyond the hill, there was a large valley, in which the tributaries of the Batshe gather. The pursuers reached the crest. They saw many homesteads in the valley. They appeared to be deserted. The men stopped briefly to eat, then returned to the base of the hill. A company of the 1st Battalion collected the wounded. A head man, Maphonsa, and one man had been killed. A lieutenant and a corporal and at least twelve men had been wounded in the fight. The enemy's loss was estimated at thirty killed, four wounded and ten captured.[2]

The 2nd Battalion and several companies of British infantry had been ordered forward about eight o'clock. They had hastened to the scene of the action, and were directed to the left of the force engaged and deployed across the valley of the Batshe. They advanced a short distance to Sihayo's chief homestead, which was deserted. They clambered up the steep cliff behind it. The caves there were empty. One of the cattle enclosures appeared to have loopholes for guns, and a large cave at the foot of the cliff had a stone wall in front of the opening.[3] At the top of the cliff was a wagon full of boxes, clothing and other articles of European manufacture – even a feather bed! The wagon could not be brought off then. (A week later Duncombe's company took up a span of oxen to haul it away down the easy southern slope of the hill.)

It was learnt from prisoners that most of Sihayo's men had gone to the Zulu King's place the day before. A number of them had been left behind to look after the cattle. Apparently the reconnaissance had taken them by surprise. The people had fled and the cattle guard fought in vain. The reconnoitring force took back to camp 413 cattle, 225 sheep, 332 goats and 13 horses. It also brought off lots of sour milk (a favourite food) and vegetables. Several guns, obsolete pieces, and a large quantity of ammunition, were also taken. On the Lieutenant General's order Sihayo's huts were burnt, but the others were not touched. The force returned to camp in the afternoon, drenched by a violent thunderstorm.[4]

Whatever the officers and non-commissioned officers of the 1st Battalion might feel about the performance of their men, the feeling at headquarters was that the regiment's behaviour was 'all that could be desired'.[5] The panic and confusion below the cliff were ignored, or perhaps put down to the inexperience of the men.

There was some grumbling among the men about the disposition of the captured cattle. A prize committee, made up of two officers of the regiment, sold the lot, including many fine beasts, to a contractor for £2 a head; also the sheep for 6s. and the goats for 2s.6d a head. The captured horses were put up for sale and fetched £139. All the money went into a General Prize Fund. The fund exceeded £1200. According to General Orders (issued in early November) livestock should be disposed of and the proceeds should be distributed among participants in the expedition, according to a scale ranging from six shares for the commander to one share for the private. In the case of 'Native Levies' provision was made for shares 'in kind', if desirable. It seems likely the men of the regiment would have preferred payment in kind to some deferred pittance in cash.

The men asked for some of the captured cattle to eke out their normal rations – the quarter beast, *sans* innards, per company per day, which they considered inadequate. The request was refused. The food which they had come upon as it had been cooking and had taken was reserved for the prisoners. The captured Zulus were fed and taken care of, then let go the next day. Such clemency was weakness to the men's way of thinking. Some men of the 1st Battalion asked for an ox for slaughter in a ceremony to 'doctor' themselves. Browne consented to this, but he regretted it in disgust when he saw the way they killed the beast .[6]

The reconnaissance revealed that the track along which the No. 3 Column was to proceed was in no condition to support heavy traffic of men, animals and vehicles, especially in rainy weather.[7] After a day's rest to dry out and clean weapons and equipment, the 1st Battalion, several companies of the British infantry, and No. 1 Company of Pioneers went out to prepare the way. The force marched beyond the Batshe on the 14th and encamped near the battlefield. They remained there for the next five days, working to make the track into a road and to make fords in the streams which would sustain the advance of the column. For the 1st Battalion the assignment was an unpleasant novelty. The officers complained. Browne had to strip off his shirt and start to work to set an example. The men had never used picks or spades before. The sun was hot and there were many flies; but once the work was underway it went well.[8]

On the 16th Browne took three companies on patrol to the east. With him went two of the Zulu prisoners, who lived at the large homestead of a petty chief Gamdane. Gamdane wanted to surrender to the British, according to report. One of the prisoners went off to give the British terms to the chief, and returned late in the afternoon with one of the chief's brothers. He said the chief was ill; he had a very bad leg and could not come in for several days. None the less he submitted. He would send part of his cattle to show it; however, the young men at his place had rejected submission. There had been a row, and they had gone off to join the King.[9]

On the 19th the Lieutenant General visited the encampment and told Browne that the Zulu army was reported to have left Ulundi that morning to attack the column. If the main column were attacked, the work detachment should move down the valley and attack the Zulu right! Browne suggested that the Zulu army would destroy the work detachment first. He asked to be allowed to put the men to work on a 'laager' – the colonists' general term for a fortified enclosure, be it of brick, stone, earth or wagons. The Lieutenant General refused. Afterwards Browne moved his wagons into place and assigned posts to the officers and non-commissioned officers. He intimated nothing to the men, for he suspected that all of them, save the isiGqoza, would bolt at the enemy's onset.[10] Rumours reached the camp that Sihayo with a large force was going to attack that night. Some small entrenchments were dug outside the exposed parts of the camp. Not surprisingly the men of the battalion became restless and seemed fearful.

Captain Duncombe was on picket with his company on top of Ngedla. He sent word to Browne to come up and look at the large number of cattle in a valley to the southeast. Browne took companies

Nos. 9 and 10 of the isiGqoza with him. They observed the cattle being herded by unarmed men, who called on them to come down and receive their surrender. At Browne's behest Duncombe shouted they must come up. He called up the head man of the isiGqoza, Mvubi, and asked his opinion. Mvubi said there was a trap, but he was willing to take the bait for a good fight, though they all should die in it. The answer startled Browne. He sent a runner up to headquarters with the information and returned to camp, leaving Duncombe with a few concealed men to watch through the night. At camp Browne found Major Black had brought up two more companies of British infantry. The major was impressed by the information and also sent a report to headquarters.

After Browne had gone, the enemy came out of the bush, some 1500 of them, and moved off to the southeast. Mvubi had been right. When they were out of sight, Duncombe's detachment descended the hill and managed to catch 150 beasts, which they brought back to camp.[11]

Reconnaissance of Malakatha

On January 20th the No. 3 Column moved forward about twelve miles. The main force at Rorke's Drift marched over the repaired 'road' and was joined by the detachment beyond the Batshe. Work parties were needed between the Batshe and the new camp eight miles beyond, but the repair of the track forward went quickly. There was a particularly difficult stream-crossing, but three officers of the 1st Battalion (Captain Krohn and Lieutenants Vane and Campbell) were expert drivers and managed to bring the wagons through it safely.

At mid-day the column reached the place selected for the new camp. It was chosen for proximity to good water and fire wood,[12] a scarce resource in this open country. It was on the sloping ground below the east face of a peculiarly shaped hill. It was likened to the recumbent sphinx which was the emblem of the 24th Regiment, the British infantry with the column. The hill was called Isandlwana.[13]

The camp extended along a line parallel to the crest of the hill, some 200 yards from the base and 200–300 yards from a dry water course which ran off to the southeast in front. The camp consisted of a series of smaller camps. The infantry battalions, the artillery battery and the mounted force each had their own. Those of the 3rd Regiment were at the north (or left) end of the line. The wagons were parked between the camps and the hill.

Ordinarily the Native Contingent would be placed 'downstream' – that is, at the southern end of the line – because 'the habits of the men were so filthy, and as their officers reported, so incurably so'. But at the southern end of the line the track crossed a rise of ground between the hill and a knoll to the south. The line of communication must be secured, and a battalion of the British infantry was placed there. The 3rd Regiment was placed at the northern end, which was considered less likely to be attacked. The men found plenty of wood behind the hill and began building shelters for themselves. In these confines they packed themselves like sardines.[14] There were two homesteads a little distance to the northeast, and a company of the 1st Battalion was sent to 'capture' them. They found some old men, women and children. These people said they were Gamdane's. A search of their huts revealed some guns and powder. They were taken prisoner and deprived of their cattle.[15]

Officers' tents were pitched and the mid-day meal was taken. Lonsdale returned to command the regiment.[16] He joined Browne and some other officers in conversation. 'My God, Maori [Browne's nickname], what do you think of this camp?' he asked. 'Someone is mad,' replied Browne. The other officers also complained about the way it was strung out. The official field regulations specified that it should be secured by a laager of wagons or a shelter trench. No preparations were made for either. Did the staff think they were going to meet an army of school-girls, asked Duncombe. Why didn't they form a laager?[17]

The wagons were not all in. About a third of the number remained at the difficult crossing about a mile west of the camp, protected by a detachment of British infantry. The camp was secured against surprise by mounted men, in a series of outposts two to three miles distant. Closer in there was another line, made up of men on foot. A company from each battalion was detailed for picket duty. At night the picket line was drawn in towards the camp. The 3rd Regiment furnished the pickets for the northern arc of the line, with a detached picket 1200 yards out, watching a path over a low ridge.[18]

During the afternoon the Lieutenant General, with some mounted troops, reconnoitred the country to the east. Some eight hundred or a thousand of the enemy were reported near the Hlazakazi mountain. The reconnoitring party went to look at the 'stronghold' of an important Zulu chief Matshana. The place, was in a gorge of a stream called Mangeni, eight or ten miles from the camp. They saw nothing of an enemy force, and returned to the camp about 6.30 p.m.[19]

Although no enemy had been found, he was reported to be in the valleys near Matshana's stronghold. The Lieutenant General wished to clear the country that bordered Natal of the enemy before the column moved on towards Ulundi. Therefore he ordered a reconnaissance in force. The mounted colonial units were to retrace his path to the stronghold. The 3rd Regiment was to go to the south, past Gamdane's kraal, round the Malakatha mountain to the west, scout the valleys eastward as far as the Mangeni valley, and ascend the valley and meet the colonial troops at the Mangeni falls.[20]

The two battalions, less two companies from each left at camp for outpost and guard duty, set out, bugles blowing, in chill dawn on the 21st. Not all the men had finished eating and they took their pots of breakfast porridge along. This slowed the pace initially. An ambulance wagon followed a short distance, perhaps to load the pots and take them back to camp. A long trailing cloud hung over the camp and extended to the horizon. It turned blood red before the rising sun, then brown and other colours as the morning passed.

The battalions headed southward across the open country and about half past seven reached a good stream. Its source is on the high ground which rose abruptly on the right, which is Malakatha, and more gently on the left, called Hlazakazi. There is a waterfall further up the stream, which descends through a verdant valley. The country thereabouts was dotted with homesteads and cornfields.

The 1st Battalion formed on the left of the stream. The 2nd Battalion formed on the right. Both advanced in skirmish order, past homesteads which had no people, and seized about seventy cattle at one of them. A few hundred yards below the waterfall the 1st Battalion moved ahead and turned right. It crossed the stream and climbed to the top of Malakatha. The 2nd Battalion also turned to the right. Again they moved parallel, the 1st along the top, the 2nd along the foot of the hill. They swept first the north side, then the west side and finally the south side of the hill. Malakatha is a plateau, so the 1st Battalion had easier going. The 2nd Battalion clambered over a slope covered with rocks and bushes and broken by intermittent watercourses. The sun was high and the dells seemed like furnaces. It was hard work for the men, harder still for the heavily accoutered non-commissioned officers.

The 1st Battalion captured many cattle in a hollow on top of Malakatha. The homesteads there were occupied by women and children and old men. Browne returned some goats which had been taken to a girl, and, through Duncombe, questioned her about the men. Where were they? She replied that they had been ordered to join the King's army. Where? She pointed with her chin to the northwest, and said that they would be attacking in two days time. Later on Browne took two youths for questioning. They were unwilling to talk. They were taken aside and made to. They said they had left the big army and come over to see their mother. Where was the big army? They pointed to the northeast. When would it attack? They did not know, but the moon would be right in another two days. Yet another prisoner indicated an army was expected daily from the King to help the people who had taken refuge in Matshana's stronghold; however, the *amabutho* he mentioned would not amount to a large force. It was also learnt that a considerable number of cattle had been driven to the stronghold that morning.

The 2nd Battalion stopped to rest and eat about noon. The 1st Battalion came down a slope with the captured cattle and joined it. Two late companies brought in more cattle. There were now several hundred head in the hands on the regiment. There was a temptation to seize more which could be seen in the direction of the Mzinyathi, about three miles distant. Instead the cattle in hand were sent off to camp in care of one company, under Captain Murray.

The sweep around Malakatha continued. The two battalions arrived at the eastern side which brought them onto Hlazakazi in late mid-afternoon. The regiment prepared to return to camp. Lonsdale, Browne and Cooper had discussed the information gleaned from the local people and they had decided this was the best course.

But the regiment did not return. The colonial mounted units which had gone along the track to the east of the camp, had crossed the watershed into the valley of the Mangeni. One group went to the west to co-operate with the 3rd Regiment, seeing its white shields gleaming against the light of the setting sun. The other crossed the Mangeni and found a large force of the enemy about a mile in front and moving to the northeast. The advance detachment fell back. The commander of the mounted men now sent to Lonsdale for support. Browne protested. Not only were the men tired and hungry – having eaten up the day's rations – but those with rifles had lost many cartridges in the scamper through rough country. Browne was wary of a trap, especially with darkness coming on. Duncombe agreed with him. Lonsdale would not have it. He seemed to want a fight. Browne thought that he must still be suffering from sunstroke. The men fell in. They moved along the Hlazakazi ridge to the east, not to the north towards camp.[21]

The regiment came up with the first part of the mounted men at the eastern end of the ridge at sunset. The officers were just in time to watch the other part make a feint at a Zulu force in the valley below. The feint drew out about a thousand men. On the crest of a high ridge beyond others were seen silhouetted against a clear sky. The men of the regiment meanwhile were kept back out of the enemy's sight. Then it was dark.[22]

Lonsdale consulted with the commander of the mounted troops. They decided to hold a position on the ridge for the night. In vain Browne, still suspecting a trap, protested against it. The mounted commander sent off a report to the Lieutenant General, telling him of the large enemy force in front and asking for reinforcements so they could attack. In due course the Lieutenant General agreed.[23]

The disgruntlement of the regiment was great. The men were fearful and restless. We know what information the officers had gleaned on reconnaissance that day. How much more must the men have learnt from talking to the people they had met on the way. All were tired, all were hungry. At least they had their blankets. The officers and non-commissioned officers had not brought theirs.[24] Two officers who were sick were permitted to return to camp.[25] They may not have reached it. Nor is it certain that Murray's company (with the cattle) did. During a moonless night the enemy was active between Hlazakazi and the camp.[26] It was later reported that Murray and the other officers who had returned to camp were killed there in the battle the following day. None of the survivors describing the battle mention them and the casualty return for the amaChunu suggest that three companies not just the two companies which were left in camp suffered heavy losses.[27]

A square was formed, the 3rd Regiment taking three sides, the colonial units the fourth, and pickets were posted. The men pulled down huts in nearby homesteads to build fires within the square. They squatted round them and talked. The enemy's fires could be seen on the distant hills. It was not Zulu practice to attack at night, but opinion favoured a battle in the morning.[28]

About two hours before dawn there was a shot on the picket line. A non-commissioned officer had fallen asleep. He awoke suddenly, mistook the man with him for a Zulu and fired at him. Most of the sentries ran away. A corner of the square caved in as one company fled after them. Then the rest followed. There was a clatter of shields. Shots were fired. Officers, sleeping behind their men, were trampled, and their horses, tied up in line in the middle of the square, were borne down the hillside in rear by the panicked mob. In the confusion some of the fugitives injured others. They all clumped together at the bottom of the hill. With a great deal of anger and rough treatment the officers and non-commissioned officers forced them back to their position. There was no telling how many might have gone.

There was not much sleep to be had after this. Again Browne urged they should return to camp. When some stirring horses precipitated another bolt, Browne's officers beat the men back. Browne told them that next time he would shoot the first man who fled and the isiGqoza would kill off his company.[29]

Daylight restored confidence. There was no attack by the enemy. The Zulu fires were smouldering. No enemy was seen on the hills opposite. To everyone's surprise, up the track from camp came the Lieutenant General himself, with reinforcements.[30]

Engagement at Phindo

The reconnoitring force, of which the 3rd Regiment was a part, appeared to be in the presence of a strong force of the enemy on the evening of January 21st. The Lieutenant General responded to the request for reinforcement by marching from the camp at daybreak on the 22nd with six companies of British infantry, a battery of four guns, a small mounted force, and No. 1 Company of Pioneers. There seemed to be no enemy near Isandlwana. A mounted reconnaissance east of the camp, towards Siphezi hill, had skirmished with only a small force on the 21st.

Before leaving the camp for the Mangeni, the Lieutenant General sent a message to Colonel Durnford, who had come up to Rorke's Drift. He informed him that he was moving off to attack a Zulu force about ten miles distant, and ordered him to move at once with the force at his disposal to the camp.[31]

The Lieutenant General's force took about four hours to march seven or eight miles. The pioneers were with the advance guard. Whenever the scouts found a difficult gully, the pioneers hurried along the track to dig and scrape away the sides before the battery arrived. (Even so the guns had to be brought down to the bottom by means of drag ropes.) The Lieutenant General and members of his staff rode ahead to confer with the leaders of the reconnaissance. Morning mist obscured the hill tops until the sun was high enough to burn it off. The imposing Zulu force of the previous evening was not to be seen – nothing but the smouldering fires and a few scouts.[32]

The Lieutenant General decided none the less to take the heights the enemy had occupied. The 3rd Regiment descended from the spur of Hlazakazi to the valley below. The battalions formed in skirmish order, men with rifles twenty yards to the front. The order was given to advance. They swept over the rough ground and up the next hill, called Silulwane. They found no enemy and halted on the crest.

To the left the column from camp could be seen moving up the valley between Silulwane and the next hill to the north. To the right the mounted colonials were moving in the Mangeni valley towards Phindo ridge. Phindo stood like a barrier to the general advance, about two miles in front.

The mounted men could not be seen, but the sound of firing indicated they were engaged. Suddenly several hundred of the enemy burst over the crest of a hill on the right. The mounted men appeared in hot pursuit. Lonsdale ordered the regiment to swing to the right and try to cut off the fugitives before they reached cover under Phindo. The bugles sounded the double. A race began, but the enemy was a mile off and had a head start. Most reached cover safely.

The enemy occupied cliffside caves and hid behind rocks in dense brush. Above was Phindo, below it a large stream. So this was Matshana's stronghold, thought Lieutenant Harford. The enemy opened fire. He seemed well supplied with firearms. The regiment prepared to dislodge him; however, only the 2nd Battalion was in fact set to the task. Harford deployed the companies and the attack began. In front of one cave thirteen men were shot in succession. The cave was bypassed. An attempt to get the defenders of another to surrender seemed to take hours and proved fruitless. The action was broken off at mid-day. Fortunately, there were only two killed. Some prisoners were taken. The men of the contingent wanted to kill them, but the colonials stopped them.[33]

Harford received an order to take the battalion to a new camp site in the Mangeni valley. Where was Lonsdale? Harford had last seen him and Browne riding off, apparently in pursuit of some Zulu chiefs. The 2nd battalion recrossed Silulwane and moved down the Mangeni valley to where the track crosses the stream. Harford warned the men not to get out of earshot of the bugle, then let them fall out. In five minutes not a man was to be seen as everyone scattered to find food at the homesteads and corn fields in the vicinity.[34]

The 1st Battalion was not engaged at Phindo. Browne had just got the men together for a charge when an orderly arrived from the Lieutenant General, who was not aware that the 1st Battalion was about to attack. Browne advised Lonsdale, and, as we have seen, left the 2nd Battalion to make the attack alone.

Browne reported to the Lieutenant General. He found him at the head of the valley north of Silulwane, at breakfast with his staff. The general politely offered him something to eat. Browne politely refused. It would not do to be seen eating before his famished men. The Lieutenant General ordered Browne to take the 1st Battalion back to camp. A report had been received from it that a Zulu force of about five or six hundred men was advancing from the north east. Browne later wrote that he also was ordered 'to examine the plains *en route*', and later still that he was ordered to assist in striking the camp and moving it to the Mangeni. He asked: 'If I come across the enemy?' The Lieutenant General's military secretary replied: 'Oh, just brush them aside and go on'. The military secretary wrote later that the battalion was ordered to skirmish through the ravines in case the enemy hung about near the camp. He did not mention anything about helping to strike camp.

The 1st Battalion moved down from Silulwane to the open valley through which the colonials and then the General's detachment had passed and took the direction of the camp. Browne and his adjutant rode ahead. Unexpectedly they flushed two of the enemy. One was shot trying to escape, but the other was taken prisoner and questioned. He had been scouting from the King's big army which was in the hills north of the camp. Several *amabutho* were going to attack the camp. Browne dashed off a note advising headquarters. He added that he would push on as quickly as possible, that the ground was good for the rapid advance of mounted men and cannon. The Zulu scout had said there were twelve full *amabutho* in the army – that would mean thirty to thirty-six thousand men. Browne accelerated the rate of march. The day was hot. The non-commissioned officers, on foot and more heavily accoutred than the men, particularly suffered.

Browne went forward again and from a rise looked at the camp through his field glasses. It seemed undisturbed. He met two boys who had been sent out by a friend at camp with some food and a couple of bottles of whisky. He halted just ten minutes, time enough to share these out among the non-commissioned officers. Ahead and observing again, he saw puffs of smoke on the hills north of the camp. They were shell bursts. A black shadow lay on the hills. No, it was not a shadow; it was the Zulu army! He dashed off another message. The enemy was attacking the north end of the camp. The guns there had opened on them. He would push on to give them support. The second messenger rode off, just an hour after the first messenger. The first messenger returned and said he had delivered the note to a staff officer. The officer had read it and told him to return and tell Browne to push on to the camp.

Men with sharp eyes had also seen something of what was happening. The battalion came to a standstill. Officers and non-commissioned officers resorted to physical force, but the men were slow to move. Mvubi suggested that the willing isiGqoza take up the rear and kill anyone who lagged. The march resumed, but very slowly.

Meanwhile Browne observed the unfolding Zulu attack on the camp. He despatched another message. The second messenger returned with the same order: push on to camp. Browne had the battalion bear to the left so it would come into camp at the southern end. Organized defence seemed to be collapsing. The camp was engulfed in dust and smoke. He turned to one of his officers: 'Ride as hard as you can, and tell every officer you meet, "For God's sake come back, the camp is surrounded and must be taken".'

The battalion itself was now in danger of attack. Large bodies of the enemy were near by and on the move. Browne reckoned he had fifteen rounds of ammunition for each man – not enough to withstand an attack in the open plain. He decided to retire towards the left rear, to find some rocky cliff the battalion could hold. He ordered the companies to form circles. The officers dismounted and with the non-commissioned officers hid among the men. In this way they retired unnoticed by the enemy to a position about five miles from the camp. During the retreat Browne observed the camp several times. The battle there came to an end.[35]

In a matter of a few hours British fortunes had changed dramatically. The advance of the No. 3 Column came to a full stop. While the Lieutenant General had been supervising an inconsequential skirmish under Phindo ridge, the main Zulu army had passed by him and fallen on the column's camp under Isandlwana hill. The result was a great victory for the Zulu, a disaster for the British.

NOTES

1 *Narrative*, pp. 12, 15–16, 26 C 2242, pp. 42, 46–47. NW, January 16: 'The Zulu War. The First Engagement;' and January 21, 1878: 'The Zulu War.' TN, January 20, 1879: 'The Zulu War.' NM, January 12, 1879: 'From Head Quarters.'

2 Hamilton-Browne, *A Lost Legionary*, pp. 101–111. *Zulu War Journal of Colonel Henry Harford*, pp. 10–21. Parr, *A Sketch of the Kafir and Zulu War*, p. 183–184. Emery, *The Red Soldier*, p. 73. *Narrative*, p. 26–27. C2242, pp. 42–73, 47. NW, January 16, 18 and 21, 1879: 'The Zulu War.' TN, January 20, 1879: 'The Zulu War.' NM, January 21, 1879: 'From Head Quarters.' J.P. Symons, My Reminiscences of the Zulu War, p. 7. *Whom the Gods Love*, pp. 103–104.

3 C 2242, pp. 43–44. Emery, *The Red Soldier*, p. 73. NW, January 16 and 21, 1879: 'The Zulu War.' TN, January 20 and 27, 1879: 'The Zulu War.'

4 *Narrative*, p. 27. C 2242, p. 43. *Zulu War Journal of Colonel Henry Harford*, p. 21. TN, January 20, 1879: 'The Zulu War.' NW, January 21, 1879: 'The Zulu War.' NM, January 21, 1879: 'From Head Quarters.'

5 C2242, pp. 43 and 48. NW, January 21, 1879: 'The Zulu War.'

6 NW, January 21, 1879: 'The Zulu War.' TN, January 27, 1879: 'With Head Quarters Column;' and November 15, 1878: GO 196. SNA 1/1/33, no. 51. Clarke, *Zululand at War 1879*, p. 157 Hamilton-Browne, *A Lost Legionary*, p. 112.

7 C 2242, p. 47.

8 *Ibid.*, p. 43. *Narrative*, p. 27. Hamilton-Browne, *A Lost Legionary*, pp. 112–113. *Zulu War Journal of Colonel Henry Harford*, p. 22.

9 TN, January 27, 1879: 'With Head Quarters Column.' Norris-Newman, *In Zululand with the British*, p. 47. *Cf. Narrative*, p. 29.

10 Hamilton-Browne, *A Lost Legionary*, p. 113.

11 *Ibid.*, pp. 113–115. Norris-Newman, *In Zululand with the British*, p. 43. *Cf. Narrative*, p. 27.

12 *Narrative*, p. 27. Norris-Newman, *In Zululand with the British*, pp. 43–44. Hamilton-Browne, *A Lost Legionary*, p. 115. *Zulu War Journal of Colonel Henry Harford*, p. 22. NW, January 30, 1879: 'The Zulu War'. *Lord Chelmsford's Zululand Campaign*, p. 71.

13 *Narrative*, p. 28. Norris-Newman, *In Zululand with the British*, p. 45. Hamilton-Browne, *A Lost Legionary*, p. 116.

14 *Narrative*, p. 28. Hamilton-Browne, *A Lost Legionary*, p. 116. *Zulu War Journal of Colonel Henry Harford*, pp. 22–23. Norris-Newman, *In Zululand with the British*, pp. 45–46. NW, January 30, 1879: 'The Zulu War.'

15 NC, January 30, 1879: 'The Isandhlwana Disaster' (from TN).

16 *Zulu War Journal of Colonel Henry Harford*, p. 22.

17 Hamilton-Browne, *A Lost Legionary*, p. 116. See also Norris-Newman, *In Zululand with the British*, pp. 46–47. The faults of the camp are dealt with by C.F. Clery in W.O. 33/34, no. 101, inclosure 1, and in C.T. Atkinson,

The South Wales Borderers, 24th Foot 1689–1937 (Cambridge, University Press, 1937), pp. 332, 335–336.

18 *Narrative*, pp. 28–29.

19 *Ibid.*, p 29. NW, January 30, 1879: 'The Zulu War.' *Cf.* Norris-Newman, *In Zululand with the British*, p. 48.

20 *Narrative*, p. 29. Emery, *The Red Soldier*, p. 74. Norris-Newman, *In Zululand with the British*, p. 48. NW, January 30, 1879: 'The Zulu War.' *Lord Chelmsford's Zululand Campaign*, p. 74. NW, January 25, 1913: Fynn, 'My Recollections of a Famous Campaign.' *Cf.* Clarke, *Zululand at War 1879*, pp. 83–84, and NC, January 30, 1879 'The Isandhlwana Disaster.' The Lieutenant General and his staff rode to Gamdane's place in the morning, but did not find him there; however, in the afternoon Gamdane came to Isandlwana. He told the general that the Zulu king had sent an army to punish him for surrendering firearms to the British and it had been expected that morning but had not appeared. The Lieutenant General talked to him about not having surrendered enough firearms and sent him away. (*Cf. Narrative*, p. 29: Fynn, 'My Recollections,' and C 2454, p. 182).

21 *Narrative*, p. 20. Norris-Newman, *In Zululand with the British*, pp. 49–50, and NC, January 30, 1879: 'The Isandhlwana Disaster.' NW, January 30, 1879: 'The Zulu War.' *Zulu War Journal of Colonel Henry Harford*, pp. 23–24. Hamilton-Browne, *A Lost Legionary*, pp. 18–120. Symons, My Reminiscences of the Zulu War, p. 13. John Maxwell, *Reminiscences of the Zulu War* (edited by Leonie Twentyman Jones; Cape Town, University of Cape Town Libraries, 1979), p. 1. The sources vary markedly in some details.

22 *Narrative*, p. 30. *Zulu War Journal of Colonel Henry Harford*, pp. 24–25. Hamilton-Browne, *A Lost Legionary*, p. 121. NC, January 30, 1879: 'The Isandhlwana Disaster.'

23 *Narrative*, pp. 30–31. Hamilton-Browne, *A Lost Legionary*, p. 121–123. *Zulu War Journal of Colonel Henry Harford*, p. 25. Norris-Newman, *In Zululand with the British*, p. 51. Maxwell, *Reminiscences of the Zulu War*, p. 1. Clarke, *Zululand at War*, p. 84. Fynn, 'My Recollections of a Famous Campaign.'

24 *Zulu War Journal of Colonel Henry Harford*, pp. 25–26. Hamilton-Browne, *A Lost Legionary*, p. 122. NC, January 30, 1879: 'The Isandhlwana Disaster.' Fynn, 'My Recollections of a Famous Campaign.'

25 Lieutenants Avery and Holcroft. NW, February 18, 1879, citing NC report. *Cf.* NC, January 30, 1879: 'The Isandhlwana Disaster,' and *Zulu War Journal of Colonel Henry Harford*, p. 26. Fynn, 'My Recollections of a Famous Campaign.' Hamilton-Browne, *A Lost Legionary*, states (p. 121) that there were four, but does not name them.

26 Hamilton-Browne, *A Lost Legionary*, pp. 125–128. The *Zulu War Journal of Colonel Henry Harford*, p. 25. Symons, My Reminiscences of the Zulu War, p. 19. Norris-Newman, *In Zululand with the British*, p. 53, and NC, January 30, 1879: 'The Isandhlwana Disaster.' C 2260, p. 99.

27 Hamilton-Browne, *A Lost Legionary*, p. 120. Maxwell, *My Reminiscences of the Zulu War*, p. 1. Norris-Newman, *In Zululand with the British*, pp. 51–52. See the casualties of the amaChunu, in NGG, XXXI, No. 1764: GN 155. Also, there is no mention of the company escorting the cattle in the order of battle; however, Gon, *The Road to Isandlwana*, states (pp. 217–218), without citing any source, that they did return to camp before dark on the 21st.

28 *Zulu War Journal of Colonel Henry Harford*, pp. 26, 28. Maxwell, *My Reminiscences of the Zulu War*, p. 1. Symons, My Reminiscences of the Zulu War, pp. 18, 19. NC, January 30, 1879: 'The Isandhlwana Disaster.' *Cf.* Hamilton-Browne, *A Lost Legionary*, p. 122.

29 *Zulu War Journal of Colonel Henry Harford*, pp. 27–28. Maxwell, *My Reminiscences of the Zulu War*, p. 2. Hamilton-Browne, *A Lost Legionary*, pp. 122–124. NC, January 30, 1879: 'The Isandhlwana Disaster.' Symons, My Reminiscences of the Zulu War, p. 20. NM, January 22, 1929: S.B. Jones, 'Haunting Memories of Half a Century.' The sources vary markedly in some details.

30 Maxwell, *My Reminiscence of the Zulu War*, p. 2. *Zulu War Journal of Colonel Henry Harford*, p. 28. Hamilton-Browne, *A Lost Legionary*, p. 125.

31 *Narrative*, p. 29–31, 38.

32 *Ibid.*, p. 38. Parr, *A Sketch of the Kafir and Zulu War*, p. 191. *Cf.* Hamilton-Browne, *A Lost Legionary*, p. 125 and *Zulu War Journal of Colonel Henry Harford*, p. 28.

33 *Narrative*, pp. 39–40. C 2454, p. 183. C 2260, p. 99. CSO 1925: Fynn to Colonial Secretary, January 23, 1879 (no minute number). NW, January 30, 1879: 'The Zulu War.' NC, January 30, 1879: 'The Isandhlwana Disaster.' Norris-Newman, *In Zululand with the British*, pp. 55–56. Parr, *A Sketch of the Kafir and Zulu War*, p. 192. Hamilton-Browne, *A Lost Legionary*, p. 125. *Zulu War Journal of Colonel Henry Harford*, pp. 28–29. Maxwell, *My Reminiscences of the Zulu War*, pp. 2–3. Symons, 'My Reminiscences of the Zulu War,' pp. 22–25 *passim*. Fynn, 'My Recollections of a Famous Campaign'. Jones, 'Haunting Memories of Half a Century.' Again, sources vary markedly in certain details.

34 *Zulu War Journal of Henry Harford*, pp. 29–30. Maxwell, *My Reminiscences of the Zulu War*, p. 3.

35 Hamilton-Browne, *A Lost Legionary*, pp. 125–132. W.O. 33/34, No. 96, inclosure 1. Browne to W. Bellairs (February 2, 1879). C 2260, p. 99. C 2454, p. 184. Also see *Narrative*, pp. 39–40 and *cf.* Norris-Newman, *In Zululand with the British*, p. 56. Hamilton-Browne's later account is an embellishment of his earlier report, and there is no other account to corroborate or to contradict it.

Chapter 5
DISASTER AT ISANDLWANA

An enemy presence near camp

At the camp of the No. 3 Column there was nothing to suggest disaster, or even danger, early on Saturday, January 22nd. The Zulu army seemed far away, or, if it was not, then it was remarkably elusive and timid. There were about eighteen hundred men, combatants and noncombatants, at the camp. The six companies of British infantry and four companies of the 3rd Regiment of the Native Contingent, a section of artillery with two guns and a mixed troop of mounted colonials seemed sufficient to look after things there. Anyway, they expected to move soon, as the column continued to make its way slowly into Zululand.

The 3rd Regiment was represented in the camp by two companies of each battalion. One company of each supplied pickets outside the camp. The other provided their relief. The camp was protected against surprise by two lines of outposts during the day and by one at night. The daytime lines consisted of men mounted, circling the camp at approximately three miles distance, and on foot, posted as sentries approximately one and a half miles out. At certain vantage points there were outposts, where officers were stationed and on which sentries could fall back in case of trouble. The mounted men were withdrawn to camp at dark, but the men on foot were withdrawn only half the distance towards the camp, where they formed the night line.[1]

No. 9 Company of the 1st Battalion, men of the isiGqoza, was stationed in front and rear of Isandlwana hill. The preceding day the men in front had occupied a conical hill about a mile and half in front of the camp and about three quarters of a mile north of the track towards the Mangeni. At night they withdrew across a small stream to a hillock about half way back towards the camp.[2] It is not clear where the men behind Isandlwana were posted.

No. 5 Company of the 2nd Battalion, Phakade's men, was stationed on some high ground where a spur juts out from the ridge to the north. This position was about 1200 yards from camp. There was a path between the ridge and the camp which an enemy might use for quick descent, and it had to be guarded, even at night. The path allowed quick communication and, if necessary, hasty withdrawal to the camp in case of danger.[3]

From these two outposts sentries were distributed in a rough arc around the north of the camp. British regulars were similarly posted to the south. In the daytime mounted men took up positions further east along the ridge several miles from camp and beyond it to the north.[4]

No. 5 Company of the 2nd Battalion had relieved No. 4 Company on picket the night before. Both were amaChunu. The isiGqoza had been on picket thirty-six hours since the column arrived at Isandlwana, and was due to be relieved by No. 6 Company of the 1st Battalion.[5] The composition of No. 6 Company is not definitely known. Very likely they were amaBhele.[6] They fell in at six to relieve the isiGqoza, but the rapid unfolding of events prevented them from doing so.[7]

The camp was secure against surprise. It was not secure against attack. It was neither entrenched nor laagered. The fighting men left at camp by the Lieutenant General numbered approximately twelve hundred. The commandant of the camp had been instructed to keep them in a compact force in defence of the camp, but neither he nor the Lieutenant General seriously considered the camp might be attacked. There was no visible evidence that a large Zulu force was in the vicinity.

The Zulu army – between fifteen and twenty thousand men – had bivouacked that night ten miles away. It was ready to attack – if not on the 22nd, because of the new moon, then on the 23rd. The Lieutenant General did not know about it. His mounted scouts had not discovered the enemy's army. The inference which might have been made from verbal information was not made.[8] The Lieutenant General apparently expected the enemy to do what he wanted him to do. His attention was focused on the opposition to his reconnaissance in front. He divided his force in the presence of the enemy and both parts were vulnerable to attack. Indeed, the part reinforcing the reconnaissance, strung out as it was, was more vulnerable than the part remaining at camp. The latter was concentrated and could at least close up quickly for a stand.

The British conception of the situation changed that morning, but not quickly enough to prevent disaster. Zulu parties were out. The men on outpost duty reported them. Phakade's men on the ridge saw armed Zulus in the broad valley before them. There were very many of them and they appeared to be moving in the direction of the camp. Some came close enough to speak to them. A report was sent back to camp. It was about seven.

The iziGqoza on the hillock were eating. Their officers told them that a Zulu army was in the vicinity and ordered them to take their blankets back to camp. The company which was to relieve them did not come. It fell in but did not move out. Instead one of its lieutenants was sent up to the prominence on the ridge where the amaChunu were posted to investigate the Zulu army numbers.[9]

The sight was unnerving. The Zulu force was dense but spread out as it advanced. It extended over five miles. The lieutenant reported to the commandant of the camp. The commandant then sent the company's other lieutenant up to look. He saw much the same thing. Large bodies of the Zulu army were on the hills of the Nquthu range, between one and two miles to the north. Others were in the shallow valley about half a mile away. The lieutenant watched the enemy movement for about half an hour before descending the ridge to report.[10]

The camp's commandant also received a report from one of the mounted men on outpost duty beyond the ridge. Zulus, thousands of them, were advancing. He sent off a dispatch by rider to the Lieutenant General at 8.50: 'Report just came in that the Zulus are advancing in force, from left front of camp.' He had 'Column Alarm' and 'Fall-in' sounded. The British infantry formed and part of it marched to the north end of the camp and about a quarter of a mile in front of the 3rd Regiment's encampment. A small Zulu force suddenly appeared on the ridge. It paused there a few minutes, and retired out of sight. Then other groups in varying numbers appeared and vanished.[11]

Two more mounted men reported to the commandant that the Zulus were in strength beyond the ridge.[12] There was a sound of heavy gun fire in the distance, now and again, from the direction taken by the Lieutenant General.[13] Yet immediately around the camp there appeared to be no threat. Nothing more could be seen of the enemy. After about half and hour the British infantry marched back to their encampments. After another three-quarters they were allowed to fall out, but told to remain under arms.[14] The oxen had been collected and tied to the yokes of the wagons.[15] There was no move to form a laager.[16] The iziGqoza arrived in camp and were ordered back to the hillock in front.[17]

It was almost ten o'clock when the commandant was informed that Colonel Durnford and his mounted men were approaching the camp on the Rorke's Drift road.[18]

Misunderstanding and false pursuit

Durnford's mounted troops had crossed the Mzinyathi on the night of the 20th and encamped a mile or two beyond Rorke's Drift. The Rocket Battery accompanied them, with its escort of two companies of the 1st Battalion of the 1st Regiment. The force was made up of the most part of amaNgwane – the two companies on foot, the three troops of Zikhali's Horse.

Durnford's force was intended to co-operate with the No. 3 Column by operating on its flank. It would help clear the Zulu country along the border of any threat to the Colony. As we have seen, the Lieutenant General's instructions and Durnford's arrangements for this purpose had changed according to circumstances. It is not clear how *exactly* the Lieutenant General intended to employ Durnford's force at this time. On the 21st he ordered Durnford to hurry forward to join the No. 3 Column. Early in the morning of the 22nd, before he departed from camp, he sent an order to Durnford to march to Isandlwana without delay with all his force. Also, if the 2nd Battalion of the 1st Regiment, near Sand Spruit, had crossed the Mzinyathi lower downstream, then it should move up on its own. The Lieutenant General explained that he was taking a force from the camp to attack a Zulu force about ten miles away.[19]

Durnford received the order while he was out foraging with the Edendale troop on the Natal side of the river. George Shepstone, his Political Assistant, had read and forwarded the order, and ordered tents struck and wagons packed. The men were at drill and thus ready to go. They quickly had something to eat, and when Durnford's foraging expedition returned about seven the lot set out for Isandlwana. Durnford and his staff led the way. Hlubi's and the Edendale troops followed. Then came the three troops of Zikhali's Horse, the Rocket Battery and its escort, and the wagons. Three baSotho rode in advance, and scouts were thrown out on the flanks, but they saw nothing of the enemy.[20] They were in high spirits. The horsemen made good time over the eight miles, but the battery, with mules to carry rockets and troughs, and the ten wagons, drawn by oxen, fell behind.

Within a mile of the Isandlwana camp Durnford and his party met an officer of the Royal

Engineers who had taken some men to the camp and was returning to Rorke's Drift. The officer told them that Zulus had been seen and also reported at the camp. Durnford told him to deliver orders to his men as he went back. The Rocket Battery, which was at the Batshe, should hurry up. One of the two escort companies should fall back to protect the wagons. Everyone should be on the lookout to the left, where it was expected the Zulus were moving. Then Durnford apparently decided to concentrate the fighting men. Fifteen minutes later the company waiting for the wagons was ordered forward post haste, leaving only sixteen men as an escort.

About ten o'clock Durnford and the mounted men rode into camp. The mounted men halted beyond the ambulances, near the centre of the camp. They were ordered to dismount and hold their horses.[21] Durnford went to see Colonel Pulleine, the commandant of the camp. Pulleine told him that the Lieutenant General had gone to reinforce the reconnaissance and what had happened around the camp. He also told him that he had been left in command with orders to defend the camp. Durnford, as senior Lieutenant Colonel, superseded him. He proposed to go out after the enemy that had been seen. Pulleine protested that that was contrary to his instructions.

It is probable that Durnford conceded the point. He did not propose to interfere with Pulleine's arrangements, yet he would not be bound by them. He wanted to strike the enemy wherever he appeared. Yet the enemy could be seen now only in the far distance, on the Nquthu range, and distinctly only with field glasses. It seemed that the Zulu forces which had appeared near the camp earlier had either retired or concealed themselves at the approach of Durnford's force. This did not mean that the earlier reports of their nearness and menace should be disregarded. There arrived a fresh report that a body of four to six hundred was to the right, in front of the camp, about two miles away and retreating. Durnford could be forgiven some perplexity at the variety of the reports. He sent six scouts of his own out in all directions to find out where indeed the enemy was.[22]

Durnford returned to his men. They mounted, 'fours right' and 'left wheel', marched along the front of the camp, halted beyond the 3rd Regiment's encampment, and formed by troops. Additional ammunition was issued. The Rocket Battery and its escort arrived, but the wagons were still out. Durnford ordered No. 3 Troop of Zikhali's Horse and Company E of the 1st Battalion to go back for them. There were Zulus lurking about, he remarked, and the wagon train was in danger of being cut off.[23]

Some of Gamdane's men came to surrender firearms and Durnford interviewed them briefly.[24] A scout came in and reported that about 6000 of the enemy were at some distance to the left. Then another report: the enemy was in three columns. And another: the columns were separating, one moving towards the left rear, the other towards the general's force.[25] This information more or less located the enemy's forces, but their precise dispositions and intentions remained unknown.

Durnford ordered Nos. 1 and 2 Troops of Zikhali's Horse to go to the left, that is, to north of camp, and to scout the ridge and the valley beyond it. He mentioned that a body of 600 Zulus had been seen crossing the ridge. He put Captain William Barton and Shepstone, in charge of the reconnaissance. The two troops, under the head man Nyanda, rode out of camp and ascended the ridge.[26]

Durnford returned to Pulleine and had something to eat. Pulleine directed an officer just in from the outpost on the spur north of camp to him. Durnford ordered the officer to send some of his men, of No. 6 Company, to the top of Isandlwana to watch the enemy. Isandlwana was not quite as high as the ridge, but it commanded the plain. Information on what was happening there would complement that from the reconnaissance on the ridge. The men climbed up the hill, but they did not report. After half an hour the officer sent another man up to find out what was happening and to report back at once. This man returned quickly. He reported the Zulus were retiring.

The officer rode to report to Durnford. 'Ah!' said Durnford, 'is that so; well then we shall follow them up.'[27] Durnford apparently thought that the retiring enemy was one of the three columns seen earlier and was going to join the enemy whom the Lieutenant General must be engaging. He decided to pursue it.[28] He asked Pulleine to let him have two companies of the British infantry as well. Pulleine refused, again pleading instructions. Durnford was not to be held back: 'Very well, perhaps I had better not take them; I will go with my own troops.'[29]

Durnford rode up to the two waiting troops and ordered them to mount and follow him. 'The enemy are retiring,' he said. He ordered the Rocket Battery and the one company left as escort to follow after the mounted men.[30] He sent another officer after the two troops on the ridge with instructions to work round the conical hill to the east of the camp on the one side while he and the others worked round it on the other. Thus they would pursue the enemy.[31] The Edendale men understood Durnford to say that there was no choice, they had to go out and meet the enemy.[32]

The two troops set out at a canter. They proceeded straight across country. The track was on their right, the conical hill on their left and the ridge further off on the left.[33] They had been in camp scarcely an hour.

Durnford and the Sotho and Edendale men were soon out of sight of the camp. They were soon out of sight of the Rocket Battery and its escort as well, for the men were on foot and the mules could not canter. The mounted men rode on, across the plain, over several streams, past the conical hill. Some Zulus were seen, apparently running away. Durnford remarked to his Sotho aide Molife: 'If they are going towards the General we must stop them at all hazards.'[34]

Durnford in fact misunderstood the enemy's movements completely. He had divided up his own small force and was setting off in pursuit of an enemy who was not really retreating. He led the two troops into a draw by which they could make a relatively

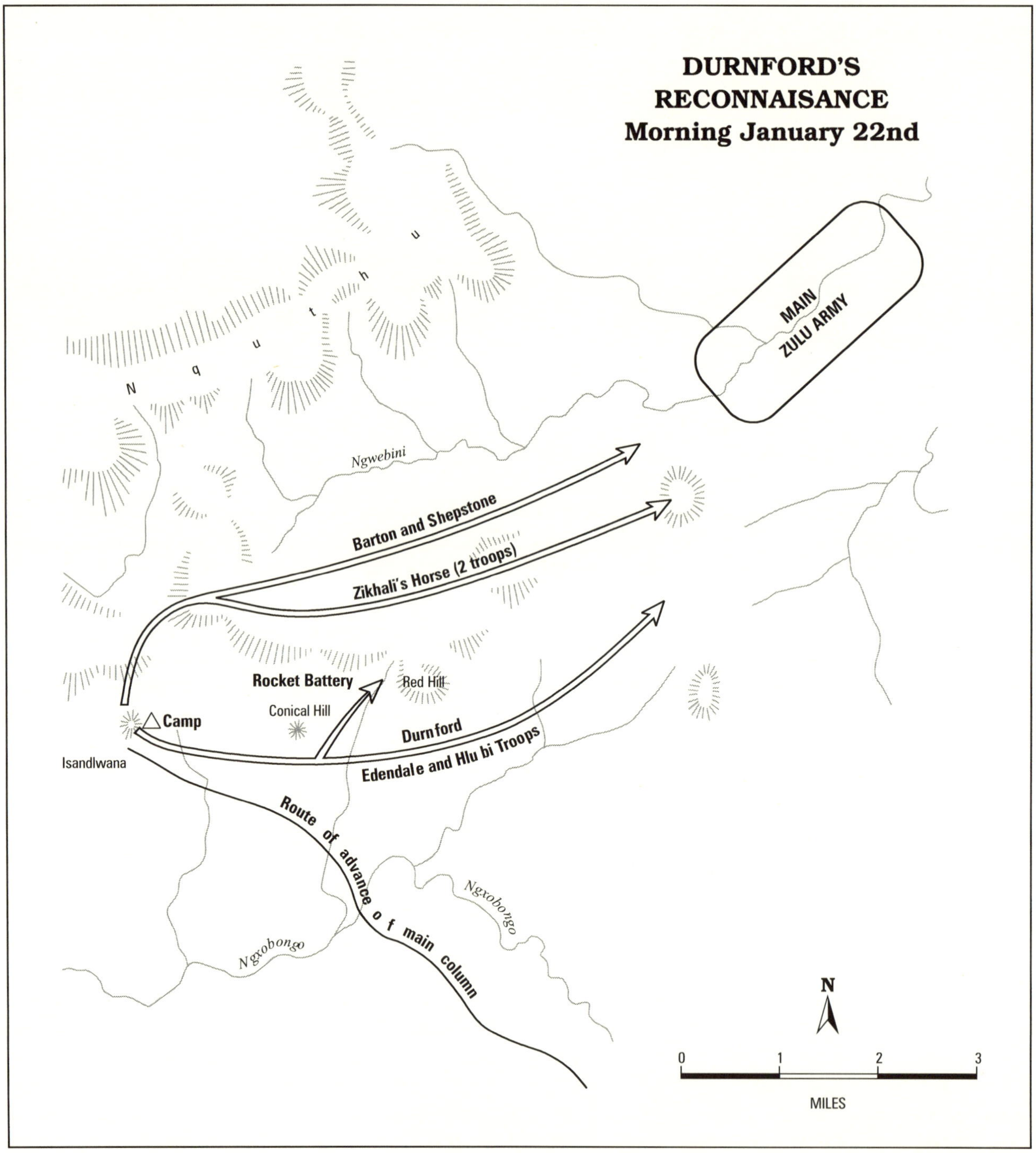

easy ascent of the ridge. They were about four miles from camp. Suddenly two mounted colonials rode down from an outpost on the ridge to the left. They brought a warning: return to the camp, the enemy is behind you, he is surrounding you and the camp. Durnford retorted 'The enemy can't surround us, and if they do, we will cut our way through them.' Where is the Rocket Battery, he asked one of his officers. A very long way behind, the officer replied. Durnford was angry. He turned and asked Molife 'What are those scouts I sent out, about?' He told the colonials to tell their officer to support the mounted troops. The colonials replied that their officer had strict instructions from Colonel Pulleine not to leave his post. 'I am Colonel Pulleine's senior,' exclaimed Durnford. 'You will please tell Lieutenant Scott to do as I tell him.'[35]

It was too late to matter. The mounted troops heard firing from over the ridge and towards their rear. Zikhali's Horse must be engaged. Hlubi approached Durnford and persuaded him to retire. The scouts came in and reported the enemy was in sight. Indeed, they were. Durnford and his men looked up at the crest of the ridge, about 1500 yards in front. There were thousands of Zulus. Their skirmish line was ten to twelve men deep. Behind it were masses in support. They looked to the left along the ridge, towards the camp. More of the enemy there – the Zulu army was beginning to descend to the plain. Zulus with rifles opened fire on them at a distance of between seven and eight hundred yards.[36]

Pursuit becomes retreat

The enemy was attacking in overwhelming numbers. Durnford must retreat. A man was sent to ask the Lieutenant General for help.[37] With his two troops, numbering a hundred men, Durnford formed a skirmish line. 'Let the enemy come a little closer, then fire and retire,' he told the troop commanders; 'keep the enemy at a distance of about 200 yards.' What range should we set our sights for, some Edendale men asked their officer, Lieutenant Davies. Four hundred yards and down to the standard sight, he replied. At about four hundred yards they began to fire.

They also started a measured retreat. The Edendale troop was on the left, Hlubi's on the right.[38] Some of their shots struck home, but the great mass of the enemy came on unaffected.[39] They fell back a little more than a mile and were approaching the conical hill when they came on what was left of the Rocket Battery and escort, Company D of the 1st Battalion.[40]

The sound of firing over the ridge had prompted the battery commander to change direction. Also, he hoped to catch up to Durnford by taking a short cut. Two mounted colonials had offered to show him to their outpost, but he wanted to go towards the firing, which meant going up the ridge short of the outpost. The colonials warned him that Zulus would be first at the brink. He disregarded the warning.

The way up the ridge was steep and rocky. At the start the mules began to baulk. Twenty-five men of the escort company were told to carry the rockets instead. With this change the amaNgwane became disorganized.

The battery commander was riding ahead. Too late he realized that the colonials were right. The enemy was at the top of the ridge. He rode back down, shouting 'Action front!' There was no time to form properly. Only one rocket was fired. Zulus rose from the rocks and bush and fired a volley at one hundred yards. It dispersed the mules and the escort. The Zulus came on, shouting 'Usuthu'. The cry blended into a buzzing sound. Two mules clambered onto a boulder. They were thrown off and killed. The men in Company D who had rifles fired them, but many could not extract the empty cartridge cases after the first shot. One of the British soldiers of the battery tried to help, but they would not part with their rifles. The company ran. The officers' horses also bolted.

Without his horse the company commander, Captain Nourse, could not even begin to rally his men. Only four or five remained. He ran down the slope. The battery commander rode down with him. They were ahead of the Zulus, but when they stopped to look around, the battery commander was shot. Nourse helped him back on to his horse. By then the Zulus were close. Nourse suggested they get away and ran again. The next time he looked back he saw neither horse nor rider.[41]

When the mounted men came into sight, the few men left in the battery and escort were fighting hand-to-hand with Zulus who had come down after them. The Edendale troop wheeled to the right, while Hlubi's still faced the front in order. The survivors were saved, and the Zulus retreated up the ridge. The men dismounted to fire from a stream bed whose bank gave them protection.[42]

Durnford asked one of the survivors where the battery was. Cut up, the commander shot, the man replied. Durnford said he had better go back and fetch the commander. The man protested they were practically surrounded. Durnford asked Nourse where the battery commander and battery were. Nourse tersely described their fate. Durnford looked very distressed. He said something about not surviving the disgrace.[43]

A man was sent after a stray mule which was carrying two boxes of rockets. The enemy was close, but the mule was brought in and sent back to the camp. Other men were told to pick up the boxes of rockets and ammunition which were lying on the ground. The troops remounted. The enemy was much closer, and the men with the boxes threw them away. Durnford's force fell into some confusion, but by the time it rounded the conical hill it had recovered. The two troops retreated and fired steadily – retire twenty yards, dismount and fire; remount, retire ten yards, dismount and fire, again and again.[44]

The Zulu army spread out on the plain. It began to extend to the south around the right flank of the mounted troops and towards the camp in their rear. The horsemen crossed another stream and the spur of the hillock on which the isiGqoza and other units were engaged to the north. They picked up more of the Rocket Battery escort on the way. A cannon near the camp fired several shots over their heads, but the shells had no visible effect on the enemy in front.[45]

The camp was only a thousand yards in the rear. There was another watercourse – deep enough to conceal them and with water for the horses to drink.[46] Durnford ordered them to get into it and fire as hard as they could. They dismounted and lined the left side and started to fire over the bank. The cannon behind them had stopped firing.[47] British infantry was off to their left. One of the British companies, apparently ordered forward from the camp, had advanced and fired into the Zulu onslaught. It had retired, apparently because it had run out of ammunition, but then another company came forward.[48] A mixed force of mounted colonials, police and soldiers, about forty strong, came down from the camp and joined Durnford's troops at the watercourse.[49] Durnford called for volunteers to try to break through to give the news of what happened to the general.[50] Apparently none came forward.

The combined fire from the men in the gully stopped the Zulu advance immediately in front. The enemy lay down, and those with rifles sought to return the fire. The enemy not in front – the great majority – swerved aside and continued to advance.[51] There was no more open country across which to retreat. The Edendale men inclined to falter. Durnford tried to inspire them. No help for it now, they must face the danger and, if necessary, die for the Queen! He rode up and down the watercourse. 'Fire, my boys.' Calm, even cheerful, he talked and even laughed with them. 'Well done, my boys.' He stood up on the bank, exposed to the enemy fire, to encourage them. Some of them told him he should keep down and not expose himself. He laughed and said 'All right' or 'Nonsense'.[52] Lieutenant Henderson, with Hlubi's troop, wondered if the Colonel had lost his head.[53] Some men brought him their rifles. Extracting an expended cartridge from a hot and foul Martini-Henry could be difficult. Durnford would dismount, take the rifle and clamp it between his knees, and with his one good hand pull out the cartridge, then give the rifle back.[54]

So successful did the stand appear to be that Lieutenant Davies ordered the Edendale men to turn their rifles towards the left, and fire at the Zulu advance against the British infantry. They fired one or two volleys in that direction, but then the Zulus in front began to advance again. Men began to call out that they were running out of ammunition.[55]

The battle on the left

The two troops of Zikhali's Horse which Durnford had sent to the ridge north of camp had arrived at the top of the ridge and begun to scout forward as directed. No. 1 Troop, accompanied by George Shepstone, followed the crest of the ridge. No. 2 Troop, accompanied by the head man, Nyanda, and Captain Barton, went on to the valley beyond it. The two troops formed extended skirmish lines, about half a mile apart but close enough to give each other support. The company of Phakade's men on outpost duty on the prominence was collected and taken along in support of No. 1 Troop.[56]

They saw only a few Zulus, who were in small groups and retreated before them. The reconnaissance proceeded two, three, four miles. The ridge flattened out slightly. The valley became shallower, but to the north, the Nquthu range formed a peak. About five miles on a small herd of cattle crossed the front. No. 1 Troop tried to capture it. The Zulu herders drove it over a hill, and the mounted men pursued to the crest. The hill fell away to a deep valley. There, in the valley, was the Zulu army – twelve to fifteen thousand men. It was silent, marshalled in perfect order. The closest men in it were several hundred yards away.

Which side fired first is disputed, but the shots stirred the Zulu army to action. As it moved, it reminded a witness of a great swarm of ants.[57]

At the sight of the enemy the company of Phakade's men ran towards camp and left their officers with the mounted troops. A hundred mounted men could not stop twelve thousand Zulus, but Shepstone told the officers to make a fighting retreat. He himself rode to camp to warn the commandant of what was coming. No. 2 Troop now joined No. 1, and together they began a methodical retreat the way they had come, dismounting and firing and remounting, very much as Durnford's troops on the plain would within the hour. The Zulus in the forefront of the advance opened fire at a distance of half a mile. Of course, they hit no one. Four times Zikhali's men stood. Nothing they could do would stop the Zulu onset. To the enemy their stands seemed like sallies, perhaps an illusion created by his own motion. By the time Zikhali's men reached the ridge where they had ascended it, the enemy was only two hundred yards away. Only one of Zikhali's men had been wounded. A number of Zulus had fallen.[58]

The sound of the firing forewarned the camp. Pulleine received Shepstone's report. At the same time he received a message from the Lieutenant General to strike camp and to send forward supplies and the equipment belonging to the force which had gone out that morning.[59] 'I am not an alarmist, sir, but the Zulus are in such black masses over there, such long black lines, that you will have to give us all the assistance you can. They are fast driving our men this way,' said Shepstone. The commandant hesitated. The young officer who had brought the general's message added: 'Under the circumstances, I should advise your disobeying the general's order, for the present at any rate. The general knows nothing of this... .'[60]

Just then Zikhali's men spilt over the ridge, Zulus at their heels. They came down to the spur below the prominence. Pulleine decided to support them. On the broad neck of ground between the spur and Isandlwana fresh forces were drawn up. There was No. 3 Troop which had brought in Durnford's wagons, dismounted and extended in skirmish order. To its right was a company of the British infantry. The men from the ridge rallied at the foot of the spur. They left their horses and altogether, the three troops supported by the infantry, they charged up the slope. The cannon from the camp threw a couple of shells into the Zulus. The enemy did not wait to fight. He laid down a hot but inaccurate fire and retreated up the ridge and over the crest, throwing aside spears and shields in his haste to escape.[61]

The amaNgwane regained the crest and the British occupied the prominence. The British were reinforced by another company on the left. The amaChunu formed along the ridge on the right of the British.[62] It is not clear whether one or two companies of Phakade's men were on the ridge, for the officers who had been abandoned by No. 5 Company apparently did not rejoin their men.[63] (Perhaps that company had not re-grouped after its earlier flight, in which case No. 4 Company would have been there alone.)

The main force of the enemy came up with the van, and the ridge could not be held against it. In front the Zulu centre was moving into and over the ridge. The left horn was taking in Durnford on the plain. The right horn was moving under Nquthu. The two artillery pieces to the left of camp fired a few shots at the turning movement, but they were ineffectual at the range of two miles. The amaNgwane, much closer and hotly engaged, tried to counter the Zulu manoeuvre. No. 1 Troop turned to the left, but the enemy was practically behind them. If the men stayed any longer they would be trapped. Also, Shepstone feared their ammunition was running out. He ordered them to fall back to their horses. The British on the right fell back at the same time. iNgwane and Briton came down the side of the ridge in a tangle. The Zulus shouted and rushed after them.

At the foot of the ridge the men sorted themselves out. The two British companies retired in good order to the artillery. A third company moved from camp to back them up on the left. The amaChunu, who had apparently got off the ridge before the others, reformed on the right of the British. Zikhali's men collected their horses and continued to fight on the spur in front of the British and to their left. Again it was a matter of dismount, fire, remount, fall back, and so on.[64]

The exposed left flank was taken by half of Company E of the 1st Battalion, 1st Regiment. The Ngwane foot soldiers, who had escorted the wagons into camp, either had been held back till now or had not been able to keep up with No. 3 Troop as it moved into action. Now they formed to the left of the horsemen, and threw out skirmishers – probably the men with rifles. There was a gap of 200 yards between them and the nearest troop. It was a terrible position. Some British infantry had been off to the right when they took the position, but evidently it had fallen back soon afterwards. The head man, Ntini, came to the young company officer, Captain Stafford, and asked to be shown how to adjust the sight of his rifle! The officer showed him, and put up the sight on his own rifle to 700 yards. He fired at a large clump of the enemy who seemed to be sitting. The bullet struck the ground just in front of them. He raised the sight to 800 yards. The bullet struck among the Zulus. They appeared to rise and advance towards the company.

The Zulu flanking manoeuvre went on apace. About two thousand Zulus swarmed over the low ground and onto the spur. The non-commissioned officers and every tenth man with a rifle fired twice when the Zulus were about 700 yards away. The men armed only with spears felt like targets for the Zulu rifles. Stafford ran over to Barton, who was directing Zikhali's Horse. He begged him to tell Durnford about the large Zulu force in front. Barton took out a notebook and wrote something, tore out the page and gave it to one of the men to deliver. He suggested that they close the gap between then. The company and troop moved to do so.

The firing was general all along the line. But the rifle men began to run out of ammunition. Barton tried to get more for the mounted men. Evidently he did not know just where in camp Durnford's wagons were. He went to one of the British infantry wagons. The officer in charge refused to give him any cartridges. He said the infantry would need it all themselves!

The Zulus were now within three hundred yards. The amaNgwane ran back towards the camp. Apparently they rallied in a slight ravine running off the neck. It seemed to Stafford that they remained there a long time, but in the circumstances minutes probably seemed like hours.[65]

The two cannon on the right pounded away at the Zulus swarming down the ridge. British infantry, lying down in line and in support, poured out a deadly rifle fire. The Zulu attack withered before it, but the Zulus were too many for the British fire to stop everywhere. The *amabutho* ran forward in skirmish lines up to twenty deep in places. The ridge and the plain below were black with them. There were Zulus as far as the eye could see. The murmur of their voices was like the buzzing of a great swarm of bees. The Zulu right horn was outflanking the amaNgwane on the left. It was behind Isandlwana. The Zulu left horn was spilling out across the plain, outflanking the Edendale and Hlubi's troops, and would soon gain the rear of the camp on the right.[66]

Stafford and Ntini left the men of Company E and hurried back to camp. Of course, they knew where Durnford's wagons were. They lugged a box of ammunition forward to the company. Too late. The amaNgwane no longer had a line. They were retreating into the camp. The British companies on their right were firing at the Zulus who were following them. The fire pinned down some of the pursuers in the ravine and caused the others to recoil over the neck.

Lieutenant Raw, No.1 Troop, rode up: 'Stafford, where is your horse?' Tied to a wagon in the rear, answered Stafford. 'You had better get hold of it as it is all up with us.' The Ngwane foot soldiers were coming into the camp. The rifle men went to the wagons to get ammunition, and found them in the hands of Zulus.[67]

The battle at the centre and on the right

Zikhali's Horse had found the Zulu army. Discovery had provoked the army to attack. The army swept forward in a great crescent – the horns and chest – to encircle its opponent. The force which Pulleine had to defend the camp and the force which Durnford had to reinforce the column could not defeat the Zulu army unless they united and set up an all-round defence. Then they could rely on the superior fire power of the Martini-Henry rifle to repel all attacks. The instructions to Pulleine to defend the camp implied such a concentration. Pulleine had started forming his men when Durnford arrived. A welter of reports had baffled Durnford, and he had launched Zikhali's Horse on a reconnaissance of his own. Before it had located the enemy's army, Durnford had seized on a misleading report and led the balance of his available force in pursuit of an enemy who was not retreating.

Whether or not Durnford told Pulleine *explicitly* to support him if he required it is debatable; but Pulleine did support Durnford's force. Instead of concentrating his own force at the camp he extended it in line some distance. His attention was directed first towards the ridge a mile to the north and approximately at a right angle to the front of the camp. On it Zulus had been seen earlier in the day. Over it Zikhali's Horse had gone to scout. As it was driven back, Pulleine deployed one British company, then a second, finally a third, and directed the cannon to support them. Durnford's wagon escort had been thrown into the battle on the left and one or two companies of Phakade's men had been formed on the right. As we have seen, the ridge could not be held against the mass of the Zulu chest. The defenders were driven steadily towards the camp.

To the right Durnford's feckless pursuit had become a retreat before the Zulu left horn. Pulleine shifted his remaining units to support Durnford's force and to meet the Zulu threat in front of the camp. This last disposition practically assured the destruction of the imperial forces. Up to this point, their survival lay in falling back rapidly on their ammunition source and forming a solid line of defence at the base of Isandlwana, flanks anchored against the steep slopes of the hill. Even then they would be endangered by a reverse fire once the Zulu right horn gained the top of the hill; however, a skillful counterfire might neutralize that. Now with the right thrown out so far from camp, there was no hope of its getting back in time for such a stand.

Phakade's men had been involved in action since an early hour. Men of No. 4 Company on outpost duty had reported the presence of the Zulu in large numbers. It had been picked up by Zikhali's Horse to support the reconnaissance on the ridge, but the sight of the Zulu army had unnerved the amaChunu and they had run away. The officers whom the company abandoned apparently retired with the Horse. When Zikhali's Horse and the British company had briefly reoccupied the ridge, the amaChunu – presumably No.5 Company and possibly No. 4 Company, if it had rallied, were posted in line on the right of the British infantry, and retreated from the ridge before it did. When the British companies reformed in line with the guns on the neck, the amaChunu, such as there were, took position on their right again. They were reinforced by the other half of Stafford's company, the amaNgwane who had escorted Durnford's wagons into camp.[68]

The isiGqoza had spent a relatively uneventful morning in front of the camp, watching the garrison form, troops go forth, and enemy appear and disappear at a distance to the left. Sikhota had asked to bring in the men who were on the west side of Isandlwana. Evidently the whole of No. 9 Company was consolidated at the right picket post, on the hillock half a mile in front of camp.[69] The company, probably amaBhele, which was to relieve it, remained drawn up just in front of the camp. At the crisis of the battle it was Pulleine's only reserve – which for some reason he did not use.

The isiGqoza observed a troop of colonial militia and police ride up the ridge in front as part of the counter attack. They observed it come down again and fight on the plain until it, too, ran out of ammunition and retired. The Zulu army was advancing on the plain as well as over the ridge. The left horn extended ever southward, threatening to envelop not only Durnford's force but the very camp itself. A British company moved up to the hillock, apparently to support the outpost. It then moved into line with it. The isiGqoza thus became part of the main line. They opened fire at the enemy at a distance of six or seven hundred yards. So great was the firing that it sounded like thunder. Against it the shots and cries of the Zulus again sounded like the buzzing of many bees.

The Zulu chest staggered under this fire. In front of the isiGqoza it was at a standstill, but the men with rifles were starting to run out of ammunition. A sergeant hurried back to the camp and brought up a supply, and the firing continued. The Zulus were moving forward again, and there was no protection on the right. Between the isiGqoza and Durnford's force was a gap of 600 yards. The Zulus were making for it. A British company moved down to the watercourse to block them. Just then Durnford's force retreated from the watercourse towards the camp, and the British company was caught by their flight and the Zulu rush.[70]

The amaChunu found themselves in the most vulnerable position – the salient formed by the British companies facing to the left and those facing to the front of the camp.[71] There was practically nothing Phakade's men could do to stop the Zulu onslaught. They were outnumbered and they had few rifles. Their position at the angle of the line meant that the British companies on either side could not give them covering fire in front without uncovering themselves. Indeed, as the enemy converged on Phakade's men, he would bring them under a cross fire! Chunu casualties were heavy. The men started to run away. Their officers could not stop them. In a few minutes there were no officers left to stop them.

The entire line, the arc from left to right now began to retire, apparently on orders, towards the camp. The Zulus were within 300 yards when the remainder of Phakade's men bolted. They looked around for the red soldiers, and did not see them. Some of the head men shouted 'Return to fight'. It was no use. The battle was running too fast against them.[72]

The Zulu army was advancing everywhere. The British line was between two and three hundred yards of the camp.[73] It was fraying at both ends and now there was the hole left by the amaChunu. There was no reserve to seal the breach, because the reserve company had fled. Its men had sat uncomfortably in front of the camp witnessing the battle. Their officers had scarcely been able to prevent them from jumping up and running when Zulu bullets fell among them. When they saw the enemy rushing towards them, they fled just as Phakade's men had.[74]

The British companies on the left were doomed. The two immediately on the left of the amaChunu were taken in flank and massacred by the Zulus scarcely before they could fix bayonets. The third, on the far left, was apparently able to form an all-round defence and fight a while longer.[75]

The isiGqoza retreated from the hillock when the Zulus were only a hundred yards away. They crossed the watercourse farther up from where Durnford's men had sheltered. They moved up the slope towards the camp. Near by them a British company knelt and fired. Further to the right and

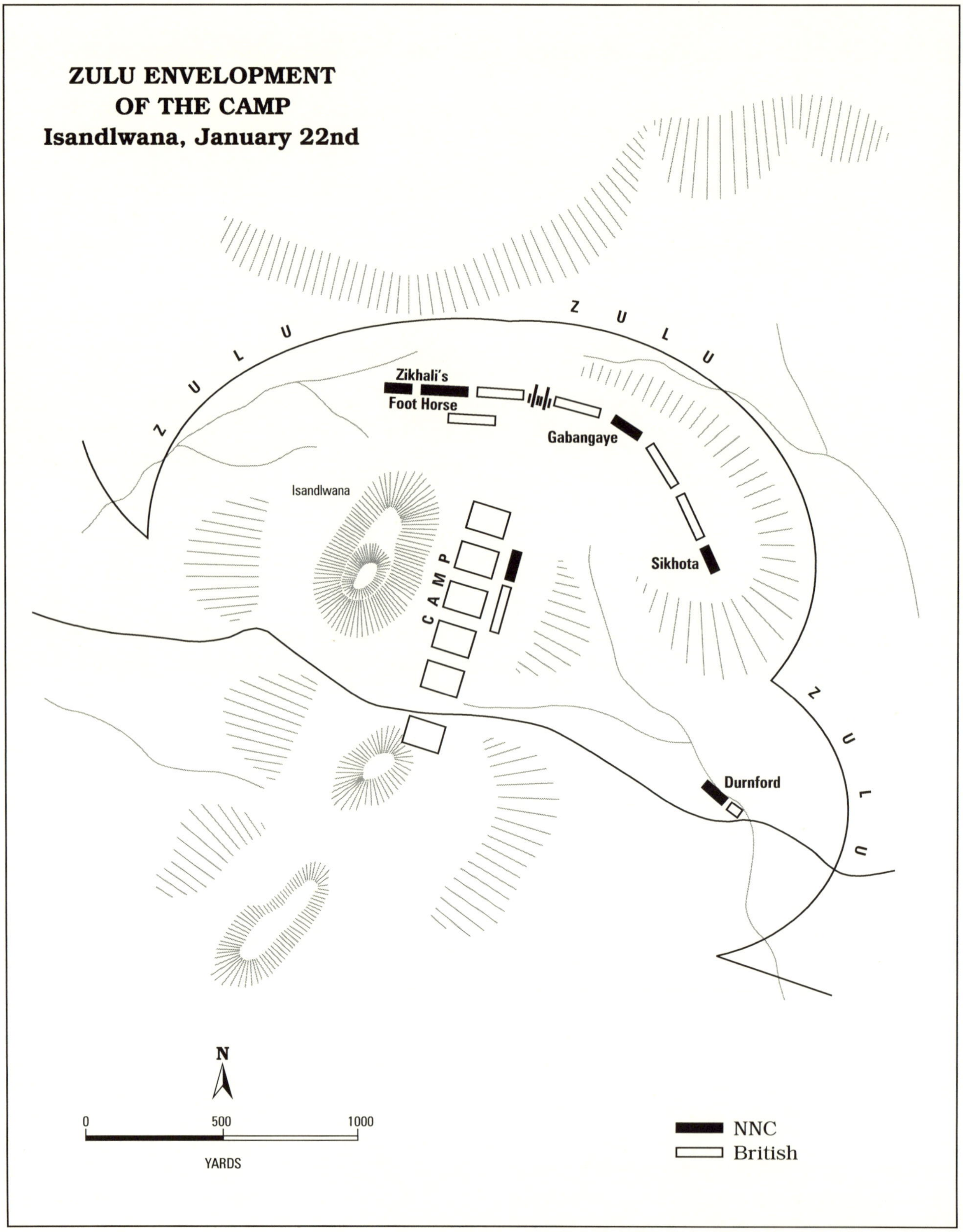

farther back, another British company, perhaps the one which had been in support earlier, was also kneeling and firing. The isiGqoza could not do the same, because the rifle men had no more ammunition. The men fled and Sikhota became separated from most of them in the flight. Their officers and at least one head man chose to stay and fight with the redcoats.[76]

Collapse and flight

The battle was now at the camp and on the neck of land over which ran the road to Rorke's Drift. The Zulus rushed into the camp. They got among the tents and the wagons, and killed man and beast. British soldiers and noncombatants fought or fled as best they could.[77] Organized resistance was at end.

Zikhali's Horse, at the north end of the camp, had to go quickly to escape. They could see the Zulus stabbing the British soldiers a little ahead. No. 3 Troop found some ammunition boxes, but they were unopened and there was no time to look for screwdrivers to open them correctly. No time apparently even to break them open. One of the men found an open box with a few cartridges. The officer quickly distributed them. The enemy was in among the tents just behind them. Zikhali's men kept close to the base of the hill as they moved down the camp, shouting to each other and firing as well as they could from the rocks. They passed a young British officer rallying his men. They reached the track at the southern end of Isandlwana. The Zulu right horn blocked the way to Rorke's Drift. The Zulu left horn was moving into the camp from the south. In a short time, perhaps a few minutes, the horns would meet and cut off any way of escape.

Shepstone left, apparently to find Durnford. Nyanda, Barton and two or three of the officers commanding the troops were left with the troops. Older men advised immediate escape through rough country to the south, and they rode into it at once. The last order Stafford heard was given by a British lieutenant: '24th fix bayonet!' Stafford and Ntini made for a break in the Zulu ranks. Spears showered round them. Ntini went down, but Stafford mounted his horse and got through. Men on foot obviously could not keep up with mounted men. Probably most of Company E which had been on the left of the line went down fighting.[78]

When his men in the watercourse had begun to run out of ammunition, Durnford had sent a messenger to the camp for more. None came. He sent Lieutenant Henderson, of Hlubi's troop, and another man back to get some. Lieutenant Davies, of the Edendale troop, took fifteen men and found about two hundred cartridges in a box in the colonials' encampment. Meanwhile Durnford, observing that his line was thin and was being outflanked, ordered the men in the watercourse to retreat to camp. He probably envisaged a rally somewhere further back.

Durnford told the Edendale men to get away quickly. They told him to come away, too, but he would not, and so they left him. Durnford was among the last to leave the watercourse. A young colonial was still looking for his horse while his comrades rode off. He was frantic. 'Here is a horse; is it yours?' asked Durnford quietly. He was holding the bridle of the horse and walking close behind the young settler. They rode together to camp.

Durnford rode into the battle at the camp and went towards the headquarters tent. It is unlikely that he met Pulleine. He did not return to his own troops. Probably he could not find them again. He fell in with some colonials and British infantry, and together they made a last stand.[79]

Hlubi's and the Edendale men emerged from the watercourse to find the battle behind them. They were practically without ammunition. They had to fend off Zulus on all sides. They saw the men of the 3rd Regiment break and run, followed by the men who led and drove the wagons. They saw the British were surrounded and the enemy was at the camp. The Zulus shouted: 'It is beaten,' and 'They are running,' and poured into the camp. 'Stab the white men, stab the pigs,' they called as they chased soldiers who were running towards the tents. Those whom they caught they stabbed, then ripped them open with their spears. They ripped up the tents and everything else they came across.[80]

Lieutenant Henderson somehow got back to his men just before or while they were retreating. He led them to their own wagons. They were able to get a portion of the ammunition they needed. Lieutenant Davies did not get back to the Edendale men. He did meet Henderson and they agreed that they must break through the Zulu ring. Hlubi's troop charged over the track towards Rorke's Drift.[81]

The Edendale troop was demoralized. Men started to drop off in twos and threes to make their escape. Sergeant Major Kambule took charge. He told them their lives depended on staying together. Anyone who strayed was lost. If it were God's will, he would bring them through to Natal. They promised to stay together for life or death. But he must get them ammunition, if possible.

Victory had rather disorganized the Zulus. Those near by were too busy in the tents to notice the Edendale men. Kambule found a wagon with ammunition but a British drummer boy was sitting on top of it. He said he was in charge. He insisted the ammunition belonged to the 24th Regiment and no one else could have it. Kambule did not argue. His men scuffled for cartridges that had fallen on the ground and been left by others. There was no time to get more. Kambule offered to carry off the drummer boy on his horse. The boy seemed surprised and hurt by the suggestion. He had been placed their by an officer and would not desert his post.[82]

Some officers told Kambule that he would have to shoot his way out. The Edendale men raised their rifles, fired into the Zulus in front of them, and charged. They broke through and rode over the neck. They passed the artillery as the enemy were dragging men off the cannon and stabbing them. Lieutenant Davies rejoined them in the retreat.

Both troops had broken through the Zulu ring. Hlubi's men would go to Rorke's Drift. The Edendale men would go to Sotondose's drift, whither Zikhali's Horse had already gone. The horsemen left the battle while it still raged on the neck, under the hill and along the paths to the river crossing, but no one on the British side lived to tell of the last stand.

NOTES

1 *Narrative*, p. 28. WO 33/34, No. 101, inclosure 1: statement by C.F. Clery.

2 CP 8-58: statement by Malindi. *The Silver Wreath* (edited by Norman Holme; London, Samson, 1979) p. 46: statement by J. Bickley. See also *Narrative*, Plate IV.

3 *Narrative*, p. 29, Plate IV. WO 33/34, 101/1: Clery.

4 *Narrative*, p. 28. *The Natal Carbineers* (edited by J. Stalker; Pietermaritzburg, Davis, 1912), p. 99: account of W.W. Barker.

5 WO 33/34, 96/3: statement by W.R. Higginson. See also WO 32/7713: statement Untabeni and Uhlolwane, and *TN*, February 26, 1879: 'The Battle of Isandhlwana as told by a combatant.' *Cf.* CSO 674: 4945/1878 and *NGG*, XXXI, No. 1764: GN 155 for Chunu casualties.

6 This is conjecture, based on the returns, which show the amaBhele the 'tribe' with the third largest number of casualties at Sandhlwana, i.e. twenty killed, dead or missing; however, Lonsdale's list (CSO 674: 4845/1878) indicates that No. 6 Company was unformed when the amaBhele were present. The list indicates that Nos. 1–4, 7, 9 and 10 companies were complete, No. 5 was incomplete, and gives no information on No. 8. The conjecture involves presumptions that the amaBhele began as No. 7 or 8 Company and the company was renumbered after less abaThembu arrived than expected and that the three companies of the isiGqoza were numbered seriatim. Yet it is quite possible that No. 6 Company could have consisted of amaChunu, too, and the amaBhele who died in combat were noncombatants, *viz.* wagon drivers, team leaders, hospital servants *et al.*

7 WO 33/34, 96/3: Higginson.

8 *Narrative*, pp. 28, 156. The number given (p. 31) is for combatants. There were also noncombatants, but their number is not given. For appraisals of the Lieutenant General's attitude and understanding of the situation, see John Laband and Jeff Mathews, *Isandlwana* (Pietermaritzburg, Centaur, 1992), pp. 29–35, and Ian Knight, *Zulu: Isandlwana and Rorke's Drift 22nd – 23rd January 1879* (London, Windrow and Greene, 1992), pp. 42–44.

9 WO 33/34. 96/3: Higginson. CP 8–58: Malindi. NW, February 18, 1879: letter of a 'A Brave Fugitive.'

10 WO 33/34, 96/3: Higginson. C2260, p. 83: statement by E. Essex.

11 *Narrative*, pp. 31–32, 39. *The Natal Carbineers*, pp. 99–100: Barker. *The Silver Wreath*, pp. 47–48: statements by J. Williams and E. Wilson. C2260, pp. 83: Essex, and 84: statement by H.T. Curling. WO 33/34, 80/1: statement by W.F.D. Cochrane, and 96/3: Higginson. Norris-Newman, *In Zululand with the British*, p. 180: extract from diary of C.D. Pope. TN, July 16, 1879: letter of J.M. Chard.

12 *The Natal Carbineers*, p. 100: Barker.

13 The firing occurred about 8 a.m. according to Smith-Dorrien, *Memories of Forty-Eight years*, p. 11; between 9 and 10 a.m. according to J.A. Brickhill, 'Survivor's Account,' in *Later Annals of Natal* (compiled by A.F. Hattersley; London, Longman, 1938), p. 150; Norris-Newman, *In Zululand with the British*, p. 180: Pope. It is referred to only as occurring before Durnford's arrival at camp in WO 33/34, 96/2: statement by H.D. Davies; and NW, January 19, 1929: 'Isandhlwana Survivors' Stories:' T.M.C. Nourse. Firing *about* this time is mentioned in Colenso, *History of the Zulu War*, p. 409 and Emery, *The Red Soldier*, p. 86: account by the Zulu soldier Uguku. Symons, My Reminiscences of the Zulu War, contains an account, 'Isandhlwana. By One Who Fell in the Battle' [*sic*], tentatively identified as J.A. Brickhill, which suggests (p. 57) that the firing occurred before Durnford's arrival and states that echoes deceived those at the camp as to its direction.

14 C2260, p. 84: Curling. *The Silver Wreath*, p. 47: Williams.

15 In WO 33/34, 80/1: Cochrane, and 91/1: statement by C.Raw; C2374, p. 24: statement by Umgohlulu, the oxen were inspanned; however, in Brickhill, 'Survivor's Account,' p. 150, and WO 32/7713: Untabeni and Uhlalwane, they were not. The latter three were better and longer placed to see what was happening at the camp.

16 NW, January 13, 1913: H.F. Fynn, 'My Recollections of a Famous Campaign' states that Pulleine was forming a laager and Durnford stopped him. George Cato wrote to Henrique Shepstone, February 12, 1879 (SP 38), that Pulleine told Durnford that he had better camp or park the wagons, but Durnford had asked if he took him for a coward and then ridden away. The information in both cases, in so far as it has

substance at all, would be based on hearsay, the reliability of which is not vouched for. Brickhill states, 'Survivors' Account,' p. 150, that the oxen were collected to get them out of the way of the troops in the event of action.

17 CP 8–58: Malindi.

18 *Cf.* Brickhill, 'Survivor's Account.' p. 151, and CP 8–14: statement by J.N. Hamer.

19 See *A Soldier's Life*, pp. 213, 222–223, and NW, January 13, 1913: Fynn.

20 WO 33/34, 80/1: Cochrane; 96/2: Davies; 91/2: statement by Nyanda. NM, January 31, 1879: 'Isandhlwana – what Lieutenant Davis [*sic*] says.' 'The Story of what Col[.] Durnford, with his troop of mounted natives did at Isandlwana, told by Jabez [Molife] – a Basuto.' R.W. Vause, Diary, pp. 4–5. *The Silver Wreath*, p. 49: account of J.M. Chard.

21 WO 33/34, 80/1: Cochrane; 91/1: Raw; 91/2: Nyanda; 96/2: Davies; 101/3: statement by C. Nourse. WO 32/7713: Untabeni and Uhlolwane. C2260, pp. 83: Essex, and 84: Curling. CP 8–14: Hamer. Vause Diary, p. 6. SNA 1/1/34, no. 159: 'statement by Chief Hlubi, residing in the Ulundi division before ASNA, July 29, 1879.' *The Silver Wreath*, p. 49: Chard, and Edward Durnford, *Isandhlwana, 22nd January, 1879. A Narrative* (London, King, 1879), p. 7, quoting Chard. NW, February 8, 1879: 'The Zulu War. The Fight at Sandhlwana. From an eyewitness.' TN, February 26, 1879: 'combatant.' NM, January 31, 1879: Davies. W.H. Stafford, 'Stirring Days of Old Times,' *cf.* Molife, 'The Story of what Col. Durnford ... did at Isandlwana.'

22 WO 33/34, 80/1: Cochrane; 90/1: Raw; and 96/2: Davies. C2260, p. 83: Essex. Norris-Newman, *In Zululand with the British*, p. 180: Pope. CP 8–14: Hamer. Molife, 'The Story of what Col Durnford ... did at Isandlwana.' Smith-Dorrien, *Memories of Forty-Eight Years*, pp. 10–11. NW, February 8, 1879: 'eyewitness,' and January 19, 1929: Nourse. NW, January 13, 1913: Fynn. *The Silver Wreath*, p. 46: Bickley. *Historical Records of the 24th Regiment* (edited by George Paton, Farquhar Glennie, and William Penn Symons; London, Simpkin, Marshall, Hamilton, Kent, 1882), p. 240: statement by a 'special Service Officer.' Cf. *Cape Times*, November 17, 1951: T. Newmarch, citing Arthur Adams.

23 See WO 33/34, 96/2: Davies, and *cf.* 80/1: Cochrane. NM, January 22, 1929: Davies. Vause Diary, p. 6. NM, January 30, 1879: 'With Colonel Durnford's Column:' private letter. TN, February 26, 1879: 'combatant.' Stafford, 'stirring Days of Old Times.'

24 Also, about this time Durnford received the surrender of eleven firearms by some of Gamdane's men, who were escorted into camp from the south under a white flag and let go in the same direction, according to Brickhill as quoted by Symons, My Reminiscences of the Zulu War, pp. 55–57, and Brickhill himself, 'How I escaped from the Fatal Field of Isandhlwana,' in *Africa Notes News*, XXIX, No. 2 (June, 1990), pp. 74–75. *Cf.* Emery, *The Red Soldier*, p. 92: letter of R. Stevens.

25 *Cf.* Davies, in WO 33/34, 96/2; and NM: January 31, 1879; also WO 33/34, 80/1: Cochrane and 101/3: Nourse and NW, January 19, 1929: Nourse.

26 WO 33/34, 90/1: Raw; 91/2: Nyanda; and 96/2: Davies. NM: January 31, 1879: Davies. CP 8–14: Hamer, and 58: Malindi. Molife, 'The Story of what Col. Durnford ... did at Isandlwana.' Nyanda states that Durnford gave the order to him, but Cochrane states (WO 33/34: 80/1) that Barton was in command. Hamer states that Shepstone was in command, and Stafford suggests ('Stirring Days of Old Times') that as well. It should be noted that Barton stayed with the troops and Shepstone went back to camp to report.

27 WO 33/34, 96/3: Higginson. Molife, 'The Story of what Col. Durnford ... did at Isandlwana;' but obviously it was too late for the 'breakfast' to which he refers.

28 Cf. WO 33/34, 96/2 NM: January 22, 1929: Davies, 'The Dash from the Stricken Field;' SNA 1/1/34, No. 159: Hlubi; and *The Silver Wreath*, pp. 46–47: statements of M. Grant, D. Johnson, and J. Trainer, with NW, January 19, 1929: Nourse and the various statements of Simeon Kambule in TN, August 15, 1879: 'Welcome to the Edendale Men;' NW, August 16, 1879: 'The Natal Native Horse: Festivities at Edendale;' NM, August 18, 1879: 'Notes from Maritzburg;' and Statham *Blacks, Boers, & British*, p. 191.

29 *Cf.* WO 33/34, 80/1: Cochrane; NW, February 8, 1879: 'eyewitness'; and Frances E. Colenso, *History of the Zulu War and Its Origin* (London, Chapman Hall, 1880), p. 281.

30 WO 33/34, 96/2: Davies, NM: January 22, 1929: Davies.

31 *Cf.* WO 33/34, 96/3: Higginson and NW, January 19, 1929: Nourse.

32 NW, August 16, 1879: Kambule. Statham, *Blacks, Boers & British*, p. 191: Kambule.

33 WO 33/34, 80/1: Cochrane, and 101/3: Hourse. NW, February 8, 1879: 'eyewitness.'

34 WO 33/34, 80/1: Cochrane; 96/2: Davies; 101/3: Nourse. NW, February 8, 1879: 'eyewitness.' Molife, 'The Story of what Col. Durnford ... did at Isandlwana.' Also see NW, August 16, 1879: Kambule.

35 WO 33/34. 80/1: Cochrane, and 96/2: Davies. NW, February 8, 1879: 'eyewitness.' NM, January 31, 1879: Davies. NW, August 16, 1879: Kambule. Molife, 'The Story of what Col. Durnford ... did at Isandlwana.'

36 WO 33/35, 80/1: Cochrane, and 96/2: Davies. NW, February 8, 1879: 'eyewitness.' SNA 1/1/34, No. 159: Hlubi. Molife, 'The Story of what Col. Durnford ... did at Isandlwana.' Wood MSS, file 81: map No. 2, marginal notation.

37 NW, August 16, 1879: Kambule.

38 WO 33/34, 96/2: Davies. NM, January 31, 1879: Davies. Also, see Brickhill, 'Survivor's Account,' p. 153; Molife, 'The Story of what Col. Durnford ... did at Isandlwana.'

39 Colenso Collection, Box 8: F.E. Colenso to J. Sanderson, April 25, 1879.

40 *Cf.* WO 33/34, 80/1: Cochrane, and 96/2: Davies; NW, February 8, 1879: 'eyewitness:' NM, January 31, 1879: Davies; Molife, 'The Story of what Col. Durnford ... did at Isandlwana;' and Norris-Newman, *In Zululand with the British*, p. 79: statement of Mehlokazulu.

41 WO 33/34, 96/2: Davies and 101/3: Nourse. NW, January, 19, 1929: Nourse. NM, January 31, 1879: Davies. *Cf.* WO 33/34, 80/1: Cochrane and NW, February 8, 1879: 'eyewitness.' *The Silver Wreath*, pp. 46–47: Grant, Johnson, Trainer. Johnson indicates that some of the men with firearms did try to fight. *The South African Campaign*, pp. 61–62. Norris-Newman, *In Zululand with the British*, pp. 79–80, 82: Meklokazulu. *The Natal Carbineers*, p. 100: Barker.

42 WO 33/34, 80/1: Cochrane, and 96/2: Davies. NW, February 8, 1879: 'eyewitness.' NM, January 31, 1879: Davies. NW, January 19, 1929: Nourse. *The Silver Wreath*, p. 47: Johnson. Molife, 'The Story of what Col. Durnford ... did at Isandlwana.'

43 NW, January 19, 1929: Nourse. *The Silver Wreath*, p. 47: Johnson.

44 WO 33/34, 9/6: Davies. Brickhill, 'Survivor's Account,' p. 153. Molife, 'The Story of what Col. Durnford ... did at Isandlwana.' NW, August 16, 1879: Kambule. WO 32/7713: Untabeni and Uhlolwane state that the left wing of the Zulu army appeared to be driving Durnford's force, in great confusion, towards the conical hill.

45 WO 32/7713: Untabeni and Uhlolwane mention the Ngwane foot being part of Durnford's returning force. WO 33/34, 9/6: Davies and NM, January 29, 1929: Davies state that Nourse retired with Durnford's force, but the sequence of events differs between the two accounts.

46 There were two watercourses in front of the camp, which met to the southeast of it and the wagon track. NW, February 8, 1879: 'eyewitness' states that the stand was at the one 'nearest to camp'; and Cochrane told the Court of Enquiry (WO 33/34, 80/1) that it was about half a mile in front of the camp. C2260, p. 101: Gardner states that it was the stream 'running across the front of our camp.' NA, January 19, 1929: 'Survivors' Stories of ... Isandhlwana': statement by Wheatland Edwards puts it at about 500 yards. *The Silver Wreath*, p. 47: Trainer states that it was 'in front.' NM, January 22, 1929: 'Survivors' Tales of Fifty Years Ago:' statement by C.M.F. Sparks puts it in front of camp, and context suggests it was near by. Molife, 'The Story of what Col. Durnford ... did at Isandlwana,' states that it was 'close' to the camp. WO 33/34, 96/2: Davies states it was about 300 yards in front, yet NM, January 31, 1879: Davies states 1000 yards, though NM, January 22, 1929: Davies states 'just in front of camp.' *A Soldier's Life*, p. 309: Nourse states that it was 1½ miles and *The Natal Carbineers*, p. 101: Barker that it was a mile in front of the camp. The weight of evidence favours a stand at the westerly watercourse. Also, it should be noted that no source mentions crossing a watercourse in the final retreat, which would have been the case if the stand had been in the easterly one.

The early maps of the battlefield also support the view that Durnford's force took up a defensive position in the watercourse closest to the camp. Gardner's sketch (CP 8–39) shows only one "spruit" in front of the camp and a mounted unit behind it, while Essex's (CP 8–26) shows "Durnford's Natives" in line but no watercourses at all. Another undated map, with an illegible signature and date (CP 8–12) shows neither Durnford's force nor watercourses. Colonel Bray's sketch based on Brickhill's and other survivor's information (C2252, pp. 74/75) does not identify Durnford's force or show any watercourse. Norris-Newman's sketch (a rough one is found between TN February 5 and 7, 1879, and a finished one is a plate in *In Zululand with the British*) shows a "gully defended throughout the morning" just in front of the camp and a "wide water course" farther in front, and an arrow indicating "Last attack of 2 Troops of Native Cavalry, under Colonel Durnford, Natal Carbineers, Volunteers, and Police" is midway between the two and pointing to the south, presumably to the confluence of the two water courses, which, however, is not shown! Jabez Molife's map, in the 'The Story of what Col. Durnford ... did at Isandlwana', shows two watercourses but does not indicate Durnford's forces standing at either. The map which appears in Edward Durnford, *Isandhlwana, 22nd January, 1879. A Narrative Compiled from Official and Reliable Sources* (London, King, 1875) seems to have been done independent of the preceeding ones, shows one "large donga" in front of the camp and the line behind it, with "Md Vanguard" on the right. (The maps in Parr, *A Sketch of the Kafir and Zulu War*, pp. 209 and 215, are elaborations on the Durnford map). A contemporary panoramic sketch of the battlefield by Inspector Mansel of the police, apparently sent to Durnford, which is conveniently reproduced (Map No. 8) in Ron Lock and Peter Quantrell, *Zulu Victory: The Epic of Isandlwana and the Cover-Up* (London, Greenhill, 2002), shows only one watercourse, which is described as the "Donga held by Police and Volunteers, and where Col. Durnford joined them when the Basutos left him [sic], and where they checked the left horn of the Zulus;" and the "Donga and small stream in front of the camp, from which it was supplied with water, about 600 yards from Neck." Captain W.P. Symons 2/24th drew a sketch map (1879), which appears in C.T. Atkinson, *The South Wales Borderers*, pp. 344/345, showing Durnford's force behind and slightly back from the nearer donga, facing to protect the British right flank.

The official maps show a remarkable change in position. Lieut. W.H. James' "Sketch of Zulu Attack at Isandlwana", dated March 18, 1879, (CP 8-30), puts Durnford's force behind the nearer watercourse, on the right of the line in front of the camp. Lieut H.G. Mainwaring's map, dated November 13, 1879 (C2676, pp. 70/71) shows both watercourses but not Durnford's force. A copy of Capt. T.A. Anstey's map, dated November 11, 1879, marked "No. 3", in the Wood Papers (in the Killie Campbell African Library), shows the two watercourses in question, but places Durford's force in two lines schematically with the notation "Hlube's Basutho under Durnford trying in vain to check the Uve.' The markings and notation are presumably Wood's and postdate the lithographed map, dated January, 1880, which itself shows only the campsite, two cairns and a graves site. But the same map, as it appears in the *Narrative*, Plate IV, shows the British line and definitely places the "Mounted men [under] Durnford" at the farther, easterly one, well in advance of the line on the right. This is the first map to do so clearly, and Durnford is shown, not continuing the British line or protecting its flank, as earlier maps indicate, but rather disjoining, extending and thus endangering it further!

47 NW, August 16, 1879: Kambule. Statham, *Blacks, Boers & British*, p. 191: Kambule. C2260, p. 101: Gardner. Norris-Newman, *In Zululand with the British*, pp. 80, 82: Meklokazulu. Also, see C 2260, p. 84: Curling.

48 WO 33/34, 96/2; Davies. Jenkinson, *Amazulu*, p. 86, quotes Charles Johnson, who received the information from Hlubi's men. It hardly need be added that such a third-hand account is suspect, but the extract still tells something of the British movements on the right-centre of the line.

49 WO 33/34, 80/1: Cochrane and 96/2: Davies. NW, February 8, 1879: 'eyewitness.' NM, January 22, 1929: Davies. WO 32/7713: Untabeni and Uhlolwane. Norris-Newman, *In Zululand with the British*, p. 80: Mehlokazulu. On who ordered the mixed force forward see and *cf.* C2260, p. 101: Gardner; WO 33/34, 69: Gardner; *The Natal Carbineers*, p. 101: Barker; NW January 19, 1929: Nourse; NM, January 22, 1929: Sparks; and *The Silver Wreath*, p. 48: Williams.

50 NW, January 19, 1929: Nourse.

51 Brickhill, 'Survivor's Account,' p. 153.

52 WO 33/34, 96/2: Davies. Molife, 'The Story of what Col. Durnford ... did at Isandlwana.' NM, January 22, 1929: Sparks. *Cf.* NW, August 16, 1879: Kambule and Statham, *Blacks, Boers & British*, p. 191: Kambule, also the transposed sequence in his accounts in TN, August 15, 1879 and NM, August 18, 1879.

53 A.F. Henderson to his father, January 28, 1879, quoted in *Henderson Heritage* (compiled by Peter Hathorn and Amy Young; Pietermaritzburg, the authors, 1972), p. 231.

54 Molife, 'The Story of what Col. Durnford ... did at Isandlwana.'

55 WO 33/34, 96/2: Davies. NM, January 22, 1929: Davies.

56 WO 33/34; 96/2: Davies. NM, January 22, 1929: Davies. *Cf.* NW, February 18, 1879: 'brave fugitive.' Also, see WO 33/34, 91/2: Nyanda.

57 WO 33/34, 80/1: Cochrane; 91/1: Raw; and 91/2: Nyanda. CP 8–14 : Hamer. Emery, *The Red Soldier*, p.87: letter of H. Smith-Dorrien to his father. Also, see Norris-Newman, *In Zululand with the British*, p. 79: Mehlokazulu and other Zulu accounts, *viz.* Emery, *The Red Soldier*, p. 86: Uguku; Symons, My Reminiscences of the Zulu War, p.75: account of Umhoti; Bertram Mitford, *Through the Zulu Country* (London, Kegan Paul, Trench, 1882), p. 28: statement by 'a warrior of the Umbonambi regiment'; Colenso, *History of the Zulu War*, p. 409: 'statement of a Zulu Deserter regarding the Isandhlwana Battle,' and George H. Swinney; 'A Zulu Boy's Recollections of the Zulu War,' *Natalia* (No. 8, December, 1978), p. 9–11: account of Umsweanto kaUzibana.

58 WO 33/34; 91/1: Raw, and 91/2: Nyanda. CP 8–14: Hamer. See Emery, *The Red Soldier*, p. 86: Uguku, and Norris-Newman, *In Zululand with the British*, p. 79: Mehlokazulu.

59 *Cf.* Brickhill, 'Survivor's Account,' p. 141, and C2260, p. 101: Gardner.

60 Brickhill, 'Survivor's Account,' pp. 151–152.

61 WO 33/34, 69: Gardner, and 90/1: Raw. C2260, p. 101: Gardner. *The Silver Wreath*, p. 46: Bickley. *Cf.* WO 32/7713: Untabeni and Uhlolwane; CP 8–14: Hamer; and NM, January 30, 1879: 'With Colonel Durnford's Column:' private letter. How far the Ngwane horse retreated from the foot of the hill towards the camp is not clear, e.g. Untabeni and Uhlolwane suggest that it did not retreat at all while Raw suggests it did retreat to a distance of about 400 yards from the camp. Vause Diary, p. 6. WO 33/34, 90/2: Nyanda. C 2374, p. 23: statement by Umgohlulu. *The Silver Wreath*, p. 48: Williams and Wilson. TN, February 26, 1879: 'combatant.'

62 *Cf. Narrative*, p. 34; C2260, p.83: Essex; and Brickhill, 'Survivor's Account, p. 152.

63 *Cf.* WO 33/34, 96/3: Higginson; TN, February 26, 1879: 'combatant;' and *The South African Campaign*, p. 263.

64 WO 33/34, 69: Gardner; 90/1: Raw; and 90/2: Nyanda. C2260, p. 83: Essex, and p. 84: Curling, CP 8–14: Hamer. Brickhill, 'Survivor's Account,' p. 152. Vause Diary, p. 6, and NM, January 30, 1879: private letter. *The Silver Wreath*, p. 48: Williams. *Narrative*, p. 23. Norris-Newman, *In Zululand with the British*, p. 63, quoting G. Barton. *Cf.* these with *The South African Campaign*, pp. 125 and 151.

65 Stafford, 'Stirring Days of Old Times.' 'Statement by Walter H. Stafford on the Battle of Isandhlwana. Dictated 60 years later (1939) then one of the two sole survivors.' WO 33/34, 90/2: Nyanda. Norris-Newman, *In Zululand with the British*, p. 63: Barton. *Cf.* these with C2260, p.83: Essex and NM, January 30, 1879: private letter. Also, see CSO 1926: 953/1879 and 1/BGV, IV, 303–304: reports by A.B. Allison to the Colonial Secretary. *Irish Times*, May 5, 1879: 'A Survivor of Isandula,' a letter by Thomas Sharp.

66 WO 33/34, 80/1: Cochrane, and 90/2: Nyanda. C2260, p. 101: Gardner. Brickhill, 'Survivor's Account,' pp. 152–154. *The Silver Wreath*, p. 48: Williams. Smith-Dorrien, *Memories of Forty-Eight Years*, p. 12. AJLC: letter by H.T. Curling to his mother, February 2, 1879. Emery, *The Red Soldier*, p. 87: Uguku.

67 WO 33/34, 90/1: Raw. NM, January 30, 1879: private letter. Stafford, 'Stirring Days of Old Times.' Emery, *The Red Soldier*, p. 87: Uguku. *Irish Times*, May 5, 1879: Sharp.

68 WO 33/34, 90/1: Raw, and 96/3: Higginson. TN, February 26, 1879: 'combatant.' *The South African Campaign*, p. 263. See *Narrative*, p. 34, which is very tentative about locating the amaChunu.

69 WO 33/34, 96/3: Higginson. WO 32/7713: Untabeni and Uhlolwane. *The Silver Wreath*, p. 46: Bickley.

70 WO 33/34, 69: Gardner; 80/1: Cochrane; 96/3: Higginson. WO 32/7713: Untabeni and Uhlolwane. CP 8–58: Malindi. *The Natal Carbineers*, p. 101: Barker. Smith-Dorrien, *Memories of Forth-Eight Years*, p. 13. Norris-Newman, *In Zululand with the British*, pp. 80, 82: Mehlokazulu. NW; January 19, 1929: Nourse. *The Silver Wreath*, p. 48: Williams. *A Soldier's Life*, pp. 309–310.

71 The position of the Chunu companies is one of the most controversial and vexatious problems in reconstructing the battle. *Narrative*, p. 34, puts them, tentatively, with the isiGqoza, but CP 8–58: Malindi makes no mention of them at all. NW, January 19, 1929: Nourse states that the Native Contingent was between the 24th in front of the camp and one company of the 24th on the left. *A Soldier's Life*, pp. 309–310, cites Nourse and officers who later surveyed the battlefield to the effect that there were no units between Durnford and the 24th, which held the hillock to the left front of the camp; however, this does not agree with Malindi or WO 33/34, 96/2: Davies. TN, February 26, 1879: 'combatant' states that he took his men to fight with Phakade's men and mentions that they were about a mile in front of the camp and on top of a hill. There is no mention of adjacent units. WO 32.7713: Untabeni and Uhlolwane state that the 24th engaged on the ridge returned to their original position on the left front of the camp and about 200 of the Native Contingent were in line with them. C2260, p.84: Essex states that the Native Contingent's retreat exposed the right and rear of the companies of the 24th on the left. *Historical Records of the 24th Regiment*, pp. 243–244, cites an unnamed eyewitness whose account of the Native Contingent's flight would seem to place it before then on the right of A and F Companies of the 1/24th, which were on the left. *The South African Campaign*, pp. 125–126, agrees with this. *The Silver Wreath*, p. 48: Williams states that the enemy turned the left of E Company, which reinforces the impression that the Native Contingent was in line between A and F Companies on the left and E Company on the right.

72 WO 33/34, 80/1: Cochrane, and 96/3: Higginson. C 2260, p. 83: Essex, and p. 84: Curling. CP 8–58: Malindi. TN, February 26, 1879: 'combatant.' NW, January 19, 1929: Nourse, and the account by R.D. McPhail. *The Silver Wreath*, p. 46: Bickley. Symons, My Reminiscences of the Zulu War, p. 76: Umhoti. *Cf.* the generalization on officers

in SNA 1/1/33, no. 50. It should also be remembered that it is impossible to tell how many casualties were suffered in the fight and how many in the flight. Swinney, 'A Zulu Boy's Recollections of the Zulu War,' p. 11: Umsweanto tells a story about Gabangaye and Sikhota. Sikhota saw the Zulu army advancing and decided that it could not be stopped. He invited Gabangaye to make a run for it, but Gabangaye preferred to wait and see what the British would do. Sikhota bade him a pleasant stay, mounted his horse, and rode quickly through a gap between the enclosing horns of the Zulu army. Gabangaye remained and was killed in the battle.

73 Brickhill, 'Survivor's Account,' p. 153. TN, February 26, 1879: 'combatant.'

74 WO 33/34, 96/3: Higginson.

75 WO 33/34, 90/1: Raw. WO 32/7713: Untabeni and Uhlolwane. C2260, pp. 83, 84: Essex. *Historical Records of the 24th Regiment*, pp. 243–244: eyewitness. Atkinson, *The South Wales Borders*, p. 344. *The South African Campaign*, p. 125.

76 CP 8–58: Malindi. See the obituary of J.F. Lonsdale in the *The Graphic*, August 16, 1879, reprinted in *The Concluding Stages of the Zulu As Reported in 'The Graphic*; (compiled by S. Bourquin; Durban, the compiler, 1965), p. 124. The obituary evidently is in error in stating that out of nine officers and 120 men only one officer and three men survived. For the confused fighting in the camp see WO 33/34, 80/1: Cochrane, and 90/2: Nyanda; C2260, pp. 84: Essex, and 101. Gardner; C2374, p. 24: Umgohlulu; Smith-Dorrien, *Memories of the Forty-Eight Years*, pp. 14–15, and the letter to his father in Emery, *The Red Soldier*, p. 87, 88. and *ibid*, p. 87: Uguku. NM, January 30, 1879: private letter. NC, February 11, 1879: 'Native Account of the Isandhlwana Disaster'.

77 WO 33/34, 90/1: Raw; 90/2: Nyanda; and 96/3: Higginson. CP 8–14: Hamer. Vause Diary, p. 7. NM, January 30, 1879: private letter. Brickhill, 'Survivor's Account.' pp. 153–154. Stafford, 'Stirring Days of Old Times,' and 'Statement ... on the Battle of Isandhlwana.' *A Soldier's Life*, p. 204. Swinney, 'A Zulu Boy's Recollections of the Zulu War:' pp. 11–12: Umsweanto. *Cf.* Nyanda and 1/BGV, IV, 320 on casualties.

78 WO 33/34, 60: Gardner; 96/2: Davies. NM, January 31, 1879: Davies. C2260, pp. 83–84: Essex. *A Soldier's Life*, p. 233n. Statham, *Blacks, Boers & British*, p. 191: Kambule. Symons, My Reminiscences of the Zulu War, p. 18. NA, January 19, 1929: Edwards. Molife, 'The Story of what Col. Durnford ... did at Isandlwana,' with which compare SNA 1/1/34, no. 159: Hlubi and Jenkinson, *Amazulu*, p. 87. For Durnford's last moments see *A Soldier's Life*, p. 235 and 237; Jenkinson, *Amazulu*, p. 87; WO 33/34, 90/2: Nyanda, and 96/2: Davies; CP 8–14: Hamer; NW, August 16, 1879: Khambule; NM, January 22, 1929: Davies; *Irish Times*, May 5, 1879: Sharp; Stafford, 'Stirring Days of Old Times;' Symons, My Reminiscences of the Zulu War, p. 77: Umhoti, and 80–81, quoting letter of Charles Tatham, March 9, 1933. For his alleged suicide see NW, January 13, 1913: Fynn, and SP 38: G.C. Cato to Henrique Shepstone, February 12, 1879.

79 WO 33/34, 96/2: Davies. SNA 1/1/34, no. 151: Hlubi. Molife, 'The Story of what Col. Durnford ... did at Isandlwana.' See also W.H. Clements, *The Glamour and Tragedy of the Zulu War* (London, Bodley Head, 1936), pp. 63–64: statement C.M. Sparks.

80 WO 33/34, 96/2: Davies. NM, January 22, 1929: Davies. SNA 1/1/34, no. 150: Hlubi. Molife, 'The Story of what Col. Durnford ... did at Isandlwana.'

81 WO 33/34, 96/2: Davies. NM, January 31, 1879: Davies; and January 22, 1929: Davies and Sparks. See Kambule's accounts in TN, August 15, NW, August 16, and NM, August 18, 1879, and Watkins, 'They Fought for the Great White Queen,' pp. 156–158. Parr, *A Sketch of the Kafir and Zulu Wars*, states (p. 217) that the 'Basutos' fired two or three rounds and charged through the weak part of the Zulu line.

82 It is difficult to determine if and where any members of the Native Contingent made a stand. Reports of later visits to the battlefield suggest that there was no stand. TN, March 21, 1879: 'Visit to the camp of Isandhlwana,' by an 'eyewitness', tells that when Major Black and a small party visited the battlefield on March 14th they found that the Zulu dead had been removed. TN, May 26, 1879: 'Visit to Isandhlwana:' the special war correspondent reported seeing no more than 200 bodies in the camp and of those no more than twenty-five were those of blacks. NW, May 27, 1879: 'Another visit to Isandhlwana:' the correspondent reported that all the bodies of the 'Natal Natives' had been removed from the battlefield and thrown into some deep gullies a short distance away. C2676, p. 73: Lieutenant M. O'Connell, commanding a burial detail in March 1880, reported finding many bodies of Europeans and Zulus, including some 'Natal Zulus', along the first half-mile of the 'fugitives' track'. Symons, My Reminiscences of the Zulu War, recalled (p. 67) that there were many bodies on the banks of the Manzinyama stream, mostly those of men belonging to the Native Contingent.

Chapter 6

ESCAPE FROM THE ZULU COUNTRY

Fugitives from the battlefield

The Zulu destruction of their camp and force at Isandlwana left the British in a desperate situation. The No. 3 Column had lost almost half of its men, much of its supplies and ammunition, and most of its transport. The Zulu army was placed advantageously to strike at the remaining parts of the column. Nor was any part capable of resisting its full weight.

The greater part of the column was on reconnaissance in front of Phindo, in broken country, without reserves of ammunition and food. The next larger part was the battalion moving up to join the reconnaissance but still outside supporting distance. It was the good fortune of both these forces that the Zulu commanders paid practically no attention to them, if, indeed, the Zulu commanders understood the strategic opportunity.

Instead, the victorious Zulu turned their attention to the British still in front of them. While those who had fought the battle enjoyed its spoils, those who had missed it pursued the fugitives from the camp. Men of the left and right horns harried their flight all the way to the Mzinyathi. Some even crossed the river. The reserve of the Zulu army moved against the British line of communication. In its path lay the weakly garrisoned posts at kwaJimu (Rorke's Drift) and Helpmekaar.

All the British forces were vulnerable. In the twenty-four hours that followed the battle of Isandlwana, the Zulu army was master of the field. The consciousness of this, as well as the calamity which had befallen the column, affected all the imperial troops. It was a crisis which fully tested courage and discipline.

When organized resistance collapsed at Isandlwana, flight was the only means of survival. Men ran, walked or rode ahead of the Zulu charge through the camp to the track which led to Rorke's Drift. They arrived there to find that the right horn of the Zulu army had come up behind the hill and blocked the track. The left horn of the Zulu army pressed into the southern end of the camp. Within a short time the two horns met and sealed off the battlefield. In the short time before they met and before the seal was tight, the fugitives of the No. 3 Column funnelled between or broke through the Zulu forces.[1] In the confusion it was supposed some had even cut their way out to the east to join the general's column.[2] Rorke's Drift lay seven miles to the west. Most of the fugitives moved to the southwest, descending obliquely the slope of the knoll just to the south of Isandlwana. The direction of the retreat was dictated by the pursuers, who swarmed after and around and sometimes got ahead of the fugitives.

The general course of retreat was across the steep-banked Manzinyama stream and around a hillside broken by several small watercourses to the bluff above the Mzinyathi and the crossing there. There was no single path or trail as such.[3] Probably a few individuals gave a lead and others followed because they had little knowledge or choice of the route. They went this way or that within the narrowing ambit. Who stood to fight died. Just so those who halted from exhaustion. Men on foot had little chance of getting away. The Zulus seemed to come from all sides, they threw long spears, they stabbed with short spears, they shot with rifles. Zulus who lived in the neighbourhood but were not part of the Zulu army apparently joined in the killing.[4]

The men of the 3rd Regiment fought much of the way. It is possible most of the regiment's casualties were suffered in flight. The way to the river was strewn with shields and spears and rifles.[5] A British officer noticed that the enemy seemed especially determined to kill the men of the Native Contingent.[6] Another observed that most of the hand-to-hand fighting was between them and the Zulus.[7] Yet some men in the contingent heard the enemy cry out: 'Leave the Kafirs, as the white men cause them to fight.'[8] In one combat, a Zulu youth, perhaps eighteen, prepared to throw his spear at one of the older men of the contingent. The older man raised his spear and glowered. 'What are you doing?' cried the youth, who drew off.[9] A Zulu overtook another man of the contingent on a cliff above the river. The two took each other's measure. The Zulu drove his spear into the man's shoulder. The man leapt into the air, and drove his spear into the Zulu's heart. Their bodies rolled together into the river.[10]

The fugitives arrived on the bluff overlooking the river after a race of between two and three miles. The crossing at this place was called Sotondose's drift. Although there had been no heavy rain in the vicinity for several days, the water was high. Men could not see any ford. To them the river seemed in flood.[11] The current was strong, but the river flowed out of a gorge at this place, reducing the force of the current over the length of a mile. A draw breaks the cliff on the Zulu side and the cliff on the Natal side gives way to a slope. There are some marshy flats along the banks.[12]

The fugitives slid and tumbled down to a narrow flat and congregated. Mounted men plunged their horses into the water. Men on foot tried to hold on to the tails, the stirrups, the saddles, but all could not make it across. Horses and men separated in the current and were carried downstream to rapids and the next gorge. Strong swimmers were able to brave the current. Others were washed away.[13] The enemy pushed down to the bank, stabbing and shooting. Their riflemen laid down a hot fire on the fugitives scrambling up the far bank. Some Zulus managed to cross the river in pursuit, but most of those determined to cross did so higher up or lower downstream. They blocked the way to Rorke's Drift again.[14] There seemed to be no getting away from them.

Zikhali's Horse had become scattered in flight. Some men got across the river on their horses; others got across without them but found riderless ones on the other side. Such of Zikhali's men who could be got to stay and the Edendale troop were rallied by Captain Barton and Lieutenant Raw.[15] Their fire enabled other fugitives to escape across the river,[16] and probably discouraged more Zulus from crossing the river at this place. Those with rifles apparently did not try. Some with spears did, and at least two were stabbed by men of the contingent on foot.[17] Sikhota and several other men exhausted from the flight were resting on the near bank when they heard a Zulu head man shout: 'He [the King] has not said that you are to cross. He is not invading. He is defending the lands of his own people. Come back! Don't cross!' In any event, the action at the river must have been brief, for it exhausted what ammunition the mounted men had left.[18]

The Edendale Horse made two or three stands during its retreat and picked up and saved several fugitives on foot. Apparently the sergeant major, Simeon Kambule, knew something of the country. He may have led the troops by a path apart from that used by the main body of fugitives.[19]

Kambule later gave two different accounts of what happened at the crossing. According to one he found that a large number of the enemy had got across the river ahead of the fugitives, whereupon he dismounted his men and ordered them to fire. Three volleys dispersed the enemy. The troops descended to the river. Kambule told the crowd of fugitives on the bank to hold on to his men's stirrups or any other animal. Then he drove the mob of men, horses and cattle into the river. The troop brought them over safely.[20] According to the other account the troop got across the river without dramatic incident and climbed to the top of the hill on the right bank. There it laid down a covering fire which allowed the fugitives to cross safely.[21] The prosaic account is the more plausible one. It fits well with other survivors' accounts. The dramatic one need not be spurious, however; it could refer to the troop's experience crossing the Manzinyama earlier on.

All of the men of the contingent on foot and most if not all of Zikhali's horse seem to have fled southward, towards distant home. Many apparently went the way they had come, by Sand Spruit and the Thukela.[22] The amaNgwane who had been wounded and could not go on fell out to be nursed at homesteads in the Msinga.[23]

Helpmekaar, the column's depot, was on the top of the escarpment twelve miles to the west of Sotondose's drift. It is a fairly easy ride across the downs, but the escarpment itself rises fourteen hundred feet and is difficult to ascend. The mounted men, including the Edendale and some of Zikhali's troops, halted several times, probably more to rest and let individual survivors catch up than to resist the enemy. The enemy did not pursue far. About twenty could be seen following Zikhali's troops, but they did not have rifles and they kept a respectful distance. After three miles they faded away.[24]

Halt at kwaJimu

Most of the Sotho troop under Hlubi had broken through the Zulu encirclement and ridden towards Rorke's Drift. Some of the Edendale men, possibly some of the amaNgwane, and a few other fugitives from the camp went with them. There were brushes with the enemy as they cleared the vicinity of the camp, but the men on horseback soon out-distanced pursuers.[25] After a while an officer of the 3rd Regiment who escaped with them rode ahead with one of the mounted colonials and told the British officer at Rorke's Drift of the disaster.[26] Within a short time a number of other mounted men passed the mission station, apparently heading for Helpmekaar, and gave information of the disaster at Isandlwana.[27] They also warned that Zulu forces were on their way to Rorke's Drift.[28] A mounted man of the contingent, sent by a British staff officer from the fugitives crossing downstream, arrived with orders to fortify and to hold the post.[29]

The British detachment at the mission station was a small one, just sufficient to protect the depot and hospital there. It consisted of a company of British infantry and a company of the 2nd Battalion of the 3rd Regiment. The mission station was not extensive. Known as kwaJimu, it had once been the trading store of Jim Rorke. Some years since it had been converted and enlarged by a Swedish Lutheran mission. There was a house and a church, now being used as a hospital and a store, respectively, and some small outbuildings. The British officers in charge of the post decided it would be safer to stand than to run in the face of the Zulu army. They set the men to building a defensive wall around the buildings.[30]

The company of the 2nd Battalion numbered almost 100 men and was supposed to provide a detachment to the pont. It provided valuable muscle in building the wall.[31] The precise identity of the company is not known. Presumably they were the hundred men which had been detailed to remain at the post eight days before. They would be abaThembu from the Klip River Division. They could hardly have had much military instruction or training. There may not have been enough officers to give any, which might also account the company's being left behind. Besides the company commander, Captain Stephenson, only three corporals appear to have been with the company. No lieutenants and sergeants are mentioned in the report.[32] The company's morale could not have been high. Stories told by fugitives from the battlefield would not have improved it. The fugitives indeed interfered with the progress of fortification.[33]

It was mid-afternoon when Hlubi's troop arrived at the mission station.[34] They were driving some cattle and were accompanied by a crowd of camp followers.[35] Lieutenant Henderson asked the British officer in command for orders.[36] Hlubi's men (and those with them) were tired and they were short of ammunition. It may have taken a little time to decide what the troop could do. In the meantime Lieutenant Henderson and a local cattle dealer were employed in bringing back absconding abaThembu and putting them to work.[37] Apparently the cattle dealer effected this by firing a shot over their heads and then telling them if they did not stay and help he would shoot at them.[38]

The British officer told Henderson to send a detachment to watch the pont and other crossing places along the river in the vicinity, also to push outposts in the direction from which the enemy was expected, and, when the time came, to check the enemy's advance. The mounted men should then fall back and help the garrison defend the station.[39] The British officer phrased his orders as a request.

The troop was drawn up on rising ground about half a mile from the station. The men offsaddled. How many were sent for the duties requested is not known. The British officer was asking too much of weary and dispirited men. Apparently Lieutenant Henderson and the cattle-dealer went off to reconnoitre on their own.[40]

They could not have been gone for more than half an hour when firing was heard from beyond Shiyane, the hill just south of the station. Whether the firing indicated skirmishing between some of Hlubi's men on outpost or a fight between the approaching enemy and some local people at a large homestead just across the river is not clear.[41]

Hlubi's men made no pretence of fighting. The feeling was that Durnford was dead and it was no use. They saddled up and rode off to Helpmekaar. As they ascended the escarpment they could see a Zulu force marching towards Rorke's Drift from Isandlwana.[42] It was part of the Zulu reserve which had missed the battle and was going to attack the garrison at the station.[43] Henderson was left to explain to the British officer that his men would not obey his orders. He and the cattle-dealer left the station but seem to have tarried a while near by. They saw the onset of the Zulu attack. They fired some shots at the enemy and rode off to Helpmekaar.[44]

No sooner had the baSotho started off than the Thembu company fled. Captain Stephenson rode off to Helpmekaar after them.[45]

It was a winding, steep road up the escarpment. As the fugitives began the climb, they met a British officer from Helpmekaar. He tried to rally them. It was a vain effort. The white men told him the station had been captured. Presently a line of Zulus deployed across the road. Smoke could be seen rising from mission buildings behind them. As it became dark, the flames could be seen. The officer was ahead of two companies of British infantry, which he meant to lead down to Rorke's Drift. They were still on the heights behind him. Two Edendale troopers sent from Helpmekaar arrived to tell him what had happened at Isandlwana. There were many black men around and in the dark it was difficult to tell whether they were friend or foe. He decided to return with the companies to fortify Helpmekaar. The redcoats got back by 9 p.m. They relieved the fugitives on guard at the laager, who at last got something to eat and slept.[46]

There was only one man of the contingent involved in the battle at Rorke's Drift mission station. He was of the isiGqoza. He had been shot in the thigh in the Batshe fight. He was in hospital and could not be moved. The Zulus set fire to the hospital building and began to break in. The wounded were evacuated from the building. The man, in the end room, tried to tear off his bandages and escape, but it was no use. He was not afraid of the Zulus, he said. He asked for a rifle. Shortly afterwards the Zulus forced their way into the room. A soldier in the next room heard them talking to him. The next day his charred body was found in the burnt ruins. No one knew his name.[47]

The lone battalion

Before he was ordered directly to the camp at Isandlwana, Durnford had been given the mission of operating against the Zulu chiefdoms on the right flank of the No. 3 Column. The 2nd Battalion of the 1st Regiment had marched from Kranskop to Sand Spruit for this purpose. It was intended that the battalion should cross the Mzinyathi when the column had advanced about twenty miles into Zululand. On January 19th the Lieutenant General had informed Durnford that the column would move forward to Isandlwana and then ten miles further towards the Qhudeni forest. He would then begin operations against the chiefdoms on the right flank. The 2nd Battalion should be ready to cross the Mzinyathi in three days time at what the general poetically but vaguely called the Gates of Natal. It should show itself at the crossing as soon as possible,[48] probably as a demonstration. Durnford told Major Bengough, the battalion commander, that he was to cross the river at a certain point and to await further orders.[49] After Durnford crossed into Zululand on the 21st, Bengough became practically an independent leader.

At certain points along the Mzinyathi were stationed units of the Native Border Guard. They each numbered several hundred men and were drawn from the chiefdoms along the border. Their role was strictly defensive. They were under the command of a district commandant, appointed by the colonial government.[50] On the 21st the Klip River district commandant received information from the leader of No. 4 unit, about eight miles below Rorke's Drift, that a large Zulu force would be gathering in the Mangeni valley during the day. He reported that it had orders to cross over the Mzinyathi into Natal during the night. His informant, ostensibly one of Gamdane's people, claimed to have seen the Zulu force. The district commandant informed Bengough, who was with his battalion at Sand Spruit, and made arrangements to concentrate the Border Guard units in the vicinity to meet an incursion. It would appear he sent a message to the Lieutenant General, but either it was not delivered or subsequently was forgotten.

There had been a rumour afloat for several days that the Zulu King was collecting a force opposite Kranskop, thirty-five miles to the southeast, but nothing had materialized and the district commandant frankly doubted the unit leader's informant.[51] Perhaps he doubted the leader, too. He was a white man – as was every one of the Natal Border Guard's leaders – but he was not one of the men the government had appointed formally. He was filling in for the man who was supposed to be there, and then because he was the only white farmer near the river on that part of the border. The commandant later recollected that he had several Zulu wives in the Qhudeni bush.[52]

Another report arrived from No. 4 – two large bodies of Zulus had been seen on the hills across the river. The district commandant reflected. Something was up. He rode towards the river. At No. 3 he learned that friendly troops had been moving along the high ground across the river. He concluded that No. 4 had mistaken these for the enemy. Indeed, the 3rd Regiment was sweeping Malakatha that afternoon. None the less he ordered No. 2 unit to move to support the others upstream.[53] Major Bengough also set his battalion in motion. When the men bivouacked late at night, they were still some distance from the river.[54]

The Lieutenant General had envisaged Bengough's battalion crossing on the 22nd.[55] The district commandant rode down to see the battalion over. The Border Guard assisted in the passage. The battalion forded upstream from the Mangeni. The river was about five feet deep but the men got through safely. They sat down on the Zulu side for their mid-day meal in high spirits, excited at being in the enemy's country. Over the high ground to the east came the sound of guns firing. The district commandant told Bengough they must be from a flank reconnaissance which the general had planned. The men of the battalion were now preparing for battle, eating medicines and sprinkling themselves.

Bengough did not intend to advance up the Mangeni valley. He intended to go up a smaller valley to the high ground and then open communication with the No. 3 Column. He had been told to cross and to wait for orders. He waited. A message arrived from Durnford: the Colonel would not be able to support him if he advanced beyond the river.

The day passed without incident. The district commandant sent his units back to their original posts, and himself rode back to the Msinga magistracy. The afternoon wore on. The battalion interpreter came to Bengough with information just brought in by a Zulu. The English army had been eaten up. The English 'baas' had been killed. A Zulu force was on its way to attack the battalion.

Bengough considered. His position was good, on a rocky point almost surrounded by a loop of the river; but the river had fallen during the day and was fordable at many points. The battalion could be cut off. He ordered a withdrawal. The men recrossed the river and marched to a high hill. It was ten o'clock before they were all on top and pickets put out.[56]

In the meantime a survivor of the disaster at Isandlwana had ridden to the Msinga magistracy about seven. The district commandant prepared the magistracy against attack and sent out warnings. Fugitives were passing through the area, among them the amaNgwane, some so badly wounded they could not go on. Zulu forces were active on the Natal side of the river just to the north.[57]

Morning came. Bengough decided to go to Rorke's Drift and join the column. A note was sent to the officer commanding there that the battalion, 1200 strong, would arrive on the old road under the Biggarsberg. The battalion marched at nine. The feeling, at least among the officers, was that some kind of reverse had occurred, but it had been exaggerated into a disaster.

If the enemy were about, then he might attack at any moment. Two hours later it was reported that six or seven thousand Zulus had occupied the hill where the battalion had camped and had been sent to 'eat them up'. Presently scouts reported there was a strong Zulu force on a hill in front. The battalion halted. Orders were given to load. The gun men stripped. The order was given: 'Gun men to the front.' The response was prompt. It appeared the battalion would have to fight its way through.

Bengough and his interpreter rode ahead. To their relief they found that the force on the hill was friendly. Probably it was the Native Border Guard No. 4 unit, whose station was near the river, but it would have retired to avoid marauding Zulus. Bengough returned the battalion. He found that men had discarded their rifles and grouped themselves around their chiefs. They were determined to fight in the traditional way.

Worse news now. The reverse *was* a disaster. The men were shocked. Fear could be read in their faces. Fortunately Bengough received orders to go to Helpmekaar, closer, probably safer, than Rorke's Drift. The battalion stuck together. In the circumstances Bengough thought it was behaving very well. It reached Helpmekaar late in the afternoon on the 23rd.[58]

Return of the column

Let us now return to the reconnaissance in force east of Isandlwana. At last the Lieutenant General was returning to find out what was happening at the camp. The 1st Battalion of the 3rd Regiment, which had been ordered back to the camp earlier, had halted. It could not go on without engaging the Zulu army. The Lieutenant General, with his staff and forty mounted men, joined it. He had received Commandant Browne's message that the camp was under attack, but none of the following messages about the progress of the battle. The general was frankly incredulous. He ordered the battalion to proceed in the belief that it and the mounted men could brush aside the enemy between them and the camp.[59]

They went a little way and a solitary man on horseback appeared before them. It was Rupert Lonsdale, Commandant of the 3rd Regiment! His pony moved at a walk. He came up to Browne and told him the camp was taken. Browne rode to the general with the report. Lonsdale followed on foot, leading his pony.

Lonsdale had left the fight at Matshana's stronghold and ridden back to the camp. He was unwell, perhaps still suffering from his recent sunstroke and fall. It is not clear whether he was permitted to go back to the camp because he was sick or was sent back to make arrangements about rations for his men and to hurry forward Pulleine. Browne later wrote that he had got lost. Adjutant Harford last saw him chasing after the enemy near Phindo. Evidently he got separated from his men, and decided to return to camp. In any case, he rode back towards the camp without informing either his adjutant or battalion commanders. He noticed no signs of battle. As he approached the camp, a Zulu shot at him, but he supposed that it was a careless member of the Native Contingent who had fired. He was almost at his tent when it occurred to him there were a great many more natives about than there ought to be. The men wearing red coats and helmets were not wearing trousers and boots. Their legs were bare and black. They were Zulus, plundering the camp! He turned his pony around and rode quietly down the hill. When he was clear of the plundering crowd, he rode fast. Some Zulus fired but did not follow him. It was just as well, for his pony soon became tired. He had to dismount and lead it most of the way. Both man and horse were plainly exhausted when they reached friends.[60]

The Lieutenant General could not delude himself any longer. Browne had told him what he had seen with field glasses. Lonsdale was eyewitness to the loss of the camp. The general sent a message for the force at the Mangeni to join him at once. Meanwhile he deployed the 1st Battalion in three ranks. Those with firearms were in the first rank – officers, non-commissioned officers and tenth men. The mounted men formed on the flanks and provided scouts. The march resumed in this order. The men crossed the plain and approached the conical hill. The ridge was to the right. Isandlwana was just over two miles ahead. The men halted in a small valley, out of sight of the camp.

Scouts were sent out. They reported that the Zulus were burning tents and taking away large quantities of stores and weapons, horses and oxen. Their number was increasing. They could be seen going over the hills to the north in their thousands, taking many wagons along with them.

The Lieutenant General was not satisfied. A strong mounted patrol was sent out. It returned with information that the enemy was in force and held the camp and blocked the track to Rorke's Drift at the neck between the hill and the knoll. The firing at the camp had almost stopped.

Against the enemy in front the 1st Battalion would make no impression. It waited for the force to come up from the Mangeni. The force arrived about an hour later with the 2nd Battalion at the rear of the column.[61] The men knew something was wrong. With them were the pioneers who had left the camp later in the morning and had seen the first stage of the battle, but the men at the Mangeni had discounted their lurid description. Now the truth was known. Moreover the reports indicated that if they returned to camp they, too, would be in for a hard fight.[62]

The Lieutenant General deployed the combined force. Artillery was at the centre. Three companies of the British infantry were in line on each side. Extending the line to the left was the 1st Battalion, to the right the 2nd, with mounted men on their flanks. Skirmishers were thrown out in front. A small guard looked after the wagons and ambulances in the rear. The general addressed the men very briefly. The camp had been taken, they must retake it and reopen the way to the river. The British infantry cheered. The men of the contingent took up the cheer.[63]

The battle-line moved forward. Men were silent, tense. The only sound they made was a click when their spears and sticks knocked against each other.[64] Four men appeared out of the grass in front and came towards the line. Mounted men went out to meet them. The four took cover. The horsemen opened fire, hitting one of them. The other three ran out with their hands up to show they were not armed. They were members of the contingent who had escaped the massacre.[65]

The advance resumed just as the sun went down. There was no moon. Night seemed pitch black.[66] The demoralized 2nd Battalion fell into disorder. The rifle men would not stay in the front rank. Officers swore and cursed, but the men gathered in clumps and company formation was lost. All Lieutenant Harford could do was ride up and down the line and keep the clumps moving forward.[67]

The whole line halted. Silhouetted darkly against the dark sky was Isandlwana, the neck and the knoll. There were two small fires burning in the camp. Large dark objects appeared on the neck. Was that a barricade of wagons? There were hoarse cries. The enemy must be waiting. The rattling sound must be made by his spears and clubs.[68]

The artillery fired shrapnel at the neck. There was no response. The order was given to take the knoll. The British companies on the left fixed bayonets. The 1st Battalion prepared for action. The line moved forward. Several shells lit up the neck. No enemy was seen. The 1st Battalion move up the knoll and cleared the crest. Browne worried that his men would come under the artillery fire. He ordered the bugler to sound 'cease fire'. The bugler could not blow. Browne shouted to the British commander, who had his bugler sound it. The British infantry had carried the crest as well. It cheered. No enemy was there, nor any on the neck. The companies of the isiGqoza accompanied the cheers by rattling their spears and shields.[69]

The line on the right also advanced. The British infantry fired several times to draw enemy attention from the left. The 2nd Battalion crossed the watercourse in front of the camp. Some of the skirmishers had to file out to the right to clear it. The battalion entered its former camp and reached the wagons. On one of them were several Zulus, apparently drunk. An officer of the battalion called to some British soldiers, who climbed up on the wagon and bayonetted them.[70]

To the front there were three large fires. A fourth fire blazed up to the rear. The way the last one blazed up suggested attack in the offing. The Lieutenant General quickly consolidated the column in a hollow square on the neck. The British infantry faced to the front, the mounted men and guns to the rear, the contingent battalions on the flanks. The men slept upon their arms. Sentries were posted.

In the darkness the men could not see the wreckage of the battlefield and the corpses which littered it. Some officers groped around the campsite and found rations for their men. A flare and small flashes of light could be seen in the direction of Rorke's Drift. Lights appeared southwards along the horizon – burning homesteads. It was said the Zulu chief Dabulamanzi and a large army was hiding behind the next hill, and there would be a fight in the morning.[71]

It was not easy to sleep. There were several alarms and some shooting at phantom assailants. Men in the 2nd Battalion breathed the stench of chemicals from a smashed medical wagon. Where was Gabangaye, the chief's son, wondered the amaChunu. They became very restless. Men crept down the slope of the neck in small numbers until no one was left on the side of the square by the hill. Harford found them in groups below the neck and drove most of them back to the position. So angry was the Lieutenant General that he himself posted two British sentries with orders to bayonet the first man who tried to leave again. No one moved.[72]

At dawn the next day the column formed for the march back to Rorke's Drift. The men marched four abreast. The 2nd Battalion led the way. The 1st Battalion brought up the rear. Mounted scouts and flankers guarded against surprises. Dabulamanzi was not waiting behind the next hill with an army. Nor behind the next.[73] The sullen inmates of a homestead constituted the only enemy. Clearing the third hill, the spur of Ngedla which overlooks the Batshe valley, the column caught sight of the Zulu army. Large numbers – three of four thousand – were moving to the east, away from Rorke's Drift. The remains of burning homesteads could be seen in their wake. The column moved into the valley. For a moment it seemed the enemy was coming at the column. The two forces were moving at an angle and passed each other, but in places the distance closed to between 250 and 300 yards. Small bucks took fright and dodged between them. A young Zulu soldier urged his comrades to attack. They would not. He ran down a hill towards the column. No one followed him. He was shot thirty yards from the column.[74]

A second time the British column passed a Zulu force. It was moving away from the river. The enemy seemed to want not to fight. Men of the 3rd Regiment wasted precious ammunition firing perhaps twenty or thirty shots at it, but the column moved on and lost sight on the enemy force.[75] As it reached the last hill before the river, cheering broke out in front. The garrison at kwaJimu was still there![76]

The mounted men forded the river and secured the pont so the British infantry could cross.[77] The 3rd Regiment forded upstream and was the last of the column to arrive at the mission station. There were Zulu corpses all around. Hundreds of them. The regiment dissolved out of curiosity, men wandering about, looking at the dead and the fortifications.[78]

The British garrison had repulsed one Zulu attack, but there might be another. A large body of men, presumably the enemy, had been seen on the heights beyond Rorke's Drift earlier that morning. The general ordered the ground cleared and prepared for further defence. The 3rd Regiment was got back together. The limited supply of picks and shovels was distributed. Pits were dug for the Zulu dead. Men were loath to handle corpses, so British soldiers collected them and dumped them into the pits. Those who did not dig carried stones to build up the fortifications. It was several hours before the work was done. Only then were rations issued.[79]

A number of wounded and exhausted Zulus were found lying in the tall grass and the cornfields near by. Men of the regiment, joined by some of their non-commissioned officers and a few British soldiers, went over the ground and stabbed or beat them to death.[80]

The 3rd Regiment was posted on Shiyane. The men bivouacked on the step-like ledges of the hillside. They were supposed to be guarding against another Zulu advance from the south, but it was very difficult to establish pickets. The officers and non-commissioned officers had to be browbeaten before they would roust the men, most of whom were skulking among the rocks and in caves. In his battalion, Browne could only get the isiGqoza to do the duty. At last the picket line, consisting of one company, was strung out.

Soon a report was sent back, that the Zulus were crossing the river downstream, portending a night attack. The officers and non-commissioned officers then drew off to a cattle pen near the fort occupied by the British. They left the men to sleep on the hill. Many men left the regiment that night to return home. An hour or so after midnight word came down from Shiyane that the Zulu army was coming. Men on picket came running into camp, firing back at an imaginary foe. The whole column stood to arms for about half an hour.[81] Another false alarm.

NOTES

1 For the completion of the Zulu movement see Brickhill, 'Survivor's Account,' p. 155; *The Natal Carbineers*, pp. 101–102: Barker; Smith-Dorrien, *Memories of Forty-Eight Years Service*, p. 15; Molife, 'The Story of what Col. Durnford ... did at Isandlwana;' WO 33/34, 96/2: Davies and NM, January 22, 1929: Davies; C2260, p. 82: Essex; and NA, January 19, 1929: Edwards. See also the Zulu accounts, Symons, My Reminiscences of the Zulu War, pp. 76–77: and NW, January 19, 1929: 'A Native Eye-Witness.'

2 NW, January 25, 1879: 'Defeat of Col. Durnford's Force.' Fynn, 'My Recollections of a Famous Campaign.'

3 *Narrative*, Plate III shows the putative route of the fugitives, and should be compared with the modern map's more accurate details of terrain. For a description of the direction and terrain see Brickhill, 'Survivor's Account,' pp. 155–158; *The Natal Carbineers*, p. 102: Barker; WO 33/34, 80/1: Cochrane; Emery, *The Red Soldier*, p. 88. Smith-Dorrien; *The Silver Wreath*, pp. 46 and 48: Bickley and Wilson, respectively; Symons, My Reminiscences of the Zulu War, p. 77: Umhoti; TN, February 26, 1879: 'combatant;' and CP 8–14: Hamer. Fynn states ('My Recollections of a Famous Campaign') that the fugitives beat a permanent path to the river. Scrutiny of the reports suggests that there were other paths besides the main one taken by the fugitives.

4 C2260, pp. 82: Essex, and 85: Curling; also AJLC: H.T. Curling to his mother, February 2, 1879. NM, January 22, 1929: Davies and Sparks. NC, February 11, 1879: 'Native Account.' *The Natal Carbineers*, p. 102: Barker. Smith-Dorrien, *Memories of Forty-Eight Years' Service*, p. 16. WO 33/34, 96/2: Davies. Incidents of the flight are described by Brickhill, 'Survivor's Account,' pp. 156–158; Smith-Dorrien, *Memories of Forty-Eight Years'* Service, pp. 15–16; Stafford, 'Stirring Days of Old Times;' CP 8–14: Hamer; Davies in WO 33/34, 96/2, NM, January 31, 1879, and January 22, 1929; TN, February 26, 1879: 'combatant;' and R.C.A. Samuelson, *Long, Long Ago* (Durban, Knox, 1929), p. 149, on Simeon Kambule. The distribution of the dead west of the 'neck' is dealt with in the reports of the later visits to the battlefield in NW, May 27, 1879: 'Another visit to Isandhlwana,' and Emery, *The Red Soldier*, pp. 114–115. Also see the report of the later interment in C2676, p. 73. Only one white soldier is reported to have escaped on foot (see Stafford, 'Stirring Days of Old Times,' and NA, January 19, 1929: Edwards); however, many blacks escaped, some perhaps by having fled early (see Stafford and Brickhill, 'Survivor's Account, p. 153), some perhaps for being spared (see n. 8), and some presumably for being more fleet-footed than the enemy.

5 Brickhill, 'Survivor's Account,' pp. 155–156.

6 Smith-Dorrien, *Memories of Forty-Five Years' Service*, p. 15. Also see *Cape Times*, November 17, 1951: T. Newmarch, recollecting a statement by David Doig.

7 WO 33/34, 80/1: Cochrane.

8 TN, February 26, 1879: 'combatant'; *cf.* NC, February 11, 1879: 'Native Account.' Also, see *A Soldier's Life*, p. 235, which states that the mounted troops escaped with little loss because the enemy was eagerly pursuing white men; and NM, January 22, 1929: Davies.

9 Brickhill, 'Survivor's Account,' p. 156.

10 TN, February 26, 1879: 'combatant.'

11 Much has been made of the terrible river which cost many fugitives' lives. Above and below the section of the river where the crossing took place are cataracts. Given the Zulu strategy, the British could retreat only to this place, known locally to settlers as 'Sotondose's Drift.' Fynn refers to Sotondose's as 'the retreating ford' (CSO 1926: 2080/1879) and the 'Melville [*sic*] drift' (CSO 1927: 2480/1879). Sotondose was chief of the Nxumalo people (see Colony of Natal, *Blue Book of Native Affairs* "Pietermaritzburg", Legislative Council, 1884), Section V, 31, and *Report of the Natal Native Commission*, p. 43). Fynn also referred ('My Recollections of a Famous Campaign') to 'Ncora Drift,' and to 'Ncora Bluff' above it, up which the fugitives scrambled. Perhaps 'Ncora' is a typographical error for Ncosa, the name of a Zulu chief across the river (see SNA 1/1/35, no. 2). Only Fynn mentions, much later ('My Recollections of a Famous Campaign'), any precipitation in the vicinity and that not much. Of course, it is possible that storms upcountry could have fed the river, which in a normal wet summer would have been high anyway. Only Fynn, Smith-Dorrien (*Memories of Forty-Eight Years' Service*, pp. 17, 18) and Sparks (NM, January 22, 1929) describe it as in full flood, though Fynn mentions it could still be crossed at at least one place. Davies (NM, January 22, 1929) and Stafford ('Stirring Days of Old Times') state that the river was very high, although Davies mentions the current was weaker higher up. Thus the swollen river as a great obstacle to escape might seem to be the invention of old memories; *however*, Brickhill told the British officer in command at Sandspruit *that day* that the river was very dangerous and unfordable at the crossing place (C2252, p. 73). Subsequently Brickhill wrote ('Survivor's Account, p. 158) that it was 'rolling high.' Curling wrote to his mother, February 2, 1879 (AJL), that it was very deep and swift. Smith-Dorrien wrote to his father shortly afterwards (Emery, *The Red Soldier*, p. 90) that it was 'little better than a roaring torrent,' and Cochrane wrote (NW, February 8, 1879: 'eye-witness') that it was high. Dangerous-but-passable sums up what is stated or implied by others who left accounts (see n. 13). It is also questionable whether or not the fugitives crossed at Sotondose's Drift at all. The crossing place later was named 'Fugitives' Drift', but few of the fugitives were aware of any ford (drift) there. They seem to have arrived at the river in the vicinity of Sotondose's and crossed where they could. Cochrane (NW, February 8, 1879) and Bickley (*The Silver Wreath*, p. 46) do refer to a ford, but TN, January 27, 1879, report: Foley states there was none at all.

12 Details of the crossing place are given in Fynn, 'My Recollections of a Famous Campaign,' and Stafford, 'Stirring Days of Old Times,' to which may be added bits from Brickhill, 'Survivor's Account,' p. 158; Smith-Dorrien, *Memories of Forty-Eight Years' Service*, p. 18; and Clements, *Glamour and Tragedy of the Zulu War*, pp. 64–65: Sparks. These should be compared with the modern map.

13 C2252, p. 83: Brickhill. C2260, pp. 84: Essex, and 101: Gardner. WO 33/34, 91/1: Raw, and 96/3: Higginson. CP 8–14: Hamer. Brickhill, 'Survivor's Account,' p. 158. Fynn, 'My Recollections of a Famous Campaign.' Symons, 'My Reminiscences of the Zulu War,' p. 46. Smith-Dorrien, *Memories of Forty-Eight Years' Service*, pp. 16–18. Clements, *Glamour and Tragedy of the Zulu War*, p. 64: Sparks, and NM, January 22, 1929: Sparks. TN, January 31, 1879: Foley. AJLC: Curling to his mother, February 2, 1879; and to his father, February --, 1879. NM, January 31, 1879 and January 22, 1929: Davies. NW, February 8, 1879: 'eyewitness.' TN, February 26, 1879: 'combatant.' NM, January 30, 1879, 'private letter.'

14 C2260, p.84: Essex. C2374, p. 24: Umgohlulu. WO 33/34, 96/3: Higginson. CP 8–14: Hamer. Vause Diary, p. 7. AJLC: Curling to his mother, February 2, 1879. *The Natal Carbineers*, p. 102: Barker. Brickhill, 'Survivor's Account,' p. 158. Fynn, 'My Recollections of a Famous Campaign.' Watkins, 'They Fought for the Great White Queen,' p. 158. Smith-Dorrien, *Memories of Forty-Years' Service*, p. 17, and letter to his father, in French, *Lord Chelmsford and the Zulu War*, p. 100. NM, January 31, 1879: Davies, and January 22, 1929: Davies and Sparks. TN, January 27, 1879: Foley, and February 26, 1879: 'combatant.' Some of the men on foot were killed by enemy fire as they climbed the hill on the right bank. NC, February 11, 1879: 'Native Account of the Isandhlwana Disaster,' paraphrases the report(s) of four wagon-drivers who crossed the river at Sotondose's drift. They said that Gamdane's men joined in attacking the fugitives, and the pursuing Zulu were haled back from crossing by a head man who shouted: 'He [the King] has not said you are to cross. He is not invading – he is defending the land of his people. Come back! Don't cross!' Among those relieved to hear this was Sikhota, who with the four others had stopped to catch his breath on the other side. The drivers made no mention of mounted men, but stated that the whites with them were exhausted and gave them their guns to fire at the pursuers! Sikhota seems to have become separated from the rest of his men, and a little further on halted at a homestead and had a goat killed to eat, while he waited for them, but they did not come and he went on his way. Unfortunately, this report has much the quality of hearsay.

15 Vause Diary, p. 7. 1/BGV, IV, 302. Allison also reported that of six men wounded in Zikhali's Horse, five were struck by bullets and only one was stabbed. *Cf.* Clements, *Glamour and Tragedy of the Zulu War*, pp. 64–65: Sparks.

16 Symons, My Reminiscences of the Zulu War, p. 47. *The Natal Carbineers*, p. 102: Barker. *A Soldier's Life*, p. 235. WO 33/34, 96/3: Higginson. TN, February 26, 1879: 'combatant'. NW, January 19, 1929: Nourse. The inference from these accounts is that the Ngwane troops were more disorganized than the Edendale troop and therefore probably played less of a role in the defence.

17 WO 33/34, 96/2: Davies, and NM, January 31, 1879: Davies. C2374, 24: Umgohlulu. French, *Lord Chelmsford and the Zulu War*, p. 100: Smith-Dorrien. AJLC: Curling to his mother, February 2, 1879.

18 NC, February 11, 1879: 'Native Account.' Watkins, 'They Fought for the Great White Queen.' p. 160.

19 *Ibid.*, p. 158. WO 33/34, 96/2: Davies. Statham, *Blacks, Boers & British*, p. 179. Samuelson, *Long, Long Ago*, p. 149. *Cf.* NW, August 16, 1879: Kambule. Davies seems to have followed the troop for a part of the way, for he collected one of its wounded men, but reached the river after it had crossed.

20 *Cf.* Watkins, 'They Fought for the Great White Queen,' pp. 158–159; Fynn, 'My Recollections of a Famous Campaign;' and French, *Lord Chelmsford and the Zulu War*, p. 99: Smith-Dorrien.

21 Statham, *Blacks, Boers & British*, pp. 178–179. NW, February 26, 1879: 'combatant.'

22 Brickhill, 'Survivor's Account,' p. 159, and 'How I Escaped from the Fatal Field of Isandlwana,' *Africa Notes News*, XXIX, No. 2 (June 1990), p. 81. TN, January 27, 1879: Foley. It is silence in the other accounts that attests the desertion of the contingent's fugitives. C2260, p. 84: Essex and Smith-Dorrien, *Memories of Forty-Eight Years' Service*, p. 17, mention that a relatively large number of blacks got across the river. No one mentions their going to Helpmekaar.

23 SNA 1/6/12, no. 1.

24 WO 33/34, 69/-: Essex; 96/2: Davies; 96/3: Higginson. C2374, p. 24: Umgohlulu. Smith-Dorrien, *Memories of Forty-Eight Years' Service*, p. 18, and French, *Lord Chelmsford and the Zulu War*, p. 89: Smith-Dorrien. Stafford, 'Stirring Days of Old Times.' NW, February 8, 1879: 'eyewitness.' TN, February 26, 1879, 'combatant.'

25 SNA 1/1/34, no. 159: Hlubi; and 1/6/12, no. 1. WO 33/34, 96/2: Davies. KCM 42538: letter of R.J. Hall to editor of *The Natal Witness* [n.d.].

26 *The Silver Wreath*, pp. 49 and 63: accounts by J.R.M. Chard and A.H. Hook, respectively. NW, February 18, 1879: 'brave fugitive.'

27 *The Silver Wreath*, p. 50: Chard. *Defence of Rorke's Drift*. January 22, 1879. By an eye witness, (Durban, Natal Mercury, [1879]), pp. 5–6.

28 *The Silver Wreath*, p. 46: Grant. NAD 504: H.C. Lugg, 'The battle of Rorke's Drift'.

29 C2260, p. 101: Gardner. *The Silver Wreath*, p. 50: Chard. TN, April 11, 1879: 'Isandhlwana. (An account by an Eye-witness).'

30 *The Silver Wreath*, pp. 50 and 63: Chard and Hook, respectively. The company's battalion is identified by WO 33/34, 96/3: Higginson; Hamilton-Browne, *A Lost Legionary*, p. 148. Stephenson is referred to in TN, December 6, 1878: GO 213, and February 21, 1879: GO 37.

31 *The Silver Wreath*, pp. 49–50, 60 and 63: Chard, F. Bourne, and Hook, respectively. KCM: Hall letter. *Cf. Eyewitness in Zululand: The Campaign Reminiscences of Colonel W.A. Dunne, CB [.] South Africa, 1877–1887* (London, Greenhill, 1989), pp. 94 and 95.

32 NW, January 18 and 21, 1879: 'The Zulu War.' CSO 680: 226/1879, and 1925: 494/1879. SNA 1/6/11, no. 20. *The Silver Wreath*, p. 50: Chard. See Chard's handwritten list of those present at the battle, in Atkinson, *The South Wales Borderers*, between pp. 354 and 355. Corporals Scammell and Schiess of the NNC were inmates of the hospital and not assigned to Stephenson's company – see Maxwell, *My Reminiscences of the Zulu War*, p. 7, and D. Blair Brown, *Surgical Experiences in the Zulu and Transvaal Wars* (London, Simpkin, Marshall, 1883), pp. 35–36, 73.

33 *The Silver Wreath*, p. 50: Chard.

34 *Ibid.*, pp. 50 and 60: Chard and Bourne, respectively. *Cf.* KCM: Hall letter.

35 *Eyewitness in Zululand*, p. 95.

36 *The Silver Wreath*, p. 50: Chard.

37 KCM: Hall letter. Symons states (My Reminiscences of the Zulu War, p. 43) that Hall was a meat contractor.

38 TN, January 31, 1879: 'The Isandwhala [*sic*] Action.'

39 *The Silver Wreath*, p. 50: Chard. *Historical Records of the 24th Regiment*, p. 248: Chard.

40 *Defence of Rorke's Drift*, p. 57. SNA 1/1/34, no. 159: Hlubi. KCM: Hall letter.

41 *The Silver Wreath*, p. 63: Hook. TN, April 11, 1879: 'Isandhlwana.' Cf. KCM: Hall letter. Chard's reports are silent with respect to the troop's performance or not of the requested task; and *Eyewitness in Zululand* mentions ([p. 96) only 'one of the outposts running back' just after the (first) shot.

42 *The Silver Wreath*, p. 50: Chard. SNA 1/1/34, no. 159: Hlubi.

43 John Laband, '"O! Let's go and have a fight at Jim's!" The Zulu at the battle of Rorke's Drift,' in id. and Paul Thompson, *Kingdom and Colony a War* (Pietermaritzburg, University of Natal Press, 1990), p. 112.

44 *Cf. The Silver Wreath*, p. 50: Chard; KCM: Hall letter; and TN, January 31, 1879: 'The Isandwhala Action.'

45 *The Silver Wreath*, pp. 50 and 63: Chard and Hook, respectively. *Defence of Rorke's Drift, p. 7. Eyewitness in Zululand*, p. 96. Maxwell, *My Reminiscences of the Zulu War*, p. 10. WO 33/34, 96/3: Higginson states that Stephenson brought off Lieutenant Purvis, who had been wounded on the 12th and was in the hospital. Subsequently Stephenson was dismissed from the service (TN, February 21, 1879: GO 37), even though Maxwell states (p. 10) that 'he was a gentleman from the Cape Colony and spoke the [Xhosa?] language perfectly.' It would appear that four corporals – Anderson, Doughty, Scammell and Wilson – of the company remained: see *Defence of Rourke's Drift. January 22, 1879. By an eyewitness* (Durban, printed by the *Natal Mercury*, 1879), pp. 8–9 and 15–16. One of them – evidently Anderson, given as killed in the battle – fled just after the men did, but before the Zulu onset, and was shot in the back by one of the garrison and fell within 150 yards of the defensive wall. See and cf. *ibid.*, pp. 8–9 and Private Hook's account in Barry C. Johnson, *Rorke's Drift and the British Museum: The Life of Henry Hook, V.C.* (London, n.p., 1986), p. 21.

46 C2260, p. 88: report of H.S. Spalding. *The Silver Wreath*, pp. 46–47: Grant and Johnson. NM, January 22, 1929: Davies. See also SNA 1/1/34, no. 159: Hlubi, and KCM: Hall letter.

47 *Defence of Rorke's Drift*, p. 10.

48 Bengough, *Memories of a Soldier's Life*, p. 113. French, *Lord Chelmsford and the Zulu War*, p. 81. C2242, pp. 26–28. CP 27–52: Chelmsford to Durnford, January 19, 1879. NM, January 27, 1879: 'With the Natal Mounted Native Contingent'.

49 Bengough, *Memories of a Soldier's Life*, p. 113.

50 J.P.C. Laband and P.S. Thompson with Sheila Henderson, *The Buffalo Border: The Anglo-Zulu War in Northern Natal* (Durban, University of Natal, Department of History, 1983), pp. 33–35.

51 C2374, p. 23. NM, January 22, 1929: W.H. Beaumont, 'Insandhlwana [*sic*] Could have been Averted.'

52 *Cf.* Laband and Thompson, *The Buffalo Border*, pp. xii, 49, and NM, January 22, 1929: Beaumont. The farm was Amoibie, whose buildings the Zulu burnt (CSO 1925: 568/1879).

53 C2374, p. 23.

54 *Ibid.* NW, January 30, 1879: 'With the Native Contingent.' Bengough, *Memories of a Soldier's Life*, p. 113.

55 CP 27–52: Chelmsford to Durnford, January 19, 1879.

56 C2374, p. 23, and NM, January 22, 1929: Beaumont. NW, January 30, 1879: 'With the Native Contingent.' Bengough, *Memories of a Soldier's Life*, p. 113. NAM 85037: R.C. Birkett to his father, March 11, 1879. It would appear, from his battalion's movements on the 21st and 22nd, that Bengough was unaware of the Lieutenant General's having ordered it to Rorke's Drift on the 21st and having changed his mind on the morning of the 22nd (see *A Soldier's Life*, pp. 222–223). If Durnford informed Bengough of the orders, there is no record of it. The crossing place of the battalion is not certainly known, but Bengough's description of the rocks and being 'surrounded by the river' suggests the loop where the kwaMahamba ford is located.

57 C2374, p. 23, and NM, January 22, 1929. CSO 1925: 568 and 664/1879, and unnumbered, Fynn to Colonial Secretary, January 26, 1879. SNA 1/6/12 no. 1. Brickhill, 'Survivor's Account.'p. 159.

58 WO 32/7726: Bengough to Senior Officer, Rorke's Drift, January 23, 1879. CP 8–19: Fynn to J.N. Crealock, January 23, 1879: 3 p.m. CP 8–19: Bengough to [Crealock], January 24, 1879. NW, January 30, 1879: 'With the Native Contingent.' Bengough, *Memories of A Soldier's Life*, p.114. *The South African Campaign*, 1879, p. 313.

59 C2260, p. 100. *Narrative*, p. 43 and n. Hamilton-Browne, *A Lost Legionary*, p. 134. NW, January 30, 1879: 'The Zulu War.'

60 *Narrative*, p. 43. *Zulu War Journal of Colonel Henry Harford*, p. 31. Hamilton-Browne, *A Lost Legionary*, p. 135. Maxwell, *My Reminiscences of the Zulu War*, p. 3. Norris-Newman, *In Zululand with the British*, p. 59. Fynn, 'My Recollections of a Famous Campaign.' Symons, My Reminiscences of the Zulu War, p. 29. NW, January 30, 1879: 'The Zulu War.' I have followed Harford's account of Lonsdale's escape, for Harford claims that Lonsdale told him what had happened, and those of the special war correspondent of the NW and Lieutenant Milner (C2454, p. 184), for they both wrote soon afterwards and likely had access to Lonsdale. Besides the other accounts in the sources cited above, there is a garbled one in CFP 8/16: Lugubu Mbata, referring to the Lieutenant General but possibly meaning Lonsdale.

61 C2260, p. 100. C2454, p. 184. Norris-Newman, *In Zululand with the British*, pp. 59–60. NW, January 30, 1879: 'The Zulu War.'

62 Parr, *A Sketch of the Kafir and Zulu Wars*, pp. 195–196. *Cf.* Maxwell, *My Reminiscences of the Zulu War*, p. 3.

63 C2454 pp. 184–185. Hamilton-Browne, *A Lost Legionary*, p. 136. *Zulu War Journal of Colonel Henry Harford*, p. 31. Maxwell, *My Reminiscences of the Zulu War*, p. 5. Norris-Newman, *In Zululand with the British*, p. 60. NW, January 30, 1879: 'The Zulu War;' also NC, January 30, 1879: 'The Isandhlwana Disaster.'

64 C2454, p. 185. Symons, My Reminiscences of the Zulu War, p. 33. NW, January 30, 1879: 'The Zulu War.'

65 *Cf.* C2454, p. 185, and Symons, My Reminiscences of the Zulu War, p. 33.

66 Hamilton-Browne, *A Lost Legionary*, p. 136. *Zulu War Journal of Colonel Henry Harford*, pp. 32–33. Maxwell, *My Reminiscences of the Zulu War*, pp. 5–6. There had been a partial eclipse of the sun during the afternoon, which occurred apparently unnoticed.

67 *Zulu War Journal of Colonel Henry Harford*, p. 32.

68 C2454, p. 185. Norris-Newman, *In Zululand with the British*, p. 61. Maxwell, *My Reminiscences of the Zulu War*, p. 4.

69 C2454, p. 185. Norris-Newman, *In Zululand with the British*, p. 61. NW, January 30, 1879: 'The Zulu War.' Hamilton-Browne, *A Lost Legionary*, pp. 136–137. Hamilton-Browne wrote that just before the advance on the knoll began he dismounted and grabbed the 'principal' head man of his battalion by his head ring and swore to blow his brains out if his men ran. The head man 'howled' to them not to. Some of the British infantry moved behind them, and if they had run, it would have been into the British bayonets.

70 Norris-Newman, *In Zululand with the British*, p. 61. Maxwell, *My Reminiscences of the Zulu War*, p. 5.

71 C2454, p. 185. Norris-Newman, *In Zululand with the British*, pp. 61–62. *Zulu War Journal of Colonel Henry Harford*, pp. 6, 33, 35. Hamilton-Browne, *A Lost Legionary*, pp. 138–139. Parr, *A Sketch of the Zululand Kafir Wars*, p. 26. Fynn, 'My Recollections of a Famous Campaign.' CFP 8/16: Lugubu Mbata.

72 C2454, p. 185. Parr, *A Sketch of the Zulu and Kafir Wars*, p. 23. *Zulu War Journal of Colonel Henry Harford*, pp. 33–34. Maxwell, *My Reminiscences of the Zulu War*, pp. 5–6. Fynn, 'My Recollections of a Famous Campaign.'

73 C2454, p. 185. Maxwell, *My Reminiscences of the Zulu War*, p. 6. Norris-Newman, *In Zululand with the British*, p. 64, and NW, February 1, 1879: 'With the Head-Quarters Column.'

74 NW, February 1, 1879: 'With the Head-Quarters Column.' Norris-Newman, *In Zululand with the British*, p. 64. Maxwell, *My Reminiscences of the Zulu War*, p. 6. Fynn, 'My Recollections of a Famous Campaign.' F. Symons, 'How Lord Chelmsford was decoyed from Isandhlwana,' in *Later Annals of Natal*, p. 149. CFP 8/16: Lugubu Mbata. *Cf.* Hamilton-Browne, *A Lost Legionary*, p. 142.

75 NW, February 1, 1879: 'With the Head-Quarters Column.' CFP 8/16: Lugubu Mbata. See Maxwell, *My Reminiscences of the Zulu War*, p. 6, on the lack of ammunition, and Hamilton-Browne, *A Lost Legionary*, p. 142, for the tale about the Zulu's believing the white soldiers were ghosts from Isandlwana.

76 Norris-Newman, *In Zululand with the British*, p. 65. Hamilton-Browne, *A Lost Legionary*, pp. 142–143. Symons, 'How Lord Chelmsford was decoyed from Isandhlwana,' p. 150.

77 Symons, 'How Lord Chelmsford was decoyed from Isandhlwana,' p. 150.

78 *Ibid. Zulu War Journal of Colonel Henry Harford*, p. 36. Maxwell, *My Reminiscences of the Zulu War*, p. 7. Hamilton-Browne, *A Lost Legionary*, pp. 143–144. CFP 8.16: Lugubu Mbata.

79 *Cf.* Chard's reports in *Historical Records of the 24th Regiment*, p.254, and *The Silver Wreath*, p. 52. Norris-Newman, *In Zululand with the British*, p. 66. Maxwell, *My Reminiscences of the Zulu War*, pp. 7–8. *Zulu War Journal of Colonel Henry Harford*, p. 37. On rations *cf.* C2454, p. 186, and Hamilton-Browne, *A Lost Legionary*, p. 151.

80 Hamilton-Browne, *A Lost Legionary*, p. 152. Cf. C2454, pp. 185–186; Colenso, *History of the Zulu War*, p. 307–308; Parr, *A Sketch of the Kafir and Zulu Wars*, p. 23; and Symons, 'How Lord Chelmsford was decoyed from Isandhlwana,' p. 150.

81 Norris-Newman, *In Zululand with the British*, p. 66–67. Hamilton-Browne, *A Lost Legionary*, pp. 152–153. Maxwell, *My Reminiscences of the Zulu War*, pp. 9–10. *Zulu War Journal of Colonel Henry Harford*, p. 37. C2454, p. 186. *Narrative*, p. 59. Symons, 'How Lord Chelmsford was decoyed from Isandhlwana,' p. 150.

Chapter 7

DISBANDING OF THE THIRD REGIMENT

Dismissal or desertion?

There was doubt at headquarters whether or not the demoralized 3rd Regiment could be kept together, let alone got to fight. The Lieutenant General must go to Helpmekaar, then Pietermaritzburg, and give a full account of what had happened to the High Commissioner and to the government at home. He left kwaJimu on the morning of the 24th. Just before leaving he apparently told Commandant Lonsdale to explain to the men of the 3rd Regiment that he intended to reoccupy the camp at Isandlwana but could not until the column again had transport, most of its wagons and oxen having been lost in the battle. The commandant should find out who were willing to re-enter Zululand with the column and disband the rest.

Lonsdale assembled the regiment and called forward the head men, but he spoke (through the interpreter) so that men could also hear. He wanted to find out which men were courageous and would stand by their officers, if necessary, even to death. They should come forward. The announcement evidently was followed by consultations.

Sikhota gave Lonsdale to understand that he was quite willing to serve. Also, Browne apparently talked to his head man Mvubi about the isiGqoza staying. The men feared that if they stayed their homes and families would be attacked by those who went home. Mvubi suggested that the isiGqoza be allowed to take the men who wanted to go home behind Shiyane and kill them. In any case Lonsdale received a reply that the isiGqoza would re-enter Zululand, but only after they had visited their homes, for they had lost many comrades in the battle. Homage to the dead was necessary.

The general consensus on Lonsdale's proposal was, we are willing to re-enter Zululand and to fight alongside the white men. The white men are our shield against Cetshwayo, the Zulu King. But now we see our shield going away. (Just then the mounted troops were riding after the Lieutenant General in the direction of Helpmekaar.) We are not going to go over the river by ourselves. No one can say that he is not afraid.

Lonsdale apparently concluded that the isiGqoza was the only part of the contingent which would stay and the rest would not and were quite useless. (He explained that the white horsemen were going away only because they had lost all of their things and were going to get new ones.) He could see that the black men were frightened, because all their wounds were in the back, whereas all the white men's wounds were in front. He dismissed the lot.

Immediately the officers and non-commissioned officers began taking in equipment. Firearms were handed in. So were the red puggarees. Blankets were also handed in, but there may have been exceptions. Some companies were allowed to take their flags home, others were not. Probably it depended on the officers. All this took some time. It may have been during this interval that Browne told the men of his battalion – except the isiGqoza – that the Great White Queen would send women's aprons when she heard of their cowardice. They should go home and dig in the fields with their wives. Indeed, they could go to a hotter place than Natal.

The formalities complete, the men were told to go home. They had eaten well that morning so they were given no rations. No officers accompanied them. They were told to keep together as far as the Msinga. There they could separate and retrace the ways they had come.

Not every man understood what was happening. Some men apparently had to be driven out of camp by the British soldiers. Some believed they were going home because there was not enough food for them. Some of the head men thought that they would be called back in two months; others knew nothing about it. According to Browne, Mvubi asked that his men be allowed to kill just a few of the 'kaffirs' who had displeased him. The Gqoza companies (the two left) formed into rings. They marched past the battalion officers, raised their shields in salute and rattled their spears against them. They broke into a war song and marched out of camp. The great majority of men in the other levies bounded off, apparently in good spirits. They were seen making their separate ways in separate groups, resembling swarms of ants going over the hillside.[1]

Lonsdale rode off to Helpmekaar. He got from the general a commission to take half a dozen officers to recruit white mercenaries in the Cape Colony. The Lieutenant General probably had not expected the commandant to disband the whole regiment. Perhaps Lonsdale lied about what he had done. Lord Chelmsford wrote to the Secretary of State for War on January 27th that the regiment had deserted.[2] On his way to Pietermaritzburg he met the Resident Magistrate of Weenen and told him that all deserters should be sent back to do their duty.[3] He certainly opposed the disbandment of the 2nd Battalion of the 1st Regiment at Helpmekaar.

Bengough had started out that morning with his battalion on the road to Rorke's Drift. Several of his officers had found it open the preceding day. His intention was to place himself and his battalion directly under the general's command. The battalion went a little way and met the demoralized men of the 3rd Regiment coming from the opposite direction. The fugitives urged the men of the battalion to leave, too. After a frightful night at the Helpmekaar fort, Bengough's men seemed to need little encouragement. Chiefs and men alike refused to go any further unless they were supported by white troops. Bengough thought, if he tried to force them forward they would disband themselves, taking rifles, ammunition, blankets and whatever else had been issued to them. The men with rifles started to go. Bengough and his interpreter hastily decided to disarm them, wondering if they would actually part with the rifles. The battalion was formed up. Bengough ordered the men with rifles to lay them down – and they did. Then he told the men they might go home and wait there until called to serve again.

Soon after this Bengough met the Lieutenant General, riding with his staff up to Helpmekaar. He explained to the general that his battalion had refused to march and he was disarming them before sending them home. He asked to put himself and his mounted officers at the general's disposal. The Lieutenant General was angry. Bengough had no right to dismiss anyone without his permission. The major must recall those whom he had let go. He, the general, would address the battalion. Bengough saluted and hastened to obey.

The battalion was got together and formed three sides of a square. British infantry formed the fourth side. The Lieutenant General told the men that the battalion was to march to the Msinga, where it would protect the magistracy and prevent the enemy from breaking over the border. There was some hesitation among the men. The general put the alternative to them without his usual tact. If he thought they were all cowards, he would have them shot on the spot. He gave orders that any men who tried to leave the battalion should be shot. Hesitation vanished. The battalion marched to the Msinga.[4]

The costs of Isandlwana

Thus ended the first British invasion of Zululand. The battle of Isandlwana was one of the great defeats of the British army. The Lieutenant General had underrated the military capacity of his enemy, deceived himself through faulty reconnaissance and intelligence as to the enemy's intentions, and then divided his force in the presence of enemy's much larger, more mobile force. A prepared, all-round defence probably would have repulsed an enemy attack, given the British advantages in firepower and manoeuvre. Neither half of the British army was prepared for all-round defence on January 22nd. The enemy could as easily have run over the portion on the march as the portion at the camp. Colonel Pulleine had time to prepare an all-round defence, but did not realize the danger until too late. Durnford contributed to his misapprehension. The British force fought in an extended line in front of the camp and could not retire in time to save itself. The result was a massacre and the collapse of the British invasion.

The British loss was given as 52 officers and 806 men, including British infantry and mounted colonials. This was the loss of the Europeans present at the battle. The imperial authorities had no idea how many loyal Africans had perished. The official guess was between 200 and 300.[5] The colonial authorities were at pains to ascertain the correct number, and arrived at 471 killed and missing and 16 wounded. These included non-combatants as well as combatants.[6]

The units of the Natal Native Contingent engaged had suffered heavy losses. At the centre of the line the two companies of amaChunu had been exposed to the full fury of the Zulu attack and flight could not save them. Not only had Gabangaye, son and heir to the chief Phakade, perished, but, according to the magistrate's count afterwards, 243 amaChunu had fallen or were missing in action. Since the two companies could not have exceeded 290 men and probably were much smaller, it would indeed appear that the amaChunu had experienced a massacre – at least in excess of eighty per cent of the companies' strength.[7]

The company of the isiGqoza on the right had come into action later. Sikhota and many of the men had been able to escape in good time. None the less the company lost 54 killed and missing in action out of 112 – almost half of its strength.[8] The company which had been in reserve and had decamped in panic, probably consisting of amaBhele, lost 23 out of 110.[9] How many fell fighting in the line, how many in flight, how many in the small unrecorded combats that marked the last stage of the battle, will never be known. Only three of the European non-commissioned officers (who were all on foot) seem to have escaped. All four of the company commanders and five of the seven lieutenants were killed.[10]

It was reported early at the Upper Tugela magistracy that the amaNgwane had lost some of their best men and most of their 'native officers'.[11] The two companies of the 1st Battalion lost 76 killed and 7 wounded out of 233 engaged.[12] Since the company with the Rocket Battery dissolved immediately it came into action and its members had ample time to flee the battlefield, most of the loss probably occurred in the company of which part fought with the mounted men on the left flank and part with Phakade's men at the centre. This company mustered perhaps 150 men and thus lost about half its strength. The two captains and two of the four lieutenants escaped the field, but most, if not all the non-commissioned officers, were killed.[13]

The mounted force fared much better because of its mobility. Zikhali's Horse had 27 killed and 6 wounded out of 157 engaged – a loss of only one-fifth of its strength; however, many horses were lost.[14] Only one officer was killed. The Edendale Troop lost two killed and one wounded.[15] Hlubi's troop apparently lost four killed.[16]

An imputation of cowardice hangs over the Native Contingent because many fled the battlefield at Isandlwana and none stayed to defend the post at kwaJimu. None of the fugitives rallied, except for two of the mounted troops. Then there were the scares at night. The European soldier had not had much confidence in his African counterpart. After the events of January 22nd he had practically none.

There is no doubting the personal courage of the men or their willingness to fight. They had stood in line to fight while there was some point to it, then they had fled. The African soldier, including the formidable Zulu, was trained to fight aggressively – to attack and defeat the enemy. His tactics were essentially offensive, not defensive. Leaders lacked experience in the control of a tactical defence. A battle started with a clash and ended with the defeated side in rout.

The psychological effect of the Zulu army advancing in great force and on an extended front should not be discounted. Firearms would keep the Zulu at bay, as the British infantry demonstrated; but only one African foot soldier in ten had a firearm. The 'gun men' were not marksmen. What would happen when the Zulu closed with them? Who would prevail in the melee?

Suppose the British infantry had warded off the Zulu with its fire, and bought the time needed to reform around the camp. The British regular soldier was trained in the manoeuvres to accomplish this, and he was disciplined to act upon orders. The African soldier had not yet acquired this training and discipline. The men of the Native Contingent had been in service just over a month. They had learned something of European drill, but not enough. Their officers might be Europeans of the right sort, but what of the non-commissioned officers? Most of the Europeans in charge could not speak the language of the men. Interpreters were few. All these things must be borne in mind when considering the Native Contingent's performance. The Native Contingent – those units engaged in action – seems to have done about as well as could be expected at Isandlwana. Some units did better than others, of course.

Return home

The war had changed dramatically in favour of the Zulu. The No. 3 Column, reduced in numbers and mobility, adopted the strategic defence. Fortunately for Natal, the Zulu strategy was essentially defensive. The people of the Colony did not know this, and a great fear existed among them that the Zulu army would invade. Rumours foretold invasion, but they proved false, and time favoured a British recovery.

Most of the men of the 3rd Regiment lived near the confluence of the Thukela and Mphafana rivers in the Weenen County. Without rations, armed as they had come, parties of the disbanded regiment set out for home during the afternoon of 24th January. There was excitement at their return. They spoke of the great defeat, then of the soldiers' driving them out of camp and telling them to go home because they were useless. There was alarm that the Zulus would invade and attack. Europeans were taking refuge in fortified places. Apparently the government was leaving Africans to their own devices.[17]

The Resident Magistrate of the Weenen Division had been told by the Lieutenant General to send back the 'deserters' of the 3rd Regiment. Instead he waited for instructions from the government.[18] The Resident Magistrate in the Klip River Division forbore as well. He saw that the returning men were ashamed. Their friends laughed at them. Even so, they set about purifying themselves, for blood had been shed.[19]

Phakade was shocked to learn that fully a third of the Chunu contingent had fallen. It was a terrible blow to him and his people. The old chief was angry with the men who returned. He grieved at the loss of two sons, Gabangaye, his heir, and Mbonjana, and sought the seclusion of a remote homestead. His people turned to mourning.[20]

The Ngwane units had disbanded themselves. The companies dissolved in action. The men who had escorted the rocket battery probably were among the first fugitives from the battlefield. The fugitives generally spread panic along the road between Helpmekaar and Pietermaritzburg. The portion of Zikhali's Horse which arrived at Helpmekaar was asked to stay but refused.[21] The first riders arrived home on the 24th. They spoke of a large Zulu army which had surrounded and defeated Durnford's column, and had caught and destroyed several companies of British infantry and two guns as well. Other horsemen returned on the 25th and told the same story. They gave the impression that the Zulus were in hot pursuit. The Resident Magistrate of the Upper Tugela Division could not stem a panic. He questioned the fugitives and told them to stay at their homes until the government decided what to do.[22]

The chief Ncwadi reported that Nyanda, commander of the mounted troops, had been detained at Ladysmith. The Resident Magistrate agreed to write for his release. After a few days Nyanda and several other horsemen who had been detained returned.[23] Meanwhile an unofficial report that the British had retaken the camp and driven the Zulus out of Natal reached the magistracy. The Resident Magistrate sent out messages with this news to stop the panic. He also had the Kahlamba passes examined. There was a rumour that they had been opened, which suggested possible action by hostile baSotho. The rumour proved false.[24]

The safe arrival home of most of the men on foot, however sensational their accounts of the defeat, probably helped to abate the panic. Many men were reported wounded and lying in the Msinga. The dead and missing were finally reckoned at 103. Thirteen wounded survived. Most of the head men had been killed. Many of the foot men had been killed, even men of Nyanda's own family. The ceremonies in memory of the dead lasted several weeks.[25]

Not all the units involved in the defeat were disbanded. The 2nd Battalion of the 1st Regiment, whose men the Lieutenant General threatened to have shot if they deserted, marched from Helpmekaar to Sand Spruit on the 24th. A detachment of British infantry and engineers was there. It was escorting a small wagon train on the way to the column, but in the emergency the colonel commanding had halted it and secured the nearby Msinga magistracy. The 2nd Battalion arrived in the evening. About the same time a large levy of the Border Guard, which had scared off some roving Zulus the previous day (and probably been scared by them), came in for safety.

The magistracy building afforded no field of fire against attack, so a rough fort of stone and earth was thrown up on top of a small hill to the south of it. The men worked hard on it all night, and next day the British engineers came to help them. None the less their morale sank as the last of the disbanded 3rd Regiment streamed past. The colonel commanding the detachment had the battalion drawn up. He told the men that 'the English could never be conquered, to stick to us, and they would in good time have their reward', but really he had no confidence in them. He decided to leave some of the engineers to encourage them after the infantry marched. Forty or fifty men deserted the battalion during the first few days at Sand Spruit.[26]

All that remained of the contingent with the No. 3 Column was the Edendale Horse and Hlubi's troop. They were at Helpmekaar with the other imperial units.[27] Several of the Edendale men did leave, but only to take a wounded comrade home.[28] Seven of the baSotho went home, but five of them reported promptly to the local magistrate and said that they had come for fresh horses. The magistrate saw that their horses were tired, their hooves were worn through and one had been wounded. The men got fresh horses and rode back to Helpmekaar after only a day at home.[29] The missionary who worked in their Location was gratified when he was told that Hlubi's men attributed their escape from the battlefield to the prayers he and the people at his station had offered to God.[30]

The Natal Native Contingent with the No. 3 Column, especially the 3rd Regiment failed, because of inadequate European leadership and training in extraordinary circumstances, not because of lack of courage or determination. We shall see the 2nd Regiment suffer a similar humiliation. Such were the fortunes of war that within a fortnight of the outbreak of the war, scarcely half the Natal Native Contingent remained in the field, and its value as a fighting force was seriously questioned.

NOTES

1 C2260, p. 4. CP 8–45: Clery to Crealock, February 2, 1879. GH 1421, p. 119. CSO 686: 818/1879; 1925: C23/1879 and unnumbered, Fynn to Colonial Secretary, January 23, 1879. SNA 1/1/33, nos. 48 and 51; and 1/6/13, no. 6. NW, February 1, 1879: 'With the Head-Quarters Column.' TN, March 17, 1879: 'Notes from the Border.' Colenso, *History of the Zulu War*, p. 321. Emery, *The Red Soldier*, p. 105. *Cf: Zulu War Journal of Colonel Henry Harford*, pp. 37–39; Maxwell, *My Reminiscences of the Zulu War*, p. 9; and Hamilton Browne, *A Lost Legionary*, pp. 154–156, which are rather vague and perhaps confused in details.

2 *Zulu War Journal of Colonel Henry Harford*, p. 37. Maxwell, *My Reminiscences of the Zulu War*, pp. 9–10. The sources do not indicate whether Lonsdale obtained his new commission conditionally before the Lieutenant General left kwaJimu or expeditiously afterwards. C2242, p. 34. Also, see *Narrative*, p. 59; GH 1421, p. 108; and CP 8–45: Clery to Crealock, February 5, 1879.

3 CSO 1925: C23/1879. The Lieutenant General expressed the same opinion to the Supreme Chief on January 26, 1879 (see GH1421, p. 109).

4 Bengough, *Memories of a Soldier's Life*, pp. 114–116. CP 8–19: Bengough to [Crealock], January 24, 1879. C2454, p. 186: Milne. It is difficult to reconcile the details of Bengough's and Milne's accounts, except by alternating between them. Also, see *Narrative*, p. 59; *Zulu War Journal of Colonel Henry Harford*, p. 38; and Maxwell, *My Reminiscences of the Zulu War*, p. 9.

5 *Narrative*, pp. 47 and 157. The figures include the Europeans in the Native Contingent.

6 *Ibid.*, p. 157. The breakdown according to chief and to magisterial division is given in NGG, XXXI, no. 1764: GN155.

7 That is 240 from the Weenen Division and 4 from the Umsinga Division, according to NGG, XXXI, no. 1764: GN155; however, the 4 was later reduced to 3 (SNA 1/1/35, no. 165). Lonsdale wrote to the Colonial Secretary, December 23, 1878, that the Mchunu companies varied in size from 20 to 145, because the existing groups objected to being broken up (CSO 674: 4945/1878).

8 NGG, XXX, no. 1764: GN155. CSO 674: 4945/1878.

9 That is 20 from the Weenen Division and 5 from the Umsinga Division, according to NGG, XXXI, no. 1764: GN155; however, the 5 was later reduced to 3 (SNA 1/1/35, no. 165). The initial strength is given by Lonsdale (CSO 674: 4945/1878). It should be noted that the presumption here is that No. 6 Company of the 1st Battalion consisted of amaBhele.

10 NM, May 16, 1879: letter of Walter Higginson. *Narrative*, p. 157.

11 1/BGV, IV, 286–187, 306.

12 CSO 1926: 1333/1879. SNA 1/1/35, no. 144.

13 *Narrative*, p. 157. Stafford, 'Stirring Days of Old Times.' TN, February 14, 1879: 'Isandhlwana. Further list of men killed in action' names five sergeants and four corporals.

14 CSO 1926: 1333/1879. SNA 1/1/35, no. 144. 1/BGV, IV, 326–338.

15 TN, February 7, 1879: 'The Edendale Horse.' *Cf.* SNA 1/1/35, no. 139, which gives three killed.

16 NGG, XXXI, no. 1764: GN155. *Cf.* SNA 1/1/35, no. 148.

17 CSO 1925: C23/1879.

18 *Ibid.*

19 C2318, p. 11.

20 NM, February 7, 1879: 'Pakadi and the Weenen Tribes.' Statement by Joko in *Evidence taken before the Natal Native Commission*, p. 354. Statement by Magadigidi kaNobebe in *Stuart Archive*, II, 85–86. SNA 1/1/33, no. 64. 1/GTN 3/2/1: G91/1879. 244 were killed or missing, according to NGG XXXI, no. 1764: GN 1SS.

21 1/BGV, IV, 289 and 305. *Cf.* Norris-Newman, *In Zululand with the British*, p. 72.

22 1/BGV, IV, 287, 288. SNA 1/6/13, no. 5. *Cf.* NM, February 7, 1879: 'Pakadi and the Weenen Tribes.'

23 1/BGV, IV, 287, 288, 305. SNA 1/6/13, no. 5.

24 1/BGV, IV, 288–289.

25 1/BGV, IV 289, 303. CSO 1926: 953/1879. NGG, XXXI, no. 1764: GN155.

26 Laband and Thompson, *The Buffalo Border*, pp. 48–49, 100. CP 8–22: Bray to Chelmsford, January 25, and to Frere, January 27, 1879. 1/GTN, 3/2/1: G91/1879.

27 See the return in CP 8–32; Symons, My Reminiscences of the Zulu War, pp. 49–50; *Henderson Heritage*, pp. 228, 231; and SNA 1/6/12, no. 37.

28 TN, February 7, 1879: 'The Edendale Horse.'

29 SNA 1/1/33, no. 74. *Cf.* 1/6/12 no. 6 and NM, February 7, 1879: 'Pakadi and the Weenen Tribes.'

30 Jenkinson, *Amazulu*, p. 87.

Chapter 8

THE SECOND REGIMENT TO ESHOWE AND BACK

The war started out well for the 2nd Regiment – good rations, short marches, little danger. The officers and non-commissioned officers were fairly lax with discipline and the men raided corn patches along the route of march with impunity.[1] No. 1 Column, to which the regiment belonged, had crossed the lower Thukela between the 12th and 15th of January. The 1st Battalion of the regiment had been last over. It took five days to ferry across supplies and to build a fort on the Zulu side of the river. On the 18th the column marched towards Ulundi. Its first objective was Eshowe, an abandoned mission station on the high ground thirty-five miles to the north.

The column marched in two divisions of about equal size. The distance between them was short, so that they could close up quickly in support of each other. One battalion of the 2nd Regiment was attached to each division. The contingent had the important task, along with the British infantry and the mounted troops, of providing flank and rear guards.[2]

The 1st Battalion was in the first division,[3] which left the lower Thukela at 6 a.m. on the 18th and camped at the Nyoni river at 2 p.m., having marched about seven miles. That night the battalion's pickets reported seeing the first Zulus.[4]

The 2nd Battalion was in the second division, which left the Thukela at 6 a.m. on the 19th. As it approached the Nyoni the first division moved off to the next river, the Msunduzi, a little over two miles ahead. Part of the second division joined it that evening, while the rest halted at the Nyoni camp to wait for the many wagons which were grinding forward over the sandy plain. On the 20th the two divisions and the wagons united at the Msunduzi camp. A work party went ahead some four miles to prepare the crossing at the next river, the Matikulu.[5]

The coastal region is hot and humid in summer. Sea breezes and thunderstorms sometimes freshen the air, but long day marches were impractical for man and beast. Moreover, the so-called road to Eshowe was no more than a traders' track, and there were many streams to cross. The ground was soft. The march was slow. The first division was encumbered by a train of fifty wagons, the second by one of eighty.[6] In addition there were ambulances and artillery vehicles. Half the company of pioneers – No. 2 Company, amaQanya from the Umgeni Division – was at the front of the column, along with a detachment of Royal Engineers. They repaired the track, such as it was. Twenty more were at the head of the second division. It was hard work but they did it well.[7]

The march had no hardships for the men of the regiment. It was more of a lark. Some of them burnt a Zulu homestead near the Msunduzi on the 19th. The redcoats did not know at first what caused the blaze. They stayed awake half the night expecting a Zulu attack! In the morning the men were up and off to forage. As the sun rose they returned from all directions, carrying corn, pumpkins and fowls. The campfires were ranged in lines between several parallel rows of branches stuck in the ground to form windbreaks. The men leaned their weapons against the branches and got down to roasting the captured corn as well as their rations of meat. They seemed quite satisfied with their lot.[8]

The column moved off again early on the 21st. The crossing of the Matikulu was not so much difficult as time-consuming. Beyond the river there was still much sand, also much bush. The train of wagons and therefore the column, proceeded at the usual snail's pace. At most it made eight miles that day. Some Zulu scouts were observed on the hills, but they kept their distance.

Wednesday, the 22nd, dawned fine. The first division marched at five. Mounted infantry scouted ahead, as usual. A company of the 1st Battalion was also in advance. The second division again followed the first. The road led along the west side of the small Nyezane river. Corn grew in abundance on the low ground. Marshiness further slowed progress. It was about eight o'clock when the head of the column came to where the track crossed the river. Just beyond the crossing, Colonel Pearson, the commander of the column, decided to halt for breakfast and a rest.[9]

The halting place was a little bushy for unhitching oxen from the wagons but seemed open enough to spot any enemy about. In front rose the coastal escarpment. The slope was not particularly steep, but it was broken up into ridges by many small streams. The track bore to the left and followed one of these ridges to the top. It was narrow most of the way. Once the column closed and started up, it would be confined to it. There were other high ridges on either side.[10]

The first division crossed the Nyezane and began falling out to rest and eat. Some of the mounted men and a company of the 1st Battalion – probably one of the amaQwabi[11] – moved up the road to scout. Captain Hart, the regiment's staff officer, led it. As the track turned and began to ascend the escarpment a half dozen Zulus appeared on the high ridge to the east. The column commander ordered the company to disperse them.

The men advanced to the base of the high ridge. The enemy scouts disappeared. An enemy party then appeared to the right, on a spur of the ridge. Captain Hart was perhaps hasty in going after it. The men crossed a wooded ravine with a marshy bottom, and as they came out onto open ground, they met a hail of bullets from the left. A large body of Zulus was coming down the high ridge towards them. The Zulus were about four hundred yards away. The company was not strong enough, either in guns or spears, to fend them off. Captain Hart ordered a quick retreat. The men ran. All but three escaped. Five of the European leaders were caught by the Zulus in the ravine. The bodies of a lieutenant and a non-commissioned officer were later found covered with spear wounds. The four non- commissioned officers who were killed may not have understood the order to retreat; at least three appear to have been Germans.[12]

The Zulu had set a trap for the column, and the contingent's scouts had sprung it prematurely. As the company retreated, the Zulu left horn rushed through the bush below the higher ridge. It aimed at the wagon park and crossing. The right horn swarmed over the track in front and onto a high ridge to the west.[13] It was the classic Zulu tactic. The first division was about to be caught in a double envelopment.

A knoll marked the near end of the low ridge which the track was following. The column commander placed the leading British infantry and artillery on it. From that central position they could see the Zulu chest and horns and guns could shift their fire against them as required.[14] The position was exposed. All the Zulus seemed to have firearms. They banged away furiously, but they hit very little.[15]

The scouting company which had been engaged and another company which had also been in the advance, formed on either side of the British infantry. The remaining eight companies were with the column closing up behind.[16] The half-company of pioneers was on the knoll, rifles in hand. They were nervous and began to fire wildly. The officer of Royal Engineers who was with them threatened to shoot them if they did not lie down. They did so.[17]

British units arrived, went into line and pushed forward to stop the left horn.[18] The Native Contingent was not expected to fight in the line in the same manner. Those with firearms seemed ready enough to go forward, but most of the men, armed only with spears, were disinclined to.[19] In any case their officers were not there to lead them. They were taken away to form a company-size detachment under Captain Hart, and posted on a rise to the left of the track. The massed fire of their Martini-Henry rifles stopped the Zulu right horn as it advanced down to the ridge to the west.[20]

The second division was arriving on the field. The crisis of the battle passed. The Zulu horns retreated, first the left, then the right. British foot soldiers, supported by Hart's band, drove back the Zulus on the track ahead. The Zulu chest gave way, and the crest of the ridge was carried.[21] The Zulus retreated with a degree of order.[22] Men of the contingent, with a little prodding, joined in the pursuit of the enemy.[23]

The battle at the Nyezane lasted about an hour and a half. In that time the first division of the British column repulsed a Zulu force twice its size.[24] The column's loss amounted to twelve killed and sixteen wounded.[25] Four men, all amaQwabi, and two officers and five non-commissioned officers of the 1st Battalion were among the dead. An officer and a non-commissioned officer were wounded. Eight of the dead fell in the first encounter.[26] The enemy lost heavily in the battle. The column commander conservatively estimated the Zulu dead at more than three hundred. Bodies were found in heaps of seven and eight. In two places ten and thirty-five lay close together.[27]

Only two wounded Zulus were captured. As one was brought in, men of the contingent called loudly to be allowed to kill him. The British, of course, would not have it. Some of the men were detailed to dig a large grave under some trees to the left of the road. The column's fallen were buried in it.[28]

After a halt of about two hours, the march resumed.[29] It was a hard climb. At the top of the ridge the column passed the bodies of several Zulus who had been horribly burnt, probably by rockets fired from the knoll.[30] The track followed another narrow ridge, higher and twisting, with many spurs and thick bush on either side.[31] Camp was made just four miles from the battlefield. There was no further opposition, but it was obvious now that the column was in hostile country. The men burnt all the homesteads along the way. Late the next morning the column marched into deserted Eshowe.[32]

At Eshowe the column would stage the last advance. A small mobile force, co-operating with the other columns of the British army, would move quickly to seize Ulundi. But first supplies and munitions must be accumulated. The buildings of the mission station, although in disrepair, would make suitable store houses. A convoy had left the lower Thukela with supplies on the 22nd. It was reported to have been attacked, and a detachment, including two companies of the 2nd Regiment, went out to escort it on the 24th. Another detachment went with empty wagons back to the Thukela on the 25th. Meanwhile the rest of the men set about fortifying the new depot.[33]

The column commander did not receive information about he Isandlwana disaster until the 27th. He did not receive instructions from the Lieutenant General until the 28th. The situation at Eshowe suddenly changed. Apparently it was assumed that the Zulu army which had defeated the centre column, if it did not follow it up by invading Natal, would turn against the left or right column still in Zululand. The Lieutenant General gave Colonel Pearson complete discretion to secure the right column.[34]

The colonel consulted his officers and decided to hold Eshowe. A forward position would afford the best defence of Natal. Of course, they anticipated a siege. The garrison must be reduced so that supplies of food and ammunition would last. There was no possibility of a flying column against Ulundi now, so the mobile troops could be sent back to the Thukela. They could look after the border there.[35] The column commander and his officers were optimistic. The presumption was the crisis would pass. In due course the Lieutenant General would raise the siege with a fresh force from Natal.

There was no telling when the Zulus would close in on Eshowe. The force defeated at the Nyezane was reported to be assembling to the northwest in

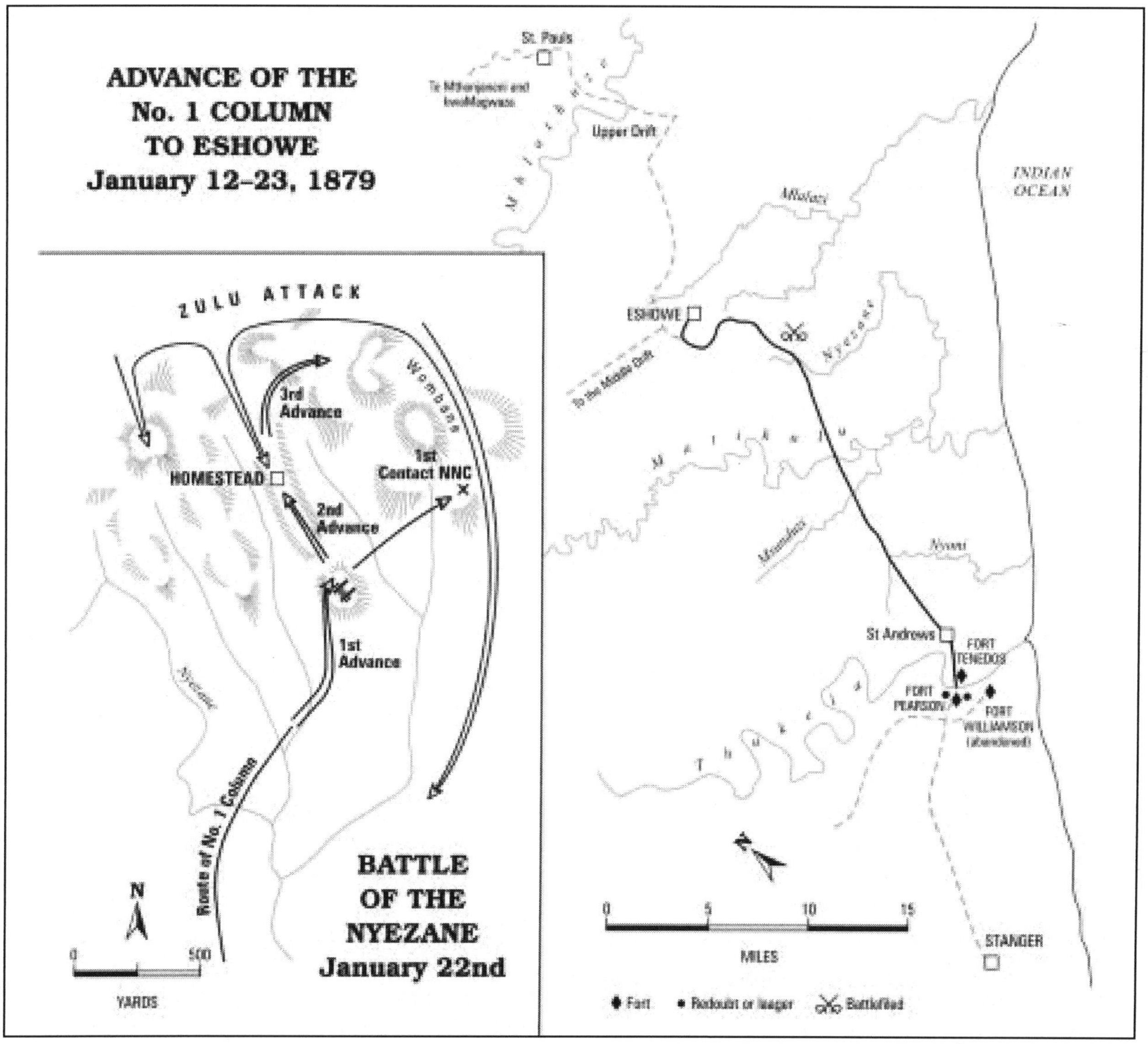

order to oppose a further British advance. Mounted troops had scouted twelve miles to the northwest on the 27th and ten miles to the southeast that morning and found no sign of the enemy. The column commander did not think there was any immediate danger.[36] The detachment taking wagons back to the Thukela had found the road clear, but at Fort Tenedos, on the left bank of the Thukela, the garrison blazed away into the night on the 25th – 26th against a putative Zulu attack. It was advisable that the mobile forces march back to the Thukela at once.[37]

It would appear the men were not informed of the object of the march.[38] Indeed, the column commander told the 2nd Regiment's commander, Major Graves, not to tell anyone where they were going until they reached the Thukela! Graves himself left Eshowe with the impression that they were hastening back to defend Natal and that the Zulus might already be across the border.[39]

Orders were given to break camp. The officers and non-commissioned officers of the 1st Battalion were told to leave their tents standing. Those of the 2nd Battalion were told to strike their tents and to put them and any baggage in the fort. They were told they were going out to meet the convoy. No rations were issued, but ammunition was issued freely, probably as much as a rifleman could carry – something between 100 and 150 rounds.

It was remarked at the time that they might have to fight their way through. Major Graves and Captain Hart expected a fight somewhere along the way. Yet no one seemed to be afraid. Some were told before they left Eshowe that there had been a disaster upcountry. Others heard about it on the road. There were no details. Some men believed they were retreating because the Zulus had got into Natal.

So quickly did the march commence, that Commandant Nettleton, having formed the 2nd Battalion, was talking to the column commander when he learned that it had gone. Graves had become impatient and ordered it to go without him.

The regiment started at about noon, 1st Battalion in the lead. The companies marched for the most part in regular order, but the pace was faster than usual. The descent from the heights was difficult and disorderly. It was asked if anyone knew a short cut. Some did and a knowledgeable captain led the way; but first the 1st Battalion had to backtrack to keep in front. The short cut saved two or three miles. As it emerged on the main track again, the regiment met the head of the convoy. Major Graves, in front, rode at a trot up to it. One of the non-commissioned officers thought he heard him tell the escort detachment to come along down to the Thukela. Someone sang out: 'The Zulus will soon be around Eshowe.' The Major seemed agitated. He passed on the column commander's orders to the convoy commander to hasten with the wagons to the fort.

As the column approached the Nyezane the men picked leaves from a certain shrub and stuck them in their nostrils. The leaves had a pleasant smell which offset the stench of the Zulu corpses on the battlefield.

The day was hot. The short cut had been hard going. A short halt was called when the column met the convoy. Major Graves ordered those who were sick and felt they could not go on to go back to Eshowe with the convoy if they wished.

Major Graves and Captain Hart, the staff officer, had decided before they left the fort that the officers and non-commissioned officers of the regiment should not march with their companies. They should form a unit at the head of the column. They had spoken well of officers and men after the action on the 22nd, and morale was high, but now the defeat upcountry put a different face on things. Graves doubted the loyalty of his men. He and Hart believed that if there were a fight they would abandon the Europeans and look out for themselves. Hart considered them "utterly useless in battle". Therefore the Europeans should band together so they could defend themselves and attack and try to force their way through to the Thukela.

The march had begun before the order to separate could be given. Now, as it resumed, the Major gave the order for officers and non-commissioned officers to go to the head of the column. Black and white were already mixed up together. The Europeans struggled to get through the mass of men. Not all of them succeeded. Some of the men pressed ahead, too, although their officers tried to keep them back. Then, black and white by turns tried to get ahead of each other.

The men did not like this. They were afraid of being left behind. Why were the white men going ahead without them? The officers had led them into Zululand. Now they were leaving them to find their way out as they could. The breakdown of control and order appears to have been greater in the 2nd Battalion than in the 1st. Demoralization set in. Officers seemed unable or unwilling to enforce discipline. Companies ran into each other, the fastest walkers getting to the front. A futile effort was made to organize a vanguard.

Graves was reduced to being a spectator rather than commander of the regiment as it struggled and became a mixed rabble. Officers and non-commissioned officers tended to stick to the track, especially non-commissioned officers, but many fell behind. The men, most of them unencumbered, took to the road sides, marching as they pleased through the long grass and corn fields. The mounted troops from Eshowe passed the mob just north of the Nyezane and vanished in front of it into the Matikulu bush.

Hart was sure they were safe after they crossed the Matikulu, but there was no stopping to regroup. Graves deemed it too risky. The march was carried along by its own momentum and a growing fear, especially with the coming of night, that the Zulu were close by and would attack. Even a small Zulu force could have routed the regiment and massacred officers and men practically at will.

Graves and the main body of the regiment arrived at Fort Tenedos at 2.20 in the morning. Graves estimated they had marched twenty-nine or thirty miles in fourteen hours and twenty minutes. Other units followed in the dark. Graves feared that the soldiers at Fort Tenedos would mistake his men for Zulus and fire on them, but there were no casualties. At daybreak mounted men went out to rescue the stragglers.[40]

The British campaign in Zululand was finished. A Zulu campaign in Natal seemed imminent. The flight from Eshowe reinforced the impression.[41] Rumours spread of misfortunes at home while men were at the front.[42] The men of the regiment wanted to go home to see and, if necessary, to protect their families.[43] They told their officers their work was done.[44] The amaQwabi, old foes of the Zulu, were among the most anxious and left without permission. There was no panic, and the men with firearms turned them in.[45] Their officers did not stop them from going. Some were sympathetic, others happy to be rid of them.[46]

In two days the 1st Battalion was reduced to about 180 men and the 2nd Battalion to about 400.[47] Most of the amaNyuswa remained.[48] Mqawe, the Qadi chief, subsequently berated those of his men who left without permission.[49] Major Graves favoured letting the rest of the contingent go. He wired the Lieutenant General on the morning of the 30th for instructions. The general replied that the men could not go without the Supreme Chief's permission. They were needed to defend the border. Those who left were deserters and liable to punishment.

The matter was referred to the Supreme Chief and sensibly resolved. Next day Graves was instructed to let the men go in batches. He told those who were left they could go. He had to make them understand that they were still required for defence. They were to have a month's pay and to keep their blankets. They seemed delighted, and said that they would turn out to defend the Colony whenever they were called to do so.[50] The Nyuswa contingent in the 2nd Battalion carried home a certificate from Commandant Nettleton stating that their behaviour had been exemplary and he would be glad to command them again.[51] The soldiers had various receptions at home. Some of them were even hailed as victors of a successful campaign.[52]

For the 2nd Regiment, as with the 3rd upcountry, dismissal in fact meant disbandment. The terrain on the coast and the enemy's forbearance had not allowed the 2nd Regiment much scope for scouting and skirmishing, but what it had done was not satisfactory. Failure in this case owed to poor leadership and training, but, unlike the 3rd Regiment, the 2nd Regiment was not ruined by a disastrous battle. The battalions would reform in due course and the men would become much better soldiers.

NOTES

1 NC, October 11, 1879: 'Libel Case. Graves v. *The Natal Colonist*.'

2 *Narrative*, pp. 13, 22, 23, 25, 53. Norbury, *The Naval Brigade*, p. 221. C2260, p. 7.

3 This is surmise. It was on the 22nd, and there is no mention of the battalions having changed division on the march.

4 C2242, p. 41. See also *Letters of Major-General FitzRoy Hart-Synnot*, p. 101.

5 C2260, p. 7. *Narrative*, pp. 22–23. According to NM, January 22, 1929: H. Sparks, 'Chelmsford's Ultimatum to Cetswayo,' the Zulu surrounded the camp of the column in the night, but then retired, apparently to the Nyezane. *Letters of Major-General FitzRoy Hart-Synnot*, p. 101–102.

6 *Narrative*, pp. 13 and 23.

7 C2260, pp. 6 and 7.

8 Norbury, *The Naval Brigade*, pp. 225–226.

9 *Ibid.*, p. 228. *Narrative*, p. 23. C2260, pp. 4, 7, 8. *Letters of Major-General FitzRoy Hart-Synnot*, p. 105. The company and battalion are determined by comparing the casualty returns in *Narrative*, p. 155 and C2260, pp. 12 and 21, also those in SNA 1/1/35, nos. 151 and 174 with the assignment of the Qwabi contingent in CSO 678: 19/1879.

10 *Narrative*, p. 23. C2260, p. 4. *Cf.* the modern map and the one in *Narrative* with the descriptions in *Narrative*, pp. 23–24; Norbury, *The Naval Brigade*, p. 228; and C2260, p. 8.

11 This is conjecture. It seems unlikely that both companies in the van would be of the same chief; and the casualty returns (see n. 9) support this.

12 *Cf. Narrative*, pp. 23–24, and C2260, pp. 4–5. *Letters of Major-General FitzRoy Hart-Synnot*, pp. 104, 105–107. NM, January 29: 'The Battle of Inyezane;' January 30: 'The Battle of Inyezane,' and May 5, 1879: letter from

'Bushranger.' NC, January 30, 1879: 'Colonel Pearson's Engagement.' Norbury, *The Naval Brigade*, p. 233. Emery, *The Red Soldier*, p. 185. H.L. Hall, 'With Assegai and Rifle: Reminiscences of a Transport Conductor in the Zulu War,' *Military Historical Journal*, IV, no. 5 (June 1978), pp. 198–199. See casualty returns in C2260, pp. 5, 12 and 21.

13 *Narrative*, p. 24. C2260, p. 8. Norbury, *The Naval Brigade*, pp. 229–233 *passim*.

14 *Narrative*, p. 24. C2260, pp. 5 and 8.

15 *Narrative*, p. 24. C2260, pp. 8 and 9. Norbury, *The Naval Brigade*, pp. 230–232. NM, January 22, 1929: 'Chelmsford's Ultimatum to Cetewayo.'

16 *Letters of Major-General FitzRoy Hart-Synnot*, p. 108. NC, January 30: 'Colonel Pearson's Engagement;' and October 16, 1879: 'Libel Case. Graves vs *The Natal Colonist*.' *Cf.* Norbury. *The Naval Brigade*, p. 223.

17 C2260, p. 6. Ian Castle and Ian Knight, *Fearful Hard Times: The Siege and Relief of Eshowe 1879* (London, Greenhill, 1994), p. 62.

18 *Narrative*, p. 24. C2260, pp. 6 and 8. NM, May 5, 1879: letter from 'Bushranger'.

19 *Narrative*, p. 24. C2260, p. 6. *Letters of Major-General FitzRoy Hart-Synnot*, p. 108. NC, October 11, 1879: 'Libel Case. Graves vs *The Natal Colonist*.' SNA 1/1/33, no. 65.

20 C2260, p. 5. *Letters of Major-General FitzRoy Hart-Synnot*, p. 109. *Cf.* Norbury, *The Naval Brigade*, p.231.

21 C2260, p. 5. *Narrative*, p. 24. *Letters of Major-General FitzRoy Hart-Synnot*, pp. 109–112. Norbury, *The Naval Brigade*, pp. 231–232. Emery, *The Red Soldier*, p. 186. The crest was called Majia's hill by the British (*Narrative*, pp. 23–24). Presumably it was named after a local chief or head man. After the battle the British were told that it was the site of an earlier battle or battles, and the Zulu called it 'Victory Hill' (Emery, *The Red Soldier*, pp. 185–187). Indeed, the Zulu name of the battlefield is *eWombane* (Carl Faye, *Zulu References for Interpreters and Student[s]* (Pietermaritzburg, City Printing Works, 1923), p. 37, and the spur referred to is also called *Wombane* on the modern map. This is a diminutive of *isiwombe*, meaning battle or encounter, charge or onslaught. The first Zulu king, Shaka, named his first *ibutho*, consisting of older, married men, the *amaWombe* (Bryant, Olden Times, pp. 124 and 642; but *cf.* p. 646).

22 Norbury, *The Naval Brigade*, p. 232.

23 NC, January 30, 1879: 'Colonel Pearson's Engagement.' SNA 1/1/33, no. 65. Castle and Knight, *Fearful Hard Times*, p. 67.

24 C2260, p. 5; but p. 8, and Norbury, *The Naval Brigade*, p. 231, give almost three hours.

25 *Cf.* returns in C2260, p. 21, and *Narrative*, pp. 24, 155.

26 *Narrative*, p. 24. See returns in C2260, p. 21 and SNA 1/1/35, nos. 151 and 174.

27 C2260, p. 5.

28 *Ibid.* Norbury, *The Naval Brigade*, pp. 224, 233–234. NM, January 30, 1879: 'The Battle of Inyezane.' TN, February 5, 1879: 'Action at Eshowe.'

29 C2260, p. 5. *Narrative*, p. 25.

30 Norbury. *The Naval Brigade*, p.235.

31 See *ibid.*, and the maps (see n. 10).

32 *Narrative*, p. 25. C2260, p. 4. Norbury, *The Naval Brigade*, p. 235.

33 *Narrative*, pp. 25 and 53. C2260, pp. 6 and 9. C2367, p. 35. *Letters of Major-General FitzRoy Hart-Synnot*, pp. 114–115.

34 *Narrative*, p. 53. C2260, p. 11. C2367, p. 35.

35 *Narrative*, pp. 25 and 54. SP. C2260, p. 11 C2367, pp. 35–36.

36 C2260, pp. 9 and 22. C2367, p. 35. NC, October 11, 1879: 'Libel Case. Graves vs *The Natal Colonist*.' Norris-Newman, *In Zululand with the British*, pp. 90–91. *Letters of Major-General FitzRoy Hart-Synnot*, pp. 116–117, puts the case for abandoning the post.

37 C2260, p. 11. NC, October 11, 1879: 'Libel Case. Graves vs *The Natal Colonist*.'

38 NC, October 14, 1879: 'Libel Case. Graves vs *The Natal Colonist*.'

39 NC, October 11 and 14, 1879: 'Libel Case. Graves vs *The Natal Colonist*.'

40 *Letters of Major-General FitzRoy Hart-Synnot*, pp. 114, 117–119. NC, October 11, 14, 15: 1879: 'Libel Case. Graves vs *The Natal Colonist*.' NM, October 11 and 14, 1879: 'The Action for Libel against the "Natal Colonist".' Also, see Norris-Newman, *In Zululand with the British*, p. 92, and NC, February 1, 1879: 'The Battle of Inyazane.' During the libel trial Major Graves testified that he was with the men and not ahead of them on the march. He did not think that the march was too severe or the men were out of control. He stated that he did not see Commandant Nettleton in the course of it. Captain Hart testified that the men conducted themselves well, and Sergeant Major Lowrie of the 1st Battalion testified that he heard no complaints about Major Graves; however, of the twenty-two other officers and non-commissioned officers of the regiment who testified, nineteen were in the 2nd (Nettleton's) Battalion and all of them were extremely critical of the major and of the conduct of the march.

41 NC, October 14: 'Libel Case. Graves vs *The Natal Colonist*;' and October 21, 1879: 'A Protest.' NM, February 1, 1879: 'Major Graves' Native Contingent.' Norris-Newman, *In Zululand with the British*, p. 92. SNA 1/1/33, nos. 4 and 65. CSO 1926: 613/1878.

42 SNA 1/1/33, no. 65.

43 *Ibid. Letters of Major-General FitzRoy Hart-Synnot*, p. 119. NC, October 11: leader, and October 14, 1879: 'Libel Case. Graves vs *The Natal Colonist*.' NM, October 11, 1879: 'The Action or Libel against the "Natal Colonist".' NA, February 5, 1879: leader. CSO 1926: 613/1879.

44 NC. October 21, 1879: 'A Protest.'

45 .CSO 1926: 613/1879. NA, January 31, 1879: 'The Native Levies Deserting.' (The same report appears in NM of the same date). NM, February 3. 'The Native Contingent;' and February 8, 1879: 'Zulu War.'

46 CSO 1926: 613/1879. SNA 1/1/33. no. 65. NC, February 1, 1879: 'The Battle of Inyazana.'

47 NC, October 21, 1879: 'A Protest.'

48 SNA 1/1/33, no. 65.

49 NM, Febryary 5, 1870: 'Our Natives at Inyezane.'

50 CSO 1926: 613/1879. C2260, p. 22. NC, February 11, 1879: leader.

51 SNA 1/1/33, no. 4.

52 NM, February 1, 1879: 'Major Graves' Native Congingent.'

Chapter 9

REMODELLING OF THE CONTINGENT

The Supreme Chief wanted to halt the alarm which spread with the news of the defeat at Isandlwana. He composed a message to chiefs, minimizing the significance of the defeat and reassuring them of the government's support. Resident Magistrates delivered and explained it and chiefs received it in good spirit and reassured the government of their loyalty and support.[1]

The Supreme Chief also wanted to know why the 2nd and 3rd Regiments had been disbanded and instructed Resident Magistrates to find out. If it was because they wanted to visit their homes or were seized by a sudden panic, then the magistrates should take steps to send them back. If the cause lay deeper, then the magistrates should exercise discretion, report and await instructions.[2]

The chiefs were consulted. Ndomba, Mganu and Mkhungo accompanied by Sikhota met the Resident Magistrate of the Weenen Division and the Colonial Commandant of Weenen County. Phakade was absent but some of his men were present. The chiefs spoke knowledgeably about what had happened. Mkhungo complained at length about the way in which his men had been organized and drilled and about the officers in whom they had no confidence. The other two chiefs agreed.

All these chiefs promised to resist to the utmost a Zulu invasion of Natal. Plans were made for the eventuality. They professed admiration for the British soldier: 'they are stones, not men.' Either at this time or later the Resident Magistrate received further complaints about organization, officers, drill, discipline, rations and treatment of prisoners.[3]

In the neighbouring Klip River Division, from which a minority of the 3rd Regiment had been drawn, the Resident Magistrate also received complaints about officers and discipline. The Resident Magistrate in Umvoti cited harassing drills and anxiety about families.[4]

The amaNgwane of the 1st Regiment and the mounted troops complained to the Resident Magistrate of the Upper Tugela Division about the way they had been organized and led into action and about officers who could not speak their language. The mounted men also complained that they were paid the same as the men on foot, which was not so.[5]

The Resident Magistrates of the Inanda and Lower Tugela Divisions interviewed chiefs who had supplied men to the 2nd Regiment. The chiefs professed loyalty, also confidence in the government, and expressed readiness to fight again. They complained about the disorganized march back from Eshowe.[6]

Head men told the Resident Magistrate of the Lower Tugela Division they doubted their men could stand up to the enemy. Under the colonial regime they had had to give up warlike practices. Their spears had been taken away. Then they had been armed again to fight the Zulu. The enemy was better trained and well supplied with firearms. Against him their men felt like women. They must have firearms, too. They also complained of the strange officers who did not speak their language.[7]

The Supreme Chief read the reports. They did not agree with what the military professed and many of the European settlers apparently believed, namely that part of the contingent had run away and the rest were useless.[8] First, the four disbanded battalions had not deserted simply because of the defeat at Isandlwana, however demoralizing the defeat had been. In the 3rd Regiment some men had deserted, but the chiefs and headmen and most of the men had stayed and the units had remained intact until they were dismissed by the commandant on January 24th.

Most of the companies of the 2nd Regiment had indeed deserted after the regiment had returned to Natal, but certain officers apparently had condoned, even connived at their desertion. Those who had stayed with the colours were let go by the commandant on the Suprene Chief's orders.

There were other considerations besides. The campaign seemed to be over. The idea of prolonged service under arms was an alien one. Men wanted to return to their homes. There were rites of purification which must follow combat. A Zulu invasion seemed likely. Men wanted to protect their families. It is unlikely that the majority of men who deserted thought of themselves as deserters. They would come back presently, when they were needed.

Whether or not the Native Contingent was 'useless' was a moot question. European settler opinion was divided and settlers did not control the government. Military opinion was what really counted. In the wake of defeat the Lieutenant General opined that the contingent was practically useless for offensive purposes. He meant the battalions of foot soldiers – there was no complaint about the mounted troops and pioneers.[9]

The military's primary concern at this stage was defence of the Colony against a Zulu inroad and organization of able-bodied men to meet it. The contingent had potential in this respect. The disbanded units should be called back into service. The Lieutenant General would see if the chiefs indeed were ready to serve again. They would be reinforced by other units from chiefdoms in the interior.[10]

At this point the Supreme Chief interposed. He had been sceptical of the Native Contingent before the war. With the accumulated complaints to hand he argued vigorously against any extension of the so-called 'regimental' system. For a month the Supreme Chief and the Lieutenant General exchanged memoranda on the question. It became a question of who would control the Colony's military manpower. The Lieutenant General accused the Supreme Chief of obstructing his preparations for defence. The Supreme Chief denied it. The dispute was marked by personal rancour.

The Supreme Chief's case against the 'regimental' Native Contingent was a strong one. It was a breach with tradition. Chiefs raised levies from among their people. Size of a unit depended on local circumstances. Men were armed with shields, spears and sticks. Chiefs and head men led them, and they fought in the traditional (or 'tribal') manner. The military authorities had tried to change all this, introducing European companies and officers, drill and discipline. No one understood why. No one liked the new system. What was the point of the drill? It was an impediment to combat. Let there be no more of it. When called out again, the levies would muster in their traditional way. They would be under control of the colonial commandant in their district. A few European settlers would superintend them. Otherwise they would be led by their chiefs and head men.

The Supreme Chief also objected to the way in which the military had displaced his authority. The Lieutenant General had styled himself Supreme Military Chief. The chiefs did not understand how loyalty could be divided, and the division seemed to weaken the Supreme Chief's authority.

The Supreme Chief objected to the military's appointment of unfit officers and especially non-commissioned officers. He had not expected that. Many were strangers. They did not know the local customs and dialect. Sometimes they abused the men verbally and physically. The Supreme Chief did not give specific instances of abuse. He could not, for the Resident Magistrates had not; however, their impression was the dissatisfaction with the strangers was widespread. Press remarks tended to support this view. The Supreme Chief passed on a copy of the report of the Resident Magistrate of the Weenen Division. It substantiated his own charges and added details about rations and prisoners.

There was one matter which the Supreme Chief skirted – use of firearms. He conceded that one for every ten men was not enough, but he doubted that men with firearms would fight any better than those with spears. More firearms would give men confidence against Zulus similarly armed, but not make them proficient in their use. It is hardly to be wondered that he did not elaborate. European technology posited European tactics. General use of firearms would knock his argument on its head.

The Lieutenant General was discredited by defeat, but his argument had force. Also, the High Commissioner who was intercessor between him and the Supreme Chief and who had had a hand in earlier arrangements, tended to support him. Tribal and regimental need not be incompatible in his view. He reflected on the experience of European and Indian armies, and stated that it was not so much a question of this and that organization as one of discipline and lack of it, raw levies and trained soldiers. The Lieutenant General pointed out that he had tried to maintain tribal units by allowing companies of uneven strength. He maintained that there was not enough evidence to discredit the regimental organization. He denied that he had ever intended to displace the Supreme Chief. He had used the term Supreme Military Chief only to distinguish exclusive command over the contingent. What else could he do? He stood upon the principle of undivided command in the field.

The Lieutenant General accused the Natal government of foot-dragging when it had come to raising the regiments of the contingent. He had been forced to get officers and non-commissioned officers from the Cape Colony because not enough were forthcoming in Natal. He insisted that there were at least some officers and non-commissioned officers in every company who could make themselves understood. He regretted not having got the government's approval, but defended the provision of non-commissioned officers as a bolstering of the European influence. He saw the need for company interpreters, but he did not think that officers who could not speak the language were necessarily useless. He mentioned that in the left column, on the Transvaal-Zulu border, some officers who did speak the language had been dismissed as useless, while some British officers who did not speak it turned out to be successful with the men.

As for the complaints catalogued by the Resident Magistrate of Weenen, he conceded a 'substructure of truth', but pointed out that Mkhungo, who had made many of them, had not been with the column, and Sikhota, who had been with it, had told the commandant of the 3rd Regiment the day after Isandlwana that he was perfectly willing to serve again with his men. Discipline and morale had been good until the 22nd. There had not been any serious cause for dissatisfaction before Isandlwana.[11]

The controversy lasted five weeks. The Supreme Chief wrote five memoranda, the Lieutenant General four, before they exhausted the subject early in March. The High Commissioner forwarded and commented on the correspondence. He was relieved when the two finally agreed to meet and talk on the 11th.[12] The Natal Native Contingent was remodelled as a result of their compromise.

In mid-February the Lieutenant General called the 2nd Regiment back into service. For the time being it could back up the Native Border Guard along the lower Thukela.[13]

He also called back the 3rd Regiment, but not as part of the contingent. Probably bearing in mind the complaints of Mkhungo and the others, he was willing to see it translated to the Native Border Guard. The Native Border Guard was organized on 'tribal' lines and divided into districts under colonial commandants. It was purely defensive. The Lieutenant General had made the colonial commandants subject to imperial officers in the districts on the Zulu border, but the imperial officers did not interfere with the organization.[14]

The response of chiefs was dilatory and of the people unenthusiastic, especially among the amaChunu, who were very bitter about the way they had been handled before. Also, many had not been paid for their service earlier, and the hut tax was coming due. It was April before the 'Weenen Contingent' or 'Weenen Corps' of the Border Guard actually took shape. It consisted of Bhele, Chunu and Thembu levies. Mkhungo's isiGqoza were left to defend Weenen. In any case they looked down upon and might not co-operate with the others.

In addition to their traditional weapons a quarter of the corps was armed by the government with Enfield muskets. Possibly it was the prospect of the firearms which changed the minds of the amaChunu. Spirits rose at the muster. Belatedly they even asked to be led across the border again to fight the Zulu. The Weenen Contingent marched on the 8th and 9th and assembled at Sand Spruit in the second week of April, but it was not to sally into Zululand. It was not even placed near the border. It remained in reserve near the Msinga magistracy until the end of the war.[15]

It was the same with additional forces required to defend the border elsewhere. They were not assigned to the Native Contingent but to the Native Border Guard. Large drafts of men from southern Natal were brought up and formed reserves in the other colonial defensive districts.[16]

This arrangement did not apply to mounted troops. These the British valued highly and wanted more of.[17] The Supreme Chief had to yield. The Lieutenant General wanted to send the Ngwane mounted men to reinforce the column on the Transvaal-Zulu border. 'They behaved very well indeed in the fight at Insalwana' [*sic*], he wrote to the column commander. 'They are willing, plucky fellows … .'

At the end of February Zikhali's Horse was ordered by the military to reassemble at Helpmekaar. The Resident Magistrate referred the matter to the Supreme Chief. He assumed that both horse and foot should muster. The amaNgwane were not keen to return to service. They did not want to be employed in a non-traditional manner. Many of the horsemen had lost horses and accoutrements in the battle and retreat. Those who had caught other men's horses in the retreat and kept them had had to give them up. Sixteen head men and thirty-eight men claimed to have lost fifty-four horses and thirty-three saddles. General Orders provided that £15 be paid to a head man for loss of a horse, £10 to a man, and £3 for loss of a saddle. Of course, once paid a man must find and buy a new mount and accoutrements. About forty men were not paid promptly. The musters proved disappointing. March passed without anyone going to the front. The notion of employing the men on foot languished.

Ncwadi insisted on the horsemen having a European leader in whom they had confidence and who spoke their language. Theophilus Shepstone, junior, son of the respected former Secretary for Native Affairs – 'Somtseu' (the mighty hunter) – was proposed. Now there would be no difficulty, Ncwadi said. Young Shepstone was sent for. He talked with the principal men of the amaNgwane on April 14th. All the men with horses – about eighty – agreed to go. He promised to try to get horses from the military for those still without. Otherwise they would have to wait until paid, then buy horses and follow. So anxious were some of them to go that they bought horses with their own money and at a personal loss. It would appear that Ncwadi himself joined them. 'Shepstone's Horse' rode out during the first week of May to join the new British column forming near Dundee.[18]

The Edendale Horse had lost two men killed and one man wounded in action. One of the dead men left a widow and seven children, the other a widow and six children as well the dependent family of a deceased brother. The wounded man had been shot through a leg, and was taken home to recover. These circumstances did not demoralize the unit. Nor did the difficulty several men had obtaining adequate compensation for horses they had lost depress spirits. The men who brought home the wounded man said that the Zulus had beaten them only because of numbers, not because of fighting ability.[19]

Thirteen men volunteered to join the unit. Six wanted horses and saddles. Apparently there was no problem supplying them. The men did not, however, join the Edendale troop. They were enrolled by young Shepstone in his troop.[20]

Some of the Edendale people had settled upcounty on the farm Driefontein, in the Klip River Division. Their leader, Johannes Kumalo, raised twenty-four mounted men for duty. Instead of joining the Edendale troop directly, the Driefontein 'section' was attached to a group of settlers called Carbutt's Border Rangers and required to patrol the farms near Ladysmith. Carbutt was a social misfit and his Border Rangers was one of the least savoury settler units. Some of the Rangers treated the Driefontein men roughly. The men's pay did not cover their rations and clothing. They wanted to go to the front. They complained to the Resident Magistrate in vain. They complained to their missionary, and so the government was led to inquire into the matter. Captain Carbutt replied that the Driefontein men were having troubles making ends meet. He denied there was any physical abuse. The Resident Magistrate insisted on their paying their taxes on time, which suggests a reason for their being detained close to home.[21]

Young Shepstone asked to have the Driefontein section. He claimed they wanted to join him. F. Johannes, who was evidently their leader in the field, and also Carbutt, claimed they did not. None the less the Driefontein section joined Shepstone's Horse early in April.[22]

The earlier discontent and the arbitrary assignment may have disillusioned the Driefontein settlers. The Resident Magistrate called on Kumalo to supply six men as wagon drivers for the military. Kumalo replied that Driefontein had no more men. The Resident Magistrate considered the reply disrespectful and imprisoned Kumalo for it, otherwise it might influence the responses of local chiefs also called upon for drivers.[23]

Two other mounted troops were assigned to Shepstone's Horse. They were the 'Amangwane Corps', thirty seven men under their chief Putsha and head man Mfinuyana, and the 'Amabomvu Corps', seventy men under their chief Siphandla and head man Mtengutana. Both had been called into colonial service and had been stationed near Pietermaritzburg, as a reserve to the Native Border Guard. They were transferred to the military late in April .[24]

The chief Hemuhemu of the amaFunzi, in the Umgeni Division, was directed to furnish men in the last week of February. He called out able-bodied men readily enough, but he wanted foot and horse to stay together. The government would not permit the combination. The horsemen mustered at Pietermaritzburg. At first they were to be called the 'Umlaas Corps' after the place where they lived, but then were named the 'Mafunzi Corps'. They were well mounted, and some had very good horses, but their only weapons were spears.

The Mafunzi Corps set out on March 4th with five days' rations, for the lower Thukela. Hemuhemu's brother Nginisa and two head men, Mnxendo and Zwelonke, were in command. There were eighty-eight in all. A special messenger showed them the way to the coast. They passed Noodsberg and Thring's Post in rainy, windy weather, and reached Stanger, the army's forward base, on the 10th. There they were to receive firearms, blankets and cooking pots. Only fifty Snider carbines were immediately available. Six men who had not been able to get saddles and expected to be issued them were disappointed. They moved to the Zinkwazi next day, thence to the Nonoti, where the 2nd Regiment was now reassembling.[25]

The infantry of the contingent was reformed. The military authorities did take the complaints of the Supreme Chief seriously. The regiments were abolished and the battalion became the highest unit.

The company organization remained. There were five battalions, the three of Durnford's old First Regiment, numbered as before, and the two of the Second Regiment, now numbered four and five.[26] Montgomery remained in command of the 1st Battalion, Bengough of the 2nd, Cherry of the 3rd.[27]

Major Graves was very unpopular with the officers and non-commissioned officers of the 2nd Battalion of the 2nd Regiment. In their eyes he had behaved badly on the march from Eshowe to Thukela. Afterwards a drunken sergeant had insulted him on parade by calling him a coward. Officers got up a petition demanding that the battalion be removed from his command. The Lieutenant General was obliged to take cognizance of it, and the regiment was separated into two independent battalions. Graves was spared further embarrassment. The government conveniently requested his return to the position of Protector of Immigrants. The general was assured that he was needed. It was quiet at the front and the 2nd Regiment existed only on paper, and the transfer was made discreetly. Captain Barton, Durnford's staff officer, was given command of Graves' old battalion, now the 4th Battalion. Nettleton remained commandant of the old 2nd, now the 5th Battalion.[28]

There was much criticism of the officers and non-commissioned officers, particularly of those in the 2nd and 3rd Regiments who had come from the Cape Colony and were ignorant of Natal. Most of the non-commissioned officers were now removed by letting them join a mercenary unit called the Natal Horse.[29] The military also ordered that at least one officer in every company must speak Zulu and that those who could speak Zulu be distributed equally among the companies. In the case of the 4th Battalion a head man was authorized as interpreter to the commanding officer at £5 a month, along with horse, equipment and clothing.[30] The net effect was to increase the importance and enhance the status of the head men and other men of social standing. They were the new non-commissioned officers, in fact if not in name.

Thus far did the military yield to criticism. It did not relent on drill and discipline. Its adamancy made better sense as firearms and uniforms were issued to the foot soldiers. The 4th Battalion was issued Martini-Henrys. The 5th Battalion apparently received Martini-Henrys and Sniders. The 3rd Battalion was issued Sniders and muzzle-loaders, probably Enfields. The 2nd Battalion was issued 200 Sniders and 300 Martini-Henrys, and evidently kept the Enfields issued earlier as well.[31] It is not clear what was issued to the 1st Battalion.

Red tunics and trousers were also issued to the 4th and 5th Battalions, but many discarded the trousers. The 2nd Battalion was issued red tunics at least.[32] It is not clear whether or not the 1st and 3rd Battalions received these basic uniforms, but there is no reason to suppose that they were not fitted out the same as the others.

The results were good. Morale and discipline improved.[33] The Natal Native Contingent could be expected in due course to perform efficiently as light infantry, scouting and skirmishing, as originally intended. It was Europeanized only to a degree that gave confidence to officers and men. Men no longer need measure themselves against the Zulu and feel inferior. They would show their mettle in the next campaign.

NOTES

1 SNA 1/1/33, nos. 53 and 63. 1/BGV, IV: 290, 296–297. 1/VLM, 3/2/1: Circular, January 25, 1879.

2 SNA 1/1/133, nos. 50 and 65; 1/6/11, nos. 57 and 69. C2318, p. 11.

3 SNA 1/1/33, no. 51. GH1421: 1053/1879. C2318, pp. 10–13. TN, February 5, 1879: 'The Native Contingent.' NM, February 7, 1879: 'Pakadi and the Weenen Tribes.'

4 SNA 1/1/33, no. 50. 1/GTN, 3/2/1: G 91/1879. C2318, pp. 11–12.

5 CSO 1926; 953/1879. 1/BGV, IV: 304.

6 SNA 1/1/33, nos. 4 and 65. CSO 1926: 613/1879. NM, January 18, 1879: leader.

7 SNA 1/1/33, no. 65. NM, February 5: 'Our Natives at Inyezane;' and March 11, 1879: leader.

8 *Cf.* NM, March 11, 1879: leader, and NA, February 5, 1879: leader. TN, March 17, 1879: 'Notes from the Border.' See also suggestions in TN, February 14, 1879: 'A Suggestion;' and NW, February 18, 1879: 'Native Levies.'

9 For the military's pessimistic outlook see French, *Lord Chelmsford and the Zulu War*, p. 120. C2260, p. 108. 1/PMB Add. 3/3/3/1: 849/1879. WC II/2/2: Chelmsford to Wood, February 3, 1879.

10 *Narrative*, p. 61. WCII/2/2: Chelmsford to Wood, February 19, 1879.

11 See the extensive memoranda, including drafts and comments in GH 1421-1423: 1053/1879. C2318, pp. 4–10, 14–19 *passim*. CSO 1926: 953/1879. French, *Lord Chelmsford and the Zulu War*, p. 162.

12 GH 1421, p. 127.

13 *Lord Chelmsford's Zululand Campaign*, p. 112. 1/VLM, 3/2/1: NA 242 and NA 330/1879.

14 GH 1423: 1222/1879. CSO 688: 1062/1878. See Laband and Thompson, *The Buffalo Border*, pp. 34–35; *Kingdom and Colony at War*, pp. 167–168; and *War Comes to Umvoti*, pp. 28–32.

15 SNA 1/1/33, no. 99; 1/6/12, nos. 77 and 88; 1/6/14, nos. 17 and 40; 1/7/12, p. 92. GH1424: 1716/1879. NC, March 27 and April 14, 1879: reports from Estcourt. TN, July 4: leader; and July 8, 1879: 'The Native Contingents.' Laband and Thompson, *The Buffalo Border*, pp. 57–59.

16 *Narrative*, p. 61. Laband and Thompson, *Kingdom and Colony at War*, pp. 168 and 170; *War Comes to Umvoti*, pp. 41–44.

17 C2316, p. 82.

18 1/BGV, IV: 301–303, 306, 321–322, 326–327, 336–337, 342–345, 357–358. SNA 1/6/12, nos. 38 and 74; 1/6/15, no. 16. SNA 1/1/35, no. 149. CSO 1926: 953/1879. TN, May 14, 1879: 'Notes by the Way.' *Lord Chelmsford's Zululand Campaign*, p. 84.

19 TN, February 7, 1870: Rev. J. Allsopp, 'The Edendale Horse.' PMB/1, 3/3/2/1: 1691/1879.

20 SNA 1/6/12, no. 20. NW, July 16, 1879: 'Natal Native Horse.'

21 SNA 1/1/34, no. 43; 1/6/13, no. 46; 1/7/12, p. 101. Ian Castle, 'Thomas Munro Carbutt: A Yorkshireman in Africa,' in *Soldiers of the Queen*, no. 69 (June 1992), pp. 9–11.

22 SNA 1/6/13, no. 46. CSO 695: 1705/1879.

23 SNA 1/1/34, no. 43; 1/7/12, pp. 101–102, 117. The case is described in Meintjes, Edendale 1850–1906, pp. 378–380.

24 See the rolls and comments in SNA 1/6/14, no. 49, and 1/6/15, no. 84.

25 SNA 1/1/33, no. 80. GH1423, pp. 136–138. CSO 692: 1475/1879; and 698: 2079/1879. Stainbank Diary, March 9, 1879. NM, March 13, 1879: 'With the Durban Mounted Rifles.'

26 NM, March 20, 1879: GO59 also describes the five as constituting a single regiment. Stainbank Diary states they moved off with the 1st Battalion to the Zinkwazi on the 10th.

27 NM, March 20, 1870: GO59.

28 NC, March 4: GO – (report), March 18: 'Explanations Wanted;' March 22: leader; April 24: 'Major Graves' Case;' October 11, 14, 16: 'Libel Case: Graves vs *The Natal Colonist*;' October 21, 1879: 'A Protest. NM, October 11 and 14, 1879: 'The Action for Libel Against the "Natal Colonist".' TN, February 26, 1879: GO43. CSO 691: 1387/1879.

29 The German-speakers in the 2nd Regiment were sent to a mercenary unit in the Transvaal. A number of officers also were reassigned to the Natal Horse and to mercenary units being raised in the Cape Colony. See WCII/2/2: Chelmsford to Wood, February 19, 1870; 1/VLM, 3/2/1: 1224/1879; and *Lord Chelmsford's Zululand Campaign*, p. 107. *Narrative* states (p. 169) that the three troops of Natal Horse, organized in February, were drawn from the officers and non-commissioned officers of the 3rd Regiment; however, the total is more than the number of officers and noncommissioned officers in the regiment. The redistribution of officers and non-commissioned officers in February and March remains unclear; bits and pieces of information are to be found in reports in NM, May 16 and June 9: TN, March 12: GO53, and April 25: GO90; and NC, April 3, 1879: GO73.

30 1/VLM, 3/2/1: 1224/1879. TN, March 29, 1879: GO68, NC, February 25, 1879: 'The Officers of the Native Contingent.' NM, February 26: 'Nettleton's Contingent;' and March 15, 1879: 'The Lower Tugela.'

31 *Narrative*, p. 170. *Cf.* Norris-Newman, *In Zululand with the British*, p. 132; Norbury, *The Naval Brigade*, p. 287; and NM, March 15, 1870: 'With the Isipingo Mounted Rifles.' Also *cf.* Bengough, *Memories of a Soldier's Life*, p. 127; CP 8–19: Bengough to [Crealock]. January 24, 1879; and Montague, *Campaigning in South Africa*, p. 203. Montague also indicates (p. 157) that some still had only traditional weapons.

32 *Cf.* Norbury, *The Naval Brigade*, p. 287, and NM, May 27, 1879: 'Latest from the Lower Tugela.' Montague, *Campaigning in South Africa*, p. 213. NW, June 12, 1879: 'Natal Native Contingent.'

33 GH 500, p. 216. C2482, p. 28. Norbury, *The Naval Brigade*, p. 287. Norris-Newman, *In Zululand with the British*, p. 132. NM, March 15, 1879: 'With the Isipingo Mounted Rifles.' NW, June 24, 1879: 'The Advance on Undini.'

Chapter 10

THE RELIEF OF ESHOWE

Gingindlovu

In March the fortunes of war turned in favour of the British. The Zulu army had not invaded Natal. British forces remained on the defensive until reinforcements arrived from abroad. The first of these were sent to the lower Thukela, where the Lieutenant General was forming a column to break the Zulu siege of Eshowe. The relief of Eshowe and the demonstrations related to it marked the recovery of the initiative by the British. The Natal Native Contingent participated in all these operations. Units of it were engaged in the battles of Gingindlovu and Khambula. They played a major role in the demonstrations.

In looking at these operations we shall focus first on the most important one – the relief of Eshowe. Two battalions of infantry, two troops of mounted men, and one company of pioneers were involved in the rescue and evacuation of the beleaguered garrison.

The orders came for the 2nd Regiment to reassemble on February 15th. Chiefs were told their men must return to duty.[1] The only recorded protest was from Isandwana, a head man of the amaQwabi in the Inanda Division, who said his people did not want to be led by Germans they did not understand. Since the Germans had been transferred from the contingent there was no problem.[2] The non-commissioned officers were kept separate and eventually reassigned to the Natal Horse. At the end of the week the first men began to assemble. Within another week large numbers of men arrived at the lower Thukela.[3]

A new camp was set up for them between the river and Thring's Post. The men were issued rifles. In the 1st Battalion, there was target practice daily at ranges from 100 to 300 yards. The commandant of the 2nd Battalion tried to organize a company of marksmen, whether as instructors or as sharpshooters is not known, but apparently without success. Drill in the European manner resumed. The turns and march past of the 1st Battalion received favourable comment.[4]

The regiment moved to the Zinkwazi, nearer the lower Thukela forts,[5] on March 10th. On the 16th the 2nd Regiment was formally dissolved. There were now two independent battalions, renumbered the 4th, under Captain Barton, 7th Foot, and the 5th, under Commandant Nettleton.[6]

The battalions were also somewhat altered in composition. The 4th Battalion was drawn wholly from the Lower Tugela Division. All but 250 men of the 5th Battalion came from the Inanda Division. At full strength at the end of March the 4th Battalion numbered 780 men, the 5th 1160. The total of the two battalions was only about eighty less than in the old regiment. The discrepancy between the two seems to have been due to the amaNyuswa's being concentrated in the 5th Battalion, whereas previously they had been divided about equally between the 1st and 2nd Battalions. It also appears that some smaller chiefdoms which had furnished men to the battalions earlier did not do so while others which had not did do so now.[7]

Also at the lower Thukela were two mounted squadrons, the Mafunzi Corps, under Captain Maclean, son of a former governor and a former company commander in the 2nd Regiment, and Jantze's Horse, under Captain Hay, former senior company commander of the 1st Battalion of the 1st Regiment.

The troops now had Martini-Henrys. Their uniform consisted of tan cord suit, half boots, leggings and felt hat with the red puggaree. That they would actually wear all that was doubtful. Also, fresh from the interior they had not yet acclimatized to the coastal plain, and their health suffered. Almost fifty men (or horses) – about a quarter of their strength – were not able to join the expedition being organized to relieve Eshowe.[8]

Another troop of Jantze's Horse had been recruited early in March. A British newspaper reporter had seen it on its way to the front, under Jantze's eldest son, and remarked that the men looked very serviceable indeed, well mounted and fairly equipped. The two troops formed a squadron under Captain Hay. They had been about to take part at Kranskop in a demonstration to distract the enemy from the relief of Eshowe when they had been ordered to the coast to join the relief expedition itself on March 24th.[9] Jantze himself led his men. As a young man he had been impetuous; now he was flamboyant. He carried a sword and conducted himself, said one European observer, like a brave captain of old. His men were drilled and disciplined, and most of them were good shots.[10]

The 4th and 5th Battalions and the mounted troops made up part of the column which the Lieutenant General was forming to relieve the besieged garrison of Eshowe which was expected to run out of food early in April. The garrison comprised most of the No. 1 Column – British infantry, some artillery and auxiliary troops, including No. 2 Pioneer Company.

British regiments from overseas began arriving in Natal in mid-March, and were ordered to join the forces at the lower Thukela.[11] By the end of March the Lieutenant General had at least 5670 men for combat. Of these some 2130 belonged to the Native Contingent. Infantry and artillery were divided into two brigades. The 4th Battalion was in the 1st Brigade, the 5th Battalion in the 2nd. Jantze's Horse and the Mafunzi Corps were part of the separate mounted force, under Major Barrow, 19th Hussars, which also included mounted British infantry and colonials and Natal Horse, which consisted of former non-commissioned officers of the 2nd Regiment. The mounted force numbered only 280 men. The smallness of their number meant they would be greatly exercised in scouting. Fortunately, this task was made easier by the attachment of 150 foot scouts, refugees from Zululand.[12]

The mounted troops opened the way into the Zulu country. They crossed the Thukela on March 15th and went about two and a half miles to St. Andrew's mission station.[13] It rained heavily on March 27th and 28th, when the relief column assembled near Fort Tenedos, on the Zulu side of the Thukela. At six on the morning of Saturday the 29th, the advance began. Jantze's Horse accompanied the 1st Brigade, the Mafunzi Corps the 2nd Brigade. The 4th and 5th Battalions escorted the 122 wagons and carts moving between the two brigades. The column did not follow the route of the old No. 1 Column. It took a course to avoid the thick bush. The weather cleared, but the ground was still soft, and the column made about ten miles and halted at the Nyoni river.[14]

The Lieutenant General was anxious that the wagons should be kept up, for he expected a fight. The column therefore camped at mid-day, the oxen were turned out to feed and the camp was secured in a laager. The experience of being caught and overwhelmed in the open at Isandlwana was a great lesson to the British. Never again would they be caught out. At the end of each day's march, the column formed a laager. Each time it experimented with the method and the size in order to perfect the defence. The laager was made by the wagons being drawn up to form a square-shaped enclosure. A shelter trench was dug around it at a distance of about twenty yards and the dug-up earth formed an inner rampart. The men bivouacked between the trench and the wagons. In this instance the 5th Battalion's camp was outside the trench. Of course, if attacked, it would come inside.

The mounted troops provided a cordon of vedettes around the camp, some four to five miles out. The 4th and 5th Battalions provided an inner cordon of pickets one and a half miles out. There were British infantry sentries at half a mile, to which men of the battalions were also added. At dusk the oxen were driven into the laager and the outposts were drawn back. Then all was confusion inside, a jumble of oxen, horses and mules kicking, carts and men. It began to rain. There were no tents, because the column was travelling light.[15]

Sunday the 30th, the column advanced nine miles. Jantze's Horse formed a screen of vedettes on both sides of the road as the column moved up. That afternoon the column laagered on the right bank of the Matikulu. The river ran high and the ford was difficult. Information was received from the lower Thukela that the Zulus were moving in force towards the column. Monday was passed in crossing the Matikulu under guard. A laager was made a mile and a half beyond the river. The distance covered that day was just three miles.[16]

While the column struggled at the Matikulu ford, the mounted men reconnoitred to the north and west. Jantze's men, again with the advance, scouted towards the Matikulu bush during the morning. They saw six to ten mounted Zulus, later on about a dozen, but the enemy avoided contact. Signal fires were observed in different directions. The most notable were three miles from Eshowe. Another part of the mounted force went ahead twelve miles to the Ngoye forest, on the upland east of Eshowe, and burnt the homesteads of one of the Zulu King's brothers. Jantze's men also burnt several large homesteads.[17]

The next day, the 1st of April, the column turned in the direction of Eshowe and the Nyezane battlefield. The 2nd Brigade took the lead. There was some bush about, but the country generally was still open; however, the grass was tall and the ground undulated so that an enemy might approach using it for cover. There were several halts so the wagons could close up. The mounted troops got so far ahead that twice the infantry had to make sweeps to see the way for the wagons was clear. The column moved

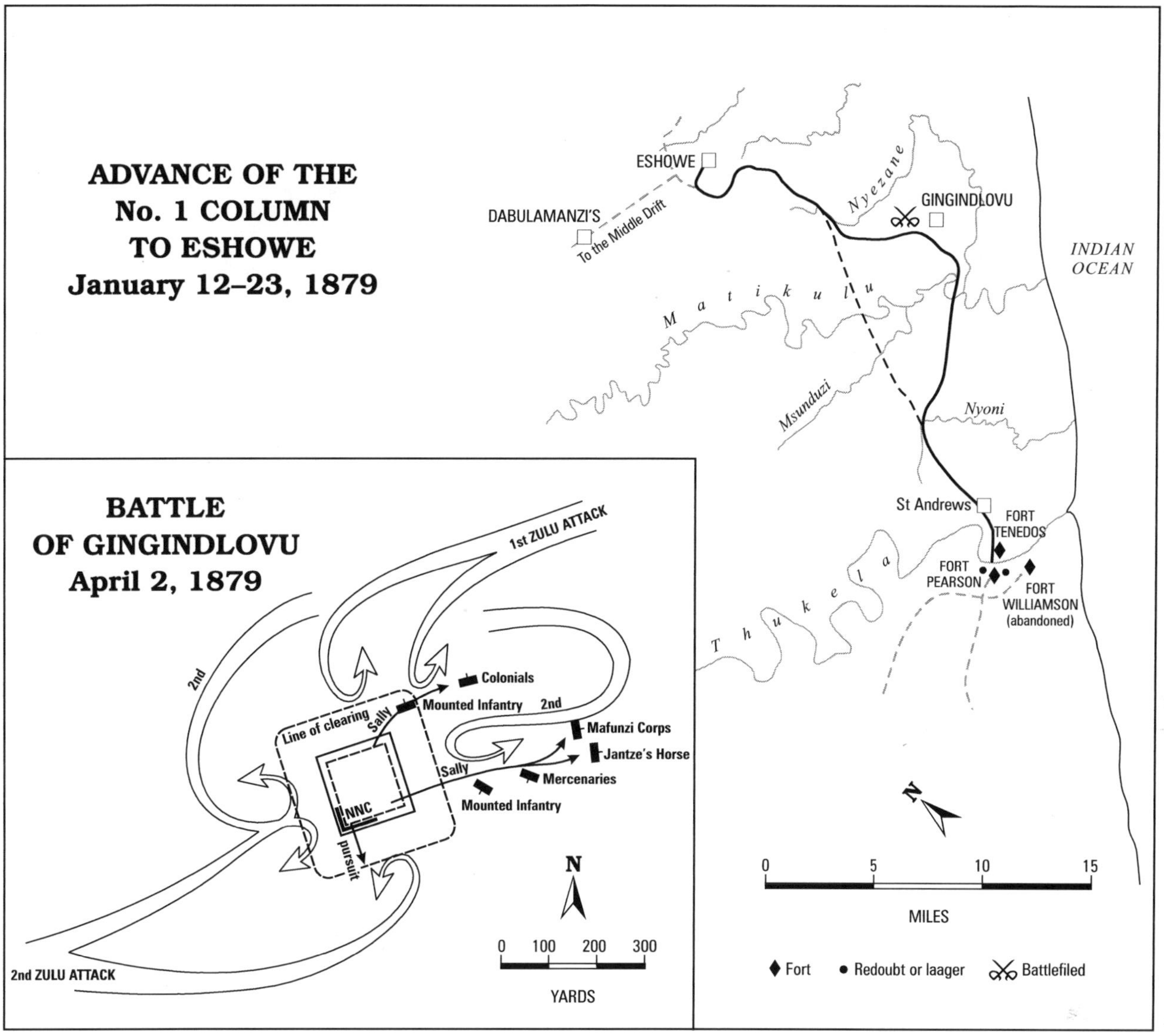

six miles and formed a laager early in the afternoon. The laager was 130 yards a side, on a small hill overlooking the Nyezane, a mile distant. It was near by the site of one of the Zulu great places, called Gingindlovu. Eshowe could be seen in the far distance. Communication was opened with the garrison by means of flashing signals.[18]

During the march Jantze's Horse scouted through the Matikulu bush and skirted the Nyezane battlefield. It found traces of many Zulus and saw a sizeable body of them on the heights east of Eshowe. Yet there was no sign of a large army. Indeed, Jantze thought that the traces might have been left as a deception. His men burnt a few homesteads and rejoined the column.[19]

There was a thunderstorm in the afternoon, but when darkness fell numerous fires could be seen on the hills to the north. These suggested the enemy was near by and in strength. There was a false alarm at quarter to eight. Then the rain came down again and lasted most of the night. The men worked to finish the laager, churning the ground to mud, difficult to move in and unpleasant to smell. Some puff-adders were killed in the commotion.[20]

The rain stopped before morning, but the column was mired in. There would be no march this day. Even so, the column was awake early. The men stood to arms at four. Preparations were made to turn out the cattle to graze. A heavy mist lay upon the ground. At five Jantze's and Mafunzi squadrons, along with the foot scouts, went out on patrol.

Just before six some of Jantze's men reported Zulus crossing the Nyezane. Pickets sent in similar reports. Several shots were fired. The sun appeared and the mist cleared. The Zulus were in force on the hills and they were moving towards the laager. The battle which everyone anticipated began as the sun rose.[21]

It was intended that the 4th and 5th Battalions should go out to bait the enemy, but obviously that was not necessary. The Zulu came on at great speed. They were not wearing their full war dress, only their loin skins. They carried spears, small shields and rifles. In units of approximately company size they ran through the bush in the river valley. They took advantage of folds in the ground and the tall grass to conceal themselves. They were enveloping the laager. The left horn had crossed the river, and was approaching the north and east sides in two columns. The right horn was apparently advancing against the west side from out of the Matikulu bush. The scouts and pickets fell back before them.

There was little to do in the laager but issue last minute commands and open ammunition boxes, which were placed behind the soldiers manning the trench. The Zulu columns broke into skirmishing order and came on in magnificent style. A Gatling gun at the northeast corner of the laager tested the range on some of them at eight hundred yards. The Zulus started to fire, and when they got between three and four hundred yards of the laager firing became general on both sides. The enemy stopped at the edge of the tall grass and bushes. They were now at the edge of the field which had been cleared for fire 100 yards all round the laager.

The left horn charged against the north-eastern corner and adjacent faces. The Zulus crashed through the kettles and pots still on the camp fires outside the trench. Above the roar of the British volleys their shouts could be heard. Rifle fire from the rampart mowed them down before they got near the trench.

The 4th and 5th Battalions and the mounted troops had been drawn up in reserve inside the rear of the laager, the mounted men near the south-eastern corner and the battalions behind the southwestern face. Behind them on the wagons were the noncombatants who had guns. The men in the two battalions squatted, their rifles perpendicular to the ground. They were told to keep the muzzles pointing to the sky and ordered not to fire.

The Zulu right horn burst from cover in front of the west face of the laager and made a furious attack against the south face. Men in the battalions began to dip their rifles and shoot, even though there was no way their shots could hit the enemy. Their officers cursed and kicked them to make them stop it – otherwise they would shoot their comrades.

Some of the mounted troops made a sortie against the left horn in front. As the right horn attacked, the rest of the mounted troops were ordered to harass its flank. Jantze's Horse, the Mafunzi Corps, and the troops of mounted infantry and Natal Horse cleared the trench on the east face, where firing had abated, and turned on the right horn's flank. Jantze's and the Mafunzi troops rode out several hundred yards to the east and encountered no organized resistance. The other two troops turned closer on the flank of the right horn and opened fire.

The Zulu right horn could not stand the fire from the rampart. A few Zulus died within twenty yards of the trench. Then the charge was broken. The right horn fell back to a slight rise sixty or seventy yards away. Both sides fired steadily at each other. Fortunately for the men in the laager Zulu marksmanship was poor. Very few men were hit. One man had his spear cut in half by a bullet.[22]

There was a lull in the fight. The force of the enemy attack was spent and was ebbing away from the laager. The contingent was ordered out in pursuit. The charge sounded. So suddenly did it come that not all of the officers in the battalions could get to their horses. The men went out with enthusiasm and the redcoats cheered them on. They leapt across the trench shouting. Just thirty yards out they crested a slight rise and found a large number of Zulus in a hollow. The Zulus fired a volley which killed three men and fled. The mounted infantry, who had swords, drew them and charged. The men of the contingent followed.

Only the Native Contingent and the mounted troops were allowed to leave the laager. They were to pursue the enemy and turn the retreat into a rout. The battle ended with a chase of about two miles. The enemy was as quick retreating as advancing, and the pursuit was careful not to take on his organized units, but killed the slow and wounded.

The Zulu units fled to the west and the north. What appeared to be the Zulu reserve, on the distant hills, retired in good order. A force rallied on a hill to the west, but dispersed under artillery fire.

The Mafunzi Corps and Jantze's Horse rode out as far as the site of Ginginghlovu. Then they turned west towards the Matikulu bush. In the pursuit Jantze's men recovered fifteen cattle which the enemy had caught outside the laager.

Some of the men on foot halted at the edge of a valley about a mile and quarter from the laager. The valley was filled with long grass, bushes and palms. Those with rifles blazed away into it or into the air. With some difficulty they were got to stop and to return to the laager. An another place a crowd of Zulus ran through a shallow ravine, passing between part of the contingent foot and the mounted men. The foot fired so wildly at the enemy that they kept the horse from pursuit. Just then an old Zulu, who had been lying near the laager, rose and made a run for it. He went at a slow pace, but passed right through the contingent. He continued on and for half a mile bullets rained down around him. The mounted men continued to fire at long range, but it was with some pleasure that they finally observed his escape.[23]

The battle of Gingindlovu lasted less than two hours. The total Zulu loss was estimated at a thousand men – just under ten per cent of their army – which was variously estimated at between 11 000 and 14 000. The British loss was nine killed and fifty-two wounded. The 4th Battalion had one killed and four wounded. The 5th Battalion had four killed and twelve wounded. Jantze's Horse had one man killed and the Mafunzi Corps one wounded.[24]

A signal, flashed from Eshowe at eight, congratulated the column on its victory.[25] At mid-morning the mounted troops and part of the contingent on foot made a reconnaissance of six miles and found the enemy had fled in all directions. Yet a nervous redcoat on picket mistook the men on foot for enemy, fired and set off another alarm at the laager.[26]

The next day, Thursday the 3rd, the Lieutenant General led a small 'flying column' across the Nyezane to relieve the garrison at Eshowe. Jantze's Horse escorted 400 oxen needed to haul the garrison's wagons. On the 4th it escorted the garrison column out of Eshowe. Meanwhile the Mafunzi Corps went out with the rest of the mounted troops and scouts to burn the nearby homestead of an important Zulu chief. The No. 2 Pioneer Company, which had been part of the Eshowe garrison, accompanied this expedition.[27]

The 4th and 5th Battalions remained with the rest of the expedition in camp at the battlefield. The laager was suitably reduced to accommodate the remaining force.[28] On the 4th five companies of the 4th Battalion scouted to the southeast as far as the Nyezane. They moved upstream and returned to camp from the west, bringing in 135 firearms the enemy had abandoned in flight.[29]

The flying column returned to the battlefield on the 6th, and formed a new laager on another hill. The Eshowe garrison moved on to the lower Thukela on the 7th. The old laager on the battlefield was no longer healthy and the country stank with dead,[30] so the garrison moved to the new one, which became the British advance post in Zululand.

Hlobane and Khambula

As the relief column advanced to Eshowe, the other British forces along the Natal-Zulu border were ordered to demonstrate in order to distract and divert the enemy. With the British threatening to cross at several separate points the Zulu King might divide his forces to meet them and weaken the vital one opposite the lower Thukela. The 1st, 2nd and 3rd Battalions of the Native Contingent were all involved in demonstrations in late March and early April. Their experiences will be described later. Let us turn now to the Edendale Horse and Hlubi's troop, attached to the column on the Transvaal-Zulu border, which not only participated in the demonstration but became involved in two bloody battles as a result of an unexpected Zulu counteroffensive.[31]

The Edendale and Hlubi's troops had remained with the centre column after Isandlwana. Captain Cochrane, 32nd Foot, who had served on Durnford's staff, was appointed to command the mounted troops of the contingent – the Natal Native Horse, as it was now called – with the No. 3 Column. He arrived on February 20th and found the two troops in camp at Vermaak's farm, about five miles from Helpmekaar on the Rorke's Drift road. Their chief activity was patrolling the country between Helpmekaar and the Mzinyathi. Both troops were under strength, with thirty-four men each. The rest – about thirty men – were on leave.[32]

On February 23rd the Natal Native Horse and the British mounted infantry with the No. 3 Column were ordered to Dundee, twenty-two miles to the northwest, thence to the No. 4 Column, which was encamped at a place called Khambula, forty-two miles to the northeast and on the Transvaal-Zulu border. The left column was operating in an open rolling country with a few large hills and mountains. The country favoured movement with speed and the column needed more horsemen.

The troops left the centre column on February 24th and arrived at Dundee on the 25th. They did not go to Khambula directly, but stopped along the way at the left column's depot at Balte Spruit. In the meantime about half a dozen men returned from leave.[33] The troops were finally played into camp at Khambula by a British regimental band on the morning of March 1st.[34]

The column commander, Colonel Wood, and the commander of his mounted troops, Lieutenant Colonel Buller, were active, restless soldiers. They were absent from camp when the Natal Native Horse arrived, having gone out with a mounted force of white mercenaries to rescue the people of a defecting Zulu chief who were hiding in caves forty-five miles to the east. The Native Horse and mounted infantry were ordered to follow that night and support the expedition, and joined it the following afternoon, as it returned with about seven hundred refugees. At this juncture several shots rang out, fired by a body of Zulus on a long, flat-topped mountain three miles to the north. The range was so great there was no danger of anyone being hit, but the Zulus came closer and their bullets began to fall around. About ten of the Native Horse were allowed to go off and engage them. This detachment shot several of them, while the expedition passed the mountain, which was called Hlobane, and bivouacked about fifteen miles from Khambula, which they reached next day.[35]

This was the introduction of the Edendale and Hlubi's men to campaigning with left column. On the 25th and 26th, they were part of another reconnaissance to the north. Swazi renegades co-operating with the Zulu King were raiding settlements there. The reconnoitring party, about 400 mounted men and 600 local levies, burnt all the crops in the Ntombe valley, from which the renegades drew supplies. A few of the enemy fired at the party from mountain caves but offered no resistance otherwise.[36]

The column commander received the Lieutenant General's orders to demonstrate in support of the relief of Eshowe. He decided to do so with a reconnaissance using the augmented mounted force and the local levies attached to the column. The object was Hlobane, which was the stronghold of some particularly bellicose Zulus known as the abaQulusi. A reconnaissance had taken five hundred cattle below the mountain in February.[37] The intention now was to get up on to the flat top of the mountain, where presumably there were more, and take them. The plateau is about three miles long but little more than a mile across at its widest. The mountain sides are steep cliffs. Colonel Buller would take the main force to attack from the eastern end of the mountain. Colonel Russell, who had brought the mounted infantry and Native Horse from Helpmekaar, would take the remaining force and attack from the western end. Both were instructed to send out scouts to look for a large Zulu army which had been reported moving from Ulundi towards Khambula.[38]

The reconnaissance began on the 27th. Russell's force contained the Natal Native Horse, the mounted infantry, a troop of German mercenaries from the Cape, a rocket detachment, and about 440 local levies on foot (including men of the recent Zulu defector). It moved at noon and bivouacked at the same place where the earlier expedition had stopped before returning to Khambula.[39]

The next morning it moved to the western end of Hlobane. Just before dawn, in misting rain, it climbed the steep slope and came on to a small plateau called Ntendeka, which is linked to the higher plateau of Hlobane by a narrow neck of land. The main plateau is about three hundred feet higher, and therefore the neck is precipitous, so precipitous in fact that Russell did not think his horsemen could go up it. He sent up a single officer who returned to report all was quiet on top. A few shots were fired at the van of Russell's force as it moved across Ntendeka. The local levies were let loose to capture cattle on the lower slopes of Hlobane and the mounted men were drawn up to support them.

Two hours passed. The morning mist had lifted, giving an extensive view from the mountain. The sound of an engagement was heard from on top of Hlobane, where Buller's main force was advancing over the plateau. The abaQulusi apparently were putting up a fight to save their cattle. Russell's mounted troops moved forward and opened fire on what enemy they could see along the edge of the mountain, then stopped lest they hit friendly troops.

Just before nine Russell received a report that the main Zulu army had been seen on a range of hills to the south. He collected his men. Meanwhile the enemy on the slope in front crept close to some nearby homesteads and put his force under a crossfire. To counteract it the Native Horse set fire to the homesteads.

The situation became ominous. In the distance the Zulu army could be seen moving rapidly from the east. It appeared to be heading towards the camp at Khambula. It was a situation reminiscent of Isandlwana. One portion of the Zulu army separated from the main body and moved towards Hlobane. Russell told his levies to leave the cattle and ordered his force down from Ntendeka. Some of the levies were sent back to Zungwini, a ridge to the west and north, closer to Khambula. The mounted men were drawn up again, on a rise at the foot of Ntendeka, ready to cover the main force when it came down from Hlobane.

For come down it must. The reconnaissance was turning into a disaster. The main force on top of the mountain was desperate to get away before the separate Zulu column joined the abaQulusi. As they hastened towards the neck more and more of abaQulusi came out of concealment to harass and chase them. Buller's force was practically pushed down the neck. It continued in disorder down from Ntendeka.

Russell's force was no longer there. Orders had come from the column commander for him to take a position at Zungwini. He moved there and Buller's force now retreated in the same direction, eluding the Zulu column but hotly pursued by the abaQulusi. In the evening both portions of the reconnoitring force returned to Khambula.[40]

It was an unhappy night at camp. Almost a quarter of the mounted men in Buller's force had been killed on Hlobane. No one could tell how many of the levies with it were dead. Most of them had been cut off in the flight by the abaQulusi. The battle was a signal defeat and reflected on the judgement of the British commanders. The Zulu army was somewhere in the vicinity and a battle was imminent. This was a daunting prospect for the levies, almost all of whom (about 750 men) deserted and thus reduced the left column by a quarter of its strength.

The camp at Khambula consisted a wagon laager, a small artillery redoubt, and a cattle pen made of wagons. They were all within easy supporting distance of each other on the level high ground of a watershed. There were 1 359 British regulars, mostly infantry, and 469 mounted men, mostly Cape mercenaries, but also the Natal Native Horse, seventy five strong. There were only 58 levies left.[41]

During the morning of March 29th, various sources informed the column commander that the Zulu army would attack the camp about mid-day. At about eleven the army came into view, moving from the southeast. It was about ten miles away and there was plenty of time to prepare to meet it. The British had rehearsed for just this battle. They had dinner, struck their tents, and took their appointed places in the laager, redoubt and cattle pen. Boxes of ammunition were opened and placed for convenience of distribution. The artillery was in the redoubt and in line beside the laager. The mounted men were inside the laager.

The Zulu army approached, but the distance was still too great for firearms. The right horn broke off and moved round towards the north of the camp. It passed on the northern slope of the watershed, out of rifle range, and seemed to wait for the left horn to complete the envelopment of the camp.[42]

The column commander sent out the mounted troops to bait the right horn. The horsemen rode into easy range, dismounted and opened fire. The impatient Zulus – they were the young men of the army – charged recklessly. The horsemen remounted and fell back firing. Then they slipped inside the laager, unmasking the infantry and artillery.[43]

Or at least most of them did. John Gama, one of the Edendale Horse, recalled later that some of the Edendale men were unable to get into the laager and remained outside to fight for the rest of the battle.[44] A European observer reported the day after the battle that the Natal Native Horse would not go into the laager.[45] Another writer, who was not present but served with the column's mounted troops later, stated emphatically that the Native Horse would not enter the laager, but stayed outside and hovered on the Zulu flank firing continually.[46]

The infantry and artillery poured a devastating fire into the right horn. Its charge stopped three hundred yards in front of the laager and redoubt. The Zulus fell back to some rocks and opened a sustained fire of their own on the camp. The right horn made another attack later in the day, when it was repulsed again.

In the meantime the battle shifted to another side of the laager as the Zulu left horn advanced under cover of the southern slope of the watershed. Its units charged onto the top within 300 yards of the laager. They took the cattle pen but came under a converging fire from the British in the laager and redoubt. Some almost reached the face of the laager. The battle raged here for several hours.

Late in the afternoon, the Zulu charges faltered. British infantry retook the cattle pen, pushed to edge of the slope and fired into the Zulus sheltering below. The Zulu army began to retreat and the column commander ordered out the mounted men to rout it.

The horsemen pursued with vigour. Many were bent on avenging comrades who had fallen on Hlobane. The fugitives were tired and demoralized, for the most part easy prey. They were shot as they fled. It is hard to aim a rifle on a moving horse, so the pursuers also picked up the enemy's spears, dropped or lost in the flight, and rode the fugitives down, driving the points home. For over seven miles the chase went on, until nightfall ended it.[47]

The Zulu army was shattered. It had numbered about 17 000. No one knows how many died. Estimates range between one and three thousand. The loss on the British side was eighteen killed and sixty-five wounded. The Natal Native Horse had one man wounded. The victory at Khambula eclipsed defeat at Hlobane. The Edendale men returned to camp from pursuit that night, and looked upon the battlefield. Victory had been grand and terrible, and they felt at last that the wounds of Isandlwana were healed.[48]

Fort Bengough

We left the 2nd Battalion of the 1st Regiment late in January, fortifying a hill just south of the Msinga magistracy. By the fourth day of occupation a stout stone fort stood upon the crest. The shape of the fort was oblong, for it followed the contour of the hill. The wall of the fort was made of loose stones piled up and stood between four feet eight inches and six feet tall. Stones and sand bags were used to make loopholes for the defenders to shoot through without exposing themselves. The entrance-way to the fort was protected by semicircular barriers of tangled brush which overlapped each other to make a circuitous outer passage. Water had to be fetched from a stream about 500 yards away. Water barrels in the fort were kept filled, but the supply was very limited. Because of that it was supposed the fort could not withstand a blockade of more than two days.[49]

Major Bengough, the battalion commander, went round the fort with the leading chief of the battalion. 'What is it for?' the old chief asked. 'This is a fort; if the Zulus from over the river attack us here, we go into the fort and shoot them down.' The chief shook his head. He gave a knowing look and said, 'No, you don't think that we are going to be caught here, like rats in a trap! Why, how are we going to run away?'[50]

In the funk that followed the Isandlwana defeat the battalion's morale was low. About forty or fifty men had deserted already. The night after the detachment of British infantry left the magistracy for Helpmekaar, January 29th, a report was received that a large force of Zulus was advancing rapidly on the fort. The order was given to stand to arms. It took only three minutes for the men to do so. A picket was sent out, and some huts at the foot of the hill were burnt to provide light.[51] The Major made the rounds of the wall. Some men opened fire. One even fired his rifle from between the Major's legs and wounded a man on picket. Bengough heard the sound of men sharpening the short spears which they carried for stabbing. He mentioned it to the battalion's interpreter. 'Yes, sir,' answered the interpreter, 'they mean to fight!'[52] But after three hours the men stood down. It had been a false alarm.[53]

Desertion continued. Some men left with rifles. Bengough wrote to the Resident Magistrate of Umvoti County, whence the men had come, to get them to return. Five days later, on February 3rd, rumours of a Zulu invasion spread along the border. There was a great scare in the Colony, affecting even Pietermaritzburg and Durban. The 2nd Battalion experienced massive desertion. Men feared for their families. Four out of six chiefs reported to the Resident Magistrate that all of their men had left the battalion and they were powerless to prevent it. The magistrate inquired after the deserters and found that they were willing to return, but obviously not now. For the moment he let them stay, pending instructions from the Supreme Chief.[54]

The remnant of the battalion set about strengthening the fort. In the centre a small redoubt with two bastions was built. The wall was three to four feet thick, and it stood six feet tall. Officers and men would retire into it to meet a Zulu attack.[55]

The Zulu invasion did not take place, although rumours of it continued to circulate at intervals. There was no Zulu attack but the garrison slept inside the fort at night, the officers fully clothed. Then apprehension waned.[56] Deserters returned to the battalion. By mid-February about a hundred had rejoined, by the end of another week 722. On March 23rd there were 980 men present for duty, on April 14th 1 059.[57]

The fort grew to accommodate the garrison. The outer walls rose to between ten and fifteen feet. It was extended to cover a greater area and was divided into three sections. At the centre was the redoubt, in which was built a square stone building to house the battalion's munitions. The bastions were taken down and elongated semicircular walls were built on each side of and connected with the redoubt. In the section on one side were quartered the men. The officers were quartered on the other side. 'Fort Bengough' was almost too big for the hill now. It is hardly a wonder that the new British High Commissioner, passing by it several months later, described it as 'a Chinese-like construction'.[58]

It took longer to rebuild the battalion. Bengough tried to see the men in a positive light. 'They are intelligent, honest, cheery and chatty. I never saw a [Natal] Zulu drunk. They have a lively sense of humour, and soon formed appropriate names for the battalion officers – my own cognomen being, I believe, "The Rock Splitter", from the rather tough marches that I used to take them [on] sometimes.'[59] The officers and non-commissioned officers saw them in a negative light. They had deserted once. Would they not desert again when it came to a fight?[60]

Even the sympathetic Major considered them fit for little more than scouting and spying. He did not think they were fit to fight side-by-side with

British soldiers. It was not because individuals lacked courage. Rather they lacked cohesiveness of a moral kind. The only thing they all had in common was hatred of the Zulu for having driven them from their former homes. The European military system, with which they were unfamiliar, undermined their self-confidence, at least in the short term.[61]

The Major did not on this account relent in his efforts to make an effective fighting unit of them. Military exercises filled most of the day. The men who had gone home had complained of harassing drill.[62] The drill now was simplified.[63] The disgruntled non-commissioned officers were transferred to the Natal Horse. By mid-April only seven remained.[64] Each company was distinguished by a flag. In due course rifles were issued to all and rifle practice was regularized. Badges were given to marksmen. Figures of merit were awarded to companies. Competition was keen. The men quickly understood how the breech-action of the rifle worked, but seemed to think that the back sight worked by magic.[65]

Another instance of magic had an unfortunate result. Divining was something of a profession and conferred great status, but it worked largely by inference. Europeans despised it but they were helpless against it. A man was suspected of stealing wood. A diviner was brought in to determine guilt. The battalion interpreter intervened. He knew how summarily justice would be meted out. It was no use. Suddenly a wild cat appeared between the suspect's feet. 'There is his familiar,' was the cry. The wild cat was killed. The suspect went missing. The Major was left with the skin of the cat.[66]

The 2nd Battalion had been formally attached to the No. 3 Column on February 12th.[67] It sent at least one patrol down to the Mzinyathi to check Zulu marauders,[68] but its first major operation after Isandlwana was to demonstrate in support of the Eshowe relief expedition. On March 26th a small mounted force from Rorke's Drift rode to Isandlwana and back. Bengough took most of the battalion to one of the fords downstream, but the river was too high for it to cross.[69] An order came from the Lieutenant General to continue demonstrating, even though Eshowe had been relieved. On April 9th, in co-operation with mounted troops, the battalion crossed the river at Rorke's Drift and burnt homesteads and crops in the Batshe river valley.[70]

A British regiment marching north along the border road from Greytown to Dundee passed Fort Bengough late in April. The 2nd Battalion turned out to greet it in a traditional manner. An officer of the regiment was greatly impressed:[71]

> … Imagine seven hundred naked savages in companies of one hundred each, their only clothing the tiny kilt of fur; perhaps a plume of ostrich-feathers on their head, or a strip of leopard-skin round the forehead. Many dress their hair in strange fashions – divided like waves of the sea, twisted into points, or peeked into a central ridge, like a cock's comb. All carry an oval shield of black and white cow-hide, four assegais [the short spears for stabbing] and a knob-kirri [a stick with a knob at one end]; some few have muskets. Amongst them stalk giants, their bodies glistening with oil, full seven feet high, true sons of Anak, magnificently built and proportioned. Many more were upwards of six feet in stature, and are models of symmetry and savage grace.
>
> Each company advances brandishing shields and assegais aloft to some native tune, slow time admirably kept, its chant being continually varied by deep gutturals, hisses, grunts, and shouts, all uttered in the most perfect time. Their eyes roll, and they give out the war-song with startling energy and ferocity as they pass. Every here and there [*sic*] a warrior dashes out of the ranks, and goes through in pantomime the pursuit, defeat, and ultimate slaughter of an imaginary foe – accompanying the performance by leaps, tumbles, crawlings, and the most hideous grimaces; his fellows in the ranks greeting him with a wild chorus of shrieks, and cries of encouragement and admiration; now whistling or giving out the deep guttural "ouf-oom-squish;" now bursting out, yelping like a pack of dogs; occasionally, when excited by some warrior more grotesque than usual, rushing out to imitate him, three and four at a time.
>
> One chief, of huge proportions, had managed to hoist himself on to a horse – the animal looking mean under the weight he carried, which was every inch the noble savage.
>
> At day break, when we marched, our allies headed us off and lined the road, as much to their own delight as to that of our soldiers, who, having picked up some bits of the native air, greeted them with the quaint "oof-oom-squish;" eliciting in return grins innumerable and the universal "Ha, ha, Johnnie!"

Bengough's battalion was not to spend the rest of the war in this quiet sector. It was to become part of the new invading army. The battalion improved in efficiency and discipline, and made excellent light infantry, suitable for scouting *and* skirmishing, a useful complement to the mounted troops in the field.

Isandlwana again

The autumn was well advanced, warm days and cool nights, less and less rain. The ground hardened and wagons and oxen moved more easily. By the end of April most of the reinforcements from overseas had arrived in the Colony and reached the forward depots. The time had come once more to invade the Zulu country.

On the 8th of May the 2nd Battalion was ordered to Landman's Drift, an important crossing of the Mzinyathi about thirty miles to the north. It left Fort Bengough and reached the crossing place the next day,[72] where it joined the 2nd Division of the invading army, the bulk of which assembled at Landman's Drift on May 10th.[73]

Zulus had been making small raids across the northern border and seizing cattle. To stop them the colonial border agent in that quarter recommended burning all the Zulu homesteads along the border between the Ncome and Batshe rivers. It was arranged that the 2nd Battalion would co-operate with the colonial border police and mounted colonials in a raid for this purpose. The evening before the raid was to take place, the border agent received reports that three or four bodies of Zulus had assembled for a raid of their own into Natal! The colonial raid was called off, and the 2nd Battalion went on as originally intended to Landman's Drift.[74]

The commander of the 2nd Division then proposed that the 2nd Battalion cross the Ncome and raid the enemy country in co-operation with a force about sixty Natal Horse and about thirty of Shepstone's Horse, which had also been attached to the 2nd Division. The battalion crossed the Mzinyathi at Landman's the evening before the raid and marched ten miles to Koppie Allein, a small isolated hill overlooking a crossing of the Ncome. The mounted men, who had come down from Conference Hill, met them there. Yet another alarming report from the border agent prompted the division commander to cancel the raid, but this time his messengers could not find the troops!

The battalion and the mounted troops crossed into the Zulu country at three in the morning of the 13th, apparently unaware of any danger in front. They halted until daybreak, then moved towards Thelezeni, the first low ridge, five miles beyond the river. It was easy to manoeuvre on the ground. The country was open. The ascent was gentle and the few hills were low ones. There were many watercourses, but they were mainly dry. The battalion spread out to form a long line between the river and Thelezeni. The mounted men went round the north end of the ridge to the other side. Then both forces worked their way southward, burning Zulu homesteads. The men of the battalion put hundreds to the torch – 'a perfect line of fire' marked their progress.

The detachment of Shepstone's Horse on the left flank kept up with the battalion, burning huts and driving out small groups of Zulus who seemed to be sheltering in them. A red hill was in front. There the horsemen halted to wait for the Natal Horse, still further to the left. The mercenaries had to overcome rough terrain and skirmished sharply with some Zulus armed with Martini-Henry rifles. After a rest at the hill all of the horsemen returned to Conference Hill. The 2nd Battalion moved on, flanks secured by the Mzinyathi and Batshe rivers. The perfect line of fire continued to Rorke's Drift.

The division commander had sent a strong force of British lancers to give the 2nd Battalion support, if it needed it. The lancers also crossed the Ncome at Koppie Allein. They found the smoking remains of huts, but did not come up with the 2nd Battalion, which bivouacked that night on the right bank of the Mzinyathi at Rorke's Drift.[75]

The battalion no sooner re-entered Natal than it set off a wild panic. Some British cavalry which had just arrived at the front were scouting along the Mzinyathi and saw the battalion crossing the river. The cavalrymen assumed it was a large Zulu force and sent posthaste to warn the base at Dundee, where a great commotion occurred to defend the place. It was an hour or two before it was realized the new troops had mistaken their enemy.[76]

The raid was the first operation in which units of the Natal Native Contingent acted independently. (The thirty-some mercenaries on the Natal Horse had a very peripheral role in the raid.) It gave proof that the contingent had recovered its morale and had benefited from the training of the past three months. The raid was also the first major punitive expedition against the enemy, and as such it was a success.

The 2nd Battalion returned to Landman's Drift on the morning of the 14th. An old man who had been captured in the raid informed Major Bengough that the Zulu King had spies on the Doornberg, midway between Landman's Drift and Conference Hill. Two companies of the battalion were ordered to go over the hill in skirmish order. They did so and brought back several prisoners.[77] On the 17th small mounted forces from Landman's Drift and Conference Hill scouted to Thelezeni again. They saw no Zulus.[78]

If the Zulus were no longer in strength across the Ncome, reports now suggested that they were in strength across the Mzinyathi further south. For several days border police passed on hearsay that a force was forming there, possibly for an incursion into Natal. Meanwhile the people in the area were seen harvesting crops without hindrance.

A party from Rorke's Drift rode to Isandlwana on the 15th and were followed back to Sotondose's drift by Zulu scouts. A detachment of the 2nd Battalion which had been left at Rorke's Drift and some of the Europeans in the garrison there went to Sotondose's to cover the party's return. There was an exchange of fire. After the party and the detachment returned to Rorke's Drift, about an hundred Zulus appeared at Sotondose's and engaged the Native Border Guard for some time. Many of the Zulus were mounted, which suggested an unusual number of leaders in the vicinity.

Next it was reported that the Zulu chief Sihayo had sent between five and six hundred men to gather crops, and to carry them off in the wagons which remained on the Isandlwana battlefield.

The commander of the 2nd Division resolved that the removal of crops, virtually in plain view of British troops, should stop.[79] He achieved this by a bold demonstration. He ordered his Cavalry Brigade to make a reconnaissance of the Nquthu ridge and Isandlwana. This force would find out what Zulus were in the vicinity and put an end to their foraging.

The 2nd Battalion was ordered to co-operate with the Cavalry Brigade. It marched to Rorke's Drift on the 19th and occupied the buildings at kwaJimu. (The British garrison had moved to a new fort, just above the ford, a few weeks before). The Cavalry Brigade, which marched from Dundee, arrived on the 20th. With it were the Driefontein section of Shepstone's Horse and the Amabomvu and Amangwane Corps.

The cavalry commander divided his force into two columns. One would cross the Mzinyathi and go up the Batshe valley, climb the Nquthu range and follow it to above Isandlwana. The 2nd Battalion would go with this column. The other column would cross afterwards and take the old track across the Batshe to Isandlwana. The mounted troops of contingent would go with it. The two columns would meet on the battlefield.

The first column forded the Mzinyathi at four in the morning of the 21st and soon reached the Batshe. The 2nd Battalion swarmed into the little valley and worked up it, burning homesteads and searching for enemy in the caves and crevices along the steep wall of Ngedla. The British cavalry moved parallel with them west of the stream. The battalion passed over the sites of the skirmish on January 12th and of Sihayo's great place. Foot and horse made their way up a draw to the top of the hill and continued along the high ground to the east. The column below marked their progress by the smoke of burning homesteads.

The second column crossed the river at 5.30 and proceeded without hindrance to the battlefield. The Amabomvu and Amangwane Corps did good service as scouts. The two columns met on the plain east of Isandlwana at about 8.30. The 2nd Battalion came down from the ridge singing a war song. Its behaviour had been exemplary. The British cavalry commander reported on its 'able co-operation' and the 'utmost coolness' of the men in difficult places where they might have encountered the enemy at any time.

No enemy was seen, but as the columns approached the battlefield fires appeared to the south. These were taken to be signals, for other fires soon appeared, as though in a line, as far as Hlazakazi. Mounted men were posted as sentries. The Cavalry Brigade concentrated on the neck where the track crossed between Isandlwana and the knoll to the south. Some corpses were buried and some abandoned but still serviceable wagons were recovered. The entire force returned to Rorke's Drift that afternoon and remained there the following day. On the 23rd the Cavalry Brigade returned to Dundee and the 2nd Battalion to Landman's Drift.[80]

It is appropriate to conclude this chapter with a reflexion on what had happened in the three months after Isandlwana. The British had remained on the defensive strategically. Latterly they had recovered the initiative. They had relieved Eshowe. The expedition revealed a change in their tactics. They formed laagers to protect their camps against attack. There would be no more surprises, such as at Isandlwana. They took great care in reconnaissance, especially in the use of mounted troops. There would be no more surprises on the march, as at the Nyezane. The pitched battles at Gingindlovu and Khambula showed the superiority of British organization and technology on tactical defence.

The Natal Native Contingent had changed. In December and January the military authorities had imposed an unfamiliar system of discipline and drill on the men. They had not issued enough rifles to give them confidence. They had degraded chiefs and head men by introducing many incompetent European officers and non commissioned officers. Their distrust of the rank and file had been made plain in the disorderly march of the 2nd Regiment from Eshowe to the Thukela. Lack of communication, lack of understanding, lack of time to overcome both had made the foot regiments of questionable value. They were not ready for the war when it came, yet they made up over half the invading army. They were fairly effective as scouts and skirmishers, but their performance in combat was unsatisfactory overall. Only the mounted troops, well armed and better led, had acquitted themselves well.

After the Isandlwana disaster the Lieutenant General and the Supreme Chief argued over the reconstitution of the Natal Native Contingent. They arrived at a compromise favourable to the military. The contingent was reduced in size and partially reorganized. The 'regimental' system was retained, but the drill was simplified. The importance of chiefs and head men was recognized. Incompetent Europeans were weeded out and those who spoke the language of the men were distributed among the units. Firearms were issued to all the men and instruction was given in shooting.

The results were promising. At Gingindlovu the 4th and 5th Battalions remained steady, though very much excited under fire. It was unfortunate that there was a tendency among the British to view this infantry as still lacking character to stand up to the Zulu in battle and to relegate it to mopping up and pursuit of a beaten foe.[81] After Gingindlovu the officers of the battalions apparently tried with little success to prevent the men from killing the enemy wounded.[82] The Methodist chaplain at Fort Tenedos wrote that British soldiers were saying that the Native Contingent was there to do what the white man could not do, for example, kill the enemy wounded. The white soldiers would defeat the enemy, the contingent would be let loose to finish them off. There was no bother with prisoners of war.[83]

The mounted troops of the Native Contingent, now called Natal Native Horse, had fought well at Gingindlovu and Khambula. They did every bit as well as the mounted colonials and Cape mercenaries. The British were ready to invade the Zulu country a second time, and the Natal Native Contingent would again play an important part in the invasion.

NOTES

1 1/VLM, 3/1/1/8, pp. 413–414, and 3/2/1: NA 295/1879.

2 1/VLM, 3/2/1: 1224/1870. WCII/2/2: Chelmsford to Wood, February 19, 1879.

3 TN, February 28, 1879: 'Border Notes.'

4 *Ibid.*, NM, March 15, 1879: 'With the Isipingo Mounted Rifles.' 1/VLM, 3/2/1: NACR 11/1879.

5 SNA 1/6/14, no. 11. Stainbank Diary, March 9 and 10, 1879.

6 NM, March 20, 1879: GO59.

7 SNA 1/1/34, no. 17; and 1/6/14, no. 11. 1/VLM, 3/2/1: 265I/1879 and 750I/1879.

8 SNA 1/6/12, no. 79. CSO 698: 2079/1879. C2367, p. 125. NM, March 15: 'With the Isipingo Mounted Rifles;' March 20: GO59; March 26; 1879: 'Major Barrow's Mounted Horse.' NC, March 15, 1870: GO –.

9 TN, January 1: GO238, March 5: report; and April 2, 1879: 'Middle Drift, Tugela.' Norris-Newman, *In Zululand with the British*, p. 113, SNA 1/6/12, no. 79.

10 NM, March 26, 1879, 'Major Barrow's Mounted Horse.'

11 *Narrative*, pp. 62–63.

12 *Ibid.*, pp. 162–163, and return in C2367, pp. 124–125, and *cf. Narrative*, p. 63. C2367, p. 121.

13 Stainbank Diary, March 15, 1879.

14 *Narrative*, p. 63. C2367, p. 121. CP 7–37: 'Order of march of the Ekowe Relief Column.' Norris-Newman, *In Zululand with the British*, p. 133.

15 *Narrative*, p. 63. Norris-Newman, *In Zululand with the British*, pp. 133–134. *Campaigns: Zulu 1879, Egypt 1882; Suakim 1885. Being the Private Journal of Guy C. Dawnay* ([n.p.], privately published, 1886), p. 9.

16 *Narrative*, pp. 63–64. Norris-Newman, *In Zululand with the British*, pp. 134–135. C2367, p. 121. CP 7–41: E.R. Courtenay to F.T.A. Law, March 30, 1879. Stainbank Diary, March 30, 1879. Charles E. Fripp, 'Reminiscences of the Zulu War,' in *Pall Mall Magazine*, XX (1920), 548.

17 CP 7–41: C.D. Hay to [Crealock], March 31, 1879. C2367, p. 121. Norris-Newman, *In Zululand with the British*, p. 135.

18 *Narrative*, p. 64. Norris-Newman, *In Zululand with the British*, pp. 135–136. C2367, p. 121. *Private Journal of Guy C. Dawnay*, p. 13. Norbury, *The Naval Brigade*, p. 269. Edward Hutton, 'Some Recollections of the Zulu War, 1879,' in *The Army Quarterly*, XVI, April 16, 1928, pp. 68–69.

19 CP 7–41: Hay to [Crealock], April 1, 1879. Stainbank Diary. April 1, 1879. *Cf.* W.C.F. Molyneux, *Campaigning in South Africa and Egypt* (London, Macmillan, 1896), p. 128.

20 *Narrative*, p. 64. C2367, p. 121. Norris-Newman, *In Zululand with the British*, p. 136. *Private Journal of Guy C. Dawnay*, pp. 11–12. Molyneux, *Campaigning in South Africa and Egypt*, p. 129. Hutton, 'Some Recollections of the Zulu War,' p. 69. Emery, *The Red Soldier*, p. 204. The sources vary in some detail.

21 *Narrative*, p. 64. C2367, pp. 43, 121–122. Norris- Newman, *In Zululand with the British*, p. 137. *Private Journal of Guy C. Dawnay*, p. 12. Hutton, 'Some Recollections of the Zulu War,' p. 69. Molyneux, *Campaigning in South Africa and Egypt*, p. 131. Stainbank Diary, April 2, 1879. Castle and Knight, *Fearful Hard Times*, p. 191.

22 C2367, pp. 43, 122. *Narrative*, pp. 64–65. Norbury, *The Naval Brigade*, pp. 269–271. Norris-Newman, *In Zululand with the British*, pp. 137–138. *Letters of Major-General FitzRoy*

Hart-Synnot, pp. 131–132. Molyneux, *Campaigning in South Africa and Egypt*, pp. 130–136. Hutton, 'Some Recollections of the Zulu War,' pp. 70–72. *Private Journal of Guy C. Dawnay*, pp. 12–14. *The South African Campaign*, p. 94. Emery, *The Red Soldier*, p. 204. For the mounted troops *cf.* the maps in C2367, p. 43 and CP 7–48. According to Nettleton's report (CP 7–43) his battalion fired 10911 rounds or an average of nine to ten rounds per man. According to Hutton (p. 71) the overall average was seven rounds and the marines' sixteen rounds per man.

23 C2367, pp. 43, 122. *Narrative*, p. 65. Norbury, *The Naval Brigade*, pp. 271–272. Norris-Newman, *In Zululand with the British*, pp. 136, 139–140. Emery, *The Red Soldier*, p. 204. Hutton, 'Some Recollections of the Zulu War,' p. 72. *Private Journal of Guy C. Dawnay*, pp. 14–15. *The South African Campaign*, p. 94. TN, April 14, 1879: 'The March to Eshowe,' Stainbank Diary, April 2, 1879. Molyneux, *Campaigning in South Africa and Egypt*, p. 136. Captain Hart described the pursuit and remarked (*Letters*, p. 133) that 'the bravest men [among the Zulu assailants] had not breath to run away, and they perished. Let me draw a veil over that part of the scene. Chivalry ends when pursuit begins; but the dire necessities of war oblige that a defeated army shall also be dispersed, so that it shall never fight again . . . .' According to Molyneux, pp. 134–135) one man of the contingent missed the chase: he lay under a commissariat wagon in the laager, unconscious and breathing loudly. A bullet had struck a barrel on the wagon and out of the hole poured a stream of rum. The man had got underneath to catch it in his mouth and evidently drunk to excess.

24 C2367, pp. 43. 122. *Narrative*, p. 65. Norris-Newman, *In Zululand with the British*, p. 141. *Private Journal of Guy C. Dawnay*, p. 16. Returns are in C2367, pp. 126–127 and *Narrative*, p. 163. A detailed breakdown for the 5th Battalion is in CP 7–48. Dawnay states (p. 17) that there were 473 Zulu dead within 500 yards of the laager. Emery quotes (*The Red Soldier*, p. 204) an anonymous officer who states that 471 Zulu dead were buried within 1000 yards.

25 *Narrative*, p. 65. Norris-Newman, *In Zululand with the British*, p. 142.

26 C2367, p. 43. *Private Journal of Guy C. Dawnay*, pp. 15–16.

27 TN, April 14, 1879: 'The March to Eshowe.' *Private Journal of Guy C. Dawnay*, p. 19. Stainbank Diary, April 4, 1879.

28 *Narrative*, p. 65. *Private Journal of Guy C. Dawnay*, p. 17.

29 CP 7–46: G. Barton to A.L. Walker, April 4, 1879. Norris-Newman, *In Zululand with the British*, p. 141. According to a report in CP 7–51 the 5th Battalion collected 216 rifles on the 2nd and afterwards.

30 *Narrative*, p. 82. C2367, p. 123. Emery, *The Red Soldier*, p. 204. *Private Journal of Guy C. Dawnay*, p. 22. Fripp, 'Reminiscences of the Zulu War,' pp. 549–550.

31 See Laband and Thompson, *Kingdom and Colony at War*, pp. 82, 133, 154, 172. *Lord Chelmsford's Zululand Campaign*, pp. 117 and 152.

32 SNA 1/6/12, no. 37. NM, February 17, 1870: GO32. Vause Diary, pp. 18–19.

33 Vause Diary, p. 19, with which *cf. Narrative*, p. 72 and CP 8–42: R.T. Glyn to Chelmsford, February 25, 1879. NM, March 31, 1879: 'With the Native Contingent.' WO32/7726: Cochrane to Deputy Adjutant General, March 4, 1879. The number at Khambula was 74 (*Narrative*, p. 161).

34 *Cf. Narrative*, p. 72; NW, March 25, 1879: 'With Colonel Wood's Column;' and NM, March 31, 1879: 'With the Native Contingent.'

35 *Narrative*, p. 72. NM, March 31, 1879: 'With the Native Contingent.'

36 WO 32/7756: Wood to [Deputy Adjutant General], March 27, 1879.

37 *Narrative*, pp. 67 and 73. WO 132/1 (Buller Papers): *Supplement to the London Gazette*, May 7, 1879: report of E. Wood. Laband and Thompson, *Kingdom and Colony at War*, pp. 9, 11, 82, 186, 188.

38 *Narrative*, p. 73. WO 132/1: Wood's report.

39 *Narrative*, p. 73.

40 *Ibid.*, pp. 75–78. WO 32/7756: report of J.C. Russell, March 29, 1879; also see reports of R. Buller and W.K. Leet. NW, August 16, 1879: 'The Natal Native Horse.' NM, August 18, 1879: 'Notes from Maritzburg.'

41 *Narrative*, pp. 78–79, 161.

42 *Ibid.*, pp. 79–80.

43 *Ibid.*, p. 80. TN, April 4, 1879: 'With Wood's Column' and 'Attack on the Kambula Court [*sic*].' NW, August 16, 1879: 'The Natal Native Horse.'

44 NW, August 16, 1870: 'The Natal Native Horse.'

45 NW, April 12, 1879: 'The Attack on Kambula Camp.'

46 W.H. Tomasson, *With the Irregulars in the Transvaal and Zululand* (London, Remington, 1880), pp. 54–55, 183.

47 *Narrative*, pp. 80–81. Norris-Newman, *In Zululand with the British*, p. 165. Laband and Thompson, *Kingdom and Colony at War*, pp. 92–98 *passim*.

48 Laband and Thompson, *Kingdom and Colony at War*, pp. 100–101. *Narrative*, p. 161. NW, August 16, 1879: 'The Natal Native Horse.' NM, August 18, 1879: 'Notes from Maritzburg.'

49 CP 8–37: report of R. daC. Porter, January 28, 1879.

50 Bengough, *Memories of a Soldier's Life*, pp. 124–125.

51 *The Graphic*, April 5, 1879: report, reprinted in *The First Six Months of the Zulu War As Reported in "The Graphic"* (compiled by S. Bourquin; Durban, the author, 1968), p. 43.

52 Bengough, *Memories of a Soldier's Life*, p. 125.

53 *The Graphic*, April 5, 1879: report.

54 CSO 1926: C18/1879. 1/GTN: 3/2/1: G91/1879. Laband and Thompson, *Kingdom and Colony at War*, pp. 284 and 309; and *War Comes to Umvoti*, pp. 38–39.

55 NW, February 13, 1879: 'With No. 2 Column – Native Correspondent.'

56 See the reports of H.F. Fynn, between February and April in CSO 1926 *passim*. Bengough, *Memories of a Soldier's Life*, p. 125. Norris-Newman, *In Zululand with the British*, p. 114. NW, March 1, 1879: 'Natal Native Contingent.'

57 SNA 1/6/11, no. 63.

58 Norris-Newman, *In Zululand with the British*, p. 114. *South AFrican Journal of Sir Garnet Wolseley* 1879–1880, p. 69.

59 Bengough, *Memories of a Soldier's Life*, p. 106.

60 NAD 1229: Commeline Papers: Charles Commeline to [Laura] Commeline, February 14, 1879. F. Francis, *War, Waves and Wanderings* (London, Sampson Low, Marston, Searle and Rivington, 1881), p. 43.

61 Bengough, *Memories of a Soldier's Life*, pp. 126–127.

62 1/GTN, 3/2/1: G91/1879.

63 Bengough, *Memories of a Soldier's Life*, pp. 127–128.

64 SNA 1/6/14, no. 8. See also NW, April 3 and 19, 1879: 'Harry's Complaints.'

65 Bengough, *Memories of a Soldier's Life*, p.127.

66 *Ibid.*, p. 129.

67 TN, February 14, 1879: GO32.

68 Norris-Newman, *In Zululand with the British*, p. 144. Also, see NAM 8503–7: Birkett Papers: R.C. Birkett to his father, March 18, 1879.

69 TN, April 7, 1879: 'With the Natal Native Horse.' CSO 1926: 1762/1879.

70 NW, April 22, 1879: 'The Zulu War. A Raid into Zululand.' CP 16–7: Clery to Crealock, April 9, 1879. CSO 1926: 1951/1879.

71 On the 94th Regiment see *Narrative*, p. 89, and *The South African Campaign*, p. 355. The quotation is from Montague, *Campaigning in South Africa*, pp. 81–83. It has a marked similarity to one of the reception given to the 94th by the Ixopo Native Contingent near Greytown a couple of days earlier by Philip Anstruther, in *War and Peace in South Africa 1879–1881*, pp. 14–15. Both Anstruther and Montague were officers of the 94th. Anstruther apparently wrote a day later, Montague less than a year later but probably relying on a diary, and both were meticulous if selective observers of detail; thus it is surprising that neither mentions the incident described by the other. Moreover Anstruther also writes (p. 16) in some detail of his reception at Fort Bengough. Scrutiny reveals dissimilarities, indeed discrepancies, between the incidents with which to argue plausibly that one of them must have been absent from the scene the other describes or did not regard it as so remarkable.

72 NW, May 10, 1879: Orders. WO 32/7735: 2nd Division Diary, May 10, 1879.

73 *Narrative*, p. 90.

74 WO 32/7735. 2nd Division Diary, May 8 and 9, 1879. See also *Private Journal of Guy C. Dawnay*, p. 30.

75 WO 32/7735: 2nd Division Diary, May 13, 1879. TN, May 23, 1870: 'Lantman's [*sic*] Drift.'

76 Norris-Newman, *In Zululand with the British*, p. 178. *Private Journal of Guy C. Dawnay*, p. 31.

77 WO 32/7735: 2nd Division Diary, May 14, 1879.

78 *Narrative*, p. 91.

79 CSO 1927: 2347, 2480, 2505, 2548 and 2648 1879. SNA 1/1/33, nos. 10 and 11. WO 32/7735: 2nd Division Diary, Newdigate to Deputy Adjutant General, May 22, 1879. *Cf.* CSO 1927: 2549/1879 and *Narrative*, p. 91.

80 WO 32.7735: 2nd Division Diary, March 19, 1879; Newdigate to F. Marshall, May 17, and reports of F. Marshall and H. Alexander, May 21, 1879. *Narrative*, pp. 91–92. TN, May 26, 1879: 'Notes by the Way.' W. Ashe and E.V. Wyatt Edgell, *The Story of the Zulu War* (London, Sampson Low, Marston, Searle and Rivington, 1880), pp. 253–254.

81 The use to which they were put after battles tends to support this, but also see Molyneux, *Campaigning in South Africa and Egypt*, p. 136, and Hutton, 'Some Recollections of the Zulu War,' p. 72.

82 Norris-Newman, *In Zululand with the British*, p. 140.

83 NAD *mf.* 2/2/1/7: Wesleyan Mission Papers: T.H. Wilkin to the Rev. Mason, April 30, 1879.

Chapter 11

WAR IN THE THORNS

Guardian of the Gates of Natal

Of all the places in Natal perhaps the most beautiful is Umvoti County. Gentle downs, steep escarpment, and the rugged valley of the Thukela form a study in contrasts. The vistas from the escarpment into Zululand are among the sublime sights of southern Africa. Into this panorama, against the backdrop of staggered hills, looping river, and wild scenery, penetrated the forces of war. The warfare was largely confined to the low borderland, in the country called 'The Thorns'.

During the afternoon of Thursday, January 23rd, reports filtered across the border into Umvoti of the disaster which had befallen the British invading column in the Zulu country. Captain Barton, Durnford's staff officer, took charge of the No.2 Column, which was in camp near Kranskop.[1]

The two battalions of the 1st Regiment were the only imperial force of any size in Umvoti County. They occupied a position blocking the most likely invasion route, via the Middle Drift and Kranskop, into the heart of Natal.[2]

Every morning at three o'clock the men stood to arms. They remained in silence until daylight. The officers slept in their clothes, rifles and ammunition beside them.[3] Commandant Montgomery had promised to tell the men of the 1st Battalion everything, good and bad. He formed them in a square and told them part of the army had been eaten up by the Zulus, but both sides had suffered heavily. 'The Queen must win in the end, and she will send plenty more white soldiers; your officers and sergeants will stick to their colours.' He pointed to the crown on the battalion's banner. 'You, my children, I also look upon as brave soldiers of the Queen, but I like you to express your confidence.' There was a pause. The head men talked to those in the ranks. Then they said: 'We will follow you to the [Middle] Drift at once.' The commandant replied that he must wait for orders. He called for three cheers for the Queen. This the battalion gave most heartily.[4]

Two companies of the 1st Battalion apparently deserted soon after Isandlwana, but afterwards desertion was negligible,[5] although officers still harboured doubts about the reliability of their men.[6] The deserters were caught and flogged.[7] Health remained good.[8] Meanwhile the infantry battalions and the company of pioneers with them were put to work fortifying the camp.

The camp was on the crest of a hill with a gentle slope, and the open ground all round gave a good field of fire. As in the case of the 2nd Battalion's fort in the Msinga, the work went on for some time. The resulting 'Fort Cherry', named after the commandant of the 3rd Battalion, was an earthwork ultimately covering 8800 square yards with a parapet 350 yards in length. From the top of the parapet to the bottom of the surrounding ditch the distance was twenty feet. The earthen wall was ten feet thick. Except possibly for the fort at Eshowe, it was the strongest fort built during the war. It was considered impregnable against a Zulu attack.[9]

Perhaps partly because of this the enemy did not take the offensive along the middle border. There were rumours of an impending raid and these culminated in a report on February 3rd that Zulus were crossing the river in force thirteen miles to the north. The settlers of Umvoti County poured into their stone laagers, leaving the defence of the county to the Native Border Guard. The garrison at Fort Cherry could do little more than the settlers, trusting to their fortifications and supposing the Zulus could not go far beyond them. The scare ended without an incursion of any sort.[10]

The main problem faced by Captain Barton and the commandants was bringing the two battalions up to full strength. There were 130 officers and non-commissioned officers and about 900 men altogether. There should have been twice that number of men. The 1st Battalion had lost the three Ngwane companies at Isandlwana. The 3rd Battalion was incomplete when the war began and amounted to no more than a couple of companies. Efforts to bring the amaNgwane back came to nothing. The 1st Battalion's strength remained at just over 700.[11] Efforts to recruit the 3rd Battalion came to nothing, and the battalion actually lost some men, probably from sickness, declining from 210 in mid February to 186 in mid March.[12]

On March 20th returns for the garrison at the fort gave the following strength:[13]

1st Battalion	290	amaNgwe
	221	amaBaso
	103	amaNyuswa
	90	abaseMbo
3rd Battalion	87	amaThuli
	70	amaZondi
	29	amaCele
No. 3 Pioneer Company	50	amaQanya
	40	amaNgcolosi
	6	amaNgwi
Jantze's Horse	37	amaXimba

There was no reinforcement of the battalions, which were imperial forces, but in March the colonial forces on the middle border were reinforced by levies drawn from chiefdoms in the south. A sizable contingent of mounted and foot from the Ixopo Division arrived in mid-March and formed a general reserve to the Native Border Guard. They were placed near Greytown and the Native Contingent had no contact with them until May.[14]

Soldiering at Fort Cherry became a monotonous life. Scares aside, the middle border was a quiet sector. The high flowing Thukela practically ruled out enemy operations for the rest of the summer. The regimen was lightened by a sports day on February 12th. Officers and non-commissioned officers engaged in foot races, a long jump, hammer throw and tug of war. Nine of the seventeen events were for the men. There were three foot races and for fun a sack race and a three-legged race. There was a spear-throwing contest for distance and one at a mark, also a knobkerry-throwing contest at a mark. The day concluded with three cheers for the Queen and for the two commandants.[15]

One day in February Commandant Montgomery, a restless man, and two others decided to climb to the top of Kranskop. The hill was an isolated knob on the escarpment reached by a narrow ridge. A steep slope was surmounted by a cliff with a bushy crown. People round about said not even a baboon could climb to the top, but Montgomery was an experienced climber. He and his friends found a fissure in the cliff and made their way to the top. There they set fire to the grass. It was a fine day and the smoke astonished those who saw it, for they could only think lightning had caused it.[16]

There was also a mock battle. The idea was to accustom officers' horses to the noise of spears rattling against shields, a feature of any attack. Some of the men were told off to be the Zulus. The officers mounted. The opposing forces drew up in lines. The order was given to charge. The lines advanced on each other. The men beat their spears against their shields. Some of the horses stopped, others reared or kicked and plunged. Many of the officers were thrown to the ground. Some horses turned and ran away. After getting sorted out, the two sides charged again, but this time the riders were cautious and the practice more successful.[17]

The Lieutenant General, on tour of the front, rode out to Fort Cherry from Greytown on February 28th. He arrived at 9.15 a.m. and inspected the fort. He said it pleased him. At 2 p.m. the garrison paraded. He was pleased with it, too. The men were 'in good fettle and anxious to cross the border'.[18] He returned immediately to Greytown.

Durnford's No. 2 Column was officially dissolved on February 12th, and Captain Barton was assigned to the staff of Major Twentyman, the British officer in command of Umvoti County, whose headquarters was in Greytown, the county seat, where two companies of British infantry were stationed.[19] The 1st and 3rd Battalions retained separate identities, but Captain Cherry, with the small battalion, was the senior commander. He was a serving officer, having been seconded from the 32nd Light Infantry to the theatre of war.[20] Montgomery did not get along well with Cherry any more than he had with Barton. Also under Cherry's command at the fort were No. 3 Company of the Pioneers and Jantze's Horse. At the end of February Barton was transferred to the coast. Jantze's Horse was transferred to the Eshowe relief expedition at the end of March.[21]

In the general reorganization of forces firearms were issued to all the men. The 3rd Battalion received Sniders and muzzle-loaders. It is not clear what types were issued to the 1st Battalion. Nor is it clear when the rifles were given over. There is also no record of the men receiving British uniforms, as did those in the battalions at the coast.[22] The non-commissioned officers were removed almost entirely from the battalions. They, and necessarily some officers, formed a troop of the Natal Horse, which was transferred to the lower Thukela towards the end of April. The 3rd Battalion was over-officered and gave up seven officers to the 4th Battalion on the coast at the end of May.[23]

Demonstration at the Middle Drift

Glancing at the map it might seem strange that the war on the middle border of Natal and Zululand was so uneventful. The shortest distance between Pietermaritzburg, the seat of the Colony, and Ulundi, that of the Zulu monarchy, is a line running through Umvoti County. Kranskop and the Middle Drift are practically on it. It is no wonder so much importance had been attached to the area initially. The British No. 2 Column had formed there. In the wake of Isandlwana came the rumours that the Zulus were going to invade the Colony along the same axis.[24]

The strategic importance of Kranskop and the Middle Drift are plain, but other factors militated against the area becoming a major theatre of operations. First, the Thukela, which was the boundary between Natal and Zululand, was a barrier, especially in the rainy season. During summer, when it rains frequently, the river is high and the fords are unusable. The Zulu King was reported to have acknowledged that the Thukela was more powerful than he and not to be trifled with; he would not send his army across the river during the summer months.[25] Second, the high ground overlooking the river valley is difficult to ascend, and in the Zulu country, it is very broken. Third, there were no good roads, and the few poor ones and many tracks followed and in places cut across tortuous contours. Therefore a large force could not take the offensive in the area; however, small forces could raid easily enough. The physical damage inflicted in such raids would be limited, but the moral effect could be extensive. The raiders of one side might gain an ascendancy on the border and undermine the credibility and power of the other, but the campaign could become long and involved. It was for this reason that the Supreme Chief preferred a defensive posture there. Probably the Zulu King did as well, for all the rumours to the contrary.[26]

The Lieutenant General ordered that forces along the entire border demonstrate in order to distract the Zulu from his expedition to relieve besieged Eshowe. If opportunity offered, they should make short raids across the river.[27] A demonstration is one thing, a raid is quite another. The Supreme Chief was willing to support the Lieutenant General in a demonstration. The colonial forces were to act at the border, but not to cross it. On March 15th the Supreme Chief ordered Colonial Defensive District Commandants to co-operate with the imperial officers accordingly.[28]

The Natal Native Contingent was not a colonial force but an imperial one, having been transferred from the command of the Supreme Chief to the Lieutenant General. The Supreme Chief no longer had authority over the contingent. Nonetheless the Acting Secretary for Native Affairs, who doggedly opposed the military authority, followed up the Supreme Chief's instruction of the 15th with a gratuitous order to the commandant of Colonial Defensive District No. VII, *viz.* Umvoti County, to tell the Natal Native Contingent at Kranskop that they would not be required to enter the Zulu country against their will. The Colonial Commandant duly informed Captain Cherry. As a professional officer, responsible to an imperial and not to a colonial superior, Cherry may well have dismissed the instruction as impertinent. We do not know.

Commandant Montgomery was no longer a professional officer. A settler, a gentleman with some pretensions in the Colony – he was a Justice of the Peace and had run (unsuccessfully) for the Legislative Assembly – it behoved him to comply with the secretary's instructions. He told the 1st Battalion on parade, through their head men, that they would not have to cross the Thukela against their will. Their reply was that they would follow him and their officers with perfect trust and willingly into Zululand. Only one person, a youth, did not agree. The feeling against him was so strong that Montgomery deemed it best to let him go home. The otherwise unanimous reply was, however, qualified. The men said that they were small in number and if required to march at once, they would be foolish to do so without the support of British troops. Let the British troops eat up the Zulu army – then they would go anywhere!

Montgomery's report was given to the Supreme Chief. The Supreme Chief pointed out to the Acting Secretary that the government could communicate with Captain Cherry or Commandant Montgomery only through the proper military authorities. He asked the Acting Secretary on whose authority he had committed such a breach of official etiquette, and bluntly told him that he would never have authorized what he had done. The secretary lamely answered that it was all a misunderstanding. The Lieutenant General was promptly informed of the mistake.[29]

The success of the Eshowe relief demonstration depended on enemy forces being distracted from the relief expedition. In fact, the Zulu King seems not to have been deceived, and it is debatable whether or not the demonstration benefited the relief expedition.[30] The demonstration assumed a provocative character after the relief and evacuation of the garrison. The Lieutenant General prolonged it and ordered raids where possible.[31] His orders were to have unpleasant consequences for the people who lived in the middle Thukela valley, for raiding invited retaliation. For the sake of grand strategy peace in the valley was destroyed. An intermittent, sometimes cruel war was introduced with a life of its own. In this warfare the 1st and 3rd Battalions and No. 3 Pioneer Company had an important if unenviable role to play.

On Sunday, March 23rd, Major Twentyman, commanding in Umvoti County, arrived at Fort Cherry. Here he arranged the details of the demonstration according to a plan he had submitted to the Lieutenant General. The contingent would go down to the Middle Drift. The Native Border Guard would mass at various fords as far as sixty miles upstream and twenty miles below. On Monday, at 4.30 in the afternoon, the garrison paraded. One company was left to hold the fort. The rest marched towards Kranskop. Then they picked their way down the escarpment on the winding road Durnford had had hacked out in December and January. The road was in disrepair. Night fell and progress was slow, but by daybreak most of the force was at the river.

They found themselves in a country very different from what they had become used to. Even in fall the climate of the middle Thukela valley is hot and uncomfortable. The soil is sandy and covered by thick scrub. There were crocodiles in the river. Some forty years before the Dutch invaders had taken the fertile, well-watered rolling uplands and left the dry infertile valley below to the people, either original inhabitants or latecomers, whose labour they did not need. Settlers called the land below the escarpment 'The Thorns' because of the number of thorn trees that flourished there.[32]

The Zulus across the river seemed surprised, in spite of a mysterious fire near Kranskop, which had appeared nightly for the last week and which the British assumed was some sort of signal to them. In any event, they quickly herded their cattle into the hills and out of sight. About a dozen men started shooting at the 1st Battalion, which had started throwing up an earthwork to secure the Middle Drift crossing. An exchange of shots followed. No one was hit, and the Zulus disappeared.

The 1st Battalion carried on with the work. A company was sent to guard a ferry about eleven hundred yards above the ford. It also threw up an earth-work. The 3rd Battalion went to a ford about three miles up the river. Natal Horse formed on a hill overlooking all, as a reserve. (Jantze's Horse was ordered to the lower Thukela to join the relief expedition, and left the demonstration.) The 3rd Battalion returned from upstream and took position on the right flank of the main force. Meanwhile, the pioneers were busy trying to fix the road so wagons with supplies could get down without mishap.

It was an exciting moment for the men. They looked straight across the river into the enemy's country, and they were eager to cross over to it, but the river was too high. A large boat, which Durnford had had sent down for the ferry, was launched. It held about twenty men. A barrel raft was also fixed up and launched the next day.

Wednesday, the 26th, was crucial. The Eshowe relief expedition would march the following day. Would the enemy be distracted? A party of Zulus appeared on the other bank, and now and then exchanged shots with the contingent. The work on the fort went on. The river began to fall. In the distance a small Zulu force could be glimpsed. Some people came down to the river on the other side waving a white flag. A ruse? The contingent fired. It was found that the people were seeking refuge!

Major Twentyman considered the demonstration a success and rode off to Native Border Guard headquarters, twenty miles away, to inspire the colonial effort. Captain Cherry was left in command at the Middle Drift.

The river continued to fall. On the 27th it was fordable at several points. There was the usual firing back and forth, but no one crossed the river. It was reported that two Zulu forces were on the other side. They had been seen through a telescope from the escarpment above. The day passed. There was rain and the river rose. The enemy need no longer fear. Captain Cherry was not so sanguine as Twentyman had been about the demonstration.

It was not only the fickle river that frustrated the demonstration. It was the Native Border Guard as well. Major Twentyman intended that it should cross the river and burn enemy homesteads. Did he not know that the Supreme Chief had forbidden it? Or did he know and suppose he could, as the imperial officer in the field, overrule the Supreme Chief's orders? Technically he was in command of all the forces in Umvoti County, but practically he could not force the Native Border Guard to do anything. The Supreme Chief retained command of it. The commandant of the Colonial Defensive District knew his orders: the Border Guard could go down to the river and demonstrate, but it was not to cross the river. Major Twentyman remonstrated in vain. What good was the demonstration now? If the Border Guard would not even cross the river, then the enemy would no longer fear it. There would be no need to keep a force against it. He wrote to the Lieutenant General to use his influence with the Supreme Chief. Unable to move the Colonial Commandant, he returned to his headquarters at Greytown to wait for the higher authorities to act.

The river ran high the next few days. Small groups of the enemy appeared in the vicinity of the Middle Drift and there was the occasional exchange. Permission for the Border Guard to cross was not forthcoming, even though some of it was willing enough. The Native Contingent must give bite to the demonstration.

Captain Cherry waited for an opportunity to put some of the contingent across the river. When he fell ill and had to return to the fort, Montgomery took

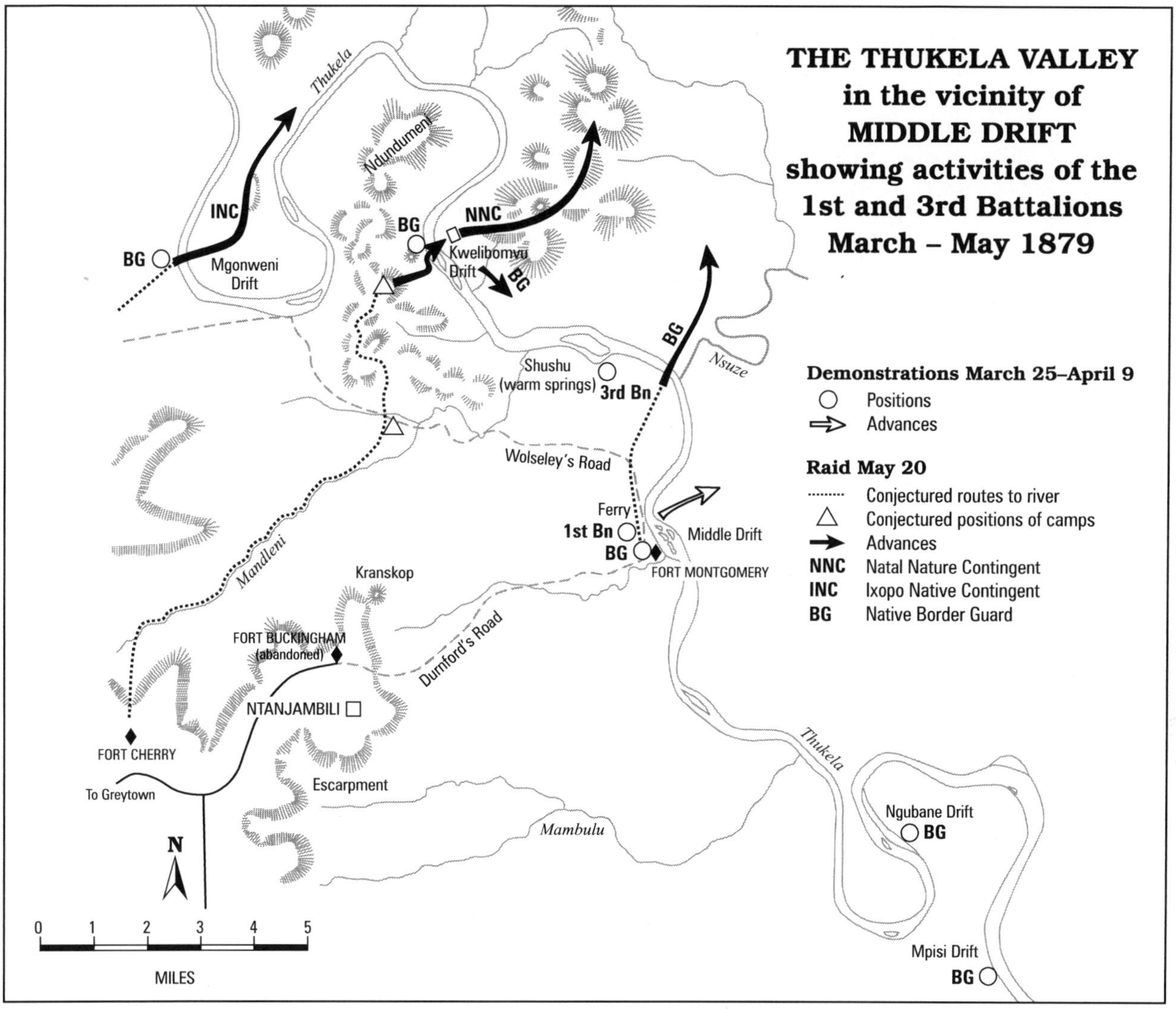

charge. On Wednesday, April 2nd – the battalions had been at the river nine days now – a small band crossed over on the boat and raft and made their way to two homesteads about a mile from the river. Presumably they harboured the enemy scouts who skirmished at the river. One was a chief's. Both were vacant, the inhabitants apparently having left a few days before, and were burnt. The officers wanted to go on, but the men refused. They had seen only a few enemy scouts, but probably knew there were stronger forces in the offing.

The telescope on the escarpment picked out several thousand Zulus about eighteen miles from the river, moving in the direction of the Middle Drift. They vanished behind a hill and did not reappear. Meanwhile the small band of raiders returned to the friendly shore unscathed.

On Thursday, April 3rd, Commandant Montgomery sent 150 men across the ferry to throw up a temporary fortification on the other side. A lieutenant and fifteen volunteers went about two miles to burn another homestead which the enemy scouts might be using. Some enemy fired at them at long range. They burnt the homestead, took some farm fowl and returned to the ferry.

The telescope on the escarpment spied a large number of Zulus about three miles from the ferry, apparently waiting to attack. A warning was sent to Montgomery. The river was still running high. The men on the other side were withdrawn. Next morning cattle could be seen on the hills several miles back and it was proposed to cross again, but the men of the contingent refused. It was a classic trick. The cattle were bait and an enemy force lay behind the hills. They recalled the Acting Secretary's message and their reply. They had been told they did not have to cross the river if they did not want to. And where were the British soldiers who had been (they now seemed to believe) promised to support them?

The demonstration no longer had much point. The mysterious fire at night on the escarpment ceased. More cattle appeared on the opposite hills. The relief and evacuation of Eshowe was accomplished, but on the 7th the Lieutenant

General's order to persist with raids was received. The river was high, but in any case the battalions were weakened since the officers' confidence had been shaken by the refusal of the men to cross on the 4th. The river front was quiet, except one night when two officers fishing by moonlight were shot at, and some Zulus fired across the river opposite the fort, causing the men camped outside to go in. There was also some shooting upstream. Morning came and all was quiet again. There were no further disturbances. Sickness was increasing. On the 10th the contingent returned to Fort Cherry. Fort Montgomery, as the earthwork by the river was called, was left for the use of the Border Guard.[33]

The monotony which characterized life at Fort Cherry before the relief demonstration returned. The officers had engaged for six months, and were not disposed to renew the engagement at the end of May. By that time the 1st Battalion had less than two officers per company.[34]

The men, of course, were bound for the duration of the war and kept in place by chiefs and head men. Desertion was negligible. The chief Somkolo of the amaNyuswa, in the 1st Battalion, died in the line of duty. He was taken ill at Fort Cherry and was carried home, where he expired.[35] The chief Nondonise of the amaThuli, on the 3rd Battalion, set an example of loyalty. He was an old man and lame. When his horse died Captain Cherry prevailed on the civil and reluctant military authorities to reimburse him, even though they were not legally obliged to do so, so that he could get a new one.[36]

Commandant Montgomery wrote to the Lieutenant General to have the 1st Battalion assigned to a sector where it might experience combat. The Lieutenant General proposed that it join the column preparing to invade Zululand in the north. The 3rd Battalion could remain at Kranskop and be augmented. It was not to be. Major-General Clifford was appointed to command the forces in Natal, and Lord Chelmsford's jurisdiction was confined to the forces immediately involved in the invasion of Zululand. An officer of the Royal Engineers toured the border and reported on its defence, and the Major General concluded that the 1st Battalion should stay where it was.[37] Indeed, the Native Contingent at Kranskop was reinforced by a mounted detachment of the Ixopo Native Contingent, which, after two months seasoning in reserve, was now being parcelled out to strategic posts in the district. Also, several units of mounted colonials were transferred to Umvoti. The forces on the border were not reduced, they were strengthened.[38]

Raid at kweliBomvu Drift

The next foray over the border was in support of the second invasion of Zululand. The Lieutenant General was of the opinion that occasional raids across the border would distract the enemy and throw him off balance there. He also abandoned the idea of making war on the Zulu King and not on the Zulu people, for the latter plainly served the King's cause. The sooner the Zulu people were made to suffer, the sooner they would seek relief in peace.[39]

The demonstration was plainly aggressive, a raid across the Thukela to destroy homesteads and food stores and to take livestock. Major Twentyman had a larger force at his disposal than before. Besides the two battalions of foot and the company of pioneers of the Native Contingent, there was the Ixopo Native Contingent, which had about eight hundred men on foot and five hundred mounted. Also, there were about a hundred mounted colonials. The men in the colonial units availed themselves of the discretion allowed by the Supreme Chief and most were willing to cross the border into Zululand.[40]

The cool season in Natal is also a dry season. During autumn the Thukela fell, making all the fords usable. The only problem was grazing, which became scarce as the season progressed. If the mounted troops were to be used to advantage, it was best to use them soon, while the horses were still well nourished.[41]

The sector chosen for the raid was upstream from the Middle Drift. Major Twentyman would lead the Native Contingent and the colonials with two troops of the mounted Ixopo men across kweliBomvu Drift, and they would work upriver to their left and meet the bulk of the Ixopo mounted contingent, moving downriver from Mkhandeni Drift. While the object was to do as much material damage as possible, there were strict orders against harming women and children. The Native Border Guard, still under the firm control of the Supreme Chief, would co-operate: a reserve levy would watch over kweliBomvu Drift until the raiding force returned. A smaller levy several miles downriver was given leave to cross and raid, evidently to avenge the enemy's shooting the son of a petty chief.

The 1st and 3rd Battalions and the pioneers marched out of Fort Cherry during the afternoon of Monday, May 20th. They carried two rocket troughs with them. Captain Cherry was in command. Commandant Montgomery was away on leave and captains commanded the battalions. They descended the escarpment, whose face is steep and in places precipitous, and joined the mounted colonials, who had taken another route. They were in a clearing near an old military road built by the British in

1875. The sun was going down and there was little time to rest. The combined force moved north towards the kweliBomvu. After a couple of hours they bivouacked in a thicket on top of a ridge, about a mile from the ford. It had been hard going all day. The Thorns lived up to its name, very broken and stony ground, much bush and, of course, an abundance of thorns. The march was made longer by the effort to keep out of sight of the enemy across the river in order to obtain surprise.

The camp was astir early. The column arrived at the river as day broke. Evidently surprise had been achieved, for cattle were in the corrals across the river. There was no time to lose. The mounted colonials and the pioneers scrambled down the bank and onto a dry part of the river bed. The mounted men splashed through the water to a bare sandy island where they stopped. They could not find the ford in the mainstream beyond! From a low ridge 800 yards away some eight or ten Zulus opened fire on them and shouted 'Usuthu!'. They hit no one, but the shots came close. The pioneers opened a counter fire, which cleared the ridge. The colonials found the ford, crossed and drew up under the steep farther bank. The Ixopo men, mounted on tough little ponies, took the lead, and the battalions of the contingent swarmed across and onto the low ridge. The units moved to left and right and also straight up the hillside. There was a long, hard climb of two miles to the top.

The Zulus, in small groups, skirmished to hold back the advance while the inmates of the homesteads fled hurriedly and spirited away the cattle. They could not stop the contingent. A small body of the enemy on the right was dispersed by a couple of rockets. In keeping with orders, the men bore to the left, approximately following the spine of a series of hills overlooking the river. They worked their way into a small valley containing several homesteads and burnt them. As the flames consumed the huts, explosions were heard from inside – cartridges for rifles. Large quantities of corn and sorghum were burnt as well. But the cattle were gone. Only some goats and a couple of chickens remained to be captured.

The advance carried two miles along the high ground. Ahead was a peak with cattle on it. The contingent and the Ixopo men wanted to get them, but Major Twentyman intervened. The force was straggling badly in the rough country. The mounted colonials with their large clumsy horses could not keep up. Moreover there was no sign of the main Ixopo mounted force supposed to be moving down from the left to meet them. The ground in that direction fell and rose steeply and was covered more densely with bush.

The men of one company asked their captain if they could go on alone and capture the cattle, but the raiding force drew in. It seemed a good time to go back to the ford. The Major directed the raiders to the left, down from the hills to the river. They followed it back to the ford. The Native Border Guard was in position there and covered their crossing. Indeed, such was the enthusiasm to raid that during the absence of the main force, a portion of the guard had gone over and burnt a couple of homesteads the main force had missed.

The main force returned to the rendezvous in the clearing. It was learned that the forces which had gone across above and below had also raided successfully and returned safely. Reports of small bands of Zulus avenging themselves on homesteads on this side of the river put everyone on alert in the evening, but the afternoon passed without further incident. The next morning the contingent returned to Fort Cherry.

Thirteen homesteads had been burnt across the kweliBomvu. Difficult terrain, not enemy resistance, had prevented doing more damage. The raiders had suffered no loss. The Native Contingent had done what it was conceived to do best, scout and skirmish as light infantry. It had done both well. Cherry's only problem with his men had been trying to get them under cover when they came under fire![42] The kweliBomvu raid enhanced the Native Contingent's reputation, especially among the Europeans prejudiced against it by its reluctance to cross the river during the demonstration in April.[43]

Most of the company officers were about to leave now, and a single successful raid was not enough to sustain morale undermined by boredom. The men declared they, too, would leave on June 21st, six months after their enrolment.[44] Somehow they were disabused of this idea, which must not have been easy to do. The remaining officers set an unedifying example by drinking heavily while Captain Cherry was sick and absent in Greytown in mid-June, but they got a good dressing-down for it from Captain Tollner, his eccentric executive officer.[45]

Commandant Montgomery returned from leave and his adjutant informed him that the head men of the battalion wished to see him. He called them up after parade. They said that they were the mouths of their men. For some time the men had been arguing over certain matters. They came to the commandant for advice and he told them to speak out. They stated that the men felt they had been deceived. They saw the majority of the officers leaving, and they were sick and restless, too. What was the cause, asked the commandant. They had been told they would be paid so much every month. They had served five months, but they had been paid for only one month. Therefore they could not buy clothes or tobacco. They had been promised they would go into the Zulu country with British troops. Instead they were kept like the Border Guard and they did fatigue work all the time. Their magistrate had told them that they would probably serve three months, certainly not more than six. They were tired of being so long at this place. They got up at 4.30 every morning in the cold to watch for nothing. If they continued to do so their feet would become so cracked none of them would be able to march.

Montgomery reminded them that the Supreme Chief's word was law and the Supreme Chief received his authority from the Queen, but the Queen did not wish to deceive her subjects. As commandant, he had made representations for them before; he would do so now with regard to pay and tell them the result, but as the Queen's soldiers they must continue to serve. The commandant duly conveighed the complaints to Captain Cherry for transmission to the Major General commanding in Natal. He added that his battalion had stood fast when others had bolted after Isandlwana. Columns were invading Zululand again, and his men saw those who had run away going with them while they stayed in Natal. The pioneers were clothed and paid every month; even the Border Guard and transport drivers were paid every month.

The Major General received the message and informed the Supreme Chief and the Acting Secretary for Native Affairs, stating that faith had not been kept with these men and they should receive their arrears in pay, also extra clothing for the winter,[46] but transfer was out of the question. The battalion was needed at Kranskop.

On June 10th two companies went down to the Middle Drift and remained there while men in the area paid the annual hut tax.[47] They left some time before the Zulu stormed across the river and took revenge on the people living in the Thorns.

Return to Static Defence

On June 25th strong Zulu forces crossed the Thukela above and below the Middle Drift and devastated the country below Kranskop. They could not have come at a more inopportune time for the battalions garrisoning Fort Cherry. There were few officers left. Captain Cherry was suffering from an illness which had set in with the cold and dry weather. It resembled colic and could be very painful. Attacks usually lasted several days. He had to go to Greytown for treatment. He had just returned and was between attacks, but he depended heavily on Captain Tollner, his second in command. Tollner was anxious to leave as his term of service expired in June, but generously remained because of Cherry's condition. Major Twentyman was at the fort when the raid occurred, but there was little he or anyone could do about it.[48]

The Zulus crossed in the morning mist, did their work quickly and methodically, and were gone before the forces on the escarpment could react. The Native Border Guard on the spot was surprised, outmanoeuvred and dispersed.[49]

The raid inflicted much greater damage than the British-led raids had done. Altogether seventy-four homesteads were burnt and more than five hundred cattle and two hundred goats taken. Twenty-seven persons were killed, including several infirm and children burnt in their huts. Forty persons were carried off, many of them relatives of Natal renegades.[50]

The raid should not have been a surprise. Since the end of April the Border Police in Umvoti and the Msinga had received several reports that the Zulus intended to raid the Kranskop sector, but rumours of raids were commonplace along the border, and for once both the Lieutenant General and the Acting Secretary for Native Affairs were in agreement in dismissing them. At the end of May the name of the Zulu King was mentioned in connection with retaliation for the kweliBomvu raid. It was reported also that he had called up men to his great place – presumably to meet the British invading column – but those on the border were apparently not responding. Whether this was due to fear of another British raid and determination to protect their homes or to preparation for a retaliatory raid is unknown. On June 20th the Border Police near the Middle Drift were fired on, and an alarm was created when an Ixopo mounted patrol went along the river and afterwards a large number of enemy was stationed above the kweliBomvu. The raiders on the 25th consisted of more than the able-bodied men of the Zulu chiefdom just across the river.[51]

The galling thing about the raid for the government and indeed for all the defenders of the border, was that it took them by surprise and they were helpless to do anything about it. Commandant Montgomery was apparently one of the first and the few to descend into the Thorns in the wake of the raid. He found a girl cowering in the bush, exhausted from running, pulled her up on his horse and carried her back to the fort.[52] That act pretty well summed up the reaction to the raids: compassion and succour. The battalions did not go down to the river, but remained on alert at the fort. On the night of the 26th there were false reports that the Zulus had crossed again and the garrison stood to arms all night.[53]

The government and the military considered and decided not to evacuate the border population. Evacuation would create greater hardship in the winter season and strain the resources of the Colony. The chief of the people in the Location adjacent to the Middle Drift asked for the Native Contingent to relieve his own men in the Border Guard so they could look after their families. Two hundred men went down to the river on the 30th. They remained for about a week, exchanging some shots with enemy scouts across the river. They also improved Fort Montgomery until it looked as though it could be held against a large enemy force. On July 10th two companies were sent to the Mpisi ford downstream to replace the Border Guard there while its men paid taxes. These detachments apparently were withdrawn when the Border Guard was able to function again.[54]

Not only did the Zulu raid give Zulus moral ascendancy along the border, but it dispelled any notion that the battalions would disband soon. They remained at Fort Cherry, and the sensitive border was reinforced by additional men of the Ixopo contingent who threw up another fort on the escarpment lower down.[55]

Commandant Montgomery went off to Helpmekaar. He had at last got a transfer, and was to become commandant of Colonial Defensive District No. 1, which included the Msinga Division.[56] The pioneers marched to Rorke's Drift in July 4th.[57] The 1st and 3rd Battalions were consolidated as the 1st Battalion, under Captain Cherry, and remained at Fort Cherry until September 24th.[58] There were no more raids and the border remained quiet. There also appear to have been no more complaints about serving there.

NOTES

1 CSO 1925: 526/1879. *The Fannin Papers: A Pioneer's Story of the Diamond Fields and the Zulu War* (edited by Natalie Fannin; Durban, Robinson, 1932), p. 33.

2 Norris-Newman, *In Zululand with the British*, p. 111. CSO 686/1879.

3 TN, February 7, 1879: 'Krantz Kop.'

4 A.N. Montgomery, 'Isandhlwana: A Visit Six Months after the Battle.' in *Leisure Hour Magazine*, XL (1892), 539.

5 SNA 1/6/12 no. 15. Twentyman's report (February 17, 1879), that the 1st Battalion had 1005 men, probably includes the Ngwane companies and therefore would be incorrect: however, Montgomery's statement (in TN, January 22, 1879: letter) that he had 887 present would exclude them. The 1st Battalion's adjutant gives 750 about the end of February (in NC, March 6, 1879: letter), which suggests that an appreciable number had deserted. NM, February 13, 1879: 'Our Natives at Krantzkop' reports that two companies deserted at the time of the 'great scare' at Helpmekaar; however, it is not quite clear whether the reference is really to the battalions at Kranskop or the one at Sand Spruit. See also, NW, February 13: 'With No. 2 Column – Native Contingent,' and April 1, 1879: report; Montgomery, 'Isandhlwana,' p. 539; and *cf.* NM, February 8, 1879: 'Natal Men or Zulus'.

6 NW, February 13, 1879: 'With No. 2 Column – Native Contingent.'

7 1/RMD, 3/2/1: Montgomery to A.C. Hawkins, February 1, 1879. *A Soldier's Life*, p. 205.

8 TN, February 7: 'Krantz Kop,' and March 19, 1879: 'Krantzkop.'

9 NW, February 13, 1879: 'With No. 2 Column – Native Contingent.' TN, March 19, 1879: 'Krantzkop.' *Illustrated London News*, June 28, 1879: report, quoted in *The Zulu War as reported in "The Illustrated London News" during January – December 1879* (compiled by S. Bourquin and Tania M. Johnston (Durban, the compilers, 1971), p. 110. *Fannin Papers*, p. 37.

10 E.S. Newmarch, Diary. February 3, 1879. C2374, p. 28. CSO 684: 666/1879; and 1926: 682, 684, 708, 709, 872/1879. *Cf.* NM, Febraury 13, 1879: 'Own Natives at Krantzkop.'

11 NW, February 13, 1879: 'With No. 2 Column – Native Continent.' NC, March 6, 1879: report. SNA 1/6/12. no. 74. 1/BGV, IV: 325–326, 328–329, 342–345, 351. See returns in SNA 1/6/14, nos. 4, 10 and 12.

12 SNA 1/6/12 nos. 15, 42, 67, 70; and 1/6/14, nos. 4 and 12. GH 1423: unnumbered memorandum by Bulwer, dated March 6, 1879. *Lord Chelmsford's Zululand Campaign*, p. 112.

13 SNA 1/6/14, nos. 4 and 12.

14 Laband and Thompson, *War Comes to Umvoti*, pp. 42–44.

15 NC, February 18, 1879: 'With the Native Contingent.' NW, March 15, 1879: report.

16 NAD/A863. J.E. Fannin letters: Fannin to his wife, February 19, 1879. One receives an impression of Montgomery as a vigorous and restless officer whose reports of his men's grievances are part projections of his own resentment at being confined to a quiet front. There is also a dark side of his character. The only suicide among officers of the contingent was that of a young man in his battalion who had been his house guest (see *War Comes to Umvoti*; pp. 111–113). Montgomery probably was not responsible for this, of course – at least not in a direct sense. More damning of him and destructive of his public career subsequently were sordid details of his personal life revealed in a confidential government investigation in September 1879 (see CSO 2554: C114/1879 and related documents). It was alleged that he had carnal knowledge of a young female house guest and she had borne a child secretly, and that Montgomery had been instrumental in its murder.

Notwithstanding this and her efforts to escape his attentions, he developed a violent passion for the girl, now since removed to her family, which may explain in part his absences from the battalion. (Montgomery was married and in twenty-five years his wife had borne him nine children.) Montgomery did not deny the allegations, but the matter was not pressed; however, the Lieutenant Governor was incensed at the probability of infanticide, and Montgomery held no position of public trust for sixteen years and even after that none of consequence.

17 *The Graphic*, May 10, 1879: 'With the Natal Native Contingent – Officer's Drill,' quoted in *The First Six Months of the Zulu War of 1879 As Reported in 'The Graphic'... January – June, 1879* (compiled by S. Bourquin; Durban, the compiler, 1963), p. 59.

18 Clarke, *Zululand at War*, p. 98. NW, March 6, 1879: report.

19 TN, January 29 and March 3, 1879: GO 19 and 43, respectively. NM, February 17, 1879: GO 32. *The South African Campaign*, p. 334.

20 Fannin to his wife, March 5, 1879. Norris-Newman, *In Zululand with the British*, p. 111. TN, December 13, 1878: GO 219.

21 See returns in SNA 1/6/14, nos. 4 and 12. TN, March 3, 1879: GO 43. Barton left on March 1st (*Fannin Papers*, p. 39). Also, see Fannin to his wife, March 14, 1879, and reports in TN, March 28 and April 2, 1879.

22 *Narrative*, p. 170.

23 TN, March 12: GO 53, and May 28, 1879: 'Military Notes.' NM, May 16, 1879: report. *Fannin Papers*, p. 45.

24 CSO 683: 545/1879; and 1926: 697/1879. C2374, pp. 28–29.

25 CSO 1926: 961/1879.

26 There were only two military roads to the Middle Drift, the one from Kranskop made at Durnford's direction, and the other, made at Sir Garnet Wolseley's direction in 1875, which entered the Dimane valley to the west of the kop and then approximately paralleled the river. Both were in disuse at this time. See John Laband, *Kingdom in crisis: The Zulu reponse to the British invasion of 1879* (Manchester, University Press, 1992), pp. 132–133; Laband and Thompson, *Kingdom and Colony at War*, pp. 154–155, and *War Comes to Umvoti*, pp. 45–46.

27 *Lord Chelmsford's Zululand Campaign*, pp. 117 and 154.

28 See Laband and Thompson, *Kingdom and Colony at War*, p. 156 *et passim* for the relevant part of the controversy over use of colonial troops.

29 SNA 1/3/33, no. 106; and 1/7/12, p. 79.

30 Laband, *Kingdom in crisis*, p. 148.

31 C2318, p. 49. *Fannin Papers*, p. 42.

32 CSO 673: 4803/1878.

33 The account of the demonstration is based on Major Twentyman's reports in C2367, pp. 50–51, and CP 26–27, and extracts in NC, April 10; NM, April 9; and TN, April 14, 1879; the various correspondents' accounts in NM, April 12; NW, April 12, 15 and 22; and TN, April 2 and 16, 1879; and Fannin's reports in C2318, pp. 41–71 *passim*; C2367, p. 104; and CSO 1926 *passim*; as well as the letters to his wife, March 26–April 10, 1879 *passim* and the *Fannin Papers*, pp. 42–43.

34 GH 569: G378 and G442/1879. TN, June 9, 1879: report.

35 SNA 1/1/33, no. 54.

36 1/GTN, 3/2/1: 1209/1879.

37 GH 569: G378/1879.

38 NM, April 12, May 17 and 21, 1879: reports.

39 *Lord Chelmsford's Zululand Campaign*, p. 154.

40 SNA 1/6/13, no. 44. CP 16–25: Twentyman's report, May 22, 1879. Reports in NC, May 31; NM, May 17, 21, 27; NW, May 15, 1879.

41 Reports in NC, August 8, and NM, May 21, June 19 and July 7, 1879.

42 The account of the raid is based on Twentyman's report in CP 16–25; W.D. Wheelwright's reports in C2454, pp. 63–65; the various correspondent's accounts in NC, May 27 and 31; NM, May 27; NW, June 3, 1879; reports in NM, May 29 and 30, and TN, June 2 and 11, 1879; Fannin's reports in C2374, pp. 90–91 and C2454, pp. 82–83 and in CSO 1927 *passim*, as well as the letter to his wife, May 21, 1879, and in the *Fannin Papers*, pp. 46–47. The location of the kwelibomvu drift on the map is problematic. Contemporary maps differ in its placement, and I have used an aerial photograph to select what appears to be the most likely one. The impact of the raid on the Zulu is assessed succinctly in Laband, *Kingdom in crisis*, pp. 184–185.

43 TN, June 4: 'The Natal Native Contingent;' and June 9, 1879: 'Greytown.'

44 CSO 1927: 2720/1879.

45 *Fannin Papers*, p. 48.

46 GH 569. G442/1879.

47 C2454, p. 207.

48 C2454, p. 152. Fannin to his wife, April 1, 3, 7, 13, 18, 24; June 4, 9, 12, 20, 23, 26; July 7 and 8; August 5, 6, 8; September 9, 1879.

49 For details of the Zulu raid see Wheelwright's reports in C2454, pp. 152–153; CSO 1927: 2185/1879; and SNA 1/1/34, no. 150; Fannin's reports in C2454, pp. 152–157 *passim*, and C2482, p. 81; and the various reports in NC, July 1; NM, July 1, 3, 4, 7; and TN, June 27 and 30, 1879.

50 C2482, p. 80.

51 CSO 1927: 2277, 2480, 2548, 2773, 2978, 3080, 3102/1879. SNA 1/7/12, pp. 94–95. Reports in NC, May 31; and NM, May 5 and 8, July 3 and 7, 1879. French, *Lord Chelmsford and the Zulu War*, p. 181. Symons, My Reminiscences of the Zulu War, pp. 59–60. Also, see the testimony in Supreme Chief vs Beje, Majingola, and twenty-two others, in CSO 835: 4758. Laband doubts (*Kingdom in crisis*, p. 187) that the Zulu king sanctioned the raid.

52 NM, July 2, 1879: report.

53 C2454, p. 156.

54 C2454, pp. 156–157. C2482, pp. 79 and 81–82. CSO 1927: 3343/1879.

55 C2482, p. 82. Fannin to his wife, July 1, 1879.

56 Fannin to his wife, June 27, 1879. NW, July 3, 1870: GO --.

57 CSO 1927: 3281/1879.

58 Fannin to his wife, June 27, 1879. *Fannin Papers*, p. 52.

Chapter 12

WAR ON THE PLAIN

The 1st Division at Fort Chelmsford

The British army prepared to invade the Zulu country again in May. The force at the coast was the 1st Division, successor to the old No. 1 Column. The forces in the interior were the 2nd Division, successor to the old No. 3 Column, and the so-called Flying Column, the No. 4 Column on the Transvaal-Zulu border with a new name. There were delays, in part because of inadequate transport and supply – a constant vexation deriving from relatively light settlement and primitive communications, and in part because a suitable route in the interior had to be found. By early June both these problems had been overcome to the extent that the invasion could begin. The 2nd Division, often called the 'Headquarters Column' because the Lieutenant-General accompanied it, and the Flying Column would converge and then move together along high ground to Ulundi, the great place of the Zulu King.

In this invasion the Natal Native Contingent played an important part. While not so numerous as in the first invasion, it still made up a large part of the invading columns. The Lieutenant General described its importance:

> ...[T]he presence of these battalions with the column ... is absolutely indispensable to their efficiency; as there is much work which native levies alone can properly perform – They are excellent scouts, indefatigable and quick witted; perform all fatigue duties most cheerfully; and can be employed with mounted men when necessary, in consequence of their wonderful marching powers – Many of the men are employed as spies; and all cheerfully and willingly perform any duty they may be detailed for such as bringing in wood, repairing roads, searching difficult country, building entrenched posts, etc, etc ...'[1]

The relief of Eshowe marked the ascendancy of British armies at the coast. The enemy had been defeated in battle, the beleaguered garrison rescued, and a foothold in the Zulu country established. What followed was a consolidation of that hold and a methodical advance along the coastal plain, which deprived the Zulu King of his power there. The campaign turned out to be more important politically than militarily. The 1st Division consisted of six battalions of infantry and smaller units of other troops. The 4th and 5th Battalions, the No. 2 Pioneer Company, Jantze's Horse and the Mafunzi Corps, made up one-fifth of its strength.[2]

The 4th and 5th Battalions had remained at the laager at Gingindlovu when the Lieutenant General led a flying column to lift the Zulu siege of Eshowe. The laager was reduced in size to accommodate the smaller garrison. The returning flying column passed it by and laagered on top of a low ridge about 3000 yards to the southeast. The garrison of the old laager joined it a day later, on April 7th.[3]

The new camp was situated on two adjacent hills. The British infantry occupied the higher one, the two battalions of the Native Contingent occupied the lower one. At night three British companies with a Gatling gun and a rocket tube came down to reinforce the battalions. It was arranged that they would do so in day-time, too, if there was alarm. A shelter trench was dug around the camp. A breastwork and a bush entanglement were added. Strong defences were in order. This was the most advanced position the British had in the Zulu country. Unfortunately, it proved to be no healthier than the old laager on the blood-soaked battlefield. Diarrhoea and dysentery became a problem and were blamed on the water, drawn from nearby streams.[4]

The Lieutenant General left camp in April 7th to superintend the British reinforcements arriving at Durban and arrangements for the second invasion of Zululand.[5] His orders to the commander of the 1st Division, Major-General H.H. Crealock, were to establish a strong forward base at the Nyezane and from it to advance and destroy the cantonments of the Zulu army at Mangweni and Ndini and to clear the district in which they lay. He should do this as soon as possible. No physical difficulties were expected in the vicinity of these strongholds. It *was* expected that the Zulu King would try to defend these places. The implication was there were battles to be fought and the 1st Division would be diverting enemy force from the main thrust of the interior columns. After it destroyed the cantonments the 1st Division should try to assist the main thrust, which, it was expected, would have reached the vicinity of Mthonjaneni.

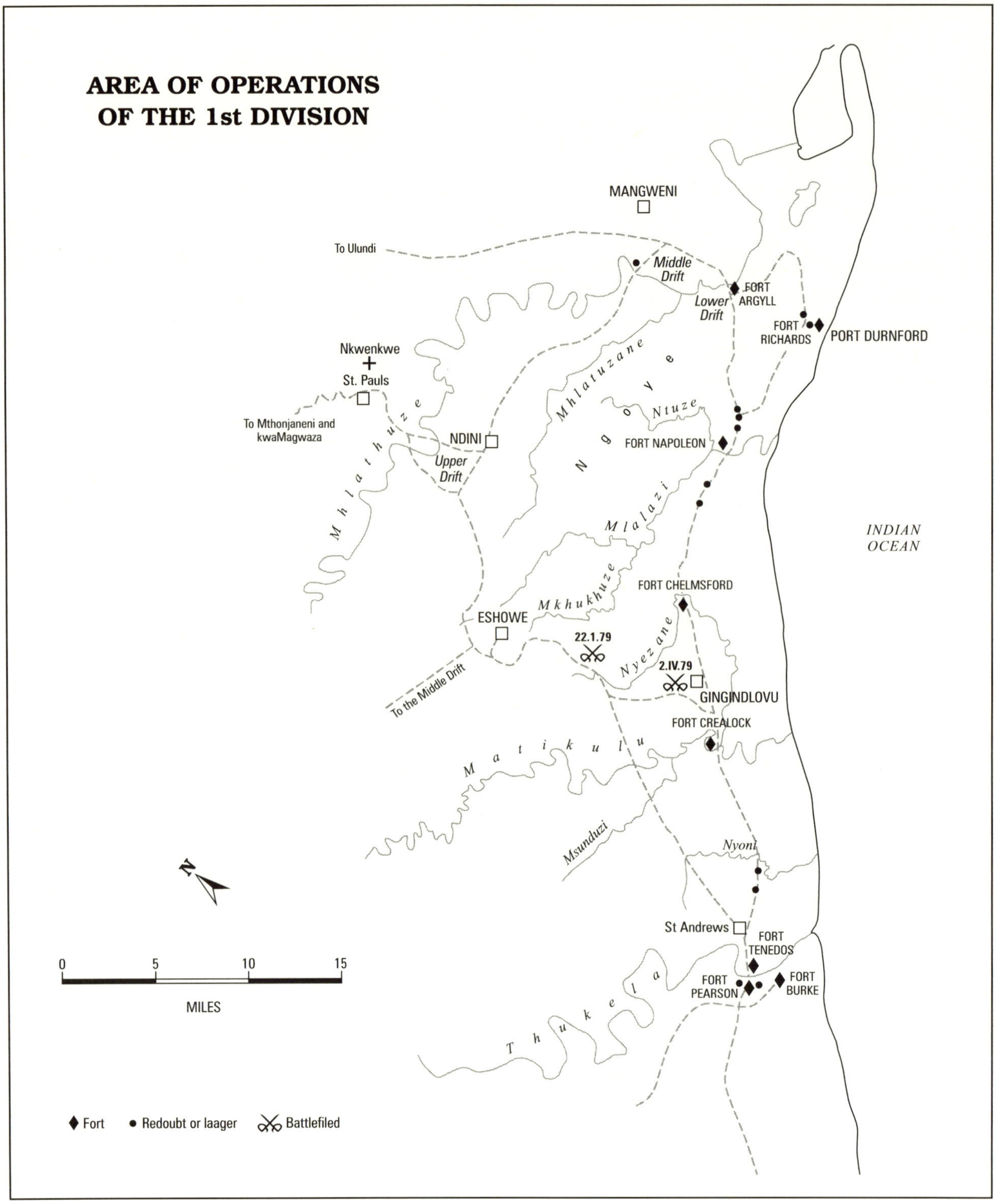

'Try' because it was presumed that rugged hill country above the coastal plain would inhibit its movement. The Lieutenant General did not envisage the 1st Division's moving further than the vicinity of St. Paul's, an abandoned mission station about fifteen miles beyond Eshowe and twenty miles short of Mthonjaneni.[6]

The 2nd Brigade of the 1st Division advanced from Gingindlovu about four miles on April 24th and 25th to a position on the right bank of the Nyezane. This was the place chosen for the strong forward base. It was on a rise of ground in a large irregular bend of the river, so an enemy must approach it from the river on three sides. The river was full of crocodiles. Fortification started at once, and was completed on May 10th. It was called Fort Chelmsford, in honour of the Lieutenant General.

Pickets were stationed around the fort and vedettes were posted on the high ground at a distance. The mounted men also patrolled the wider vicinity. They went up the coast to the Mlalazi river and inland to the Mvutshini stream. The local people, overawed, tended to avoid them. There was no chance of a surprise enemy attack. Indeed, no enemy force was found in the vicinity. Garrison duty at Fort Chelmsford consisted of improving the earthworks, guarding horses, and escorting convoys.[7]

Convoys were all important to the 1st Division. The Lieutenant General had ordered that it should advance against the Zulu strong places as soon as possible, but also that it should store two months' provisions at the fort and advance with one month's supplies. So the garrison could only make a quick advance after it had accumulated the supplies. The first convoy, carrying three weeks' supplies for the 2nd Brigade, left the lower Thukela on April 21st and reached the Nyezane on the 24th. Meanwhile a convoy of empty wagons left Gingindlovu for the lower Thukela. At the Matikulu the escorts exchanged convoys. This was the pattern, exchanges of convoys taking place between the Matikulu and the Nyoni for the next eight weeks. Several earthworks were built along the convoy route for protection. The most important of these was Fort Crealock, at the Matikulu.

A fully laden convoy carried from seven to nine thousand pounds. 802 wagon loads of supplies and 84 of ordnance stores were sent from the lower Thukela to Fort Chelmsford. The average number of wagons in a convoy was 102. There were 3500 oxen and about 250 wagons initially available for transport. When a convoy arrived at Fort Chelmsford as many as 1600 oxen had to be corralled. Still, there were not enough oxen to move all the provisions at once in the available vehicles.

The oxen, from Natal, were not used to being worked very hard. Now, they were being worked six days out of every eight. The sandy soil of the coast made heavy going. When it rained, though it did not rain often in the fall, the way became heavier still. The Matikulu crossing was difficult, but lesser streams could be difficult, too, requiring double teams to get across. There were not enough drivers for the wagons, and many of them did not know their work. Inexperienced transport officers leaned heavily on experienced conductors, but the conductors usually were not mounted, horses and mules being in short supply.

The convoys followed a well beaten track, along which the oxen ate up most of the grass. Some grass was burnt to grow sweet, but pickets and patrols had to keep the oxen from feeding on the new growth too soon. Undernourished and overworked, the oxen fell prey to sickness in the moist warm coastal climate. Many collapsed. A convoy usually lost fifteen to twenty, sometimes thirty oxen. They died at the rate of ten a day. No wonder then that the 1st Division was not ready to leave Fort Chelmsford until the third week in June. By then the convoy route was littered with rotting carcasses. The smell made men sick.[8]

The 4th and 5th Battalions had a relatively easy war. The 4th Battalion was regularly engaged in escorting convoys between Fort Chelmsford and Fort Crealock. The entire battalion was employed for the first three convoys, half of it for the next six. The 5th Battalion left Fort Chelmsford on May 10th. Half of it garrisoned Fort Crealock, along with a battalion of British infantry. The other half of the battalion went on to the lower Thukela for fatigue work there.

Garrison and escort duties were hardly onerous. The men working on fortifications soon made them as well as British soldiers did. They built the corrals for the cattle and kept them in repair. They cut timber and grass and built sheds. They unloaded the wagons when convoys arrived.[9]

Returns for April 21st and July 7th show that the strength of the 4th Battalion declined from 789 to 720 and that of the 5th Battalion from 1107 to 879; losses of 8,7% and 20,6%, respectively, suggesting that sickness or desertion or both were more serious in the 5th Battalion than in the 4th. Sickness does not appear to have been so much a problem as it was for the British soldiers, for the men of the 4th and 5th Battalions were acclimatized to the coast. Desertion was a problem, although again statistics are fragmentary and for the 5th Battalion only. Some deserters probably were men granted leave who did not understand that they had to return promptly at the end of it. Whatever the case, Commandant Nettleton, of the 5th Battalion, sent a detachment of amaQadi to bring back deserters on June 14th. The detachment was armed. The Commandant explained to the Resident Magistrate of Inanda that desertion had become so frequent that strong measures were becoming necessary to stop it.

The Commandant did not attribute desertion to any particular cause, but it reflects on the discipline and therefore the leadership of the battalion. In May and June many officers were leaving the contingent as their commissions expired. Their departure may have had a demoralizing effect on the men. There is no record of how many officers left the 4th and 5th Battalions at this time, but on May 18th two companies of the contingent had to be sent back to the lower Thukela from Fort Chelmsford because their officers were about to leave and they would be "unserviceable" without them.[10]

The mounted troops were tested to the limit during the build-up period. Outpost duty, patrolling and reconnoitring were not normally burdensome tasks, and at the beginning of April horse-sickness which had plagued the mounts since February ended. Yet the coastal climate still seemed to affect many of the horses badly. The main problem was lack of forage for the horses. The allocation was five pounds a day. In mid-May it was doubled. The division commander ordered that the horses be fed out of courses or troughs, or that feed bags be used and sheets be spread on the ground to prevent the loss of corn or grain! The condition of the horses improved when their rations did. Then, at the end of May many were affected by a skin disease. Several showed symptoms of a form of glanders and had to be shot. Twenty per cent of the horses were unserviceable. Sickness accounted for eighteen percent in May alone. Remounts came in dribs and drabs and did not begin to make up the losses.

Janze's Horse and the Mafunzi Corps were hit hard by horse sickness. Also, the men's clothing and equipment were in poor condition, until rectified in May. On April 21st the two corps mounted ninety-five men. A week later they mounted only fifty-six. The Mafunzi Corps apparently was sent back to the lower Thukela early in May. The reason is not clear. It returned early in June. Jantze's Horse remained at Fort Chelmsford. It mounted forty-four men in mid-May. In June conditions improved. The two corps mounted 114 men at Fort Chelmsford on the 16th, just prior to the division's advance onto the Mlalazi plain.[11]

The enemy was no longer entirely absent. On May 19th a company of the 5th Battalion was sent from Fort Crealock to reconnoitre the valley of the Matikulu. Ten men from the company were 'foraging' on their own account when they came across a party of thirty Zulus who fired and killed one of them. A reconnaissance of the Matikulu bush was made on May 21st. The detachment of the 5th Battalion at Fort Crealock assisted the mounted troops by working up the Matikulu valley towards the crossing of the Eshowe track. No enemy was seen. On the 23rd the mounted troops made another reconnaissance up the coast, in the direction the division would move in when the build-up of supplies was complete. They skirted the Mlalazi river and tested the water supply (which was very poor) at the middle ford.[12]

Five days of rainy weather set in, but on the 28th Jantze's vedettes observed a party of twenty Zulus near their post and larger parties across the Nyezane. The weather cleared on the 31st. On the 1st of June six men of the 4th Battalion were collecting wood about two miles from Fort Chelmsford when they were surrounded and surprised by the enemy and one of them was shot. The mounted men hastened up but failed to find the attackers. They noticed that the homesteads in the hill country to the north along the Mkhukhuze stream had been reoccupied. Two days later a party scouting from Fort Crealock to Gingindlovu saw some Zulus whom they took to be enemy soldiers. A detachment of the contingent went after them and searched the bush in vain. The alarm was sounded at Fort Crealock that night. British infantry manned the breastworks, while the men of the 5th Battalion squatted in silence in the centre of the fort, waiting for an attack. None came.[13]

A prisoner taken by a mounted patrol on June 11th said that a force of 5000 men had been waiting across the Mlalazi until the end of May, when the Zulu King had called it to Ulundi. As it left, many of the people in the vicinity also had left their homesteads for the interior again.[14] On June 12th, telegraphic communication between Fort Chelmsford and the lower Thukela was interrupted several times and inspection revealed a length of wire had been cut out of the line. It was supposed Zulus had done it.[15] The country had been secured, but it was not entirely safe.

By mid-June the 1st Division was ready to advance against Mangweni and Ndini. It had taken two months to accumulate the stores considered necessary to support this advance. By this time the columns in the interior were well on the way to Ulundi. The 1st Division had yet to divert any significant force of the enemy from them. Nor was it likely that it would, now that the invading force was in the heart of the Zulu Kingdom. The strategic relevance of the 1st Division's mission was doubtful, in a military if not political sense. The men of the Native Contingent suffered chiefly from boredom and homesickness, except for the mounted men, who had to worry about horse sickness.

Advance to the Mlalazi plain

At last the 1st Division was ready to make the advance against the Zulu cantonments. Between June 13th and 19th the 1st Brigade marched from the lower Thukela to Fort Chelmsford. It was delayed by rain on the nights of the 14th and 15th and sodden roads on the 16th. Meanwhile mounted patrols went forward to test the crossings and draw samples of water at the Mlalazi on the 14th and 17th. The division commander arrived at Fort Chelmsford on the 19th, and the division assembled there on the 20th.[16] The 4th and 5th Battalions were uniformed in scarlet tunics and armed with Martini-Henry rifles.[17] The 5th Battalion marched into Fort Crealock on the 18th singing – the men of the battalions often did – a war song. The refrain boasted their greater prowess and promised to make short work of the Zulu King and his army.[18]

Spies now reported that strong Zulu forces had been waiting to oppose the advance, but lack of food in the vicinity had made many leave. It was supposed that an appreciable number was still in the vicinity. Mounted patrols frequently exchanged shots with enemy hidden in the dense bush.[19]

The very afternoon that he arrived at Fort Chelmsford, the division commander went out on a reconnaissance to the Mlalazi and chose a camp site and a crossing place. Next day, the 20th, half of the 4th Battalion, British infantry and detachments of engineers and artillery began the march forward. Mounted men, including Jantze's Horse and the Mafunzi Corps, as well as companies of the 4th, covered the flanks. It was a difficult march. The distance was about eight miles, but the route deviated from the track to the upper ford of the river and followed the line of the river. There was such a delay that the column bivouacked a mile short of its destination. There was a storm during the night, but the weather cleared the following day, and the advance column reached the chosen site. The rest of the division came up after it, though the rear of the column was also delayed. On a hilly ridge above the river the British dug in in two camps. The mounted force was in between, and a wagon laager and the stores behind. At the very rear bivouacked the Native Contingent. Half the 5th Battalion was left behind, with a detachment of British infantry, to garrison Fort Chelmsford.[20]

As the division marched to the new camp on the right bank of the Mlalazi, several hundred Zulus gathered to observe it from the left bank. There was a large homestead on a rounded hill from which the enemy earlier on had fired on mounted patrols and reconnoitring parties. He fired from it now. It was an easy target for the British artillery, which shelled and burnt it that night. Next day a local chief made submission to the division commander. The mounted men were drawn up in line as he came in. He was given a new homestead in which to live with his people, and a guard was put on it. He brought in no cattle, he explained, because of lungsickness. None the less the horsemen were ordered to scour the country for any.[21]

It poured with rain on the 22nd. A detachment of the 4th Battalion and some of the foot scouts searched the woods along the river bank. Then several companies of British infantry occupied the woods. Pontoons were brought down and launched in the river. A detachment of the scouts and a company of the infantry were ferried across and climbed the hill to the burnt homestead. Pickets were posted to cover construction of a bridge by the Royal Engineers. The river was thirty-five yards wide at this point. Small bands of Zulus watched the building from hills in the distance. The bridge was completed before noon. Men of the contingent and scouts crossed first and spread out on the other side, burning homesteads and plundering.[22]

The 23th was a beautiful day. A convoy of empty wagons started back to Fort Chelmsford for more supplies. Detachments of the 4th and 5th Battalions and the pioneer company made up part of the escort. They returned with the convoy on the 25th.[23]

The division commander paraded the mounted troops at daybreak and took them across the bridge and along the hilly ridge beyond the river. A force of infantry and artillery crossed and took up a position on the left bank to give them support. The mounted men proceeded along the ridge, then descended to the coastal plain and crossed it to the ocean shore. A British warship was riding at anchor some distance beyond the surf. They returned to the Mlalazi along the low ridge which paralleled the shore and reached camp at sunset.

The reconnoitring party had encountered no enemy in force. People in the vicinity appeared to be trying to get out of their way. The mounted men had burnt several homesteads, and brought back an assortment of firearms, spears and shields, pots and baskets, and strings of beads. Quite by accident they came upon 250 Zulus driving away a large number of cattle. There was a short skirmish in which no one was injured, and the herd changed hands. The booty included 170 cattle, 20 sheep and 9 goats. Between sixty and seventy prisoners were taken. Most of them were women, some with children. The women looked half-starved and pleaded with the division commander for protection. Biscuits and corn were served out to them on the ground.[24]

The British warship was off shore for a good reason. It had been taking soundings to find an anchorage from which supplies could be landed. It would be quicker to deliver supplies by sea than by land from Durban. An Intelligence Department map showed a potential port at the mouth of the Mlalazi, but apparently the navy had mistaken a smaller stream for the river. 'Port Durnford', as the landing place was called, was almost five miles further up the coast, as the warship had belatedly determined.[25] So much the better for his arrangements, rationalized the division commander.[26] Just why is not clear. Instead of going straight towards the Zulu cantonments, in conformity with his instructions, he directed the division at a sixty-degree angle to the right towards Port Durnford.

Until they communicated with the warship no one ashore could be sure of the exact location of Port Durnford. Next day, the 24th, the division commander made another reconnaissance, to establish contact. The mounted men followed practically the same route as the day before. To divert any enemy there was an infantry demonstration. Two companies of the 4th Battalion crossed the Mlalazi bridge in company with a British regiment and two pieces of artillery. They scoured the bush for several miles to the northeast. Then they wheeled left towards the river and swept the hilly ridge. They remained there to cover the flank of the reconnaissance.

The mounted force advanced below the ridge. The ground was marshy, but otherwise there was nothing to stop them. They pushed through the bush on the plain and reached the beach where the warship had been seen the day before. The ship was still off shore. It stood in close and put out a boat from which signals were exchanged with the party.

The mounted men now divided. One portion, probably the larger, went with the division's engineering officer to find a way between the Mlalazi camp and the so-called port. Two tracks were discovered. It is not clear whether or not the Mafunzi Corps was in this group, but Jantze's Horse was with and perhaps made up the other division of mounted men, which pushed across the plain towards the next large river, the Mhlathuze. About a mile short of it, it saw hundreds of armed Zulus in several groups, halted, and returned to camp probably by way of the bridge. Both groups returned to camp before dark. Homesteads were burnt and fifty-three cattle and some sheep were taken during the reconnaissance. Also, more women and children were brought in.[27]

The war was being brought home forcibly to the people of the Zulu kingdom. Reconnaissances were also raids, meant to sap their will to resist. Moreover the Zulu King did little to encourage them, and practically nothing to counteract the raids. It is not surprising that the trickle of surrenders which began when the division reached the plain soon became a stream. People seemed ready to hand over spears and firearms; however, they had driven most of their cattle into the dense bush beyond the Mhlathuze for safekeeping. It was reported that the Zulu King had gone to the confluence of the White and Black Mfolozi rivers, where he intended to fight, and had ordered all the young fighting men from the vicinity to join him there.[28]

The horses needed a day's rest after two days work on the plain. On June 26th another reconnaissance was made, this time into the populous hill country. The mounted force had instructions to sweep the area, burn homesteads, seize cattle, and destroy opposition. They crossed the upper drift of the Mlalazi and skirted the hills for about five or six miles. The broken ground slowed their progress. They stopped short of the Mhlathuze, circled round, and headed back to camp, crossing the Ntuze river, a small tributary of the Mlalazi, under cover of infantry. The infantry, including three companies of the contingent, had crossed the Mlalazi and advanced in a northeasterly direction about three miles to the upper fords of the Ntuze.

Never before had so many homesteads been put to the torch. At one time, twenty-one of them could be seen burning from the Mlalazi camp. The infantry destroyed thirteen. The mounted men destroyed more than thirty-five. The people in the vicinity were taken by surprise and hurriedly drove off their cattle, but 105 cattle and 20 sheep were taken, most of them by the Mafunzi Corps. A few firearms and a quantity of spears were taken. An even larger number of women and children than before was brought in.[29]

Jantze's Horse and the Mafunzi Corps were the admiration of British officers. A detailed rendering of their operations has been given to show why. They were perfect as light cavalry, suited to the work at hand. Wiry men on shaggy ponies, they were imperturbable as they dashed through bush and galloped over stony ground. They were expert at penetrating the enemy's country and quick in setting on fire his homesteads.[30] What offensive edge the 1st Division had owed very much to these troops.

For the first time since Gingindlovu the mounted men had a brush with the enemy. When the Mafunzi Corps burnt a chief's homestead a small group of Zulus attacked it. The officer commanding the corps, Captain Nourse, killed two Zulus and the others fled. Altogether five of the enemy were killed that day and nine were captured. On the forested heights several miles to the west a large number of armed Zulus, perhaps 700, was seen, along with herds of cattle. They did not come down to fight, and the reconnoitring force's orders did not allow them to go up after them.[31]

It was a surprise when the mounted troops also came upon emissaries of the Zulu King. The emissaries were seeking headquarters and brought with them a dozen fine cattle and a long elephant tusk, earnest of the King's desire for peace. They were told the King must communicate with the Lieutenant General. They returned, all except one, who tendered his submission![32]

The reconnaissance on the 26th was also a demonstration in favour of the small column, consisting of British infantry and 200 men of the 4th Battalion, which plodded towards Port Durnford, leading the way for the rest of the division. The column crossed the Mlalazi early in the afternoon, but ascent of the ridge on the other side was slow. It was a long haul over a soft road. The crossing of the next stream, though small, was difficult. The oxen were strained to the limit. Camp was made scarcely two miles from the river.

On the 27th the main body of the 1st Division marched for Port Durnford. Two companies of the 4th Battalion were in the van, and four with the main body. A detachment of the 5th Battalion formed part of the rearguard, but most of the battalion seems to have been left behind. Why is not clear. A small fort had been built on the burnt-off hill above the bridge. It was left with a garrison of half a battalion of British infantry, with a Gatling gun and a few mounted men, and twenty-five men of the 5th Battalion.

It was about seven miles to Port Durnford by road, but there were several marshy places. Details of British infantry cut trees with which to corduroy the road, and mounted troops and men of the Native Contingent were sent in advance to look for more wood. It took two days (27th and 28th) to reach the new camp ground and to close up.[33]

The site was on low ground with marshes about. It would be hard to move on the plain in wet weather. It was hard enough to build a fort in the sand in dry weather. At least there was a good supply of water, from a stream that flowed through the dunes to the sea near the landing place. There were also a few lakes of fresh water. Much of the ground was open, but there were tall palm trees and places where the bush thickened into forest, yielding a supply of fire wood.[34] Occasionally the long grass caught fire. Sometimes the night was illuminated by long lines of flame moving across the plain. On the night of July 15th a line of fire perhaps five miles long burnt itself out within a mile of the camp.[35]

Port Durnford failed to meet expectations. It was a narrow stretch of beach off which the rough surf inexplicably moderated so that small boats could land and take off men and material in small quantities in good weather. A cart-road was cut between the landing place and the camps one and a half miles inland. The first provisions were landed on June 30th. Next day the wind changed and transfer ceased in the afternoon. That evening it began to rain. It poured with rain the next two days. Not until July 5th could a few stores be landed. On the 7th and 8th it rained heavily again.[36] The 1st Division thus continued to draw on Fort Chelmsford for supplies, with the little fort on the Mlalazi and several laagers between forts, as way stations. Half the 5th Battalion arrived as part of the escort of a large convoy on the 2nd. During the next week small convoys with empty wagons or carts left Port Durnford and returned full from Fort Chelmsford, the 4th and 5th Battalions furnishing one or two companies for escort duty.[37]

Destruction of the Zulu cantonments

The 1st Division was now well placed to achieve its primary objective, the destruction of the Zulu cantonment at Mangweni and the clearing of the district around it, to be followed by the destruction of the nearby cantonment at Ndini. Division instructions anticipated that the Zulu King would try to defend these important places. The cantonment at Mangweni was reported to have a thousand huts and the surrounding district to be highly populated. The road to Mangweni was stated to run through perfectly open country, and the road from it to Ndini to be fit for a light carriage. The 1st Division should have no difficulty with such terrain,[38] but it turned out the country was not so easy and the cantonments were not so close, but neither was the Zulu King determined to defend them.

The cantonments lay beyond the Mhlathuze river. The division commander wanted to reconnoitre the Mhlathuze as soon as the division arrived at Port Durnford; however, the horses were exhausted from the exertions of the last few days. He had to put off the reconnaissance till the morrow, June 30th. The objective of the reconnaissance then was the Lower Drift of the Mhlathuze. A good track was found to the river and the country in the direction of Mangweni and Ndini was examined. Twenty-seven homesteads, including those of two chiefs, were burnt. No cattle were seen. The reconnaissance then shifted down river four miles, as far as a large bay into which the river flowed, after which the force returned to camp.[39]

On July 4th, the cantonment at Mangweni was destroyed. The task was assigned to the mounted troops, because it was fifteen miles from the camp and the same distance back. 251 mounted men were available. Jantze's and the Mafunzi each mustered forty-five men. The horsemen were to be assisted by the 200 foot scouts.

The troops drew one day's rations and paraded just after midnight. They left camp at one o'clock and made good time under a fine moon, crossed the Lower Drift of the Mhlathuze, and proceeded four miles before halting to rest at four.

At 5.30 they remounted. In a little over an hour it would be light. They moved quickly, covering the last mile before dawn, and deployed around the cantonment. The mounted infantry and a troop of mercenaries formed in front. Jantze's and another troop went round the left rear. The Mafunzi and two others moved round the right rear. At seven, just as the sun rose, the signal was given to attack. The troops galloped into the great circle of huts. Jantze's Horse was there first, made its way through, and formed up again in front. The huts looked as if they had not been used for a long time.

The cantonment, impressive even in abandon, contained more than three hundred huts. Seven appeared to be those of chiefs: each one was surrounded by smaller huts and enclosed in a paling. There were also two large square buildings with windows and white washed inside.

The troops set to work firing the huts. By nine the cantonment was destroyed. The scouts remained to watch the ashes, while the mounted men went on to 'clear out' the district. Twelve homesteads within a radius of six miles were burnt. Half of the troops went in pursuit of some herds of cattle which were being driven over hills about three miles distant. It was a hard gallop to catch them. The pursuit carried into a long valley of about four miles. The herders, though armed, fled, and six hundred cattle were taken. The Mafunzi Corps meanwhile raided the adjacent homesteads for cattle. Another hundred head were picked up elsewhere, also eleven donkeys, said to be the personal property of the Zulu King. Perhaps as many as 500 Zulus were seen, but it was difficult to reckon the number as they kept their distance. About 200 retired into the bush of the Ntombanana river valley to the west. Only five men were captured, along with about forty women and children.

The reconnoitring party recrossed the Mhlathuze and offsaddled at two o'clock. At three they resumed the ride to camp. The scouts and some of the mercenaries went ahead with the cattle and donkeys. The rest of the mounted men followed shortly. All were back in camp at 6 p.m., almost an hour after the sun had set.[40]

The cantonment at Ndini was burnt next. It was twenty miles to the west of Port Durnford, but the way to it was much longer. The mounted troops rested on the 5th. A strong force of infantry marched from camp in the middle of the afternoon to the Lower Drift of the Mhlathuze and formed a laager. This force consisted of British infantry and details to man a Gatling gun and a cannon and 500 men of the 4th and 5th Battalions.

Major Barrow, the commander of the mounted troops, asked the officers commanding the different troops what strength they could turn out for a three-day patrol, whose ostensible purpose was to try to open communication with the Lieutenant General in the interior. 230 mounted men turned out. Jantze's Horse and the Mafunzi Corps each turned out forty men. 150 foot scouts and a rocket tube and rockets on horseback under an artillery officer accompanied them. So did the division commander.

The force left camp at 9 p.m. Moonlight made the march easier. The troops crossed the Lower Drift. They offsaddled and rested two hours at an abandoned mission station near Mangweni. The division commander returned to the Mhlathuze. At four in the morning of the 6th the expedition was on its way, crossing the Mhlathuze again at the Middle Drift and following a track through thick bush along the north edge of the Ngoye forest. At 9.45 they reached Ndini. The cantonment contained 640 huts. It was unoccupied and there was no sign of the enemy. The main force offsaddled and rested.

A small party tried to find a way to St. Paul's, the mission station which was the division's ultimate destination according to the Lieutenant General's orders. The party went four or five miles but did not reach it. A few Zulus were taken prisoner. They spoke of the advance of the Lieutenant General's column, and one said he had been in a battle which had taken place at the King's great place at Ulundi.

Ndini was put to the torch and the expedition returned the way it had come, offsaddling at the mission station at four for an hour and a half, and bivouacking at the laager just after eight. The division commander had gone with the British infantry and details back to camp earlier in the evening. The detachment of the Native Contingent held the laager. The laager was on a hilltop, exposed to rain and a cold wind during the night, but the mounted troops slept soundly in spite of the elements. In the morning the entire force at the laager marched back to camp.[41]

The mounted troops were exhausted. They had travelled over sixty miles in seventeen hours. Six horses had collapsed on the way (the raiders got home on the spares brought along). Jantze's Horse had forty effective horses and thirty-five non-effective ones on the 7th. The Mafunzi Corps had thirty and thirty-six, respectively.[42]

The main objective of the 1st Division had been achieved. During the first week of July Zulu refugees continued to flow into camp, until there were about 1400 of them. The British were using the carrot and the stick. The division commander promised the people if they submitted at once, and did not oppose his advance, he would give them protection of life and property and freedom to live wherever they liked. If they did not and fired on his men, then he would have their homes destroyed and their cattle seized.

The people of the coast were Zulu subjects, but they were treated as inferiors by their Zulu overlords. They had served the Zulu in battle, but the prospect of further service, of casualties and destruction of possessions in the cause of the King must have made the British offer attractive. So many came in to tender submission that a large number had to be sent back whence they had come (presumably after their submission was accepted). They could not all be fed. Also, it was believed that a large number of refugees would add to the sickness in camp.[43]

On the morning of July 4th, no less than six chiefs arrived to surrender. They brought their families, followers, and cattle. They said that other chiefs, indeed the people of the region as far north as St. Lucia, were coming to surrender. The next morning the division formed to receive eight chiefs and 300 fighting men with perhaps twice that many women and children and the usual cattle. The division was drawn up in a line almost a mile long, with the commander and his staff front and centre. Those who were making the submission were arranged in front of him. They made it and laid down their arms. Through an interpreter the commander gave a speech. In the course of it he told them that they were good men, but the British were better and had beaten them fairly. He accepted their submission and expected henceforward there would be peace in the district. He gave them their cattle and protection on condition of their good behaviour, but if any Zulu were found in arms among them they would be punished.

The majority of the people squatted in the grass and seemed entirely uninterested in the proceedings. Two dogs played on top of a pile of spears.

Swords were drawn. The band played. The British Political Agent gave the men passes to go wherever they liked and the others pieces of paper. The soldiers stood down and the people went home. For all practical purposes the war on the coast was over.[44]

The 1st Division commander had been trying for some time to communicate with the Lieutenant General in the interior. He used runners, but it was only on July 5th that they got through. They returned on the 6th with information that the Lieutenant General and his forces had defeated the army of the Zulu King.[45] Victory and peace appeared at hand.

Men of the 4th Battalion liked to sing, even on the march. Now they held a war-dance in the moonlight and sang splendidly, with deep voices and rich mellow notes. They clicked and whistled, and as they danced, they jumped and tumbled, and they seemed to do all this at once.[46] They had much to be joyful about. They could not know that it would be almost three more months, with many more hardships, before most of them would see homes and families again.

NOTES

1 C2482, p. 28.

2 2042 out of 8579, i.e. 23,8%, according to the return of April 21st in C2505, p. 133. *Narrative*, pp. 84–85.

3 *Narrative*, pp. 65–66, 83. C2505, p. 184.

4 C2505, pp. 147, 184.

5 *Narrative*, p. 83. C2381, p. 82.

6 C2505, pp. 146, 154–155. *Narrative*, p. 86. *Lord Chelmsford's Zululand Campaign*, p. 202.

7 C2505, pp. 157, 184–186. *Narrative*, p. 86. Stainbank Diary, April 26 – June 17, 1879 *passim*.

8 C2505, pp. 148–149, 155–158, 166–169, 171–176, 185, and Plate VIII. *Narrative*, pp. 86–87. WO 32/7754: 1st Division Diaries, May 19–28 and June 9–18, 1879 *passim*. Norbury, *The Naval Brigade*, p. 284. Also see Hutton, 'Some

Recollections of the Zulu War,' pp. 77–78, and NW, June 24, 1879: report.

9 C2505, pp. 166–169, 171–176, 184–186. *Letters of Major-General FitzRoy Hart-Synnot*, p. 137. Stainbank Diary, April 22 and 30, 1879.

10 1/VLM, 3/2/1: 435I, 538I, 543I, 558I, 567I/1879. C2505, pp. 153–154. Sickness affected the British severely and 493 men were sent back from Fort Chelmsford to the division's main hospital at the lower Thukela (*Narrative*, p. 87). There are no returns for the sick in the 4th Battalion, but messages from the adjutant of the 5th Battalion to the Resident Magistrate of the Inanda Division give 40 men discharged medically unfit on May 25, 1 on the 10th, 4 on the 18th and 8 on the 23rd, total 53 or 4,8% of the battalion's strength on April 21st (See 1/VLM, 3/2/1: 539I, 543IO, 558I/1879). Three or four horsemen given sick leave on June 27th arrived in Pietermaritzburg in a state of near collapse. The horses stumbled into town, the riders asked for a hospital; both appeared in dire need of medical attention. (TN, July 4, 1879: 'From the Front. Sick.')

11 C2505, pp. 142, 194–195; *cf.* returns, pp. 153 and 192. WO32/7754, 1st Division Diary, May 24, 1879. Stainbank Diary, May 15, 1879. *Lord Chelmsford's Zululand Campaign*, p. 180. It was arranged that a troop of fifty men, amaXamalala of the chief Lugaju, stationed near Pietermaritzburg, should join the 1st Division. It was to march on May 8th, but no record of its joining the division has been found. See SNA 1/6/14, nos. 18 and 45; 1/7/12, p. 84; and NW, May 8, 1879, GO --.

12 WO 32/7754: 1st Division Diary (2nd Brigade) May 19 and 21, 1879. Stainbank Diary, May 21, 1879.

13 Stainbank Diary, May 27 – June 3, 1879. NC, June 7, 1879: 'Fort Chelmsford.' *The Zulu War as reported in the Illustrated London News*, p. 154.

14 Stainbank Diary, June 11, 1879.

15 WO 32/7754: 1st Division Diary (2nd Brigade), June 12, 1879.

16 *Narrative*, pp. 87–88, 104. C2505, pp. 149, 160–161. WO 32/7754: 1st Division Diary, June 15 and 16, 1879. Stainbank Diary, June 14–17, 1879.

17 Norbury, *The Naval Brigade*, p. 287.

18 NC, June 26, 1879: 'The Advance on Ondini.'

19 NW, June 24, 1879: report from Fort Crealock.

20 C2505, pp. 149, 161–162. *Narrative*, p. 104. Stainbank Diary, June 21, 1879. NW, June 26, 1879: 'The Zulu War. With Gen. Crealock's Column.'

21 C2505, p. 149. TN, July 11, 1879: 'Advance of the Lower Column and Establishment of Point [*sic*] Durnford.' *Cf.* Ashe and Wyatt Edgell, *Story of the Zulu War*, p. 215.

22 C2505, pp. 149, 167. *Narrative*, p. 104. Norbury, *The Naval Brigade*, pp. 287–288.

23 C2505, p. 150. *Narrative*, p. 104. NW, June 28, 1879: 'Napoleon Hill.'

24 C2505, pp. 149–150, 162. *Narrative*, pp. 104–105. Stainbank Diary, June 23, 1879. NW, June 28, 1879: 'Napoleon Hill.' Ashe and Wyatt Edgell, Story of the Zulu War, pp. 215–216. Cf. *Letters of Major-General FitzRoy Hart-Synnot*, pp. 144–146.

25 C2505, p. 162. *Narrative*, p. 105.

26 C2505, p. 150.

27 C2505, pp. 150, 162. *Narrative*, p. 105. Stainbank Diary, June 24, 1879. TN, June 27, 1879: 'Latest from the 1st Division.'

28 *Narrative*, p. 107. NW, June 27: 'Latest Telegrams. The Advance of the Lower Column;' June 28: 'Napoleon Hill;' and July 8, 1879: 'The Zulu War. With Gen. Crealock's Column.' A local chief, Maquenda, reported to be a half-brother of the Zulu king, surrendered to the commander of the 2nd Brigade on April 21st (C2505, p. 186).

29 C2505, pp. 150, 162–163. *Narrative*, p. 105. Norbury, *The Naval Brigade*, p. 290. Stainbank Diary, June 26, 1879.

30 C2505, p. 145. NW, July 3, 1879: 'The Zulu War. With Gen. Crealock's Column.'

31 C2505, p. 162.

32 *Ibid.*, pp. 151–152. *Narrative*, p. 105. Norbury, *The Naval Brigade*, p. 290.

33 C2505., pp. 151, 158, 163. *Narrative*, pp. 105–106. NW, July 5, 1879: 'The Zulu War. With Gen. Crealock's Column.'

34 C2505, pp. 158, 163. TN, July 14, 1879: 'Port Durnford.'

35 W. Clifford Holder, *British Rule in South Africa* (London, Wesleyan Conference Office, 1879), p. 187.

36 C2505, pp. 151–152, 164, Plate IV. *Narrative*, pp. 105–108. Stainbank Diary, June 30 – July 9, 1879.

37 *Narrative*, p. 107. C2505, pp. 169–170.

38 C2505, pp. 155–156.

39 C3505, p. 151. *Narrative*, p. 106. Stainbank Diary, June 30, 1879. TN, July 2, 1879: 'Reconnaissance by Gen. Crealock.' Even with a day's rest there were only 371 mounted men for duty. Jantze's Horse and the Mafunzi Corps together had eighty mounted men. Fifty-four other men could not ride because of the poor condition of their horses (C2505, p. 192).

40 C2505, pp. 152, 164–165. *Narrative*, p. 107. Stainbank Diary, July 4, 1879. NW, July 8, 1879: 'More Cattle Captured.' TN, July 11, 1879: 'Advance of the Lower Column and Establishment of Point [*sic*] Durnford.'

41 C2505, pp. 152, 164–165. *Narrative*, pp. 107–108. Stainbank Diary, July 5, 1879, which gives some different times. TN, July 11: 'Advance of the Lower Column and the Establishment of Point [*sic*] Durnford;' and July 14, 1879: 'Port Durnford.' Also see and cf. *Letters of Major-General FitzRoy Hart-Synnot*, pp. 153–155.

42 C2505, pp. 154, 165. *Cf.* return of mounted troops (p. 192), which gives seventy mounted men in both troops.

43 C2505, pp. 141–142, and *cf.* p. 152. *Narrative*, p. 107. TN, July 14, 1879: 'Port Durnford.'

44 C2505, pp. 141–142 and 152. Holden, *British Rule in South Africa*, pp. 185–186. TN, July 9, 1879: 'General Crealock's Division.'

45 NW, July 12, 1879: 'With Gen. Crealock's Column.'

46 Holden, *British Rule in South Africa*, p. 186.

Chapter 13

WAR IN THE HILLS

Entering into Zululand

The invasion of the interior depended on the discovery of a route by which the Flying Column and the 2nd Division, which in Zululand became the Headquarters Column, could approach the Zulu King's great place, Ulundi, with the least difficulty in the shortest time. The route by which the 2nd Division would invade Zululand had still to be determined. The way from Rorke's Drift in January had proved more difficult than anticipated. A course following higher ground to Ulundi was preferable. It appeared that the division might have to take a northerly route along with the Flying Column. An advance depot was being prepared for it at Conference Hill, on the right bank of the Ncome river.[1]

The discovery of a more direct route was largely the responsibility of the mounted troops attached to the columns. Reports of spies and sojourners might provide valuable information but only personal inspection could verify it. Reconnaissance was the method of verification, and it was the duty to which the mounted troops were best suited.

Reconnaissance fell initially to the mounted troops of the Flying Column, which were already organized and in the field, while those of the Headquarters Column were still forming. The bulk of the Flying Column's mounted troops consisted of small units of colonial mercenaries and the Natal Native Horse, under Captain Cochrane, consisting of the Edendale and Sotho troops. These two troops had been tested from the start on patrols and scouts and in battle at Khambula. Colonel Buller, commander of the Flying Column's mounted arm, pushed his men and horses to the limit of endurance. He was active, inquisitive, even reckless at times, apparently never happier than when in action.

The Native Horse stood out in character from the mercenaries, whom an English gentleman of the general's staff noted were 'the greatest set of rogues I ever met, and they compare badly with the Zulus, in both sentiments and language'.[2] (Presumably he meant by 'Zulus' the men of the Native Horse). An officer of one of the mercenary units remarked that the 'Basutos' – British and colonist alike used the term generically – were courageous as well as invaluable as scouts. Their only weaknesses were a tendency to become overexcited and a habit in combat of levelling their rifles over their horses' heads with one hand and firing wildly.[3]

The Edendale men and their fellows from Driefontein, in Shepstone's Horse, also stood out as Christians. Every morning and evening they held divine service. It was then presumably that Simeon Kambule yielded to John Gama. They were Methodists and their hymns were memorable. The British soldier understood not a word, but he would stop to listen.[4] Edendale would be the hammer of the heathen, nemesis of the Zulu King.

The Flying Column was to co-operate with the 2nd Division in the invasion. It moved south from Khambula to Segonyamana hill on May 5th. Yet the northerly route to Ulundi from Conference Hill, by way of Nhlazatshe mountain, appeared to lead into a formidable massif. Geography dictated finding a way through easier terrain just east of the Ncome and picking up the track from Rorke's Drift further into Zululand.[5]

Before dawn on May 10th a mounted force of 140 men, including forty men of the Edendale and Sotho troops under Captain Cochrane, left the Segonyamana camp. The column commander, General Wood, accompanied the force, which was to find a track for wagons in the direction of Babanango, a mountain overlooking the track between Rorke's Drift and Ulundi.

It was still dark when the mounted men rode through a bushy ravine. A few Zulus watched from concealment. One on a hill above jeered at them to visit his home. The Native Horse wanted to shoot him, but orders were not to fire unless fired upon, and they were restrained with some difficulty. The party emerged from the ravine, and by sunrise they had ridden ten miles. The sun raised and burnt off a heavy mist and the day was warm and still. The horses cantered along to a high hill called Munhla. Just west of it the force came upon a track, approximately following a north-south line, and halted for breakfast.

The march resumed along the track. The troops kept up against the steep hillside, and entered a wooded defile between Munhla and another, higher hill to the west, called Nkanda. Flanking

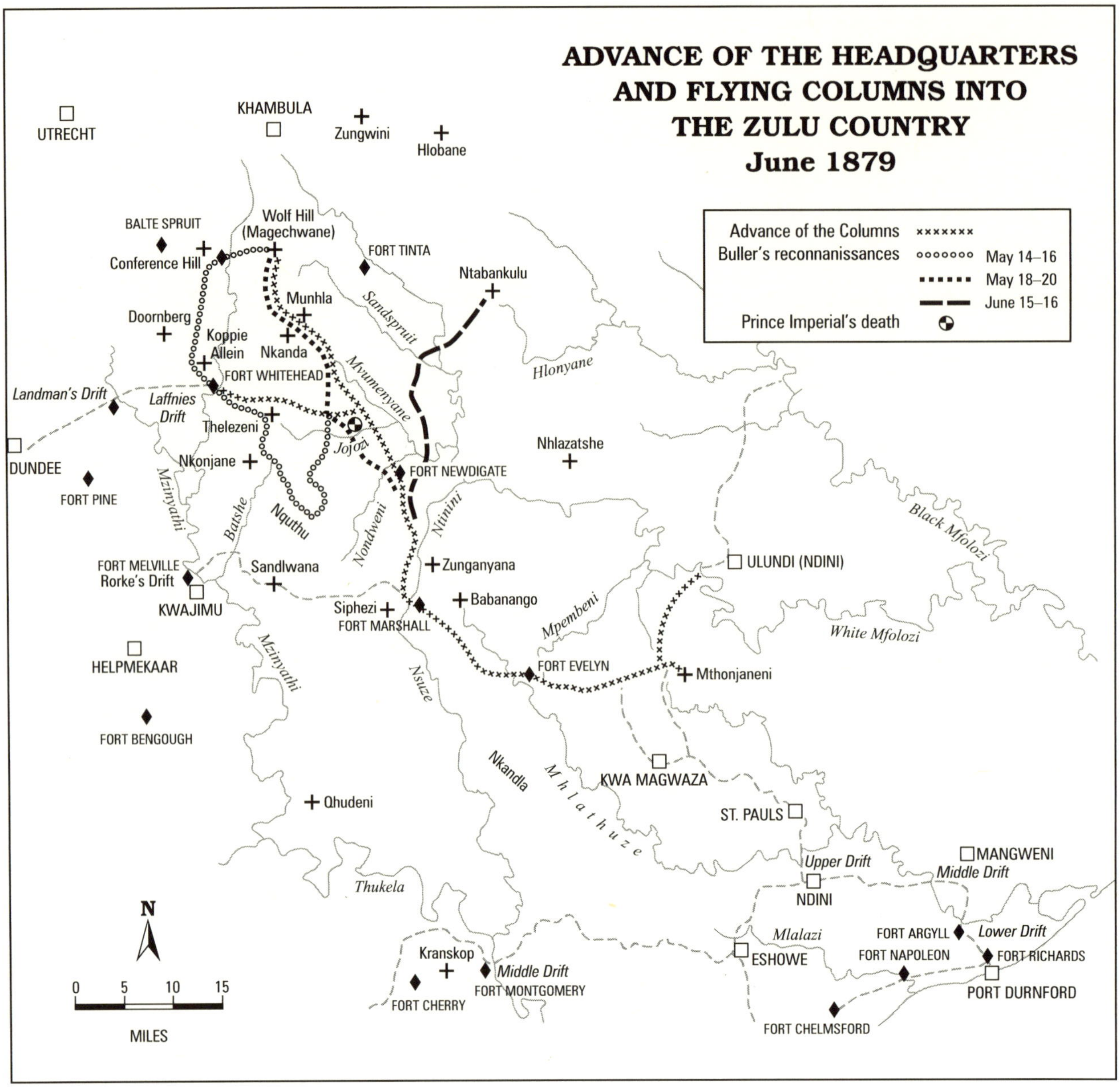

parties were thrown out and skirmishers closed up in front and rear. An ambush was expected at any moment. As the men in front reached the mouth of the defile, shots rang out in the rear, followed by a great shout. Zulus swarmed on the steep sides of the hills, apparently intent on taking the men in the rear. The bugle sounded halt. The column commander went back, and Colonel Buller picked twenty men from the column and followed. A fierce skirmish took place. The troops in the rear, now reinforced, attacked the Zulus on the hillsides, wounding several and driving off the rest. The enemy retired in groups of six or eight. Recall was sounded and the scattered pursuers reassembled. Again the march resumed.

The track wound out of the defile down a steep hill and into a valley. At this point the column commander left Buller to carry on and returned with a small escort to camp. The reconnaissance continued to the Mvunyane river, where the horsemen offsaddled and cooked dinner. The day was hot and haze obscured Babanango, to the southeast. Colonel Buller and a staff officer, with six of Cochrane's men as escort, rode to a hill three miles ahead to get a better view, but the haze was still too thick. The escort chased off several Zulus. The Colonel returned to explore the river banks. The homesteads there were deserted, but there was plenty of firewood and corn. Men and horses helped themselves to the extra rations. The homesteads were not burnt.

It was the Colonel's practice on reconnaissance to choose a camp site for the night, then move from it after dark to another one relatively close by. The object was to deceive an enemy contemplating an attack at night or, more probably, at daybreak. In this instance he chose a small stony hill and then some ground in the loop of a deep gully. The Native Horse were at the rear of the little column and became scattered while watering their horses in the pools of the river bed. When Cochrane had collected them, he found the rest of the column had disappeared into the dark. The night was moonless and there was no finding the others. He and his men made for the little hill, but arrived after the main force had left. They did not offsaddle, but lay down to sleep. A sentry saw something in the dark, called to another, and all came to their feet, revolvers and carbines at hand. It was a false alarm. About half an hour before day break the main force appeared through the morning mist and the column was re-united.

There were better atmospheric conditions on the 11th. Observations were made of Babanango and Nhlabamkhosi, another hill in the same direction. The Colonel concluded that wagons would have no difficulty over the route reconnoitred so far. The mounted force returned to camp that evening.[6]

The Flying Column advanced to a new camp, on a hill overlooking Magwechwana stream, six miles northeast of Conference Hill, on May 12th.[7] The possibilities of the route beyond Munhla and towards Babanango were further explored in another reconnaissance on the 14th. Buller's force was much stronger this time – two hundred, including forty of the Natal Native Horse. They drew the usual three days' rations and set out in high spirits. It was an easy ride to Conference Hill, where two strong forts protected the advance depot. The Colonel's force was joined there by several important officers of the Lieutenant General's staff, among them the young prince imperial, pretender to the throne of France. The augmented force rode southward about six miles and camped for the night near Koppie Allein.

The reconnoitring party was on the move before sunrise on the 15th and crossed the Ncome into Zulu country at about six. It continued over the same open country that Bengough's battalion had covered two days before, and ascended the southeastern spur of Thelezeni, where there was a draw. The Natal Native Horse took position on the left while another group of men scoured the steep hillside on the right. The object was to drive any enemy down towards the Native Horse, which was waiting to take them in, but no enemy was found. The mounted force reached the top of the hill and turned to the right.

Thelezeni is one of the hills that make up the watershed between the Ncome and Mzinyathi rivers to the west and the White Mfolozi river to the east. The reconnaissance continued southwards along this watershed for several miles. It saw nothing of the enemy, but came upon a homestead which had been recently vacated and offsaddled to rest before climbing the wooded slope of another, higher hill in the chain.

It was then they saw a man on a grey horse on top of the higher hill. He began to call out, as though to gather a force. Men emerged from caves and crevices: about fifty Zulus appeared to the left, eight on horseback appeared on the right. Would they stand and fight? Experienced opinion was that they were bluffing. Lieutenant Raw and six Edendale men were sent to drive them. The little party dashed up a winding footpath, cutting in and out of some tall mimosa trees on the edge of the woods. When they reached the top of the hill, the enemy disappeared.

The impetuous prince imperial galloped ahead to join the Edendale men. The Zulus reappeared, perhaps a hundred strong, halfway up the cliff. Was it a trap? One of the enemy ran as if to communicate with those no longer visible. He was shot by a man in the main force below. Another Zulu tried to go, but turned back under fire. The rest of the enemy fled. The prince overtook the Edendale party on the flat top of the hill. He rode here and there. He spied a Zulu on a small hill in the distance. He rode for him. Lieutenant Raw and the Edendale men followed at a gallop. Colonel Buller sent up a troop of mercenaries to make sure they – that is, the prince – were safe. The lot arrived at the small hill. On the other side the main ridge fell away sharply. The fleeing Zulus looked like specks on the plain below. The mercenaries fired at them, apparently without hitting anyone.

The reconnaissance proceeded without further hindrance. It was spectacular country. From the high ridge there was a glimpse of Isandlwana, peeping through the hills, ten miles to the south. Thirty miles to the west Nhlazatshe was visible on the horizon. The mounted troops descended the ridge into the basin of the Jojozi river and its tributaries. The mercenaries went down one way and burnt several large homesteads at the foot of the ridge.

Buller and the Natal Native Horse went down another way. They arrived at a deserted homestead. The occupants had lately been shelling corn, and the horses ate their fill. Then the corn was destroyed, and the march continued. The two forces met at another homestead. The destruction continued. Some oxen nearby were shot, but the shooting was poor and it took six shots to kill one of them, at a distance between six and thirty yards. The Colonel wanted to bivouac in the Mvunyane valley again, but the ground the force would have to cross over was so eroded, with numerous watercourses, that he had to make camp east of Thelezeni. The night was cold, made bitter by wind. Next day they returned to camp by way of Munhla hill.[8]

On the 18th the Colonel made another reconnaissance, aiming deeper into the Zulu country, for he had yet to come upon the Rorke's Drift – Ulundi track. The reconnoitring force consisted of about two hundred men, including the Native Horse. It followed what was becoming a familiar route past Munhla, crossed the Jojozi and pushed on towards the Nondweni river. The region appeared to be thickly populated, but the homesteads were deserted.

Out of a hut cried a lone voice. Some of Cochrane's men halted and found an old woman inside. She was blind and apparently starving. She said her people had left her many days ago. She did not know where they had gone. One of the men offered her a biscuit, but she could not eat it. An old dog howled beside her. There was nothing they could do for her. The reconnaissance continued. Another abandoned wretch was found further on. At least she could see to get from her hut to a corn patch. The homesteads were not burnt. The expedition bivouacked a few miles from the Nondweni and crossed the river next morning. This region was even more populous and the inhabitants seemed to have just fled. A blind man was found crouching at a homestead. He appeared to be about thirty years old. He trembled violently and his teeth chattered. The soldiers tried to reassure him and asked questions about those who had fled. Had the men gone to Ulundi? They might have, the man answered, the women and children had gone to hiding places in the hills. The force moved on and halted for breakfast near a small tributary of the river.

The Native Horse and mounted British infantry provided an escort to the Colonel, who rode to the crest of a hill seven or eight miles away. They looked down upon a broad valley with a great number of homesteads. All of them seemed to be deserted. There was not a Zulu to be seen. A small herd of cattle was visible, about some six miles up the valley, probably bait for some trap. The scouting party reckoned (incorrectly) that they were about thirty miles from Ulundi. Evidently they did not see the Rorke's Drift track. The Colonel took cross-bearings on Babanango and Nhlabamkhosi and rejoined the main party. The reconnaissance was over. The force retraced its steps and bivouacked near the Jojozi. Most of the men could not sleep that night because their feet were cold. Heavy frost covered the ground several hours before sunrise. The party made good time getting back to camp, offsaddling only once and arriving in time for dinner. Buller did not return with them, but went off alone to look for the best route between the Munhla track and the Doornberg.[9] His tireless energy amazed the men of the Natal Native Horse. They had a nickname for him, likening him to a steam engine.[10]

The reconnaissances by mounted troops of the Flying Column and the 2nd Division revealed feasible wagon routes for the invading force from Conference Hill and Koppie Allein to the neighbourhood of Thelezeni and beyond to the Nondweni. The Lieutenant General decided that the two forces would converge and take the single route eastward. He was reliably informed that the columns could follow with relative ease a long ridge from Siphezi hill, just west of Babanango, to Mthonjaneni, the mountain overlooking the Mahlabathini plain on which stood Ulundi and other great places.

The Flying Column would move south from the Magwechwana. The 2nd Division north from Landman's Drift and east from Koppie Allein, and the two would meet beyond Thelezeni. No more time should be lost. Reconnaissance had not revealed the exact way from the Nondweni to Babanango and the main track from Rorke's Drift to Ulundi, but presumably it could be found in due course. On May 25th, the Flying Column marched to Munhla hill, where it waited several days for detachments to come in. The 2nd Division formed a new depot at Koppie Allein, which required the shifting of supplies from Conference Hill and Landman's Drift. The first force ordered to the advance post was the 2nd Battalion of the Natal Native Contingent, on the 24th, just after its return from the reconnaissance to Isandlwana. The Lieutenant General arrived the same day and the division concentrated there between the 27th and 30th. Shepstone's Horse, which had gone from Dundee to Conference Hill on May 24th and 25th, rejoined the division on the 30th, just in time to be in the vanguard as it forded the Ncome the following day.[11] With that act the second invasion began.

Confrontation at Zunganyana

The second British invasion of the Zulu country was underway. The Headquarters and Flying Columns were in motion. The columns of soldiers, foot and horse, variously arrayed and armed, the large trains of wagons drawn by many teams of oxen and mules, converged on the crossing of the Nondweni river. The Natal Native Contingent provided the army's eyes and ears. The 2nd Battalion, the Natal Native Horse and, to a lesser extent, Shepstone's Horse were toughened by training and discipline, experienced in scouting and skirmishing. Still before them was another test in battle.

The Flying Column, including the Natal Native Horse under Captain Cochrane, moved from Munhla hill and crossed the Mvunyane. The 2nd Battalion of the Contingent was attached to the Cavalry Brigade of the Headquarters column, when it crossed the Ncome river on June 1st. The column moved to the neck of high ground north of Thelezeni.[12] Shepstone's Horse provided van and rear guards for the advance.[13]

Six men of Shepstone's Horse were to make up half the escort of a small reconnoitring party under a British lieutenant of the staff. The party included the young French prince imperial. They did not arrive at the appointed time (8.30 a.m.) and the prince was impatient to start. It is not clear whether a message sent to Captain Shepstone or the reply to it stated that the six men would join the party on the neck above Thelezeni. A guide was obtained from the 2nd Battalion. What the qualifications of the guide were is not known. Presumably he had some knowledge of the country in advance.

The reconnoitring party, consisting of the young staff officer and the young prince, the guide, and an escort of six mercenaries, crossed the Ncome and made its way up to the neck. There it met another reconnoitring force under a senior staff officer. The six men of Shepstone's Horse still did not arrive and another message was sent to Captain Shepstone.

The reconnoitring party, nine men strong, proceeded along a low spur of the ridge to the east. One account says it met some 'Basuto' horsemen on the way. Both the Natal Native Horse under Captain Cochrane and Shepstone's Horse, and even possibly the Amabomvu and Amangwane Corps, were involved in scouting ahead of their respective columns in the area. The horsemen might have belonged to any one of these units. In any event, the party waited about an hour and the prince sketched. The rest of the escort still did not arrive.

The nine then continued along the spur and down to the Jojozi. It was mid-afternoon and they were about eight miles in front of the columns. They came to a deserted homestead on the left bank of the river. They were resting there when they were ambushed. The lieutenant and four troopers saved themselves in flight. The others were neither so swift nor so fortunate.[14]

The death of the prince imperial was a serious blow to British prestige. The regret in higher quarters was great. If only the men from Shepstone's Horse had accompanied the party! They would never have allowed it to be surprised. If only they had arrived as expected. If only the party had waited for them! The infantry of the Headquarters Column remained in camp the next day while the Cavalry Brigade was sent to find the missing members of the reconnoitring party. The Flying Column advanced to a new camp site near the Jojozi, only a few miles from where the ambush had occurred. Its mounted men also joined in the search for the missing.

Captain Cochrane and a few of the Natal Native Horse discovered the body of the prince in a gully. It was naked and had sixteen stab-wounds. It was Zulu practice to stab a fallen prey repeatedly in the heat of battle, but the customary ripping open of the abdomen to release the baleful spirit had not taken place. (This was not the case with the bodies of the dead troopers near by). The leaders of the search converged at once on the place where the prince's body lay. It was examined, covered and solemnly taken away. The other two bodies were buried near a cairn erected to mark the place where the prince's body had been found.[15]

On June 3rd the Flying Column crossed the Jojozi. The Headquarters Column came up to the river, and camped near the place where the prince and his companions had been killed.[16] There was occasion to visit the site. The homestead had been damaged but stood intact. In a hut was a shirt, rent and bloodied, said to have been the prince's. There was the usual crone in the hut entrance, and there was no difficulty persuading her to talk. She spoke readily and gesticulated, through the interpreter giving the British soldiers to understand that her sons had killed the prince. 'They killed your great Nkosi. They are gone now to the king's kraal to fight you white men. What do you come here for? We don't want you. This is Zululand. Keep to your own side!'

Some men, probably of the 2nd Battalion, went round the cattle enclosure, tapping the ground with their spears to find out where the grain store was. An officer sat on the wall, sketching.

The body of the guide was found about a mile away. Evidently he had been overtaken by the Zulus there. His body had the usual stab wounds. Around it were broken weapons which suggested he had put up a hard fight. There is no report how his body was disposed of.[17] Next day a detachment of Shepstone's Horse burnt the homestead and eight others near by.[18]

The Flying Column crossed the Nondweni on June 7th. The Headquarters Column followed in its path, crossing the Jojozi and camping under Mhlungwane hill.[19] Henceforth the two forces operated as parts of a single army, under the Lieutenant General. The mounted forces of both were active in front and on the flanks. Shepstone's Horse burnt homesteads in the vicinity.

The Natal Native Horse, had a more exciting mission. Colonel Buller made a reconnaissance with a relatively small force to examine the wagon track towards Babanango. The Edendale troop and Hlubi's men made up the advance guard and flankers. The bulk of the force consisted of mercenaries. The advance guard was about six miles south of the Nondweni crossing when it saw large bodies of Zulus. The Zulus were in a valley and on a stony hill called Matshamhlophe. On the hillside were five on horseback.

The van reported what it had seen and gave chase to the enemy horsemen. Buller came on with the mercenaries and went around the east side and behind Matshamhlophe. Evidently the Zulus were no longer to be seen on the hill, and the Colonel caught up with the Native Horsemen on a spur south or southeast of the hill.

Thirteen Zulu horsemen rode into view, apparently intent on finding out where the reconnoitring party had gone. As soon as they saw it they galloped away, firing a few shots. They crossed a valley about three miles wide and headed towards a long flat-topped hill called Zunganyana. At the front of the hill were four homesteads, one quite large, out of which men swarmed in great numbers.

The reconnoitring party doubled back around Matshamhlophe, and not a moment too soon. The Zulus covered the front slope of the hill and extended across the valley to Zunganyana. A rough estimate put their strength at about 2500 men. The nearest were about 500 yards off. It appeared that the troop had just escaped from a trap.[20]

Both sides exchanged shots. Buller ordered the reconnoitring party to retreat and try to draw the enemy on. He himself hastened back to the column for reinforcements. The Native Horsemen and mercenaries retired slowly, from time to time firing at the pursuers, and they met the reinforcements on a crest about four miles from Matshamhlophe and about three miles from camp. Every horseman in camp had come forwards, in all there were about 500. The enemy was not to be drawn further and the skirmish came to an end.[21]

The Zulu force was unusually large. No large force had been seen in that quarter of Zululand since the battle of Khambula, and there was speculation that it was the vanguard of a larger army. The laager in which the Flying Column bivouacked was entrenched in anticipation of attack. The Lieutenant General ordered the Cavalry Brigade to support Buller's mounted men on a reconnaissance next morning. It was important to find out just how strong the Zulu force in front was and to learn something about it.

The Colonel, as usual, was off before dawn. He took 300 men, including the Native Horse, to Matshamhlophe and into the valley beyond. The Cavalry Brigade, which started at 4.30, would catch up. As the sun rose over Zunganyana to the east, his men arrived on the eastern slope of Matshamhlophe. It was a fine scene. The valley between the hills slipped out of shadow and the sun glittered in the little Ntinini river which ran through it. Sun shone on Babanango in the distance to the right and on green Nhlazatshe far away to the left.

The Zulus were mustering for action at the homestead at the foot of Zunganyana. One body was estimated at 600 men, another at between 300 and 400.

Buller drew up his men and ordered them to attack. The descent to the river was easy. Crossing was also easy, for the river was dry except for pools here and there. The homesteads on the other side were in the centre of small plain beyond which was dense thorn bush at the base of Zunganyana. The horsemen found the plain broken by gullies and pitted with holes. It was also dotted with ant heaps and rocks. Horses tripped and threw their riders, but the charge continued into tall grass and corn patches, right up to the huts.

The horsemen burnt the huts. The angry Zulus retreated to the bush and opened fire. The range was only two or three hundred yards. The troopers dismounted, every fourth man taking back horses, and lay down to return the fire. They took advantage of the irregularities of the ground for protection. The hillside was covered with small puffs of smoke. No one could see the Zulus. One could only fire at the puffs.

The men dared go no further. It seemed a wonder none had been killed, but the enemy was

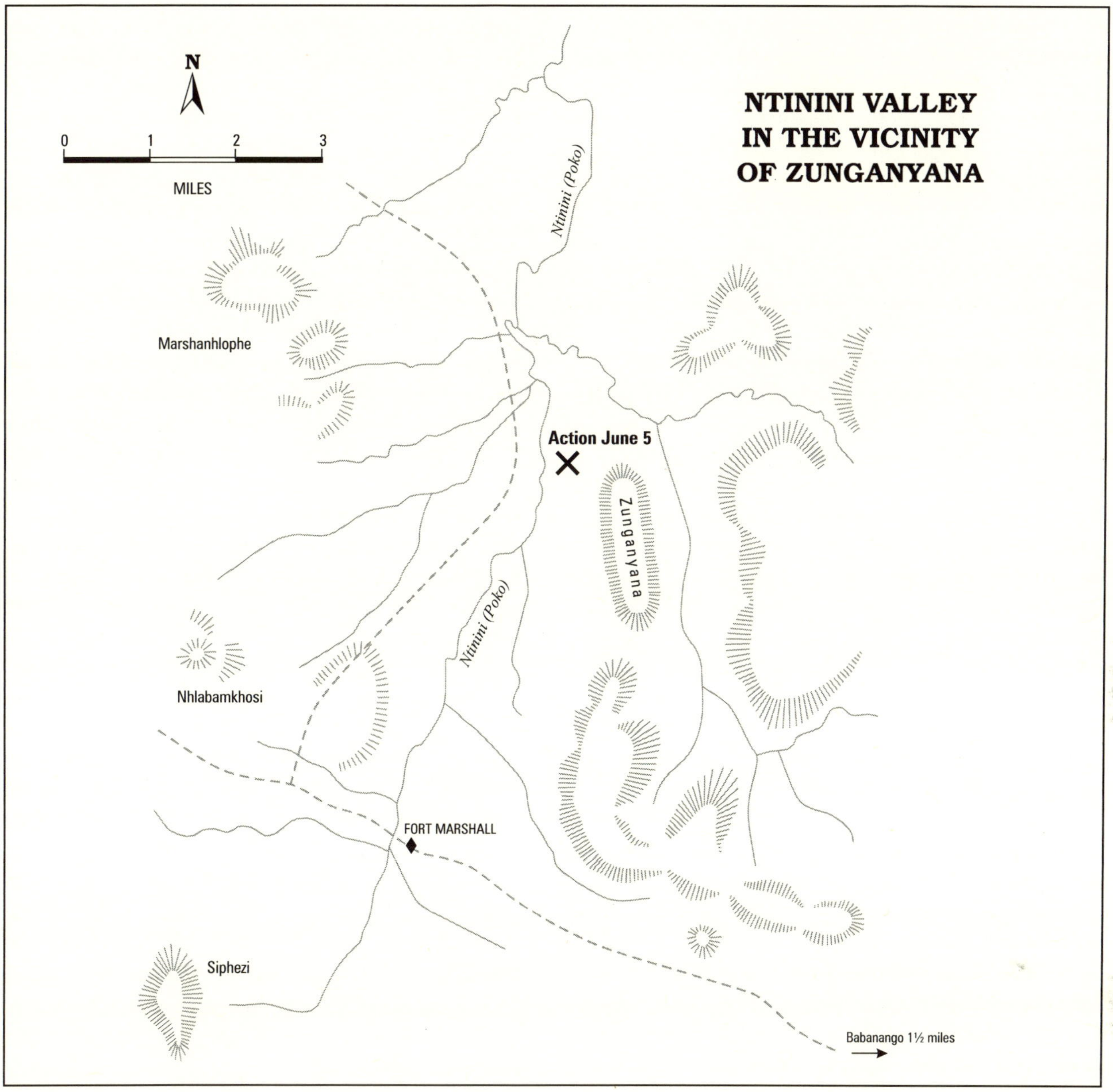

firing high again. They were greatly outnumbered and as time passed their position became precarious. Some of the enemy went down a gully on the right and opened a cross fire on them. The Colonel ordered them to fall back. They did so in good order and remounted. A few men were wounded and several horses were killed and wounded. Some of the enemy sallied into the open to fire at the retreating troops, but not so far that they could suddenly be ridden down, and they fell back when the horsemen returned their fire. The troops recrossed the river and drew up on the left bank. They offsaddled out of range of the Zulu rifles. The British cavalry was forming behind them. The Lieutenant General was on a hill, watching the action.

There was no point in the British cavalry – 17th Lancers in front, King's Dragoon Guards in support – getting into the fight, but they advanced through the Colonel's line with the *élan* of professionals. They crossed the river and the plain. They took up the same position the Colonel's men had earlier. The Zulus dared not come out to attack them and they dared not go in to attack the Zulus. The Zulus fired at them and killed a British officer. Both sides were wasting their ammunition. The cavalry duly retired across the river.

Meanwhile more Zulus had crept down another gully to the river bed and fired a volley into some of Buller's men who were resting at a homestead. The surprised mercenaries scattered to left and right, but the attackers were beaten off by a troop of Shepstone's Horse, which had come up with the Cavalry Brigade. Buller's men saddled, mounted, and retired by sections to rising ground about 500 yards to the rear, where they again dismounted and formed a skirmish line.

The battle, such as it was, was over. The enemy's strength had been tested. The homesteads, including the larger ones, which were said to belong to the chief Sihayo, had been burnt. The mounted forces had lunch and returned to their respective camps.[22] It was just after noon and the rides were short. The infantry had moved up during the morning. The Flying Column bivouacked on the north side of Matshamhlophe and the Headquarters Column on the right bank of the Nondweni.[23]

The Lieutenant General calculated there were 1500 Zulus in front on the 5th. If the Zulus clung to the hills and fought in the bush this way, then British infantry would have to clear them out. The advance would be slow. Food and ammunition would be eaten up at a great rate and the army must be provided for accordingly. The invasion came to a halt, and wagons were emptied and sent back to the depots at Landman's Drift and Conference Hill to be loaded. The Flying Column, plus detachments from the Headquarters Column, including part of Shepstone's Horse, escorted the train as far as Koppie Allein, where the wagons were sent in sections to the respective depots. The expedition left the Nondweni on June 7th and returned on the 17th. In order to protect the supplies at the front two small redoubts were started, on opposite sides of the pile. The fortification was called Fort Newdigate, for the 2nd Division commander.[24]

The first close encounter with the enemy, then the apparent necessity to work on the fort, probably told on the nerves of men in the column. During the night of the 6th there was a great scare in the camp of the Headquarters Column, notwithstanding the remaining wagons were properly laagered and a trench dug round, with pickets and sentries placed at the right distance.

The moon rose a few hours after sunset, but at first was obscured by cloud, so that the night was dark when the scare occurred. A company of the 2nd Battalion was on guard duty along with two companies of British infantry, although many of the latter included new recruits. They were posted in small groups alternating with each other. A squadron of mounted men, including a troop of Shepstone's Horse, were on duty beyond the infantry pickets.

It was about 9 p.m., on the east side of the camp, that one of the battalion's sentries thought he saw a Zulu creeping forward. It was not clear whether he fired the three shots which were the signal the camp was under attack or he pointed out the supposed Zulu to a British soldier who fired. In any case the British sentries double-quicked back to their pickets and the officer-in-charge ordered them to fire two volleys and then fall back to the camp.

The camp was outside the laager. In the event of danger, the men would retire into the laager and units would take up prearranged positions. (The fortifications which had been started did not form part of the defence yet). The men struck their tents, clearing a field of fire, and did so, but there was much confusion and noise. On one side of the laager, the British thought they saw many Zulus running about and they fired a volley. If they saw anything, it was probably the men of the contingent or drivers and conductors trying to get into laager.

The firing quickly spread to the other sides of the laager, and the artillery joined in with a couple of rounds. Excited horses and oxen crowded towards the narrow entrances. Conductors joined in the shooting. One British regiment fired 1200 rounds. Squatting inside the laager the men of the 2nd Battalion put their rifle butts on the ground and pulled the triggers. The discharge of so many firearms created a thick white cloud over the laager. The tents and equipment in the camp were riddled with bullets.

Suddenly the moon appeared from behind a cloud and illuminated the battlefield. General and staff trying to reassert control found it easier once they could see. 'Cease fire' sounded and order was restored. At 10.45 the men were dismissed and returned to camp. The pickets returned to their posts.

The scare had cost seven men wounded and three or four horses killed. The Amangwane Corps lost five horses and saddles to the friendly fire. The head man, Putsha, lost his uniform, boots and gaiters. Two of the mounted men, caught outside the laager during the firing, dismounted and eventually crawled, with their horses, up to and under the protection of a wagon. It was a wonder none of the contingent was killed. It was a problem, generally admitted, that it was difficult to distinguish them from the enemy when they came off picket at night. The difficulty would be compounded, of course, by the fear of a night attack.

No enemy was to be seen. It was suggested that a cloud or a stray ox had alarmed the sentries. Indeed, Fort Newdigate was nicknamed 'Fort Funk' by the soldiers for its inauspicious baptism of fire. None the less a report circulated afterwards that 15 000 Zulus, under an important chief, had been moving to attack the camp but had withdrawn when they saw how well defended it was. It was also reported later that thirty-five Zulu dead later were found in a gully, not far from the camp.[25] At this stage of the invasion it was hard to verify or to disprove such reports. In any event there were no grounds for complacency. The action at Zunganyana indicated the enemy would make a fight of it before he let the columns get to Ulundi.

The Headquarters Column left a garrison of two companies of British infantry, two Gatling guns and crews, and a company of the 2nd Battalion at Fort Newdigate, and advanced on June 7th to a position on the left bank of the Ntinini river. It had a good view of Zunganyana, a little over two miles to the southeast.[26] The enemy still appeared to be in force there. People could be seen in some unburnt homesteads and gullies beneath the hill. They left when one of the British cannon opened fire on them, but re-emerged in small groups later and annoyed parties going from camp to the river for water. It was feared that these groups might become bolder and begin to interfere with work parties and take cattle and horses near the camp. The Lieutenant General ordered a full reconnaissance of the hill, with the object also of driving the enemy away and destroying the homesteads which gave him shelter.[27]

The reconnaissance succeeded completely. Colonel Buller moved out with 240 mounted men, including the Native Horse, followed by Major Bengough with the 2nd Battalion. Strong detachments of British infantry and cavalry moved to support them. Artillery took position to support the whole. In their red coats the men of the 2nd Battalion struck a colourful contrast to the drab corduroy of the mounted troopers. In extended order the advance moved up the Ntinini valley, burning homesteads as they came upon them. The British infantry, also in extended order, followed. The British captured quite a few Zulus, who turned out to be drivers, leaders and servants from Buller's camp. Some of them were looting the sites of homesteads. Others said they were collecting firewood in the bush at the foot of the hill.

The mounted troops were well in front of the infantry. Now they could be seen silhouetted against the sky. They passed by the hill on the west. They rounded it to the south over a neck of land which separated it from the next hill in the range. The men on foot toiled after them.

The mounted men entered a narrow valley formed by Zunganyana on the west and the next hill to the east. The sides of the valley were cut by streams and, especially under Zunganyana, by numerous gullies. The main body of horse, consisting of mercenaries and mounted infantry, proceeded down the valley, thus circling Zunganyana. Buller directed the Native Horse to the left. It was to keep under the steep side of Zunganyana and burn homesteads there. This the Edendale and Sotho troops did admirably. They cantered along, throwing out detachments to burn the homesteads as they came to them, neither breaking their pace nor falling behind the advance of the troops in the valley.

So swift was their progress that they surprised a group of the enemy intently watching the British cavalry and guns, which had entered into the valley round the north end of Zunganyana. The artillery was shelling some large homesteds at a great distance. Three of the Zulus were mounted, one on a white horse. The horse had been observed several times in the last few days and given rise to speculation that the rider was a chief of some importance. Six other men were on foot. There was half a mile between them and the Native Horse. Edendale and Sotho went for them at full gallop. The Zulus fled across the valley, whether in front of or behind the line of the horsemen is not recorded. Three on foot were run down and shot. The other three on foot and one on horseback escaped.

Edendale and Sotho pursued the man on the white horse and the other horseman, who raced up the hill on the east side of the valley. The hillside become too steep for them to go directly over the top. They followed the contour round to the north end. They laid their rifles across the saddle bows and fired at their pursuers. The Native Horse laid their rifles across the bows and fired back. The distance closed to twenty yards. The enemy turned the end of the hill and rode desperately towards the homesteads, the same ones which the artillery had been shelling in the next valley. The pursuit did not relent, but after half a mile it was in danger of an ambush. Even then it was difficult to get the men to stop. They returned to the main body, where Colonel Buller praised them for the work.

The reconnaissance had circled round Zunganyana. The mounted troops, Bengough's contingent and the British infantry had burnt sixteen homesteads on the west, south and east sides of the hill. The British cavalry had burnt four others to the north. Zulu resistance had been negligible. Small groups had formed out of rifle range and had dispersed under artillery fire. Under a lowering sky the British forces returned to camp.[28] The immediate Zulu threat in the Ntinini valley apparently had been removed, but there was still the possibility of a large enemy force moving down from the hinterland.

NOTES

1 *Narrative*, p. 90. *Lord Chelmsford's Zululand Campaign*, pp. 159–160.

2 *Private Journal of Guy C. Dawnay*, p. 53.

3 Tomasson, *With the Irregulars*, pp. 71, 128.

4 *Ibid.*, p. 128. Molyneux, *Campaigning in South Africa and Egypt*, p. 190. Montague, *Campaigning in South Africa*, p. 157. SP 41: Theophilus Shepstone, jr., to William Shepstone, July 17, 1879. TN, August 15, 1879: 'Welcome to the Edendale Men.' NW, August 16, 1879: 'The Natal Native Horse.'

5 *Narrative*, p. 100.

6 TN, May 23, 1879: 'With General Wood's Column'. Ashe and Wyatt Edgell, *Story of the Zulu Campaign*, pp. 241–148.

7 *Narrative*, p. 101.

8 NW, May 24, 1879: 'The Zulu War With General Wood's Flying Column.' TN, May 30, 1879: 'Landtman's [*sic*] Drift. With Bettington's Horse.' Ashe and Wyatt Edgell, *Story of the Zulu Campaign*, pp. 248–252.

9 TN, May 30, 1879: 'With General Wood's Column.'

10 Tomasson, *With the Irregulars*, p. 76.

11 *Narrative*, pp. 90, 92, 101–102. *Lord Chelmsford's Zululand Campaign*, pp. 172–176, 181, 185, 191. WO 32/7754: 2nd Division Diary, May 20, 31, 1879: also see the map, May [21?], 1879. NAM 6302-48-2: Diary of W.H. Fairlie, May 24–25, 30–31, 1879.

12 *Narrative.*, p. 102. *Cf.* pp. 92, 149 and Bengough, *Memories of a Soldier's Life*, p. 134.

13 Fairlie Diary, June 1, 1879.

14 *Cf. Narrative*, pp. 93–95: *The South African Campaign*, p. 38; Ashe and Wyatt Edgell, *Story of the Zulu Campaign*, pp. 275–276; and Bengough, *Memories of a Soldier's Life*, p. 132.

15 *Narrative*, p. 95. Molyneux, *Campaigning in South Africa and Egypt*, p. 162. *Private Journal of Guy. C. Dawnay*, p. 40. Fairlie Diary, June 2, 1879. TN, June 13, 1879: 'With Genl. Wood's Column.'

16 *Narrative*, pp. 95 and 102.

17 Montague, *Campaigning in South Africa*, pp. 176–178. In this quotation I have changed the woman's term of address from 'Inkoss' to 'Nkosi'.

18 *Ibid.*, p. 178. Fairlie Diary, June 4, 1879.

19 *Narrative*, pp. 96 and 102.

20 Fairlie Diary, June 4, 1879. *Cf.* T. St. Lo Malet, *Extracts from a Diary in Zululand* (Upper Norwood, Platt & Burdett, 1880), p. 16.

21 Tomasson, *With the Irregulars*, p. 105. TN, June 20, 1879: 'With Gen. Wood's Column.' Also, see *Narrative*, p. 96, and Fairlie Diary, June 4, 1879.

22 The action is described in *Narrative*, p. 96; Tomasson, *With the Irregulars*, pp. 105–110. WO 32/7754: 2nd Division Diary, June 5, 1879; Fairlie Diary, June 5, 1879; NW, June 14, 1879: 'With General Wood's Flying Column;' TN, June 18: 'With the Natal Light Horse,' and June 20, 1879: 'With Gen. Wood's Column.'

23 *Narrative*, pp. 96 and 102.

24 *Ibid.*, pp. 97, 98 and 102. *Private Journal of Guy C. Dawnay*, p. 47. Fairlie Diary, June 5, 1879. WO 32/7754: 2nd Division, June 6, 1879.

25 The 'scare' is variously described in *Narrative*, p. 97; Malet, *Extracts from a Diary*, pp. 16–17; Molyneux, *Campaigning in South Africa and Egypt*, pp. 168–169; Montague, *Campaigning in South Africa*, pp. 187–191, 201–202; *Private Journal of Guy C. Dawnay*, pp. 46–47; Edward D. McToy, *A Brief History of the 13th Regiment (P.A.L.I.) in South Africa during the Transvaal and Zulu Difficulties, 1877-8-9* (Davenport, Swiss, 1880), pp. 71–72; WO 32/7754: 2nd Division Diary, June 6, 1879; and Fairlie Diary, June 6, 1879.

26 *Narrative*, p. 97. *Private Journal of Guy C. Dawnay*, p. 47. WO 32/7754: 2nd Division Diary, June 7, 1879.

27 WO 32/7754: 2nd Division Diary, June 7–8, 1879. *Private Journal of Guy C. Dawnay*, pp. 47–48. Malet, *Extracts from a Diary*, p. 18. NW, June 17, 1879: 'The Zulu War. With Gen. Newdigate's Column.'

28 The reconnaissance is described in *Private Journal of Guy C. Dawnay*, pp. 48–49; WO 32/7754: 2nd Division Diary, June 8, 1879; NW, June 17, 1879: 'The Zulu War. With Gen. Newdigate's Column;' TN, June 20, 1879: 'With Gen. Wood's Column;' and *The Concluding Stages of the Zulu War as Reported in "The Graphic"*, p. 165. Also, see Malet, *Extracts from a Diary*, p. 18, and Montague, *Campaigning in South Africa*, p. 213.

Chapter 14

IN THE ZULU HEARTLAND

Raid on Ntabankulu

From June 7th to 17th the invasion of Zululand was in abeyance. The Headquarters Column, with part of the Cavalry Brigade and the mounted troops of the Flying Column, remained in laager at the Ntinini river. The line of communication extended thirty miles back to Koppie Allein, and the forward depot established at Fort Newdigate had supplies to sustain the invading army only for a fortnight. More supplies must be brought up. The Flying Column, with some infantry from the Headquarters Column and the other part of the Cavalry Brigade, convoyed the supply train back and forth.[1]

The need for more supplies, especially of ammunition, was magnified by the Zulu resistance at Zunganyana on June 4th and 5th. Yet it was rumoured that the Zulu King wanted to negotiate, and his envoys came to camp on the 4th and left on the 6th.[2]

The reconnaissance on the 8th showed that the Zulus were no longer in force in front, but there was no telling when or where they might gather to fight again. Soldiers worked to improve the laager at the camp.[3] There was another alarm on the morning of the 9th, but the men took their places as though it were a drill.[4]

The mounted troops made several reconnaissances. Colonel Buller's rough mercenaries grumbled at being under the temporary command of the Lieutenant General. They complained of being kept under arms for an indefinite period every morning, and they did not like false alarms. They even suggested their horses were not given the usual corn or grain.[5]

The onset of winter, the dry season, turned the grass from green to yellow, then to brown. The ground hardened and the surface became dusty. Streams dried up or became trickles. The Ntinini ran from pool to pool between high banks covered with ferns and creepers. Mimosa remained green on the sides of the hills, and a certain cactus bloomed in scarlet flowers, but overall the country seemed bleak. The hills, formed from antiquity by erosion, were mostly flat topped and their slopes were scarred with gullies. The valleys had many boulders and outcrops of rock. The homesteads in the vicinity had been burnt or abandoned, but their food pits yielded corn and melons and fruit resembling pomegranates.

A few Zulus were seen occasionally on Zunganyana. Sometimes they took shots at wood cutting parties. The caves in the hillsides and the holes in the sides on the gullies were searched, and yielded rifles, helmets, belts, saddlebags, broken Martini-Henry cartridges, valises and an assortment of personal items belonging to Europeans. All these articles were presumed to have come from the battlefield of Isandlwana, seventeen miles to the west.[6]

The 2nd Battalion fell in with the camp routine. Its own encampment was about one hundred yards off the northern face of the laager.[7] The rifles of the battalion were muzzle-loaders and they were kept loaded and plugged for action. Now and then the riflemen were given leave to fire to empty the old charges. On one occasion when they did so, the noise brought forth from the river an ample British officer, stark naked but for the pistol he brandished. No one had told him they were going to fire their rifles. He had heard them while he was bathing, assumed it was an attack and hastened back to the laager.[8]

The men were better with spears than rifles, of course. There was little game about, somewhat to the irritation of the British officers, for gentlemen must hunt.[9] While encamped at the Nondweni, some officers' dogs had flushed a springbok (a type of small antelope) near the camp. It had fled towards the river, where some of the men were drawing water. One of them had set down his buckets, drawn a short spear and crouched. The buck dashed by. At twenty yards he sprang up and threw and brought the animal down.[10]

Every morning the battalion paraded by companies, each company with its small calico flag before it. The mornings were cold, sometimes frosty. Each man turned out wrapped in his blanket, legs sticking out at the bottom, spears at the top. They got to know the British soldiers in a general, friendly way. 'Halloa Johnnie!' They were all Johnnie to one another.[11]

There may still have been some uncertainty as to the route ahead. The track from Rorke's Drift to Ulundi – which the column was to follow eastward – was only about five miles to the south, but there is no mention of patrols finding it. The omission is best explained as oversight of something now taken for granted. Meanwhile a half troop of British cavalry and a hundred men from Rorke's Drift reconnoitred the country between the crossing and the headquarters camp in June 7th, and reported that the district was deserted.[12]

From the evening of June 7th the weather became showery and cold, made bitter by wind. On the 10th patrols went out, evidently to investigate the way forward. One reported seeing Zulus in some strength, so the next day three patrols set out towards Isandlwana and towards the White Mfolozi to find them. One patrol observed a few enemy and gave chase to two horsemen who were thought to be spies. About thirty of the Native Horse, in another patrol, rode about twenty miles from camp without seeing anyone. Reports persisted. This time they said the enemy was only a few miles off. On the 13th two patrols went out to search and found nothing.[13]

The Flying Column was returning with the supply train. On the 13th it marched to Thelezini, on the 14th to the Vumenkala, and on the 15th to the Nondweni.[14] The Lieutenant General evidently was concerned for its safe return, especially if there was a strong Zulu force in the offing, and on the 14th ordered Colonel Buller with part of the mounted troops to the White Mfolozi to cover its left flank.[15]

The result was an expedition thirty-five miles deeper into the enemy's country, the riskiest adventure which the restless colonel had undertaken yet. Its objective was the mountain Ntabankulu, beyond and to the north of the White Mfolozi. The adjutant of one of the mercenary units had the impression that the main object was simply to harass the enemy, but noted as well that a large herd of cattle was reported to be at the mountain. The strength of the expedition was between 195 and 250 men, including seventy men of the Native Horse.

The men drew the usual rations: fresh beef for two days, tinned beef for a third day, some biscuit, coffee and sugar. They rode out of camp in a northeasterly direction at eleven in the morning of June 14th. It was cold and rainy, with poor visibility. It took three hours to reach and cross the lower Mvunyane, perhaps ten miles from camp. The men offsaddled and rested an hour. Another ride of almost three hours and eleven or twelve miles brought them to the right bank of the White Mfolozi. The short winter day was over. A search was made for the ford in the dark, but the guide, a Dutch farmer, apparently could not find it.

They made camp in the usual way, shifting from one place to another. Sentries and vedettes were posted. The men ate what they could. It was bitterly cold, but no fire or lights were permitted. Orders were passed in a low voice, and the horses were ringed together in groups of thirty or so, fastened so none could break loose. Saddles and bridles were left on. At eight the men lay down to try to sleep, each under his one blanket and with his head next to his horse's in the circle. It did not rain, but a very heavy dew came down, and after midnight the cold became so intense no one could sleep. A dog was heard barking across the river. Had a homestead there been alerted?

A few hours after midnight the men were roused. It was pitch dark. They loosed their horses and fell in for a hushed roll call. Orders, necessarily short and pithy, were whispered. In an instant the men mounted.

The party now moved to the river. It was broad and, notwithstanding the recent rain, fordable, but the banks were steep on either side. The nimble horses slid down to the water, and then clambered out with ease. The rain started again. The cold increased, and wind drove it into the bones. Dawn came, and the pace quickened to a canter. The party diverged from the river line and rode to the right six or several miles.

About seven the expedition arrived before Ntabankulu. Apparently the rain had stopped. The mountain rose abruptly from the plain to a height of 1500 feet. The mounted men were opposite the western end. The homesteads at the foot were deserted, as if the inhabitants had been alerted and fled. Those on the terrace above, under the cliff, still had fires burning in front and people swarmed from the huts. Some climbed the mountain face and others fled to the sides. A number could be seen driving a herd of cattle along the terrace and up the mountain.

The attack began. Every unit was given orders, a sentence or two, what to do and headed towards their objectives. Some mercenaries rode directly at the mountain. Others turned to right and left to climb it. They pursued the fugitives up the side, notwithstanding the enemy's advantage of higher ground.

There was no organized resistance. The defenders were surprised and seemed bewildered. Some fired from behind rocks, others from the mouths of caves, and a few were foolish enough to venture out to shoot, but apparently forgot to take out the paper they had wadded in the muzzles of their rifles to keep out the rain. One man fired wildly at the leader of the mercenaries. The distance between them was less than six yards. The mercenary captain fired his pistol at the man's head and the bullet went flat against his skull. The man went down mortally wounded. Enemy fire was in fact light and sporadic. The mercenaries blazed away whenever they saw a foe.

Buller led a group of men to the left. In a valley between the mountain and the next large hill to the west, they burnt homesteads and took cattle. The Native Horse rode quickly to the right and captured many of the cattle on the terrace. Then they climbed the mountainside and got on top of the first cliff, commanding the terrace below. The action was now a standoff. The troops on the mountain were occupied with mopping up.

The men in the valley had run afoul of some exceptionally difficult gullies and marshy ground. Headway was slow and the enemy could be seen gathering in front. The advantage of surprise was gone. The alarm had spread throughout the neighbourhood. The hills were dotted with men. Their number was increasing. The Colonel contented himself with burning one more homestead, a large well built one which was said to belong to the Zulu King, and retired.

The expedition regrouped at the place where the attack had begun. It had no casualties, but an estimated dozen Zulus had been killed and fifteen to twenty homesteads had been burnt. Some of the huts had been full of corn and grain. Three herds of cattle had been captured, totalling over 300 head. More than a hundred sheep and goats and a couple of horses had been taken. For the first time prisoners were taken – a couple of men and ten women and children, all flushed from one gully. Many others overtaken in flight had been let go.

Zulus on the mountain were yelling furiously, but they did not venture onto the plain. They fired a few shots as the mounted force withdrew towards the river. They did not follow it. About noon the men halted for breakfast near the place where they had bivouacked the previous night. Sentries were posted and vedettes placed on rising ground, and the rest of the men offsaddled and let the horses out to graze. Some went to fetch water for coffee in their billy cans, others dismantled the nearby homestead for firewood, still others emptied the remaining rations from their haversacks. The sheep and goats which obviously would not make it back to camp were killed. Some were cut up to roast and eat. The carcasses of the others were slung over the spare horses.

The prisoners had the task of driving the cattle. One of the prisoners was a good-looking young woman who wore a leopard skin about her shoulders. One of the mercenaries bantered her about marriage. Would she marry him? – Would he make her work in the fields? – No – Was he a chief? – Another of the men joined in. He was a great chief. She abandoned the first for him, then tried to make up, since breakfast was at stake – coffee, meat and biscuit. She was disagreeably displeased that her coffee had no sugar, but her beaux were put off by her choice of cuts and the way she ate them.

The meal was soon over. The horses were brought in and saddled and the women and children were released. The young woman with the leopard skin burst into tears and begged to be allowed to go with the horsemen. Her chaffing had evidently not gone down well with the other women. Of course, she could not go. At 1.15 the expedition started for camp. The countermarch took almost nine hours, the last four in darkness over rough ground.

The two men captured were apparently let go soon after. One of them was charged to take a message to his chief – if the chiefs did not come and submit, then the British would destroy their homesteads and crops everywhere and take their cattle.[16] The war had reached the brutal stage, and the expedition to Ntabankulu drove the point home. Militarily it might be insignificant. Psychologically, and therefore politically, it had great significance for those who would resist.

The high road to Ulundi

The Headquarters Column marked time for ten days in the Zulu country, and the enemy made no effort to dislodge it. On Tuesday, June 17th, the Flying Column rejoined it with 660 wagons laden with supplies to sustain the invasion.

As the invading army moved further into the Zulu country and farther from its bases on the border, its line of communication would become more extended and vulnerable. Elements of the invading force would have to be detached to hold posts strategically located along the line, providing safe bivouacs for individuals and units shuttling back and forth between front and rear. The posts would serve as secondary depots for supplies in transit. They must be fortified and garrisoned in sufficient strength to ward off Zulu attacks. In order to man the line the Headquarters Column was reconstituted. One of the two brigades of the 2nd Division was broken up to provide infantry. The Cavalry Brigade was broken up to provide cavalry. Artillery was supplied as well from the divisional troops. Fort Newdigate was the first such post. Others were established as the invasion proceeded.[17]

The bulk of the British cavalry – the King's Dragoon Guards and the 17th Lancers – was assigned to the line of communication. In due course, only two squadrons of the Lancers remained with the army when it reached Ulundi. In contrast, most of the colonial mounted troops stayed with the column. Only a few units were assigned to the line of communication.

The campaign so far had given the British cavalry little opportunity to fight in its usual way. A pitched battle on the European model seemed entirely unlikely. English horses were, of course, used to English oats and hay. Fodder was supplied from base, mouldy oats and pressed hay-chaff uneconomical to forward with a limited number of wagons and oxen. Inevitably the horses had to eat grass and corn, when sufficient was captured. At halts on the march they had to be unsaddled and their panoply of war removed, so that they could graze; and then, of course, they must be saddled and all the trappings put back, which took more patience than time warranted. Quite apart from marching through the increasingly rugged country, scouting and sentry and escort duties exercised them to the limit. The English horses were acclimatizing, but too slowly to justify their concentration in such a large force. They could acclimatize without being pushed relentlessly at the posts along the line of communication. There they could be used for patrols, escorts and occasionally expeditions into the neighbouring countryside.

In these circumstances the burden of the army's reconnaissance and security on the march fell upon the Natal Native Horse, Shepstone's Horse and the various mercenary units all under the command of the indefatigable Buller. The mounts of the Natal Native Horse and the colonial mercenaries were indigenous products. Small but hardy, the 'Basuto pony' won the admiration of the British for its serviceability. Not much to look at, but it could outmanoeuvre and outlast the sleek, pampered hay burner of the dragoon or lancer. The Basuto pony thus became a mainstay of the army and was used to the utmost – until, as we shall see, it, too, wore out in the rugged Zulu country.[18]

The invading army resumed its advance on June 18th. The Flying Column, followed by the Headquarters Column, marched up the Ntinini valley. It reached the main track between Rorke's Drift and Ulundi near the head of the river, and the Flying Column crossed it. Part of the Headquarters Column followed and began building Fort Marshall, named after the former Cavalry Brigade commander, now placed in charge of the line of communication.[19] The Native Horse and some of the 2nd Battalion scouted, beyond Babanango, the mountain below which the track passed to the east. About mid-day they saw some 300 Zulus and exchanged shots with them. The Zulus cried out, rather cryptically: 'Never mind to-day. Come again to-morrow and you will see.''[20]

That night there was another alarm in the camp of the Headquarters Column. It was set off by a dog's barking outside. The dogs in camp answered, and a sentry fired, on the supposition the dog outside belonged to Zulus who were lurking about. The soldiers quickly took their places in the laager and there was no disorder.[21]

Henceforth the march was to the east, along the track to Ulundi. The morrow held no terror. On the 19th the Flying Column marched five miles and encamped two miles to the southeast of Babanango, on a spur of the mountain. The mounted troops scouted in advance. Zulus appeared in small numbers, but there was no action. The Headquarters Column finished crossing the Ntinini and completed Fort Marshall. Its garrison consisted of a small company (sixty men) of the 2nd Battalion, two companies of British infantry, a section of artillery (two guns), and a squadron of cavalry.[22]

There was rain during the night and the morning of the 20th, but the Flying Column marched five miles during the day, moving around the base of Babanango onto a flat ridge narrowing towards the crossing of the Mhlathuze river. One reason why the Flying Column led the way may have been that it had No. 1 Company of the pioneers, which was very useful on the track. The Headquarters Column had no pioneers. It followed over the wet spur of Babanango for six miles and bivouacked just south of the mountain.

On the 21st the army descended the ridge to the Mhlathuze. The Flying Column forded the river and bivouacked. The Headquarters Column camped on the near side. The last of its wagons got in after dark. The track ahead was more difficult. There was an ascent of seven hundred feet in less than two miles, and the top of the next ridge turned out to be very narrow. The Flying Column could manage no more than about two miles on the 22nd. The Headquarters Column remained at the Mhlathuze. Detachments from both, including part of the 2nd Battalion, were sent to build a fort on the ridge near the Flying Column's camp. It was named Fort Evelyn Wood, shortened to Fort Evelyn, after the Flying Column's commander. The next day the Headquarters Column joined the Flying Column on top of the ridge. The fort was completed, and another company of the 2nd Battalion was assigned to the garrison, along with two companies of British infantry, a section of artillery, and a troop of mercenaries.[23]

From the ridge the soldiers saw, or thought they saw, Ulundi for the first time. The ground fell away into deep valleys, interspersed with hills and little rivers. Those that still had water glistened in the sunlight. In one valley, which was estimated to be thirty miles long, many large places could be seen, presumably the enemy's cantonments beyond the White Mfolozi. Straining to see beyond them, men perceived a circle of huts far away, said to be the great place of Cetshwayo, the Zulu King.[24]

A period of fine weather had set in on the 20th and lasted over a fortnight. The army moved forward slowly, but methodically. The rate of advance was determined by the wagons and oxen. The almost six hundred teams covered thousands of square feet of ground on the move, but the area of movement was restricted by the width of the narrow ridge. At places it was only a few hundred yards wide, at others half a mile. Laagering took hours, as teams pulled abreast and wagons were shifted end to end or axle to axle. The oxen were grazed (and then interned) while hasty entrenchments were thrown up. It took time to unlaager as well. It was not at all like the first invasion, but the time-consuming procedure insured there would be no repetition of the Isandlwana disaster.

On the 24th the army marched about five or six miles to a high point on the ridge. The Flying Column camped there, the Headquarters a mile behind and below it. The two columns always kept in supporting distance in the event of an enemy attack. The march on the 25th was an arduous one. There were rises and dips along the ridge, and early on the track crossed a small stream with steep banks and a soft bed. The Flying Column ransacked some deserted homesteads for grass mats to throw down in the ford and passed on. Four hundred wagons crossed one-by-one. The Headquarters Column followed. Altogether it took between six and seven hours for the army to get over the stream. The Flying Column bivouacked almost six miles ahead. The Headquarters Column closed up to within two miles and bivouacked.[25]

The rugged country and tortuous track into the heartland of the Zulu kingdom often put the invading army in exposed positions. There were places where the contours of the ground favoured an attacker, although the open grassland afforded little opportunity for ambushes. Whatever opportunities there were, the Zulu seemed to ignore or to let slip after no more than a gesture of resistance. There was skirmishing in advance every day, but the enemy did not stand and fight. A report received on the 22nd had stated that the Zulu army was waiting to do so at Ulundi. The Natal Native Horse was in the van; Shepstone's Horse, along with the detachments of British cavalry, covered the flanks and rear of the invading army. The enemy could not deceive or deflect the efficient, ruthless men on horseback. Zulu spies and scouts found it difficult if not impossible to get near the main British force.[26] The army came upon deserted homesteads. Large quantities of corn indicated that their occupants had only lately fled. Perhaps the enemy had meant to resist but at the last moment demurred.

Colonel Buller's troops scouted the way in the early morning of the 21st, spreading on to the hills to either side of the track. To the south the mercenaries got into a sharp skirmish, but got the best of about 700 Zulus.[27] British cavalry saw about 400 Zulus the following day and skirmished with them on the 23rd.[28]

Zulus in small groups set fire to the dry grass in front of the army. The aim seemed to be to burn up the invader. The mounted troops were hard pressed to root out incendiarists on the line of march. When the army bivouacked, the men cut the grass in broad swaths around the camps.[29] They became selective, too, about burning homesteads. The Lieutenant General worried that there would not be enough wood along the route to make fires. Therefore homesteads along the way were, when possible, to be dismantled for their wood rather than simply burnt.[30]

During the morning of the 24th Buller and his men dispersed a number of the enemy burning grass in front, when a spy reported that he had seen two bodies of Zulus, which he believed were the vanguard of an army moving towards the columns. The Colonel sent a message warning the columns to go into laager as soon as possible. In the time before the enemy force appeared the troops offsaddled and rested.

Several hours passed. The Zulu army did not come on. A number of Zulus, some of them mounted, did gather on a crest four miles to the front. They appeared to be scouts. Considering that the laagering must be well under way, the Colonel had his men mount and go on. Alongside the track was a stick in the ground. On it hung the hide of a small animal, perhaps a tabby cat. Hlubi's troop was in advance, and Lieutenant Henderson looked at the pelt. It was, he told a British companion, Zulu 'medicine', which some witchdoctors had put it there, believing that it would paralyse the army, perhaps even stop it altogether.

The mounted troops arrived within about half a mile of the crest where the Zulus had collected. At Buller's command, they galloped towards the enemy. The Zulus fled. There was a chase over three miles. The enemy ran down the north side of the ridge onto a spur covered with aloes and bush. The horses could not overtake them in the thicket. The mounted men opened fire, but at a range of between 800 and 1600 yards they hit no one. The thrill of the chase gave way to excitement at the view of the valley below. It stretched towards the White Mfolozi, and the mounted men looked upon what plainly were many of the great places the Zulu nation.[31]

The following day, the 25th, the mounted men pushed further along the main ridge. They passed over the same crest. They burnt several homesteads in a small semicircular valley, which opened out into the larger one with the historic Zulu cantonments. Smoke was seen rising from the nearest of them, Dukuza, which was estimated to have four or five hundred huts.[32] A detachment of Shepstone's Horse scouting on the left burnt some large homesteads.[33]

The enemy was being challenged on sacred ground. The cantonments in the Mkhumbane valley were keepers of the burial places of early Zulu Kings. They had great political as well as military significance. The Flying Column commander decided to destroy them.

On the morning of June 26th, as the Headquarters Column toiled forwards to join the Flying Column, the commander of the latter gathered a mixed force on the ridge overlooking the cantonments. It consisted of the mounted men and some foot levies from the Flying Column, and two squadrons of British cavalry, a section of artillery, and two companies of the 2nd Battalion from the Headquarters Column.

The mounted men went down the spur over which the enemy had retreated on the 24th. As they picked their way down the steep slope, through the aloes and bush, they lost sight of Dukuza, but saw columns of smoke rising in the sky ahead. The Zulus themselves were burning the cantonments! The troops arrived at the foot of the slope, passed over broken ground and climbed a hill. From the top they saw Dukuza again. It was abandoned and many of the huts in the great circle were in flames. A detachment was sent to fire the others.

About three miles to the north lay another cantonment, Ngwegwe, consisting of hundreds of huts in five or six concentric circles. It, too, appeared to be deserted. A unit of mercenaries was dispatched to burn it. One of the Natal Native Horse, apparently in a frenzy, dashed ahead and got to it first. Hearing someone or something inside one of the large huts he fired into it and killed a woman. She had a heavy rug about her. Presumably she had been sick and therefore left behind. The mercenaries came up and looted the huts. They found many relics which they supposed came from the Isandlwana battlefield – baths, buckets, canteens, cooking pots, also some prints of saints and a hymnal. They put the huts to the torch.

The rest of the mounted troops pressed on towards a third cantonment, Klebha. As they approached it they saw the huts were in flames. Just leaving them were between five and seven hundred Zulus, who retreated over a hill behind the cantonment. The troopers galloped after the enemy silhouetted briefly against the sky, and overtook a few stragglers. There was a sharp skirmish. At least seven of the enemy were killed. The mounted men suffered no loss. They could not see that another, larger body of Zulus, perhaps 2000 strong, was starting to move towards them from the hills beyond.

On the spur of the ridge the artillery section observed the enemy force advancing. The range was very long – perhaps six miles – but the guns opened fire. Two shells exploded just in front of the enemy, whose advance ended abruptly in quick retreat, presumably in the direction of the Ulundi. The horsemen were puzzled by the cannon fire. They did not see the enemy force, but in any event, they were ready to give up the pursuit. The enemy knew the country well. The ground was very bad for horses. The air in the valley was hot, and had an unpleasant fragrant smell. The order was given to withdraw and the troops climbed back up the ridge.

In the few reports of the action no mention is made of what the two companies of the 2nd Battalion did on this expedition. Apparently they were active elsewhere in the valley, perhaps burning other cantonments. Altogether nine or ten cantonments were destroyed.[34]

On June 27th the columns marched seven to eight miles and came to Mthonjaneni, a mountain which rises two thousand feet above the White Mfolozi and commands the Mahlabathini plain. The men could see Ulundi clearly from it. The rugged slopes extend several miles. For the most part they were covered in thick bush. Its top is level, and though the contour is irregular, the columns were able to form a laager fairly easily on it. For two days the British army remained on the mountain, perfecting the laager from which it would sally forth. Some wagons were sent back to Fort Marshall on the 27th to bring up more supplies. The enemy did not interfere with its occupation of this strategic height.

Buller's horsemen moved down towards the river and encountered envoys from the Zulu King, bringing two elephant tusks and 150 cattle as tokens of peace. They were sent back with the ivory the next day. The invading army was poised to strike at his capital. The Zulus must surrender or fight: the King could not bargain.[35]

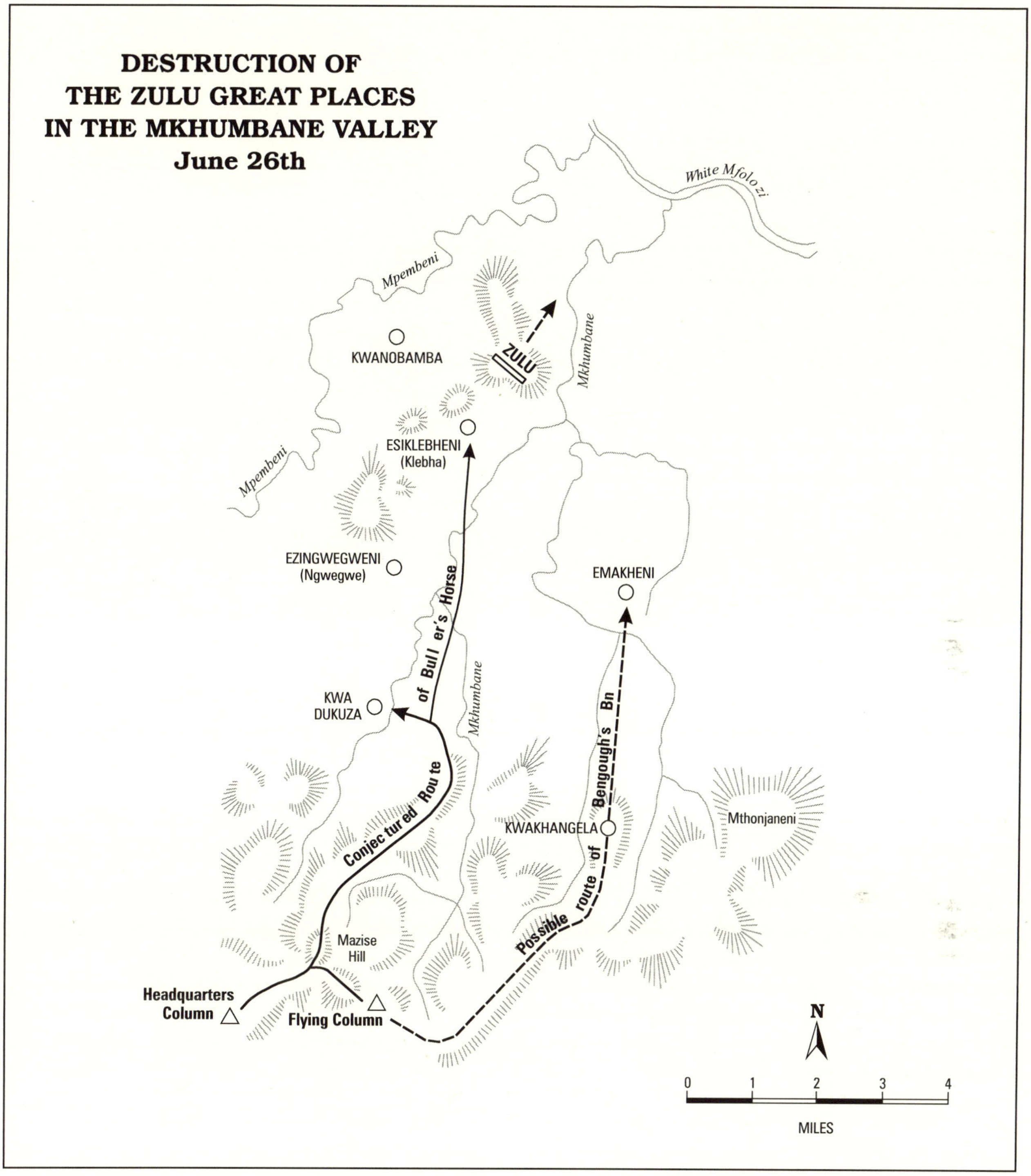

The British army was sixteen miles from Ulundi. The way to it lay along a track through dense bush and over rough ground as far as the river. The country beyond appeared to be open. That evening some spies from the 2nd Battalion reported that a large Zulu army was in the bush on the lower slopes of the mountain and just to the east of the track.[36] Perhaps the Zulus had realized that such terrain would favour them in combat. Or would the Zulus wait beyond the river to fight the British in the open?

The line of communication

The lifeline of the army in Zululand was the track along which the army advanced. The units responsible for maintaining communication between the army and the bases in Natal were stationed in the forts along the track. There were three now – Fort Newdigate on the right bank of the Nondweni river, Fort Marshall at the head of the Ntinini, and Fort Evelyn on the ridge just east of the Mhlathuze crossing. The distance between the army at

Mthonjaneni and Fort Evelyn and between the different forts was sixteen or seventeen miles.

The forts were garrisoned by units of the Headquarters Column. Major General Marshall, commander of the Cavalry Brigade, was put in command on the line of communication when the brigade was disbanded. Each fort had two companies of British infantry, a section of artillery, a squadron of British cavalry or a troop of colonial mercenaries, and a company of the 2nd Battalion of the Native Contingent.[37]

The country to some distance on either side of the line of communication had been deserted by the population. The homesteads – those which had not already been burnt – dotting the hillside here and there, were uninhabited. The only signs of recent occupation were rank grass and piles of rubbish, partly picked bones and broken pots, outside their perimeters. The dome shaped huts, whitened by exposure, the corn patches with overripe and dropping ears, the cattle pens built of stones, all bespoke abandon. The exception was the dogs lurking about, looking forlorn and hungry. Around Fort Newdigate they gathered in packs of about twenty. They came out at night and could he heard barking, howling and fighting over what was left of slaughtered oxen.

Winter enhanced the appearance of desolation. The grass was brown or yellow and a yellow-brown haze often hung over the hills. In some places there were buck and a variety of birds, but a disquieting number of vultures skulked about Fort Marshall.[38]

The companies of the 2nd Battalion at Forts Newdigate, Marshall and Evelyn provided scouts and spies as well as pickets, patrols and escorts.[39] There were also the troops of mounted men lately drawn from Natal – the Amabomvu and Amangwane Corps stationed at Forts Newdigate and Marshall. Together they numbered about one hundred men. Not all of them were mounted. So poor was the condition of their horses that the Amabomvu at Fort Newdigate could do little proper work.[40] There is no report of the condition of the horses at Fort Marshall. Early in July another mounted unit arrived at the fort from Natal. This consisted of Teteleku's amaMpumuza, about 130 men from the Umgeni Division west of Pietermaritzburg, which had been serving at Msinga, Helpmekaar and Rorke's Drift.[41] Probably the amaMpumuza assumed the duties which the Amabomvu were no longer able to perform.

Garrison life was monotonous. We have a description of the daily routine at Fort Marshall, which probably differed little from that at Newdigate or Evelyn. The company of the 2nd Battalion had about sixty men, under Captain Worthington and Lieutenant Heathcote. The camp was outside the fort, and the contingent's huts were on a slope going down to a small stream. Reveille sounded at 5.15. The men fell in for roll call. It was dark – very dark when there was no moon – and was often misty. There might be a cold wind. The foot soldiers filed into the fort, taking assigned places, and fixed bayonets. The mounted men stood to their horses and saddled up. The commanding officer and his staff then made an inspection. There was no talking. Cooking fires were lit outside the fort. A frost appeared at dawn.

The sun rose over the mountains. No enemy could be seen, so the men stood down. Rations were issued and vedettes were posted. The men who had been on the outer picket line came in. They had spent the night in snug crannies about a mile out. The mail was loaded on ponies, and the Amabomvu provided an escort. The horsemen were almost naked in the sunlight and rode with their toes in the stirrups. (The head man had a spur on one heel.) Whatever convoy or set of wagons was to go off was got ready.

There was a pause for breakfast. Then convoys, wagons, mail, dispatches and the like were got on their way. Work parties went out. Wood for the fires had to be brought from a distance. Worthington's men fetched six loads of thorn bush on July 2nd and spent July 4th cutting wood in the Ntinini valley. The men who remained at the fort cleaned the area. Dinner. More work. At four the fort was manned again. 'Tea' followed, and free time until tattoo at eight.[42]

The enemy was in the vicinity. He was seen occasionally, in groups from two to ninety, just off the main track. A young British officer accompanied by a corporal started on a ride from Mthonjaneni to Fort Evelyn. The bodies were found a few miles short of Fort Evelyn. A group of thirty Zulus fired on the Amabomvu detachment carrying mail between Fort Marshall and Fort Evelyn on June 27th, but could not be found by a troop of British cavalry which escorted the mail next day. The Zulus had to keep on the move, for British expeditions continually sought them. Though information of these expeditions is patchy, we have glimpses of a few of them.

For instance, on July 8th, an expedition comprising fifty-five British cavalry and seven Amabomvu set out towards Ntabankulu. About four miles from the fort it saw a group of twenty Zulus at a distance of one and a half miles. An effort was made to catch it, but it disappeared in the hills above the Jojozi. The expedition crossed the White Mfolozi, but did not go as far as Ntabankulu. It burnt six homesteads and seized six cattle.

Meanwhile the company of the 2nd Battalion went out in the opposite direction. It scoured caves on the Nquthu range, and brought back what were presumed to be personal belongings of British soldiers killed at Isandlwana. On the 7th half the company was sent to search for the Zulu near the Jojozi, but the enemy apparently had left the vicinity. The signal station above the fort reported seeing a large force of the enemy, about five hundred men, near Ntabankulu.

Expeditions from Fort Marshall went out towards Babanango, five miles to the east, and beyond in June 24th and July 5th, respectively. Others went to the Phindo range, four miles to the west, on June 26th, and beyond it on June 27th and July 2nd and 3rd. The Amabomvu Corps and Worthington's company were involved in most of these expeditions. After July 1st the men of the 2nd Battalion provided a colourful contrast to the horsemen, for on that day a detachment brought a wagon full of winter clothes, including uniforms, for the contingent. Thereafter they sallied forth wearing new red coats.[43]

Nearby homesteads, even if deserted, could be used by the shifting enemy and therefore should be burnt. The typical homestead was sited on the rocky ledge of a hillside, difficult of approach because of rocky outcrops above and gullies below. The punitive expedition would make its way to the circle of thatch huts surrounding the cattle pen. Sometimes an old woman would be found, apparently abandoned by her kin. The huts were searched. The insides were usually black from smoke and dirt and the thatch was infested with flies, fleas and cockroaches. They contained few articles beyond some wooden headrests and grass mats.

If time allowed the men searched for store pits of grain. They were usually concealed, but tapping and probing in likely places would disclose them. Part of the corn might be eaten, the rest would be destroyed. Imagine the surprise of one man who opened a store. He pulled away the stone cover and put in both arms to pull out a bundle of corn. Instead he pulled out the head of a baby. The pit had been used for burial.

It was quick work to burn the homestead, especially in the dry winter weather. Put a match to the weather side and in a few minutes the hut was ablaze. In a few minutes the huts of the circle were so many fiery cones. A little longer and they collapsed into ashes. The grass outside the circle would catch fire. The flames moved along to the corn patches, jumped gullies and climbed around the rocky outcrops. It reached the tall grass in the valley and would go on until extinguished by the damp of night.

Some men of the contingent were shouting from rocks at a distance. They had found where the valued possessions had been hidden. They waved them aloft – mats, gourds, dresses, pillows, guns, things from Isandlwana.[44]

If garrison duty in the forts was monotonous and forays provided diversion, the security of the line of communication still could not be taken for granted. It is surprising that small Zulu forces were not more active, seeking to wear down the mobile forces as well as pick off individuals and small groups outside the forts. Such an enterprising strategy would soon have isolated the garrisons and required further detachments from the main force to keep up communication. Fortunately for the British, there was no Zulu strategy in this respect, and the garrisons' winter idyll continued uninterrupted.

NOTES

1 *Narrative*, pp. 97 and 192.

2 *Ibid.*, pp. 96–97. Tomasson, *With the Irregulars*, p. 113. Laband, *Kingdom in crisis*, pp. 195–196.

3 Malet, *Extracts from a Diary*, p. 18.

4 NW, June 17, 1879: 'The Zulu War. With Gen. Newdigate's Column;' with which *cf.* Tomasson, *With the Irregulars*, p. 122; *Private Journal of Guy C. Dawnay*, p. 49, and WO 32/7754: 2nd Division Diary, June 6, 1879.

5 Tomasson, *With the Irregulars*, p. 122.

6 *Narrative*, p. 98. WO 32/7754: 2nd Division Diary, June 8, 1879. Malet, *Extracts from a Diary*, pp. 18–20. Montague, *Campaigning in South Africa*, pp. 192–193, 196 and 206. *Private Journal of Guy C. Dawnay*, pp. 49–53.

7 The return of the 2nd Battalion on June 16th gives seven companies proceeding with the 2nd Division (C2454, p. 125) and the map of the division's camp (2nd Division Diary) shows seven lines or ranks, suggesting seven companies. One company had been left at Fort Newdigate (*Narrative*, p. 97). Another 'detachment' (presumably a company, for two officers were in charge) left Pietermaritzburg on June 11th, escorting a supply of winter clothing for the battalion (NW, June 12, 1879: 'Natal Native Contingent'); it is doubtful that it reached the battalion by the 16th, if indeed it was destined to – it may have been the same company earlier assigned to the base at Dundee (CP 16–7: Clery's report, April 9, 1879; and 16–10: return of April 30, 1879). There also appears to have been a company left with the garrison at Rorke's Drift (see CSO 1927: 2549/1879 and *Private Journal of Guy C. Dawnay*, p. 48).

8 Montague, *Campaigning in South Africa*, p. 203.

9 For game and hunting in this region generally see Bindon Blood, *Four Score Years and Ten: Sir Bindon Blood's Reminiscences*

(London, Bell, 1933), p. 200; *War and Peace in South Africa*, pp. 21 and 43; Malet, *Extracts from a Diary*, p. 11; and Montague, *Campaign in South Africa*, p. 252.

10 Malet, *Extracts from a Diary*, p. 16.

11 Montague, *Campaigning in South Africa*, pp. 262–263.

12 *Cf. Narrative*, p. 98, and *Private Journal of Guy C. Dawnay*, p. 48.

13 This is a conflation of several short and rather vague reports in WO 32/7754: 2nd Division Diary, June 10 and 11, 1879; Ashe and Wyatt Edgell, *Story of the Zulu Campaign*, p. 304; *Private Journal of Guy C. Dawnay*, pp. 49–50; and Tomasson, *With the Irregulars*, pp. 113–114. Also, see *Narrative*, p. 98.

14 *Narrative*, p. 103. Fairlie Diary, June 13–15, 1879.

15 WO 32/7754: 2nd Division Diary, June 14, 1879.

16 The expedition is described in *Private Journal of Guy C. Dawnay*, pp. 50–53; Tomasson, *With the Irregulars*, pp. 115–121; and NW, June 24, 1879: 'With Gen. Newdigate's Column.' Also, see Malet, *Extracts from a Diary*, p. 19.

17 *Narrative*, pp. 98 and 103; *cf. Private Journal of Guy C. Dawnay*, p. 53. WO 32/7754: 2nd Division Diary, June 14 and 17, 1879, respectively. Fairlie Diary, June 17, 1879. At Fort Newdigate the garrison consisted on one company of the 2nd Battalion, two of British infantry, two Gatling guns and crews, and a squadron of British cavalry (C2454, p. 97; *Narrative*, p. 97; WO 32/7754: 2nd Division Diary, June 14, 1879).

18 WO 32/7754: 2nd Division Diary, June 15, 22, 1879, respectively. *Lord Chelmsford's Zululand Campaign*, pp. 195–197. Montague, *Campaigning in South Africa*, p. 212. Also, see Statham, *Blacks, Boers & British*, p. 179; *War and Peace in South Africa*, pp. 10 and 13; and Tomasson, *With the Irregulars*, p. 128.

19 *Narrative*, p. 109. *Lord Chelmsford's Zululand Campaign*, pp. 197–197. WO 32/7754: 2nd Division Diary, June 18, 1879. Fairlie Diary, June 18, 1879.

20 CP 26–34: Bengough to Quartermaster General, 2nd Division, June 19, 1879.

21 Malet, *Extracts from a Diary*, p. 20.

22 *Narrative*, p. 109 and n. WO 32/7754: 2nd Division Diary, June 19, 1879.

23 *Narrative*, p. 109, 110 and n. WO 32/7754: 2nd Division Diary, June 20–23, 1879. McToy, *Brief History of the 13th Regiment*, p. 75.

24 *Cf.* Malet, *Extracts from a Diary*, p. 21; S. McToy, *Brief History of the 13th Regiment*, p. 78; Tomasson, *With the Irregulars*, p. 135; and Fripp, 'Reminiscences of the Zulu War,' p. 556.

25 *Narrative*, pp. 110, 173 and Plans of Camps, facing p. 173. WO 32/7754: 2nd Division Diary, June 22–25, 1879. McToy, *Brief History of the 13th Regiment*, pp. 78–79. Absence of reports of inclement weather is taken to mean there was fair weather.

26 *Narrative*, p. 109. Fairlie Diary, June 22, 1879. SP 41: Theophilus Shepstone, Jr., to William Shepstone, July 17, 1879. TN, July 11, 1879: 'With Genl. Wood's Column.'

27 Tomasson, *With the Irregulars*, pp. 132–134; but the dating sequence for the latter part of June seems to be two days off and there are gaps in the account. See Fairlie Diary, June 21, 1879.

28 Fairlie Diary, June 19–23, 1879. On the 19th and 20th part of Shepstone's Horse was on escort duty to Rorke's Drift and back. On the 21st a detachment burnt several deserted homesteads, including two large ones, apparently in the vicinity of the mercenaries' skirmish the same day. On the 23rd part of Shepstone's Horse was on patrol to the left of the Flying Column.

29 Tomasson, *With the Irregulars*, p. 135.

30 *Lord Chelmsford's Zululand Campaign*, pp. 185 and 199.

31 TN, July 11, 1879: 'With Genl. Wood's Column.'

32 *Ibid.*

33 Fairlie Diary, June 25, 1879. They had burnt some on the 24th as well (*ibid*).

34 *Narrative*, p. 110. Tomasson, *With the Irregulars*, pp. 136–137. C2482, pp. 43 and 98. WO 32/7754: 2nd Division Diary, June 27 [sic:26], 1879. TN, July 11, 1879: 'With Genl. Wood's Column.'

35 *Narrative*, pp. 110–112. Tomasson, *With the Irregulars*, pp. 140–141. WO 32/7754: 2nd Division diary, June 27 and 28 [*sic*: 26 and 27], 28, 1879. TN, July 11, 1879: 'With Genl. Wood's Column.' Fairlie Diary, June 27, 1879. *Cf.* McToy, *Brief History of the 13th Regiment*, p. 78.

36 Fairlie Diary, June 29, 1879. See Laband, *Kingdom in crisis*, p. 197.

37 *Narrative*, pp. 97 and 109. The distance between Koppie Allein and Fort Newdigate is twenty-five miles, and a fourth fort, called Fort Warwick, was built by a company of British infantry on Thelezeni, ten miles from Koppie Allein and fifteen miles from Fort Newdigate (Atkinson, *The South Wales Borders*, p. 36).

38 Malet, *Extracts from a Diary*, pp. 32–33. Montague, *Campaigning in South Africa*, pp. 211, 214–216, 223, 251, 253.

39 Montague, *Campaigning in South Africa*, pp. 198–199. Bengough, *Memories of a Soldier's Life*, pp. 127 and 134. TN, August 6, 1879: 'The Second Division.' NW, October 4, 1879 Supplement: Newdigate's report.

40 See the roll in SNA 1/6/14, no. 49, and WO 32/7767: Diaries of Officers commanding posts in frontier and lines of communication, Zululand. *Cf.* SNA 1/6/15. nos. 75 and 84; *Private Journal of Guy C. Dawnay*, p. 60; and Montague, *Campaigning in South Africa*, p. 262. There is no reference in the records to the whereabaouts of the Amangwane Corps after the scare at Fort Newdigate during the night of June 6-7, 1879 (see SNA 1/1/35, no. 189).

41 *Private Journal of Guy C. Dawnay*, p. 73. TN, August 6, 1879: 'Latest from the Front.' For background see SNA 1/6/12, no. 78; CSO 1973, pp. 135 and 186; Norris-Newman, *In Zululand with the British*, p. 187; and the various reports in TN, March 31 and August 20, 1879, and NW, April 22 and May 10, 1879.

42 Montague, *Campaigning in South Africa*, pp. 207–208, 242–245.

43 WO 32/7767: Diaries of Officers commanding posts on frontier and lines of communication, Zululand, *passim*. Montague, *Campaigning in South Africa*, pp. 213 and 217. *Narrative*, p. 167. *Lord Chelmsford's Zululand Campaign*, p. 269, n. 67. P.H. Butterfield, 'The Letters of Colonel Davies of the Grenadier Guards, 1879,' Africana Notes News, XXX, no. 1 (March 1992), pp. 26–27. NW, June 12, 1879: 'Natal Native Contingent.'

44 Montague, *Campaigning in South Africa*, pp. 194, 213–217, 248–251. See Malet, *Extracts from a Diary*, pp. 20 and 33.

Chapter 15

VICTORY AT ULUNDI

Advance to the White Mfolozi

From the vantage of Mthonjaneni one could see the end of the war. The mountain overlooked the Mahlabathini plain. There were the great places of the Zulu nation and Ulundi, seat of the Zulu King. The British attached great political importance to Ulundi. Whether the Zulu attached the same or not we cannot tell, but he could not very well leave it without a fight, lest he impair the cohesion and morale of the kingdom. Thus Ulundi assumed symbolic as well as strategic significance. The battle for it was the climax of the war.

The Zulu army on the plain was in great strength. On June 28th about 20 000 warriors were seen advancing from the cantonment near Nodwengu. They formed three bodies and advanced towards Mthonjaneni. They reached the White Mfolozi and some crossed it. Next day scouts from Bengough's Battalion reported that a large force was in the Pathe bush, five to six miles down the slope. The hilltop was fortified: two wagon laagers were formed and details from the units of the Headquarters and Flying Columns were told off to man them.[1]

On the 30th the two columns – the Flying Column in the lead, the Headquarters Column following – marched down the northern spur of the mountain. They still followed the track which traders had made to Ulundi. The men were lightly equipped. There were no more than a hundred wagons with each column, and they carried ten days' rations and ammunition.

Thorn bush enclosed the columns and the soil became sandy. The sun shone brightly and the air was still and hot. Small numbers of the enemy observed their progress from close by. No skirmish occurred, but scouts in front reported a large force of the enemy was moving towards the river again. Once more the Zulu King sent emissaries. The Lieutenant General's terms were tantamount to a demand for surrender. The King had three days to comply, during which time his army should neither oppose nor provoke the British army, which would not burn any more homesteads and not cross the river.

The two columns camped on a flat near a small flowing stream. They had gone only four miles and were only a third of the way to the river. The march continued on July 1st, over ground covered with thorns, cactus, and long grass, under a hot sun. Water was scarce. The track was bad and had to be repaired to carry the wagons, which could only pass one at a time as they approached to the river. It took all morning to go about six miles. The Flying Column reached the vicinity of the river a little after noon. The Headquarters Column was about a mile and a half behind it. Shepstone's Horse was scouting on the left flank of the army.[2]

Buller's mounted men were in front. Starting in darkness as usual, they had reached the river at dawn. A large number of watch fires were burning on the other side, but as the sun rose, the enemy left them and moved off towards a cantonment a little upstream and farther from the river. The mercenaries formed a line of vedettes along the right bank. The Edendale and Sotho troops took position on a small stony hill overlooking the river.

The Zulus who had moved off were observed to form a strong column, which moved to Nodwengu and then east to Ulundi. Once they were inside the great place of the King a cloud of dust rose over the place and hung there for an hour. The enemy was seen marching to and fro between cantonments. The mounted men estimated about 15 000 in all.

The Zulus formed a large circle, from which issued a column which moved round some hills to the west. The remainder of the circle moved towards the river, on a line to the laager which the Flying Column was making.[3] The Flying Column hastily made ready to receive them. The Headquarters Column halted abruptly and laagered on its leading wagons.

Yet the Zulus did not attack and the defenders of the laagers eventually stood down. During the course of the afternoon the laagers were strengthened, but the enemy threat receded. Horses and cattle were watered at the river without interference and brought back to the laagers before dark.[4]

The laager of the Headquarters Column had been formed so hurriedly that the wagons were parked in some disarray and the enclosure was rather too small to accommodate the men without crowding. It was strengthened by a shelter trench and a barrier of entangled thornbush. The ground was cleared all round, but only to a distance of about twenty yards. The cattle were driven inside the laager for the night. British infantry bivouacked between the rings of wagons and thorn bush. Bengough's battalion lay down outside the barrier. A gap had been made in it to give them access to the laagers. As usual, redcoats made up the first line of sentries. The second, outer line was drawn from the battalion.[5]

An almost full moon illuminated the landscape. Around the laager the tall grass, bush and small trees seemed to close in. About midnight an officer of Bengough's battalion went to visit the outposts. He failed to tell the British officer in charge of the sentries. One of the sentries heard a sound. Later it was supposed to have been made by the returning officer's horse, but in any case the sentry could not see what had made it. He challenged three times and received no reply. The sentry fired. 'Guard turn out!' 'Stand to arms!' The men in the bivouac seized their weapons and scrambled to the laager.

None moved faster than the men of the Native Contingent. Some grabbed their spears, some did not. Some dashed through the gap in the entanglement, others vaulted over and through it. It was a warm night and they had been sleeping naked. Naked they ran, over and through the British soldiers who lay between them and the laager. They shouted as they ran. Many of the British soldiers first thought they were Zulus attacking. There were several hundred new men in the column, and some of them apparently panicked.

Fortunately, alarm was no longer a novelty. Discipline quickly prevailed and there was no shooting, though several of the battalion were injured when some of the officers beat and kicked them, partly to restore discipline.[6] Major Bengough himself was knocked down by the rush when he rose from sleep. As he staggered to his feet, one of his officers exclaimed: 'They are not worth a rap.' 'Who?' asked Bengough. 'Our men, sir,' the officer replied.[7] Not long before General Wood, commander of the Flying Column, had told him: 'Don't believe that your Zulus will fight. They are all right for scouting, but would run away if there was any fighting.'[8] This latest experience must have been disconsoling.

On the 2nd the Headquarters Column moved down to form a larger laager in conjunction with the Flying Column. A stone fort was built on the hill just above it and the men of both columns spent the rest of the day perfecting the defence. Small bodies of Zulus moved about on the other side. Occasionally they fired across the river, truce notwithstanding. A herd of white cattle was seen coming from the direction of Ulundi. White cattle belonged to the Zulu King. There was speculation that the herd was a peace offering but then enemy soldiers drove it back from the river. That night there were Zulu camp fires all round the laager.[9]

Reconnaissance to Nodwengu

The track to Ulundi crossed the White Mfolozi about 1400 yards in front of the British laager. It ran between two sides of a loop in the river to a shallow, sandy ford at the bend and then emerged on the other side in thick bush under a bluff 150 feet high.

On the morning of July 3rd the enemy resumed firing from across the river, even though the truce was not to expire until noon. His marksmen concealed themselves in the crannies on the cliff face and shot at water parties from camp and men washing and bathing in the river. The British had to give up the loop and fall back to the bush in front of the laager. Two companies reinforced the picket. Two groups of Zulus arrived to reinforce the snipers. A British cannon was directed to fire at the bluff. The skirmish became quite lively. Some of the enemy bullets even fell inside the laager.[10]

While the skirmish was taking place at the main ford, Colonel Buller was preparing to cross the river at another ford downstream. The Lieutenant General ordered him to scout towards Ulundi and gather vital information for the battle which would take place the following day. He was to take the main track as far as he could and see what it was like. He was to look for a place where the army could take up a good position and fight. The enemy was expected to react to the reconnaissance. The Lieutenant General was anxious that he do so, to show his strength, his gathering points and his plan of attack.[11]

The mounted men dined early. At 11 they were ordered to saddle their horses. Just before noon they mounted. A few minutes before the expiry of the proffered three-day truce Buller and another British officer cantered down to the river's edge to join them. The fording place he had chosen was almost a mile below that of the main track and below the loop. There was no high ground opposite and apparently the enemy ignored it.

Probably the enemy was distracted just at this time. The Zulu King had sent a small herd of cattle, ostensibly captured at Isandlwana, to the Lieutenant General on the 27th, as a token of good faith in negotiations. As we have seen, the Lieutenant General had pledged not to cross the White Mfolozi before noon of the 3rd, giving the Zulu King the interval in which to come to terms. As the time expired, this herd was returned, presumably at the main ford where obviously there was someone to receive them.[12]

At noon Buller looked at his watch. He gave the order: 'Forward'. The horses plunged into the water. It was about two feet deep and in a short time they were through and climbing the opposite bank. There were 530 troopers – all the men and horses in the Flying Column still serviceable. There were four bands of mercenaries, a unit of mounted infantry, and the two troops of Natal Native Horse.

The ground rises gently to the spur of a hill. One face of the hill is the bluff which was infested by snipers. The Colonel sent one of the mercenary units to the left to clear and hold it. With the main force he struck out straight towards Ulundi.

The reconnaissance proceeded over the spur, across a small stream and up a low ridge. The Colonel directed it along the ridge to the left in order to reach the main track. The troops did so about a mile in advance of the main ford, where he collected them, as they had become somewhat scattered. The separate band was then engaged in clearing the bluff. A few of the enemy, who apparently had fled from the hill, were headed in the direction of Nodwengu and passed in front of the main force. It went after them at a gallop. The mounted men emerged on the Mahlabathini plain – open, rolling country, with fine views. Just over half a mile on the troops came to Nodwengu. They rounded the edge of the large circle of huts and saw the fugitives again. The runaways were joined by others from Nodwengu itself. There were a hundred of them. They were taking the ridge line towards a hill a mile to the north. Some enemy horsemen appeared in the distance and seemed to be headed in the same direction. Also, a few men could be seen driving a large tribe of goats in that direction. Buller sent a band of mercenaries towards the hill. With the rest of his men he bore to the right, keeping to the track and the general direction of Ulundi.

The ground was open, but the grass was quite long, and the goats seemed to take their time escaping. The Colonel called out: 'Halt and fire without dismounting, they are foxing.' The leading troop did so, and almost at the same time about 300 Zulus in a line sprang up and started to shoot at it. They had been lying in wait 150–200 yards ahead, in a dry watercourse at right angles to the track.

The reconnaissance had stopped just short of an ambush. Not only was the enemy in strength in front, but another line appeared to the right, in the direction of Ulundi. They caught the mounted men in a crossfire, but they were shooting high as usual. Their first volley, at 150 yards, knocked over only a few horses and men. The stricken horses rolled on the ground and there was a scramble to rescue the riders. The enemy seemed to be coming on in a semicircle. Buller had to order a hasty retreat to avoid being trapped.

The retreat was orderly, but the Zulus pressed closely. The Edendale and Sotho troops were in the rearguard and at one stage were almost cut off. Pursuing Zulus taunted them: 'You curs! To-morrow we will drive you across the Ncome River, and we will eat up all the red soldiers!' Buller staged a rally on the rise of ground near Nodwengu, then retired down the ridge. The pursuers appeared on one side of the cantonment. Fire from the rearguard drove them back out of sight. They reappeared as the troops fell back, coming down the slope after them.

The Colonel sent another unit to reinforce the mercenaries on the hill overlooking the river. Together they laid down a fire to cover his retreat to the crossing. Three companies of infantry and two pieces of artillery were also sent down from the camp to give cover. It was none too soon, for a large body of the enemy had appeared on the hills to the left and was descending, evidently to co-operate in the effort to cut off the horsemen at the river.

The mounted men escaped the converging forces of the enemy. The Native Horse came down the hill in a loose formation, rifles at the slope, firing recklessly in the direction of the pursuers. The mercenaries from the hill were last to cross and there was some worry they might be hit by the fire, but everyone returned without injury. The enemy reached the far bank and an exchange of small arms fire ensued.

The Colonel ordered the troops back to camp and losses were counted: three men killed, three wounded, thirteen horses killed or missing. The Edendale and Sotho troops had suffered no casualties at all. Half an hour later the horses were turned out to graze and the men took the second meal of the day. The rest of the afternoon was spent cleaning rifles and filling ammunition pouches.

The reconnaissance was a complete success. All the information the Lieutenant General desired had been obtained by the troops or by himself and his staff as they observed the action from the laager.[13]

That night the army slept in expectation of the decisive battle. Enemy fires burnt all round again. The full moon illuminated the laager once more. The bush nearby again assumed mysterious and fantastic forms. The river reflected the moonlight, though the bluff at the crossing was a dark mass. The hills beyond Ulundi stood out against the sky.[14]

Between eleven and midnight the sleepers were awakened by the rising sound of singing. The Zulu army must be gathered in thousands, presumably at the great places. Perhaps they were moving about, or

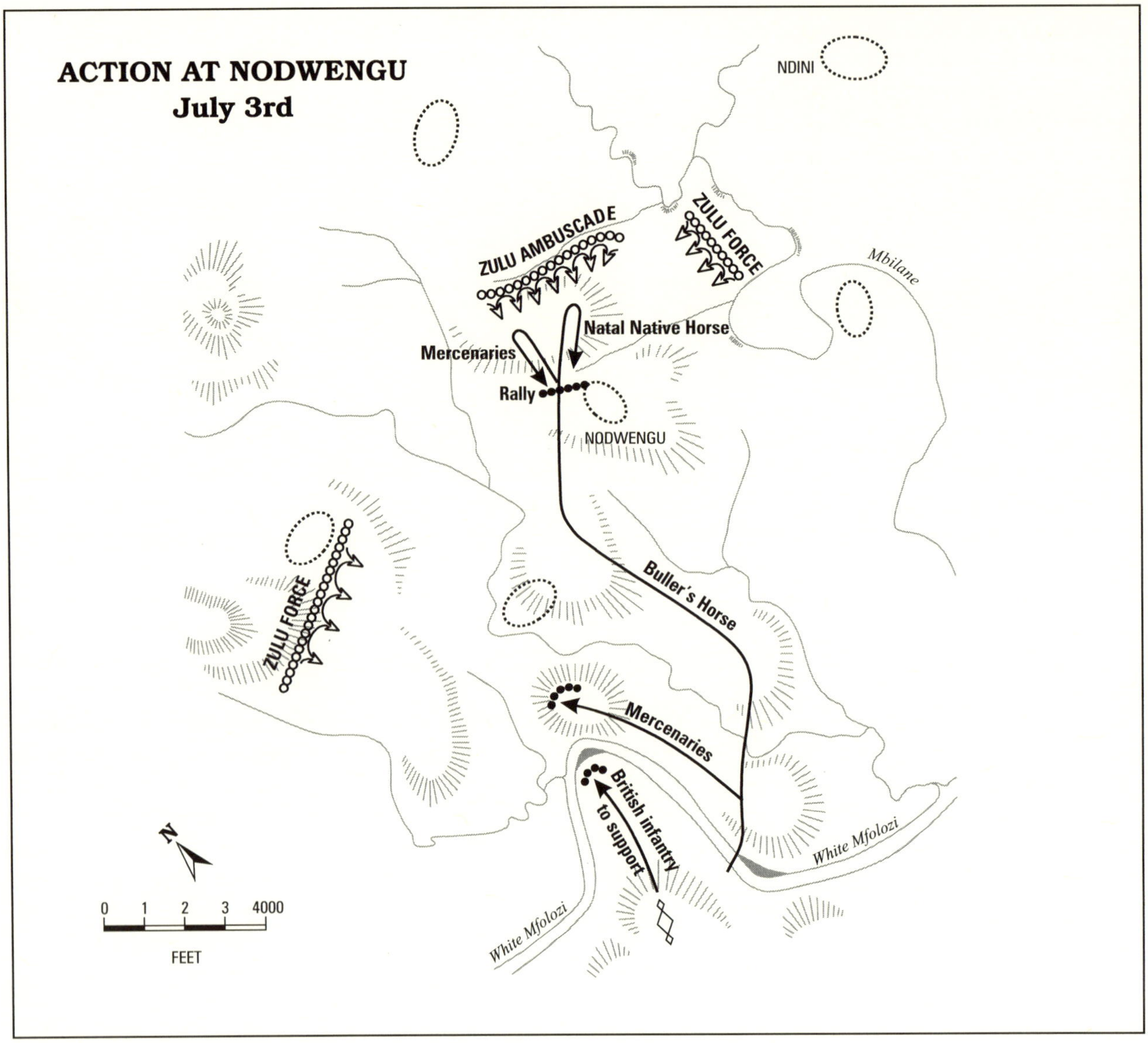

the night wind bore the sound uncertainly first as a murmur, then loud and distinct. The singers seemed to be drawing closer, to be approaching the river. Few could sleep, most lay still and listened. Some stood quietly to arms as if expecting an attack. Sentries were particularly vigilant. The songs were of war, of devotion to the King. They were exultant and powerful. Against the roar of the basses tenor voices could be heard, some individually. The powerful rhythm was punctuated by shouts and shrieks. Occasionally there were rifle shots. Some men – who may have been of Bengough's battalion – said that this was the enemy's last feast before battle: if the British did not attack him the next day, then certainly he would attack the British.

There was a general expectation that the enemy would attack at daybreak, but then, one officer reasoned, if he spent the night singing, he would be late rising in the morning. It is difficult to say at what hour the singing ceased. It may have gone on all night, but the loudest part seems to have lasted perhaps three-quarters of an hour. The martial sound faded, but its portent was clear to all listeners. Those who had stood to arms lay down again. Men were lulled back to sleep by the low murmur of the cattle inside the laager.[15]

The battle on the plain

The British army rose early for the battle on July 4th. Men were awakened quietly and prepared silently for the day's work.[16] Troopers were in the saddle and at the lower drift long before dawn. Each one carried a day and half's rations in his saddle bags and 100 rounds of ammunition.[17]

The last hours before dawn were cold. A heavy dew settled. A mist rose and hung over the river. There was nothing on the opposite bank to indicate the enemy's presence or awareness of the army's movements. At quarter to six Buller's horsemen splashed through the stream and turned to the left, making for the main track. The various troops took up positions and spread out in a semicircle to cover the infantry,[18] which started crossing at the main ford about six. It took almost an hour for the column to clear the river and form up in the bush on the other side. The Flying Column was first, then the Headquarters Column, but they continued on in a single column. Mounted troops brought up the rear. There were 5170 fighting men and fourteen guns in the column.[19] The Natal Native Horse, the Edendale and Sotho troops, were in front. No. 1 Pioneer Company was with the men of the Flying Column, the 2nd Battalion with those of the Headquarters Column. Shepstone's Horse was with several squadrons of British lancers in the rear.

A detachment of 632 officers and men was left to hold the fort and laager against an expected Zulu attack. The bugle sounded in the laager at daybreak. The enemy apparently took the cue to rise as well, and found the main British force already among his cantonments.[20]

The mounted men in front could not see the main column at the river, but they learned it had crossed and therefore advanced. They followed the track past Nodwengu and took position on the high ground beyond it. The sun was up and they could see the enemy gathering on the hills in front and to the left. At first he seemed to be trying to conceal his movements. This, of course, was impossible, for the small bodies soon combined into large ones which could not be concealed.[21]

The British column struggled up the track and emerged from the bush onto the open ground. The rearguard burnt an abandoned cantonment – Ndabakawombe – as it passed. The sun just topped the hills in front and glinted on the steel of the soldiers' bayonets. The column formed a 'square', in fact a rectangular laager whose sides were double lines of infantry.[22]

The sun was well up. The square moved, passed Nodwengu, halted on the rise which had been chosen for battle, and wheeled slightly to the right to get an advantage of the ground. Cannon and Gatling guns went into line with the infantry. Ammunition boxes were unloaded from the carts and opened. Inside the square the pioneers began to dig.[23] Bengough's battalion was in the centre, in reserve. The men crouched down and held up their shields.[24]

In the distance the Zulus could be seen moving to surround the position. The enemy's strength was estimated at ten, fifteen, then twenty and even twenty-five thousand. Large bodies descended from the hills in open order. They were in long lines rather than in dense formations, but these thickened as they compassed the square. The British cannon fired a few shells at long range. The shells burst among the enemy without retarding his movement. The speed of movement, the order with which the enemy advanced, impressed the waiting British.[25]

Large numbers of the enemy also emerged from the low ground near the river. The mist rose and revealed a strong force moving towards the British laager. Some men had already crossed the river, but discovered the British were in their rear. The attack on the laager across the river was being redirected to the square on the plain.[26]

The British expected the Zulus to attack in the usual way, chest and horns in a double envelopment. It was essential that the enemy should attack as soon as he had concentrated and that his attack be repulsed with the greatest possible loss of life and injury to morale. The British could not be detained on the plain. The enemy could not be indulged in second thoughts about his tactics. The mounted men went to bait the *amabutho* into a precipitate and reckless attack. Then, as at Khambula, they would escape into the square and leave the rest to the infantry and artillery.

The cordon of horsemen around the square pushed outwards to make contact with the enemy. All along the line firing started. In front and on the flanks were Buller's troops, the Native Horse on the right. In rear and also on the flanks were the British lancers, a small band of mercenaries, and Shepstone's Horse, also on the right and in the rear.[27]

The Edendale and Sotho troops engage the *amabutho* coming from the direction of Ulundi. The Zulus cry out, 'Now we have you at last, some few of the mounted men among you may get away, but the red soldiers will all die.' The ground, though open, is covered by the tall grass and broken by gullies, which hinder the horses. The horsemen seem little bothered by it. They fire at the enemy. Colonel Buller's line is falling back to the square. They fall back without the least hurry. In a short time they are at the square.

The British soldiers have told them: 'This battle will be fought to the death.' They are loath to enter the square. At Khambula they drew aside from it. They cannot do that here. They will be left outside and die. They stand fast. They fire a volley into the Zulu line in front. Another, and another. The British soldiers then make an opening in the square and they pass through it. It is not a moment too soon. The enemy taunts them: 'Gallop on, but we will overtake you. We are going to kill everyone of the red men. Perhaps some of you wild men may escape. But go

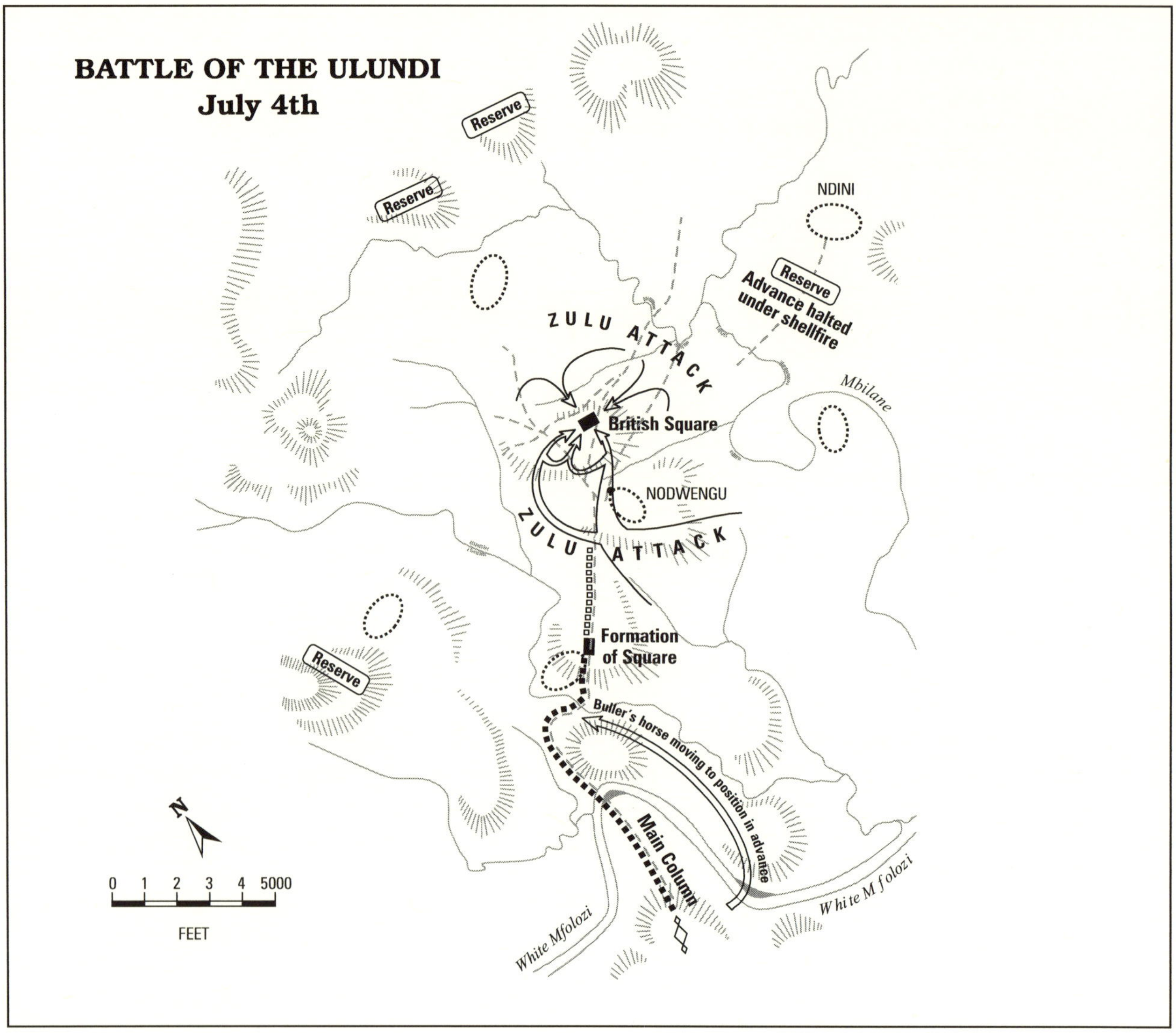

quick, for we will chase you over the Mzinyathi.' Inside they dismount. What are they to do? Red soldiers tell them: 'Eat your biscuits, Johnny, and lie down.'[28]

Shepstone's Horse has a similar experience. The enemy is a quarter of a mile distant and advancing in skirmish order. There appear to be two *amabutho*. Their lines are thirty and forty deep. They fire and run forward, shouting 'Usuthu' and waving their shields. Captain Shepstone will not let his men fire. The amaNgwane wait patiently.

The enemy is within three hundred yards. Captain Shepstone gives the order. The rifles flash. The Zulus do not stop. They fire, too. The fire is heavy, but the bullets go overhead. The Captain continues to give orders and the men listen. They are silent while they fire. At 150 yards the Zulus hesitate and dodge about. Hlubi's baSotho, on their left, fire and retire into the square. The British on the right face of the square open fire. The cannon on the rear face send shells over the horsemen's heads. The British in front and on the left face of the square are now engaged with the enemy.

The amaNgwane are in a cross fire from the Zulus attacking the right face and rear of the square. The British infantry on the rear face cannot fire until they come into the laager. The Zulus are within a hundred yards. Shepstone orders his men to fall back into the square. They won't. They are checking the enemy. They are afraid to go into the square. The Lieutenant General and his staff are watching anxiously.

The horsemen are retiring, slowly, at a trot. The Zulus rush forward after them, shooting and yelling. The amaNgwane slip in through a passage the infantry has made. They are the last to enter the square. The rear face of the square blazes with rifle and cannon fire. Shepstone's men have not been inside four minutes before one of them is killed, three others wounded, and four horses struck by enemy bullets.[29]

The Zulu encirclement is complete. The enemy beats against every face of the square. Nowhere can he close with the British infantry. Volley after volley from the rifles, bursts of bullets from the Gatling, explosions of shrapnel from the cannon, stagger the *amabutho*. Through the smoke Zulu head men can be heard with hoarse voices urging their men on. Dark figures can be seen brandishing spears. At times it is hard to tell what effect this terrible fire is having because of the noise and clouds of smoke. It is easier to see a Zulu formation at a distance than close at hand. From time to time cease-fire sounds along parts of the line. The smoke clears. The Zulus, evidently perceiving a weakness, redouble their effort. The battle continues.[30]

The Zulus demonstrated a considerable firepower for the first time. From the surrounding hills their marksmen laid down a heavy fire, using a great variety of rifles. There was a great sound of bullets passing overhead, also the howl of flying pot legs and pieces of broken wire. The square was a splendid target, but the Zulus were shooting high again. The chance of being hit in the square amounted to less than one in fifty.[31]

Bengough's battalion was drawn up at the centre of the square. Its value as a reserve in the event of a crisis was questionable. The men were plainly unnerved by the battle. It was, after all, their first one. They could see little or none of it outside their ranks, but they could certainly hear it. Many of them lay down. They put their faces to the ground and their shields on their backs. They gave loud vent to their feelings, probably a mixture of tension and fear. Their officers, whom Bengough had had dismount (unlike the generals and their staff), were seen looking on and apparently laughing at them. It is unlikely Bengough would have tolerated *that*. The officers may have been joking and affecting a certain nonchalance.[32]

Edendale and Sotho were drawn up behind the front face of the square, near the right corner. Each man held his horse's bridle and stood by its head. Four cannon were in the line with infantry and the ground in front was good. The enemy attack stalled under their fire without getting close. The Edendale men observed that the British soldiers laughed while they fought and cheered as the Zulus charged. They admired such spirit. The red soldiers made a laager of their bodies, protected *them* and did not call for their help.[33]

Shepstone's Horse was drawn up near the right rear corner of the laager. For several minutes it seemed the enemy might break in there. Nodwengu was 600 yards away and screened his movement. Low ground between it and the square afforded cover for an advance. The *amabutho* worked their way through the long grass and rushed the square at a distance of 130 yards. The British fire did not stop them at a hundred yards, not at eighty.

The Lieutenant General galloped up and ordered the infantry to fire faster. Cannon fired canister, but the shells did not burst at the short range. They continued with shrapnel. The men in the line braced themselves for the enemy's onset. The Gatling section and engineer company in reserve were sent for from the front of the square. At sixty yards the enemy faltered. A few brave men carried on. They fell within forty yards of the square. The rest of the Zulu line wavered. Suddenly the charge collapsed.[34]

The company of pioneers had started throwing up an earthen wall against a cross fire, which suggests a certain stolidity under fire. One of their officers was grazed by a bullet through his helmet. The wall was only three feet in height, when the battle ended.[35] The Zulu attack on the square began at 8.50 and ended before 9.30. The *amabutho* which led it were retreating before those in reserve had time to support them.[36]

Pursuit and destruction

The British lancers led the pursuit. Issuing from the square they charged towards the Nodwengu ridge. There was no organized force to resist them. They carried the ridge and turned against a large body of the enemy which was still firing at the right face of the square as it started to retire. One *ibutho* stood its ground long enough to let loose a last wild volley. The collision of the forces could be heard in the laager. The Zulus broke and ran. The lancers pursued, plucking away the enemy as both dashed towards the hills. There rough ground, a steep slope, and Zulu reserves put an end to the chase.[37]

As the enemy fled across the front of the laager, Buller had his mounted infantry fire into their flank. A few minutes later his men issued from the square in pursuit. The Native Horse dashed through an opening in the laager and the British soldiers cheered them on. The two troops galloped directly towards Ulundi.

They soon caught up with the rearmost of the fugitives. The easiest way to bring one down was to dismount at, say, one hundred yards, and shoot him. The Zulu could run as fast as a horse could gallop. By the time one shot him the range was between two and three hundred yards again. Then mount, ride, dismount and shoot again. As the enemy tired he was caught more easily. The carbine was used as a pistol. It was hard to avoid bodies. The horses trampled them underfoot.

The pursuit ceased at the foot of the hills. The grass on the slope was short but the enemy rallied in small groups and fired. In an exchange of shots they gave way, then came back for a parting volley as the horsemen rode off.

The pursuers began to pick about in the tall grass on the plain, where some Zulus were hiding. Sometimes a man on foot surprised the man on horse and drove him off with a shot. Some troops found a number of Zulus hiding in a gully and drove them down it towards a group of mercenaries who cut them off and killed them.

There was no Zulu stand. The Edendale Horse chased an *ibutho* beyond Ulundi. It was the one which had followed it to the square. They killed about fifty men and called out: 'Well, and are you going to the Mzinyathi now?' There was no reply. The Native Horse took three prisoners. They were the only ones who did so.[38]

Shepstone's Horse left from the rear of the laager, also cheered by redcoats. Captain Shepstone's horse galloped into a hole and both took a tumble. It was feared he had been shot, but he promptly remounted. Only his dignity was injured.

Pursuit became butchery, Shepstone's own word for it. He estimated that his men killed at least three hundred Zulus – fugitives who could not flee fast enough or conceal themselves well enough in grass, gullies and ant-bear holes. The lancers by-passed about seventy Zulus who were hiding in a ravine. The amaNgwane killed every one of them.[39]

A British officer on picket near the river observed two mounted men ride to the edge of a corn field and fire into the middle of it. Three or four Zulus jumped up and ran. The mounted men fired a couple of shots without hitting them. Each picked a man and rode for him. One was practically on top of his man, ready to spear him, when the quarry turned and fired his rifle almost point blank and missed. The horse pivoted round on its hind legs and then the chase continued. The Zulu stopped at last. The horseman jumped down and speared him. A similar fate overtook the other fugitive.

The same officer reported two other incidents, evidently hearsay. In one, a mounted man found a Zulu sitting helpless, shot through both legs. He dismounted and sat down in front of him. In leisurely manner he questioned him about the King and his recent activities, evidently gleaning all the information possible. At length he asked if there was anything more. The wounded man answered there was nothing. The mounted man calmly got up and stabbed him with a spear. In the other incident, a mounted man found a Zulu, wounded and in great pain, who asked if he would take him to an English doctor. The mounted man tapped his carbine. 'This is all the medicine you must expect,' he said, and shot him.[40]

Men of Bengough's battalion, along with irregulars from the Flying Column, went out to mop up where the mounted men had passed. Some of the enemy rallied momentarily against them, and they fell back to the square, but as the mounted men cleared the field of resistance, the men on foot went forward again to ferret out and kill stragglers. For hours the British heard shots across on the open plain,[41] presumably the sounds of personal combats and executions.

The mounted troops and cavalry chased the enemy as far as they safely could. The Zulus who collected on the hills were dispersed by artillery. In another hour not an enemy was to be seen.[42] It was not yet noon. The British square advanced to a stream, halted and dined. The Lieutenant General directed the mounted men to burn the cantonments on the plain. Ulundi, the great place of the Zulu King was fired at 11.40. Two other places a few miles northeast were fired soon afterwards.[43] After these were set on fire, Shepstone's Horse was ordered to burn Khandempemvu, on the side of a hill about two miles to the west. The extreme of the Zulu right horn had occupied the hill before the battle. It was reported that there were Zulus still in the vicinity who were going to cut them off, so one of the mercenary units was sent to cover them.[44]

About two in the afternoon, the British square marched back across the battlefield, and towards the laager beyond the river. Nodwengu was burnt on the way. A cloud of smoke hung over the plain. The return to camp took less than two hours. A British band played for the march and there was a general feeling of exultation. All were conscious of the decisive victory.[45] There was a pause. During the march the Edendale Troop halted briefly to bury one of their men who had been killed. Their hymns gave men pause up to a mile away.[46]

The Lieutenant General had avenged the defeat at Isandlwana. The British army had triumphed over the Zulu and destroyed the great place of the Zulu King. To the victors the war seemed over. It would take time to work out details of the peace, but the fighting was at an end. In fact the peace would take longer to work out than anyone expected. The fighting had ended, but the war would go on for another two months, and the Natal Native Contingent, which had fought first and last, and played a part in every battle, would witness its conclusion.

NOTES

1 WO 32/7767: 2nd Division Diary. Fairlie Diary. (In the case of both these sources, references to dates appear in the text and therefore are omitted in the notes). It had been intended earlier (the 28th) to leave a troop of Shepstone's Horse and a company of the 2nd Battalion (or perhaps Wood's Irregulars) at Mthonjaneni (see 2nd Division Diary; *Lord Chelmsford's Zululand Campaign*, p. 200), but it was not done (see *Narrative*, p. 111n).

2 *Narrative*, pp. 111–112. C2482, p. 54. *Lord Chelmsford's Zululand Campaign*, p. 200. Malet, *Extracts from a Diary*, p. 23. Molyneux, *Campaigning in South Africa and Egypt*, pp. 180–181. 2nd Division Diary. Fairlie Diary.

3 TN, July 18, 1879: 'With Gen. Wood's Column.' Fairlie Diary. Also, see *Narrative*, m p. 112 and C 2482, p. 54. A similar account of Zulu movements is given in Mitford, *Through the Zulu Country*, pp. 165–167, but evidently is misdated July 2nd, for which there is no support in other sources, except possibly Molyneux, *Campaigning in South Africa and Egypt*, p. 182. See Laband, *Kingdom in crisis*, pp. 210–211 on Zulu activities at this time.

4 *Narrative*, p. 112. C2482, p. 54. Malet, *Extracts from a Diary*, pp. 23–24. Molyneux, *Campaigning in South Africa and Egypt*, p. 181.

5 Malet, *Extracts from a Diary*, p. 24. Bengough, *Memories of a Soldier's Life*, p. 165. Norris-Newman, *In Zululand with the British*, p. 209. Smith-Dorrien, *Memories of Forty-Eight Years' Service*, p. 28. Fairlie Diary. See NW, July 10, 1879: 'The Battle and Sacking of Ulundi,' which, however, gives the time as the following night. Also, *cf.* McToy, *Brief History of the 13th Regiment*, p. 81.

6 2nd Division Diary. Emery, *The Red Soldier*, p. 222. Norris-Newman, *In Zululand with the British*, p. 209. Malet, *Extracts from a Diary*, p. 24. Molyneux, *Campaigning in South Africa and Egypt*, p. 181. Smith-Dorrien, *Memories of Forty-Eight Years' Service*, p. 28. Bengough, *Memories of a Soldier's Life*, p. 135. NW, July 10, 1879: 'The Battle and Sacking of Ulundi.' There are discrepancies in details among the sources.

7 Bengough, *Memories of a Soldier's Life*, pp. 135–136.

8 *Ibid.*, p. 134. A British traveller, F. Francis, saw the army on the eve of the invasion and recalled (in *War, Waves and Wanderings*, pp. 43–44): 'Here we have Major Bengough's battalion of the Native Contingent on parade for an inspection of arms. As far as physique is concerned they are superior to our own men, but except as scouts they are utterly useless .... Possibly with discipline they would become useful troops, notwithstanding the fact that their hearts fail them at Ketchwayo's [the Zulu king's] name. No one who has not been in Natal and Zululand can realize the enormous influence Ketchwayo possesses. Against any other power they would fight well enough, for the pluck of the Zulus is unquestionable, and these fellows are simply renegade Zulus.'

9 *Narrative*, pp. 112–113. C2482, p. 54. Molyneux, *Campaigning in South Africa and Egypt*, p. 182. 2nd Division Diary. Fairlie Diary.

10 *Cf.* Malet, *Extracts from a Diary*, p. 25; *Private Journel of Guy C. Dawnay*, pp. 63–64; and Tomasson, *With the Irregulars*, pp. 154–158 *passim.*

11 C2482, p. 55. Tomasson, *With the Irregulars*, p. 156.

12 *Narrative*, p. 110. Laband, *Kingdom in crisis*, pp. 209 and 212.

13 There are few first-hand accounts of the reconnaissance and these differ in detail. The account here is based on Tomasson, *With the Irregulars*, pp. 154–168; NW, July 17, 1879: 'The Zulu War. Genl. Wood's Division;' and TN, July 18, 1879: 'With Gen. Wood's Column.' Second-hand information comes from C2482, pp. 54–55 and *Narrative*, p. 113; 2nd Division Diary; Fairlie Diary; *Private Journal of Guy C. Dawnay*, pp. 63–64; and Molyneux, *Campaigning in South Africa and Egypt*, pp. 183–184. John Gama alluded to the reconnaissance in a speech paraphrased in NW, August 16, 1879: 'The Natal Native Horse,' which is amplified by the anecdote of the taunt in Montague, *Campaigning in South Africa*, p. 234.

14 2nd Division Diary. Fripp, 'Reminiscences of the Zulu War,' p. 555.

15 The impressions of the Zulu movement and sounds that night are recorded variously and sometimes irreconcilably in *Narrative*, p. 114; C2482, p. 55; 2nd Division Diary; Malet, *Extracts from a Diary*, p. 26; Molyneux, *Campaigning in South Africa and Egypt*, p. 184; McToy, *Brief History of the 13th Regiment*, p. 85; Fripp, 'Reminiscences of the Zulu War,' p. 555; TN, July 18, 1879: 'With Gen. Wood's Column;' and Frank Emery, 'At war with the Zulus 1879. The Letters of Lieutenant C.E. Commeline RE,' in *The Royal Engineers Journal*, XCVI, No. 1 (March 1982), p. 37.

16 C2482, p. 55. 2nd Division Diary. Emery, 'At war with the Zulus,' p. 37.

17 Tomasson, *With the Irregulars*, p. 172.

18 *Ibid.*, 172–174. *Narrative*, p. 114. 2nd Division Diary. WO 32/7764: report of R. Buller. Molyneux, *Campaigning in South Africa and Egypt*, p. 185. Mitford, *Through the Zulu Country*, p. 168. Emery, 'At War with the Zulus,' p. 37.

19 *Narrative*, pp. 114–115. 2nd Division Diary.

20 *Narrative*, p. 114. C2482, p. 55. Malet, *Extracts from a Diary*, p. 27. The force left behind included 93 'native troops', but whether they were a unit or from several units is not clear. The 2nd Battalion had 385 in the battle, which suggests four companies; however; 19 officers suggest five (*Narrative*, p. 164).

21 Tomasson, *With the Irregulars*, pp. 174–175. WO 32/7764: Buller's report.

22 *Narrative*, pp. 144–155. C2482, p. 55. 2nd Division Diary. Tomasson, *With the Irregulars*, pp. 176 and 182. There are certain inconsistencies with regard to when and how many times the 'square' was formed – *cf.* C2482, p. 55; Molyneux, *Campaigning in South Africa and Egypt*, p. 185; *Private Journal of Guy C. Dawnay*, p. 66; Mitford, *Through the Zulu Country*, p. 168; and Fairlie Diary.

23 *Narrative*, p. 115. C2482, p. 55. Emery, 'At War with the Zulus,' p. 37. Molyneux, *Campaigning in South Africa and Egypt*, pp. 185–186. McToy, *Brief History of the 13th Regiment*, p. 90.

24 NW, October 4, 1879: Newdigate's report. Bengough, *Memories of a Soldier's Life*, p. 137.

25 *Narrative*, pp. 115, 117. C2482, pp. 54–56. 2nd Division Diary. Fairlie Diary. Tomasson, *With the Irregulars*, pp. 175, 177. *Private Journal of Guy C. Dawnay*, p. 66. Malet, *Extracts from a Diary*, p. 27. Mitford, *Through the Zulu Country*, pp. 168–169. McToy, *Brief History of the 13th Regiment*, p. 88. Fripp, 'Reminiscences of the Zulu War,' pp. 557–558. SP

41: Theophilus Shepstone, jr., to William Shepstone, August 17, 1879. Emery, 'At War with the Zulus,' p. 38.

26 C2482, p. 55. Tomasson, *With the Irregulars*, pp. 177, 187. McToy, *Brief History of the 13th Regiment*, pp. 88–89. Mitford, *Through the Zulu Country*, p. 168. Malet, *Extracts from a Diary*, p. 27. The battle is dealt with at length by J. Laband in *The battle of Ulundi* (Pietermaritzburg, Shuter and Shooter, 1988) and from the Zulu viewpoint in *Kingdom in crisis*, ch. 11.

27 C2482, p. 55. 2nd Division Diary. WO 32/7764: report of E. Newdigate. Molyneux, *Campaign in South Africa and Egypt*, p. 186. NW, July 10, 1879: 'The Battle and Sacking of Ulundi.'

28 McToy, *Brief History of the 13th Regiment*, pp. 88. Tomasson, *With the Irregulars*, pp. 182–184. NW, August 16, 1879: 'The Natal Native Horse'. NC, Sepember 18, 1879: account from *Journal*.

29 SP 41: Theophilus Shepstone, Jr., to William Shepstone, July 17, 1879. Fairlie Diary.

30 *Narrative*. p. 116. C2482, pp. 55–56. Tomasson, *With the Irregulars*, pp. 180–191 *passim*. *Private Journal of Guy C. Dawnay*, p. 66. *Memories of Field Marshall Lord Grenfell* (London, Hodder & Stoughton, 1925), p. 61. Fripp, 'Reminiscences of the Zulu War,' pp. 559–560. Emery, 'At War with the Zulus,' p. 38. SP 41: Theophilus Shepstone, jr., to William Shepstone, July 17, 1879.

31 *Narrative*, pp. 116, 164–167. Tomasson, *With the Irregulars*, pp. 180–181. SP 41: Theophilus Shpestone, jr., to William Shepstone, July 17, 1879. The loss was heavy according to the Lieutenant General (C2482, p. 56).

32 *Bengough, Memories of a Soldier's Life*, p. 137. Tomasson, *With the Irrregulars*, pp. 183–184. Molyneux, *Campaigning in South Africa and Egypt*, p. 112.

33 Colenso, *History of the Zulu War*, p. 449. TN, August 15, 1879: 'Welcome to the Edendale Men.' NW, August 16, 1879: 'The Natal Native Horse.' Tomasson, *With the Irregulars*, pp. 183–184. Montague, *Campaigning in South Africa*, p. 239. There is an anecdotal account of a 'Basuto' praising the brave British soldiers for making a laager with their bodies and fighting the Zulus and letting the Basutos sit and eat their biscuits as spectators, given with slight differences by Montague (p. 239) and Tomasson (p. 183).

34 C2482, p. 56. 2nd Division Diary. Molyneux, *Campaigning in South Africa and Egypt*, p. 186–187. *Private Journal of Guy C. Dawnay*, p. 67. Emery, 'At war with the Zulus,' p. 38. Mitford, *Through the Zulu Country*, p. 171.

35 McToy, *Brief History of the 13th Regiment*, p. 90. Tomasson, *With the Irregulars*, p. 191.

36 *Narrative*, pp. 115–116. C2482, pp. 55–56. Molyneux, *Campaigning in South Africa and Egypt*, pp. 187–188. Tomasson, *With the Irregulars*, pp. 190–191. *Private Journal of Guy C. Dawnay*, p. 66. McToy, *Brief History of the 13th Regiment*, p. 90.

37 *Cf.* C2482, p. 56; *Narrative*, p. 116; Molyneux, *Campaigning in South Africa and Egypt*, p. 188; Mitford, *Through the Zulu Country*, pp. 171–172; and *Private Journal of Guy C. Dawnay*, pp. 67–69.

38 *Narrative*, p. 116. C2482, p. 56. WO 32/7764: Buller's report. Clarke, *Zululand at War*, pp. 233 and 238. Tomasson, *With the Irregulars*, pp. 192–198 *passim*. Mitford, *Through the Zulu Country*, pp. 172–173. TN, July 18, 1879: 'With Gen. Wood's Column.' TN, August 15, 1879: 'Welcome to the Edendale Men.' NW, August 16, 1879: 'The Natal Native Horse.' NC, September 18, 1879: *Journal* account.

39 SP 41: Theophilus Shepstone, jr., to William Shepstone, July 17, 1879. There are references in *Narrative*, p. 116 and C2482, p. 56 to 'mounted natives' killing the trapped Zulu. According to *Private Journal of Guy C. Dawney*, p. 69, 'Buller's horse' killed them; but Buller's troops did not follow in the wake of the Lancers, whereas Shepstone's Horse did.

40 Malet, *Extract from a Diary*, p. 29. *Cf.* a variant of the anecdote in NC, September 18, 1879: *Journal* account.

41 *Private Journal of Guy C. Dawnay*, p. 70. Montague, *Campaigning in South Africa*, p. 236; however, this is hearsay. The assistant adjutant general of the 2nd Division wrote privately a few days later (Clarke, *Zululand at War*, p. 238): 'Our irregulars and native contingent went out also in pursuit – after a while, for at one moment the Zulus rallied and renewed the attack a little – and I fear spared few wounded. We have only 2 in all.' Tomasson states (*With the Irregulars*, p. 199) that 'the native contingent' rushed out of the laager after the horsemen, but a few Zulu turned on them and their officers could not keep them from bolting back to safety; later they emerged again and searched the pools of the Mbilane stream, which flows between Ulundi and the battlefield. Malet mentions (*Extracts from a Diary*, p. 29) a member of 'our native contingent' spearing a Zulu hiding in an ant-bear hole. In both cases 'the native contingent' might be taken to mean Wood's Irregulars as well as or rather than Bengough's battalion. Bengough makes no mention of his battalion in the pursuit, which suggests the battalion was not in it; however, Bengough does not mention the aftermath of the battle at all. The reason may be found in the aforesaid adjutant's letter: 'In fact I saw them [the contingent and irregulars] assegai several [Zulu], with my glasses. Don't mention it generally or they will think us awful brutes … .'

42 *Narrative*, p. 116. Tomasson, *With the Irregulars*, p. 206. McToy, *Brief History of the 13th Regiment*, p. 89. *Private Journal of Guy C. Dawnay*, p. 70. Molyneux, *Campaigning in South Africa and Egypt*, p. 188.

43 *Narrative*, pp. 116–117. C2482, p. 56. *Private Journal of Guy C. Dawnay*, p. 70.

44 SP 41: Theophilus Shepstone, jr., to William Shepstone, July 17, 1879. Fairlie Diary. Tomasson, *With the Irregulars*, p. 205.

45 *Narrative*, p. 117. *Private Journal of Guy C. Dawnay*, pp. 70–71. Molyneux, *Campaigning in South Africa and Egypt*, p. 189. Mitford, *Through the Zulu Country*, p. 173. McToy, *Brief History of the 13th Regiment*, p. 89.

46 Molyneux, *Campaigning in South Africa and Egypt*, p. 190.

Chapter 16

THE KING CHASE[1]

Reduction

The battle of Ulundi marks the climax of the war. It demonstrated once more the military and technological superiority of British over Zulu. This British victory differed from the earlier ones in one important respect: it occurred at the seat of the Zulu King, in the heart of the Zulu kingdom. The moral effect was overwhelming. Organized Zulu resistance to the British invader collapsed. Chiefs in threatened areas were ready to forsake the King and to make peace in order to spare their people further ravages of war.

In the hour of victory, Lord Chelmsford, the Lieutenant General commanding the British army in the field, was subordinated to Lieutenant General Sir Garnet Wolseley. Lord Chelmsford had been much criticized at home after the disaster at Isandlwana. His differences, not least over the use of the Natal levies, with the Supreme Chief and Lieutenant Governor of Natal, Sir Henry Bulwer, raised questions about his ability to conduct the campaign. The High Commissioner, Sir Henry Bartle Frere, who had worked to bring on the war, had also been discredited when the reverse occurred. In these circumstances Wolseley was appointed Governor of Natal and the Transvaal and Special High Commissioner to the Native Territories to the north and east of them on May 28th. He had a reputation for getting things done. Now he had plenipotentiary power to end this unwanted war, which had gone on too long and cost too much money. He arrived in Natal during the last week in June. He could communicate with the Lieutenant General, deep in the Zulu country, only with difficulty, which difficulty gave the Lieutenant General time enough to retrieve his reputation at Ulundi.

The British army could not remain in the heart of Zulu country without further supplies. The Lieutenant General proposed that it should move to a post near the coast, where it could be reduced to a size appropriate to police the country and supplies could be sent up from the coastal plain. The Special High Commissioner had no choice but to fall in with the proposal, though he preferred Mthonjaneni as a forward post.[2]

The victorious army left the Mahlabathini plain and the smoking ruins of the enemy's great places and returned to the laager on the right bank of the White Mfolozi. The following day, July 5th, the Headquarters Column led the way back up the mountain to the laager at the top. Extra oxen had been sent down to help move the wagons up the steep grade. The Flying Column followed and spent the night at the campsite of the 30th. It reached the top of the mountain on the 6th. The laager there was broken up and the army prepared to move.

It was cold on the mountain top and there was a strong wind on the 5th. It was windy and dusty on the 6th. The fine weather that had aided the British advance was ending. That night a violent storm broke over the mountain. For the next two days the columns were immobilized by torrents of rain, gale-force winds, and bursts of hail. The mud became knee-deep. Large black worms, some four feet long and thick as broom handles, wriggled out of the muck. It was intensely cold. Many horses and hundreds of oxen perished from exposure. The carcasses lay all around the camp.

Rain and cold notwithstanding, Colonel Buller set out with his horsemen on patrol at three in the morning of the 7th, and they were out all day. The Natal Native Horse made up a part of the force. It met no enemy, although some of the mercenaries were almost struck by lightning, and returned at dark with a herd of about three hundred cattle, which made up for some of those lost at the laager. Next day a ration of rum was served all around in celebration of their victory on the 4th. During the night the horses broke loose from the picket line and wandered over the mountain in the rain and fog. In the morning the troops scoured the mountainside for several miles to get them back.[3]

The weather cleared on the 9th, but it was still bitter cold. The Flying Column left Mthonjaneni during the afternoon. At kwaMagwaza, where the Lieutenant General wished to locate the new advance post, it halted and built a small fort on the 11th and 12th, then proceeded to St. Paul's, a mission station nearer the coast which had been abandoned and destroyed before the war. It reached the station on the 15th and was reviewed there by the Special High Commissioner on the 16th. Lord

Chelmsford returned to Natal. Having vindicated himself at Ulundi, he resigned command. His resignation was accepted.

The Special High Commissioner was determined to reduce the size of the army (and thus expenses). All the units not needed should be sent home. Most were not needed now, for the Zulu no longer posed a threat. The Flying Column was disbanded piecemeal during the last half of July.[4] Among the units which were let go were the Natal Native Horse. The two troops returned to Natal by way of the lower Thukela. On July 25th, they arrived in Pietermaritzburg, where they were paid off and disbanded. Hlubi's troop returned to the foothills of the Khahlamba, the Edendale troop to the village a few miles west of the city. The Christian soldiers held a thanksgiving service and then greeted their families and friends.[5]

Shepstone's Horse was again the eyes and ears of the 2nd Division – without the Lieutenant General it was no longer the Headquarters Column – as it left Mthonjaneni on July 10th and marched back along the invasion track. A small force was detached to garrison the little fort at kwaMagwaza. The division proceeded to the Ntinini valley, where it remained from July 15th to the 26th. A convoy of sick and wounded was sent on to Natal on the 18th, escorted by a detachment of British infantry. Because of the poor conditions of horses and oxen, two companies of Bengough's battalion were ordered to go along as bearers. One troop of Shepstone's Horse was ordered to Rorke's Drift on the 21st and was sent home from there.[6]

On the 24th the day was given over to sports and races. Among the contests was one of spear throwing. (Unfortunately, men crowded about and got in the way and one of them had a calf cut.) The high point of the occasion was the so-called First Zululand National Races and Steeplechase. This was a British affair, or course, but there was a special race for Shepstone's Horse. The horses were tired and in poor condition, but nonetheless twenty-five of Shepstone's men entered the contest, which started well, but at the first fence almost all of the riders fell off their horses or stopped. Only two men rode it out. They finished in a dead heat, but not in the set time.[7]

On the 25th the order came from the Special High Commissioner that Shepstone's Horse should go home at once and be disbanded. It started at 7.30 the next morning. The march followed the track to Landman's Drift, then on to Dundee, Waschbank and Ladysmith, where the troops were disbanded on the 30th.

The 2nd Division was disbanded officially on July 16th. Its units returned to Natal except for one regiment of British infantry which was to escort a supply train from Landman's Drift and to provide garrisons for the forts. The destination was Mthonjaneni. The train would supply a flying column which the Special High Commissioner was organizing for a return to Ulundi, where he intended to force the Zulu to make peace.[8]

Final orders were issued to the 2nd Division on July 27th. Respective units received their meed of praise from General Newdigate. Shepstone's Horse was praised for its scouting and Bengough's Battalion for its good service during the recent campaign.[9] By this time, of course, Shepstone's Horse was on its way home, but Bengough's Battalion was not. Several companies remained on the line of communication and those in the field were assigned to another new flying column which was to operate in northwest Zululand. The battalion nearly mutinied. Head men declared that the men had been engaged for six months; their time was up and they wanted to go home. The amaBomvu especially wanted to go because the Zulu raid across the middle Thukela on June 25th had cut into their territory. They said their homesteads had been burnt and wives had been carried off. Agitation increased during the next few days. Finally part if not all of the battalion at the Ntinini camp announced it would desert next day; however, Homoyi, the elderly chief of the amaBomvu and devoted to Major Bengough, wanted to shake hands before he went.

At this juncture the Special High Commissioner arrived at Fort Marshall, on his way to join the flying column which was to operate in central Zululand. Major Bengough, the chiefs and head men of the 2nd Battalion were summoned to meet him on August 5th. He listened to their representations concerning the terms of service and the Zulu raid. Then he told them, through the Acting Secretary for Native Affairs who accompanied him, that no term had been specified when they were engaged for service. Now was a time when their services were most required. But under the circumstances he would allow some of them to go home for a short period of time. This promise placated them, and they returned to camp evidently much pleased.[10] It is not recorded which men in the battalion got to go home, but it would seem likely they included amaBomvu. Also, the records contain no reference to the mounted Amabomvu and Amangwane Corps after this time. Probably they, too, returned home.

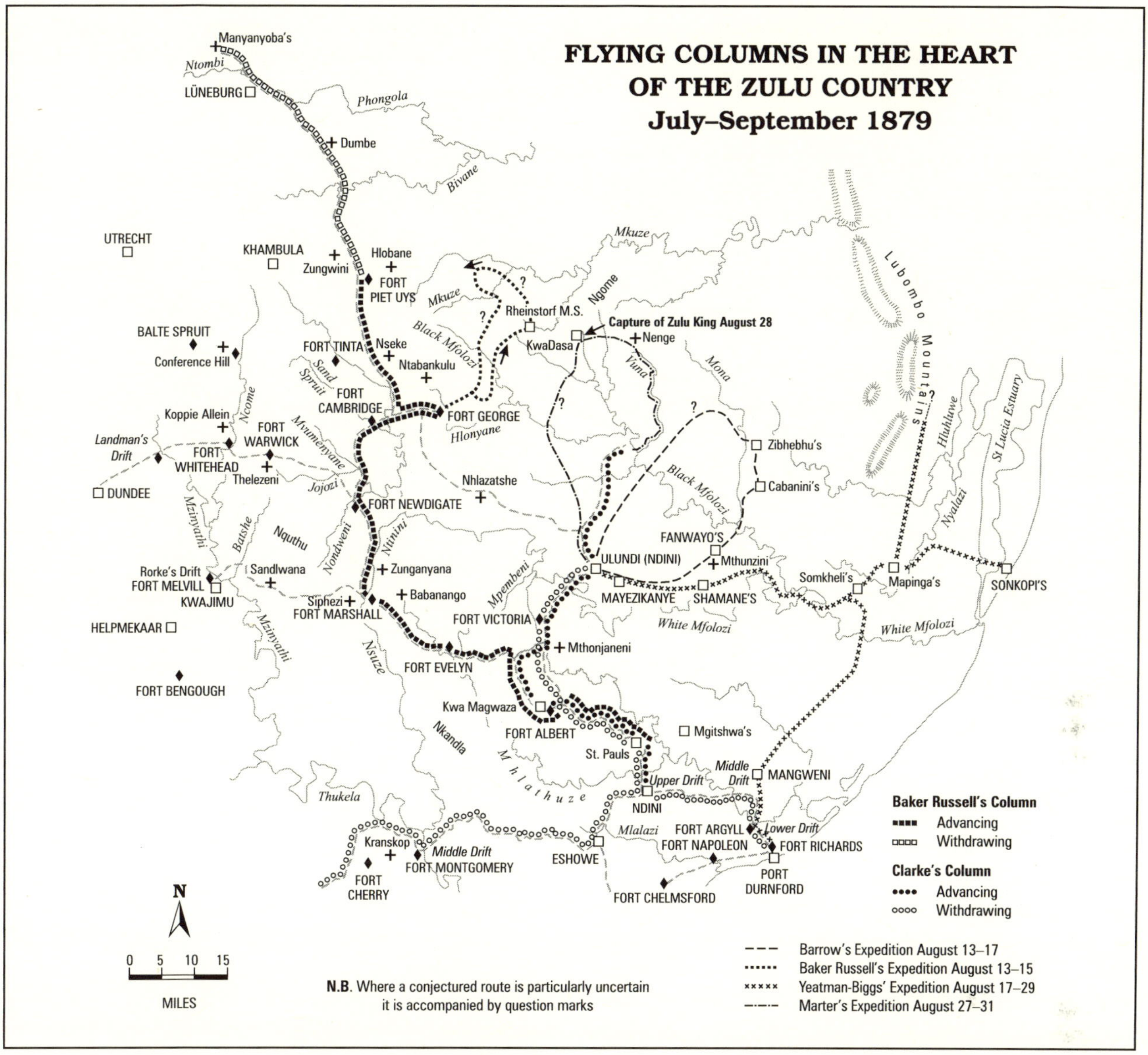

There was also dissatisfaction in another unit – No. 1 Pioneer Company. It was part of the new flying column to go to Ulundi. It consisted of older men who wore head rings, amaNgangoma and amaNgcolosi from the coastal Locations. 'The war is all over, why can't we go home?' 'Is it all over? We only wish it were, as we want to go home, too,' their officers replied. The reason the company was not disbanded, as were the mounted troops and the Swazi levies of the old Flying Column, was because they had worked so well and had behaved so well. This explanation did not mollify them, but their dissatisfaction seems not to have become a problem.[11]

Redeployment

The British army was reduced in order to deal more efficiently with the enemy. It was unlikely that a Zulu army would take the field again. It remained to be seen whether or not the Zulu King could give effective direction to any continued resistance. The British were determined on the removal of the King, the end of the monarchy and the military system, and a stop to wanton killings in the Zulu country. Many chiefs were inclined to make peace and the British were ready to confirm their authority, if only they submit and surrender any royal cattle and firearms in their people's possession.

The Special High Commissioner devised the strategy to bring the war to a speedy conclusion. Priority was given to catching or getting rid of the Zulu King. So long as he was at liberty there could be no peace in Zululand. He must be hemmed in and the Zulu chiefs enticed or intimidated into abandoning him. Small 'flying columns' would take up advance positions at Ulundi and under Ntabankulu and operate in the heart of the Zulu country. A small static force would hold the lower Mhlathuze crossing. The Zulu King's half brother, who had gone over to the British at the outbreak of the war, was to lead his people into the country between the Black Mfolozi and the Phongola rivers in the north. The amaSwazi, historic enemies of the Zulu, were to assemble beyond the Phongola and descend into Zululand. Unspecified 'measures' were to be taken to assure that the King did not escape to the northeast, into the country of the amaThonga.

The Special High Commissioner began to implement the strategy during the third week of July. The garrisons of the forts along the lines of communication were put under the Major General responsible for the defence of Natal. The 1st and 2nd Divisions and the Flying Column were disbanded and most of their units ordered to return to Natal, by stages to take ship for other stations in the British empire. The new flying columns were organized and moved forward. Thus the commissioner could give his full attention to hunting down the Zulu King. By July 26th, when General Orders for the redistribution of forces in Zululand were issued, the redistribution was already well underway.

The flying column which moved to Ulundi consisted of troops of the 1st Division, which ceased to exist on July 23rd. It marched from Port Durnford on the 24th, under the command of Lieutenant Colonel Clarke, of the 57th Regiment, and proceeded by way of the various crossings up the Mhlathuze river to St. Paul's, where it was supplied by a convoy from Fort Chelmsford on the 30th. Adding some of the units that had been in the old Flying Column, Clarke's column marched on the 1st of August for Mthonjaneni, where it received the supplies from Landman's Drift on the 6th. It moved down the mountainside on the 7th to the flat where the earlier columns had bivouacked and started an earthwork, called Fort Victoria. That afternoon the Special High Commissioner arrived in camp, having ridden from Rorke's Drift by way of Fort Marshall. Further advance was delayed by another two-day storm which killed 452 oxen, but on the 10th the weather improved and the column moved down to the White Mfolozi. The commissioner went with a mounted escort to Ulundi and pitched camp in the very centre of the great place. The next day he joined the column, which arrived and made camp some distance away. The neighbourhood of the great place was found to be too dirty for a campsite.

Mounted patrols found no enemy force on the Mahlabathini plain. They roamed at will, and discovered in a ravine the two cannon which had been captured at Isandlwana. In a cave they found a quantity of ammunition and gunpowder which the enemy had cached for future use. The cannon were retrieved, the ammunition and powder were exploded. A deserted cantonment near by was burnt.

Clarke's column consisted of the equivalent of three battalions of British infantry, a detachment of British cavalry and a squadron of mounted infantry, three troops of mercenaries, a Gatling gun section, and a small detachment of Royal Engineers. Some Native Guides from the coast were also with it. The Natal Native Contingent was strongly represented. From the old 1st Division there were the 4th Battalion, Jantze's Horse and the Mafunzi Corps. From the Flying Column there was No. 1 Company Pioneers. In all, including the noncombatants, the column numbered about 3500.

The column which moved to Ntabankulu comprised units drawn chiefly from the old 2nd Division and the Flying Column. The column, under Lieutenant Colonel Baker Russell of the 13th Hussars, started from St. Paul's on July 26th and added units as it passed along the invasion track and on to Fort Cambridge, a new work near the White Mfolozi. It rested there for three days, August 6th – 8th, and was joined there by three companies of Bengough's battalion. It left two of these, with a company of British infantry and a dozen mercenaries to garrison the fort, and on the 9th crossed the White Mfolozi. It marched to a deserted mission station at the southeast foot of Ntabankulu and built Fort George, which would be its base for operations in the vicinity of the Black Mfolozi for the next eleven days.

Baker Russell's column, including the garrison at Fort George, contained the equivalent of a battalion of British infantry, a battery of artillery, a company of Bengough's battalion, and a motley mounted force, which consisted of a squadron of British cavalry, one of mounted infantry, a band of mercenaries, and the Mpumuza troops under Teteleku.[12]

The Flying Column at Ntabankulu

Fort George was an earthwork in the shape of an elongated diamond or flattish parallelogram. The opposite faces were forty-seven and sixty-five yards, respectively. There were two small redoubts at the acute angles. Ammunition, stores and tools, and a hospital were put inside them. The mounted men and the artillery made camp in the large enclosure. The infantry made camp outside the northern redoubt, on a slope above the ruins of the mission station.

August is the least pleasant month of the year in Natal and Zululand. Winter has left the country dry and withered. Grazing is poor. Nights are still cold but days are warm. Hot winds blow off the mountains. At Fort George the weather seemed uncomfortably warm for the season. The yellow grass, breast high, had been burnt to a distance around the fort and camp for security, not only against the Zulu but against grass fires. On one occasion a grass fire swept up from the direction of the White Mfolozi on a six-mile front and continued for several days over a distance of twenty miles, eventually burning out at the Black Mfolozi.

Five miles to the northwest Ntabankulu rose to a height of 2000 feet. The mountain, with many terraces and partly wooded, was believed to be a refuge for thousands of Zulus. Thirteen miles to the southeast Nhlazatshe rose abruptly to a height of 1600 feet. To the north and east of the fort there was a broken ridge, beyond which was the valley of the Black Mfolozi and a range of high hills. Somewhere beyond them the Zulu King was believed to be in hiding.[13]

On August 13th, the day after his column arrived and started building the fort, Colonel Baker Russell led out the mounted men of his column in an expedition to try to catch the Zulu King, who the commissioner had informed him was reported to be at a place called Mkhondo. Its distance from the fort was not known.

This expedition was the first taste of serious campaigning in the enemy's country for Teteleku's contingent. There were eighty of them, a quarter of the force. There was about the same number of mercenaries. Just over half the force – 170 men – consisted of British troops – cavalry, mounted infantry and artillery drivers. Horses were not in good condition, and the foray proved to be an ordeal.

The expedition left Fort George at daybreak with local guides. It crossed the Black Mfolozi and made its way up a steep path towards the top of the range of high hills. Near the crest Zulus formed as if to resist, but fell back as the advance guard approached. Then a number came forward to talk. They said their chief had gone to Ulundi to meet the Special High Commissioner. The Colonel thought it would be unwise to demand that they surrender their firearms or supply his men food, because the expedition would be returning by the same route and he did not want resentful people in his rear. The Zulus for their part decided not to dispute the way.

The expedition proceeded along a chain of hills eastwards. It was reported that the Zulu King had with him a large armed force, and all but one of the guides who had accompanied the expedition from the fort deserted. A new guide was picked up at an otherwise deserted homestead. Evening was coming on and the horses were exhausted. The expedition arrived at the ruins of another mission station and bivouacked. It had marched about twenty-seven miles. It was now in country once inhabited by the people of the Zulu King's half brother who had defected to the British at the outbreak of the war. During the night the last guide from the fort deserted, presumably also frightened by the prospect of meeting the King's force.

In the morning it was learnt that Mkhondo, the place where the Zulu King was supposed to be, was twenty-five miles away. What appeared to be two Zulu cantonments could be seen only a few miles ahead. Were they manned? The Colonel decided to go no further. He also decided that the expedition would not return by the same route. Instead he took a northerly direction, for the most part through the half brother's territory, and crossed the headwaters of the Mkhuze river. The country had very few supplies and several horses had to be abandoned. People in the locality said that the Zulu King had sent men to take their corn after his half brother had defected and they had devastated the country. The expedition halted for the night about ten miles east of the source of the Black Mfolozi.

On the 15th the expedition returned to Fort George, passing over the range of high hills, abandoning several more horses, and reaching the fort in mid-afternoon. Fortunately, trains had arrived from the base with supplies and ammunition. Also, many Zulu chiefs had come in to surrender arms and cattle.[14]

During the following week several reconnaissances were made from the fort, but none so ambitious as the Mkhondo expedition. Perhaps the horses were not up to the effort. The reconnaissances had the effect of securing the submissions of the local chiefs who had hitherto held back. Men came in batches, surrendering cattle, spears and, of course, guns, all of them useless old pieces. The Zulu people in the vicinity were loyal to the King, but they wanted peace. Some of the homesteads in the vicinity were reoccupied and Zulu cattle grazed along with the army's and its horses on the hillsides. The garrison needed fire wood, but had to be careful about dismantling homesteads to get it since some were no longer the enemy's. On one occasion Teteleku's mounted men escorted a wood cutting party about five miles to the southeast of the fort, near the Hlangabende stream. No. 1 Pioneer Company, from Clarke's Column, was set to work in the same area, improving a track under Nhlazatshe.[15] Baker Russell's flying column thus pacified the country on the upper Black Mfolozi, but found no sign of the Zulu King in the district.

At the other end of the front a British infantry regiment had moved up from Port Durnford to the lower Mhlathuze on July 24th and built a fort overlooking the Lower Drift. 200 men of Nettleton's 5th Battalion formed part of the garrison.[16] In mid-August the Special High Commissioner's unspecified 'measures' took the form of a small expedition up the coast to cut off any attempt by the Zulu King to escape in that direction. This expedition, under the command of a British artillery officer, Captain Yeatman-Biggs, consisted of a large party of officers, some men from the artillery and engineers, all mounted for the mission, and a company of Nettleton's battalion under Commandant Nettleton himself. It left Port Durnford on August 17th with a week's provisions on pack mules. It crossed the Mhlathuze ten miles from the mouth and passed through Mphangweni and pushed on north-northeastward to the Mfolozi.

Homesteads were numerous in this area. There was plenty of cattle, sheep and goats, and the people seemed quite friendly, although no girls were to be seen in any of the homesteads. Nor were the men going to give up their firearms and spears as a sign of submission. Many men were still suffering from bullet wounds received at the battles at Nyezane and Gingindlovu.

The expedition crossed the Mfolozi about twenty miles from the sea and headed towards the southern spur of the Lubombo mountains, which roughly parallel the coast at about twenty-five miles and extend north into the Swazi country. At the place of the chief Somkheli it was learnt that a patrol from Ulundi had recently been in the vicinity. Yeatman-Biggs turned more to the east, crossed the Nyalazi river, and come to the place of Maphinga, where his men were well received.

The Captain determined to divide his force to search in different directions, but Nettleton's men baulked at this point. They would not go down into the flat country around St. Lucia Bay. Not only was the country very broken and full of thorns, but it was unhealthy. Men of the company were frightened by reports that many of the people there were stricken by fever. There was no moving them. The company thus remained at Maphinga's for four days, while the rest of the expedition split in two, one party going north into the Thonga country and the other crossing the narrows at the lower end of the bay and reaching the coast at the place of Somkheli's father. Nothing was heard of the Zulu King. Apparently he had not come that way.

The expedition reunited at Maphinga's. Yeatman-Biggs decided to go to Ulundi rather than go directly back to Port Durnford. The expedition turned west and crossed both branches of the Mfolozi near their confluence, and arrived at Ulundi on the 29th, just in time to see the Zulu King brought in as a prisoner. The horses were rested and on Sunday the 31st the expedition started back to Port Durnford by way of St. Paul's and Eshowe.[17]

The Flying Column at Ulundi

Lieutenant-Colonel Clarke's flying column took position on the Mahlabathini plain near the site of the Zulu King's great place at Ulundi. The Special High Commissioner accompanied it. The show of force and diplomacy by the British led to the submission of the various Zulu chiefs in the surrounding country on August 25th and September 1st.

There was no rain and only once was there a threat of it during the three weeks the flying column was on the plain. The days became warmer in the last week of August and the last day at camp was hot. The men were in excellent health. The undestroyed stores at the great places provided food. Flowing streams provided sufficient water. There was grazing for cattle and horses. The latter were in poor condition when they arrived, but the condition of both improved, except for horses kept on patrol. The camp did have to be moved at intervals for hygiene, and latterly it was affected by a swarm of flies. With the increasing heat the smell of the decaying carcasses of oxen became unpleasant – indeed, Fort Victoria, next on the line of communication south of the White Mfolozi, had to be abandoned by its garrison for that reason.[18]

The Natal Native Contingent made up a third of the strength of the column. Both foot and horse of the contingent were involved in various expeditions to track down the Zulu King. The 'king chase' depended on timely information and very prompt action. This meant hard work for the mounted men, whose horses already were in a poor condition.

For Jantze's Horse and the Mafunzi Corps the chase was an endurance test. They were joined with an equal number of British cavalry and mounted infantry, all under Major Barrow, who had commanded the mounted troops of the 1st Division and now commanded those of the flying column.

Barrow set out with the mounted troops, some 400 strong, with two days' rations, on the afternoon of Wednesday, August 13th, for Mkhondo, where the King was supposed to be. His orders were to track down the King, no matter if he killed all his horses and men in the process. The expedition crossed the Mahlabathini watershed and descended into the thorn bush of the Black Mfolozi valley. Night fell, but a Dutchman who had been a Zulu prisoner led the way with a lantern and at midnight the men crossed the river and dismounted for a short rest. Then they pushed on along a narrow path, stringing out and closing up and finally reaching a rolling country, open and almost treeless. At dawn they passed a burnt cantonment.

They crossed several small streams and some difficult hills, and came on the upper reaches of the Mona river, a tributary of the Black Mfolozi. It was about eleven when they saw the Mkhondo homestead, a mere ten huts, high on a hill partly surrounded by two gullies. They encircled it and closed in. It was deserted, but they turned up a head man in the neighbourhood. He told them that the King had slept there night before last and had left yesterday afternoon.

The expedition rested. The Dutchman said that the King might be at another homestead which he knew of, ten miles distant. About 200 royal cattle were reported to be there. A small party resumed the march, probably at a quick pace since the trail of the King seemed fresh, while the majority of the expedition, including the British cavalry, remained at Mkhondo to rest their horses. At mid-afternoon the tracking party, ninety strong, arrived at the other homestead, which was also deserted. The King had spent the night there and had gone that morning. The party pushed on to a third homestead. There it lost the trail and night descended.

The next morning an old man, whom the Dutchman recognized as one of the King's personal attendants, was seized. He was induced to act as a guide. The tracking party made straight for a homestead, called Cabanini, in the direction of the Lubombo mountains. There it took some royal cattle. They appeared to have been abandoned by the royal party in flight. Major Barrow divided his force, sending Captain Hay with Jantze's and the Mafunzi – those whose horses had lasted – in one direction, and Lord Gifford, an officer on special service, with the rest of the detachment in another. Both brought back servants of the King. The following morning they were made to take the force to where the King had slept Wednesday night. This was in the bush along the lower Mona. The trail was picked up and followed almost to the Black Mfolozi. Then it was lost again.

The Major headed for the trader's track north of Ulundi. The party crossed the Black Mfolozi and bivouacked. Lord Gifford rode off with ten men to continue the chase. The trail, so far as it had gone, suggested the King might be heading south. Thither went Gifford.[19]

The Special High Commissioner, doubtless following reports closely, arranged to send 350 men of Barton's 4th Battalion from Ulundi to raid and the search for the King in the country down to the confluence of the Black and White Mfolozis. He also ordered Major Barrow, whose expedition to Mkhondo returned to Ulundi on Sunday, the 17th, to divide the mounted men into small hunting parties of about twenty.[20]

Jantze's Horse was sent off with some provisions to reinforce Gifford. It was a long and hard ride, for Gifford's detachment made thirty-five miles that day, going almost to the Mhlathuze, and next day turned north by a different route. Jantze's men arrived in time to help it capture ten women of the King's household returning to their homes. They expressed surprise that the King was being hunted so far south. They thought he had been captured at the Black Mfolozi. The chase had been so hard upon him there that the royal party had scattered.

Back towards the Black Mfolozi went Gifford's augmented force. It took supplies from pack mules specially sent from Ulundi on the 20th. It picked up a trail at the Black Mfolozi. Jantze's men headed upstream towards the Mngeni bush. Another clue, and they hared off to Cabanini, under the Lubombo. There they found a hot water bottle and some rugs, which were believed to belong to the King. The head man had decamped, presumably fearing what they would do to him for having misled Barrow's expedition.

Lord Gifford determined to take hostages at each homestead, seize cattle, and harass the people until the King was captured. One of the men at Cabanini was seized. Some girls were reported to have taken beer and meat out on a recent night. Next morning the hostage was made to guide them to the place they had gone. It was in a draw of difficult access. They dismounted and went up to a small hut, whose appearance suggested a hiding place. It was empty.

The horses of the flying column were now worn out by the hunting expedition. Jantze's rested a day, while Lord Gifford and a few men scouted to the north and Major Barrow joined them with a few men. Next day, the 23rd, Jantze's and the others were back in the saddle, pursuing another false lead in the Mngeni bush. They had to rest a day again, except for short patrols to collect information.[21]

The hunt for the King so far had left the hunters tattered and weary. Their sense of frustration was revealed in Gifford's harsher policy towards local people. Jantze's Horse had been on a cross-country chase of between 180 and 200 miles in twelve days, with only two days of rest. The Mafunzi Corps fared somewhat better. Between the Mkhondo expedition's return to Ulundi on the 17th and the 22nd it was scouting and patrolling the valley of Mfolozi, but on the night of the 20th the corps lost three horses, including one belonging to Captain Nourse, to lions.[22]

A sense of frustration was also revealed in the strategy of the Special High Commissioner. The King was still at large. The weather, which had been fine so far, threatened to change. Rain would make search difficult. The country remained unsettled. He ordered Lieutenant Colonel Clarke with 400 British infantry and 300 men of Barton's battalion and Major Barrow with 300 men (those not with Lord Gifford), from Ulundi to the Black Mfolozi on August 22nd. The following day the column arrived at the wagon-crossing on the trader's track near the confluence with the smaller Vuna river.

The fugitive king seemed to be moving among the people with impunity. If necessary, then their homesteads should be burnt and their cattle seized. Pressure would be extended to the powerful chiefs beyond the valley as well. The commissioner addressed an assembly of important chiefs on the virtues of submission. As long as the King was at large there could be no peace. He ordered them to send men in all directions to catch him.[23]

On August 25th Jantze's Horse, the Mafunzi Corps, and a small party under Lord Gifford started at three in the morning to take the war home to the people under the Lubombo mountains. They searched for the King. They seized cattle, prisoners, and almost 200 firearms. They smashed the firearms. Seizure of their cattle provoked some local people to fire at them. They were not deterred. The cattle were turned over to Major Barrow and a party at Cabanini. The raiders prepared to move on.

Lord Gifford led them towards Clarke's camp on the 26th. They halted two miles from it and drew two days' rations, then marched all night through wild country. At daylight they descended on the homestead of the chief Mnyamana, the King's principal advisor, and obtained information that the King was only six miles away. He no longer had any horses and was travelling on foot. They spent the night at Mnyamana's. Next day, Thursday, the 28th, Lord Gifford sent scouts to find out where precisely the King was. The scouts reported the hiding place was about eight miles distant, at a homestead, called kwaDwasa. It lay in a small valley, with high hills on three sides. It was approachable from the fourth side, which was open ground, but the King's spies were there.

Lord Gifford did not consider his force sufficient to try to capture the King by daylight. He, and apparently Hay and Nourse, consulted and decided to wait until night and then surround the hiding place. He sent messages to two other small expeditions known to be in the vicinity, asking for assistance. Some men were sent to watch the homestead to make sure the King did not leave it. They returned at five and offsaddled. Just then a Zulu rushed in to Mnyamana's to say that another mounted force had surrounded the hiding place and captured the King that afternoon![24]

The capture of the King

The successful expedition was led by Major Marter, of the King's Dragoon Guards. On the evening of the 26th it was reported at Clarke's camp at the Black Mfolozi that the King was heading towards the Ngome forest. Major Marter was ordered to try to catch him on the morning of the 17th. He took a squadron of British cavalry, a squad of mounted infantry, a troop of mercenaries and – the only infantry – Captain Plesh's company of Barton's 4th Battalion. The force crossed the river and moved up the Vuna, marched twenty-four miles and bivouacked at Nenge mountain. The following morning, on the 28th, it turned to the west and crossed the Bululwane stream.

Just beyond the Bululwane or a stream flowing into it, the force encountered a man, evidently of the locale. He came down the hill in front and engaged in conversation. The conversation was long and peculiarly aimless, until at length he said: 'I have heard the wind blows from this side to-day' – he pointed to the west, towards the Ngome forest – 'but you should take that road' – he indicated a track leading up and skirting the range in front – 'until you come to Nisaka's homestead.'

The hint was clear. The expedition took the track to Nisaka's. It met another man who delivered a piece of paper – from Lord Gifford. It was addressed to another officer supposed to be leading an expedition in the vicinity, but Major Marter read it. It stated that Lord Gifford was on the track of the King and hoped for a speedy capture, but it did not tell where the King, or Lord Gifford, was. The Major sent the man on his way and the expedition continued. It was well up the range when about mid-day it reached Nisaka's. Another long and general conversation followed. The Major did not mention the King. At length he said: 'I suppose you know why we are in your country, I want guides.' Nisaka replied: 'You had better go to my brother Mhlungulu, whose place is on top of the mountain;' but he directed two men to guide the expedition.

On the crest of the range was Mhlungulu's. There was no parley. The guides indicated the force should halt near some tall trees. They were at the edge of the Ngome forest. The horsemen dismounted. The guides led the Major through the trees to the edge of a precipice. They crawled along and stopped. The guides indicated the Major should continue as far as a certain bush, which he did. From it he looked down and saw, 1700 feet below, a small homestead on the floor of a narrow valley. It must be the hiding place of the King.

The Major decided to try to capture the King straightaway. But how to do it? The valley ended abruptly in a draw, and forest covered the steep slopes on three sides. The ground down the valley was open and doubtless watched. Any enemy approaching from that side would be reported in time for the King and his retinue to escape into the forest.

The Major decided to surround and surprise the homestead. The squadron of British cavalry would take the crest of the mountain to the head of the draw and work down it, concealing itself all the while in the forest. The cavalrymen left their steel scabbards and other metal equipment which might rattle, with the pack horses, under guard of the other mounted men. The company of Barton's battalion was ordered to strip off their uniforms and as much else as possible, save their rifles and ammunition. Captain Plesh was ordered to lead them over the edge and down the steep slope of the mountain in front, also concealed in the forest. When they reached the foot of the mountain they were to remain concealed in the edge. When they saw the cavalry emerge from the forest behind the homestead, they were to emerge from it in front. They were to run, quickly form a line across the open valley, and advance to meet the cavalry and complete an encirclement of the homestead.

The two forces went their respective ways. The company went down the precipitous slope and got into position. There was a wait while the cavalry, which had much farther to go, picked its way along the crest of the mountain and scrambled down into the valley.

Perhaps two hours after they had started, past mid-afternoon, the men of the company saw some of the homestead's occupants, presumably royal attendants, run from a small outlying group of huts to the main grouping. They must have seen the cavalry and were running to warn the King! Captain Plesh ordered the men forward. They rushed into the open ground and began the encirclement. The cavalry appeared from the woods, galloping recklessly through tall grass, over boulders, across gullies. The Captain called to the royal attendants not to shoot. If they did they would all be killed. He wanted only to capture the King!

The cavalry closed the ring. The Major arrived and through the interpreter warned the occupants of the homestead that if they resisted everyone of them would be shot down and the huts burnt. Not a shot was fired. The Major dismounted. With a few men he entered the narrow passage into the homestead. There was another wait, while he persuaded the King to surrender. About twenty firearms were found, with a large amount of ammunition, and many spears, but, aside from the King, there were only seventeen persons in the homestead, ten men and five women and two children. Resistance would be futile.[25]

At last the mission was accomplished. The King and his retinue emerged from the homestead. He was a tall, dignified man.[26] He looked at the men of the Native Contingent and smiled contemptuously. When they approached he drew himself up. None should touch him. He rebuked their insolence. 'And you, too, Qwabe, do you take part against us?' he asked. 'Are you still harbouring feelings of revenge against us?'[27]

The King was a handsome man, but he was also very much overweight. His fat thighs had chafed each other so that he could not walk quickly nor ride comfortably. He and his retinue moved slowly down the valley. Five miles on the expedition reached another homestead. It was only four in the afternoon, but they halted for the night.

The march resumed in the morning. Lord Gifford's force came up and looked at the trophy which had eluded them, then rode off to take news of the King's capture to Ulundi. (Gifford's clothes were in shreds when he met the Special High Commissioner that evening. Very probably his men's were, too.) Major Marter also dispatched a request to Colonel Clarke at the Black Mfolozi for a mule cart the King could ride in.

The King was being difficult. He asked repeatedly to be allowed to send attendants to homesteads at some distance for beer or snuff or other items. His captors suspected he was trying to arrange a rescue and refused. The prisoners were told they would be shot if they tried to escape. Towards evening of the second day the expedition came to dense bush. A narrow path permitted passage only in single file. The soldiers were given orders to shoot anyone who tried to escape or who tried to rescue the captives. The file extended as the distance between captives became greater. The captives seemed to be exhausted. Suddenly four of them bolted. Guards fired. Two men were shot. The carrier of the royal snuff box and one of the women escaped. Major Marter, sabre in hand, went up to the King: 'Look here! I shall begin with you, if I find that you are deceiving me.' The shooting and the threat had an effect. After this the King was compliant.

The next day the mule cart arrived, with an escort of British infantry. The King and his female attendants had a bumpy ride to the Black Mfolozi. Apparently the crossing place was upstream of the main British force. The expedition lined the bank as the cart crossed the river. The King, lest he be jolted and pitched into the water, got out and crossed on foot. The amaQwabe he professed to despise burst into a war song, 'The Bones of the Ndwandwe'. It was a song that told of a triumph in battle, several generations past. The King was visibly shaken. There was nothing regal in his mien as he waded through the water and went up the bank and climbed into the cart. He seemed to realize at last that he was truly a captive.[28]

The Zulu King returned to Ulundi on August 31st. He had a brief, unceremonious interview with the Special High Commissioner, who announced that he had been deposed and the Zulu kingdom was at end. Four hours after he had arrived, he departed under guard for the coast and foreign exile. On September 1st the commissioner addressed another meeting of 250 chiefs and head men, and they put their marks to an agreement which ended the war. Among the spectators were men of the Natal Native Contingent. Their curiosity at the spectacle was shown by questioning looks and other signs.[29] What particularly they marvelled at has not been recorded. Perhaps they realized that the Zulu power was broken. The lingering fear of generations, that the Zulu army would descend upon their homes and eat up their people, was laid to rest. The British – and they, too, were British subjects – had triumphed.

NOTES

1 The term 'king-chase' seems to have been coined by Norris-Newman, *In Zululand with the British*, p. 239.

2 *Narrative*, pp. 98, 106–107, 111, 112, 114, 117–118. *Lord Chelmsford's Zululand Campaign*, pp. 200–203, 215. *South African Journal of Sir Garnet Wolseley*, pp. 32, 49, 53–54. Wolseley's commissions are in C2318, Appendix.

3 *Narrative*, p. 117. WO 7767: 2nd Division Diary, July 4–7, 1879. Malet, *Extracts from a Diary*, pp. 30–31. Molyneux, *Campaigning in South Africa and Egypt*, p. 191. Tomasson, *With the Irregulars*, pp. 207–208. Fairlie Diary, July 4–8, 1879. Stainbank Diary, July 15 and 16, 1879.

4 *Narrative*, pp. 118, 122–123. *South African Journal of Sir Garnet Wolseley*, pp. 54–55, 57. *Lord Chelmsford's Zululand Campaign*, pp. 217–218.

5 *Narrative*, p. 169. NC, July 26: 'Military Notes;' and July 29, 1879: 'Natal Native Horse.' NW, July 24: 'Natal Native Horse;' July 26: 'The Natal Native Horse;' and August 16, 1879: 'The Natal Native Horse.'

6 *Narrative*, p. 124. SP 41: Theophilus Shepstone, jr., to William Shepstone, July 17, 1879. Fairlie Diary, July 10–26, 1879.

7 SP 41: Theophilus Shepstone, jr., to William Shepstone, July 17, 1879. Malet, *Extracts from a Diary*, p. 33. Fairlie Diary, July 24, 1879.

8 *Narrative*, p. 125. Fairlie Diary, July 25–30, 1879; *cf. Narrative*, p. 169.

9 TN, August 6, 1879: 'The Second Division.' Also, see Newdigate's report in WO 32/7764 and NW Supplement, October 4, 1879, and his comments on Native Levies in *Précis of Information concerning Zululand with a Map prepared in the Intelligence Division of the War Office. Corrected to December, 1894* (London, Her Majesty's Stationery Office, 1895), p. 131.

10 TN, August 4: 'The Native Contingents;' and August 20, 1879: 'With Sir Garnet Wolseley.' NM, August 15, 1879: 'second Battalion N.N.C.' *Cf.* Bengough, *Memories of a Soldier's Life*, pp. 139–142, and Montague, *Campaigning in South Africa*, p. 294, which do not mention insubordination but contain anecdotes which may be related to it. Although sources do not state that the companies remained at the three forts, neither do they mention their withdrawal. TN, September 15, 1879: 'With Sir Garnet,' mentions Capt. Dellamore, the commander of the company at Fort Evelyn there as late as August 28th.

11 NW, August 21, 1879: 'The Zulu War. With Brigadier Clarke's Column.' Blood imputes (*Four Score Years and Ten*, p. 200) drunkenness and fraud to the company commander, which, of course, would have had an adverse effect on morale.

12 *Narrative*, pp. 120, 121, 124, 126–129, 153, 154. *South African Journal of Sir Garnet Wolseley*, pp. 57, 58 and 83–91 *passim*. TN, July 28, 1879: GO 14. *Paula Dlamini: Servant of Two Kings* (compiled by H. Filter and edited and translated by S. Bourquin; Pietermaritzburg, University of Natal Press, 1986), p. 70.

13 Montague, *Campaigning in South Africa*, pp. 304–306, 313–315. *War and Peace in South Africa*, pp. 45–47.

14 *Narrative*, pp. 129–130. WO 32/7779: Diary of Colonel Baker Russell's Column August 13–15, 1879. Also, see *South African Journal of Sir Garnet Wolseley*, pp. 87–89.

15 *Narrative*, p. 130. Montague, *Campaigning in South Africa*, pp. 306–309 *passim*. *War and Peace in South Africa*, p. 44. WO 32/7779: Diary of Colonel Baker Russell's Column, August 16–17, 1879. TN, September 24, 1879: 'With No. 1 Company Natal Pioneers.'

16 *Historical Records of the 91st Argyllshire Highlanders* (edited by G.L. Goff; London, Bentley, 1891), p. 289.

17 TN, September 15, 1879. 'With Sir Garnet. Return of Capt. Biggs's Expedition.' *South African Journal of Sir Garnet Wolseley*, pp. 89 and 101. *The South African Campaign*, pp. 305–323. Norris-Newman, *In Zululand with the British*, p. 241 and 'Military Map of Zulu Land.'

18 *Narrative*, pp. 128, 132–133. *South African Journal of Sir Garnet Wolseley*, pp. 78–105 *passim*. Norris-Newman, *In Zululand with the British*, p. 240. NW, September 11, 1879: 'The Capture of Cetywayo.'

19 *Narrative*, pp. 132–133. *South African Journal of Sir Garnet Wolseley*, pp. 85–89 *passim*. Norris-Newman, *In Zululand with the British*, pp. 239, 243–244. NW, August 28, 1879: 'The Cetywayo Hunt.' Also *cf. A Zulu King Speaks* (edited by C. de B. Webb and J.B. Wright; Pietermaritzburg, University of Natal Press, 1978), pp. 35–36, and *Paula Dlamini*, pp. 71–72.

20 *Narrative*, p. 133. *South African Journal of Sir Garnet Wolseley*, p. 89. Norris-Newman, *In Zululand with the British*, pp. 240 and 246.

21 *Narrative*, p. 134. *South African Journal of Sir Garnet Wolseley*, p. 93. Norris-Newman, *In Zululand with the British*, pp. 240, 244–246. TN, August 29, 1879: 'With Head Quarters at Ulundi.'

22 *South African Journal of Sir Garnet Wolseley*, p. 93.

23 *Ibid.*, pp. 92, 94, 95, 97. *Cf. Narrative*, p. 133.

24 *South African Journal of Sir Garnet Wolseley*, pp. 97–99. Norris-Newman, *In Zululand with the British*, pp. 246–247. TN, September 3, 1879: 'With Sir Garnet'. See also *Letters of Major-General FitzRoy Hart-Synnot*, p. 166.

25 *Narrative*, pp. 134–135. Norris-Newman, *In Zululand with the British*, pp. 248–251. *South African Journal of Sir Garnet Wolseley*, p. 191. *Cf.* NW, September 9, 1879: 'Capture of Cetewayo.' I have changed the word 'kraal' in the quotations to 'homestead'.

26 *South African Journal of Sir Garnet Wolseley*, p. 101.

27 NW, September 9, 1879: 'Capture of Cetewayo'. *Stuart Archive*, II, 255: statement by Mayinga kaMbekuzana. See also *Letters of Major-General FitzRoy Hart-Synnot*, pp. 166–168.

28 *Narrative*, pp. 135–136. *South African Journal of Sir Garnet Wolseley*, pp. 100–101. Norris-Newman, *In Zululand with the British*, p. 242, 251–252. TN, September 15, 1879: 'With Sir Garnet.' Ian Knight, *The National Army Museum Book of the Zulu War* (London, Sidgwick & Jackson, 2003), pp. 268–274, quoting a letter of Lieut. H.A. Amyatt-Burney. CFP 7: 'How We Captured Cetywayo. Told by Martin Oftebro and set down by Carl Faye' (an account which appeared in NW, August 27, 1927). The crossing place is conjectured.

29 *Narrative*, p. 136–138. *South African Journal of Sir Garnet Wolseley*, pp. 103–105. NW, September 11, 1879: 'The Capture of Cetywayo.'

Chapter 17

THE RETURN OF PEACE

Pacification

The war formally came to an end when the great chiefs of the Zulu kingdom agreed to British terms at Ulundi on September 1st. The Zulu monarchy was abolished. The King left the country for foreign exile on September 4th. The Special High Commissioner left Ulundi with a small force on the 4th for the Transvaal. The flying columns were assigned the task of pacifying certain areas where chiefs and people so far had avoided or refused submitting to British terms. All British forces – the flying columns and the garrisons on the lines of communication – withdrew from the Zulu country during September.[1]

Baker Russell's column, having pacified the region on the upper Black Mfolozi and not found the King in the vicinity, had been ordered to pacify the country about Zungwini and Hlobane, where the abaQulusi remained staunch supporters of the monarch. A company of British infantry, a company of Bengough's Battalion and a dozen mounted mercenaries were left to garrison Fort George on August 25th, when the column marched.

The column moved to Nseke mountain on the 26th and remained there a day, drawing in detachments. Teteleku's troops reconnoitred the White Mfolozi valley and protected a small wagon train returning to Fort Cambridge on the 27th. The column moved to near Zungwini on the 28th and to near Hlobane on the 29th. The mounted troops patrolled around the mountain. They met no enemy, but reports indicated the people still intended to fight. News that the Zulu King had been captured occasioned rejoicing in camp and local submission followed.

The column moved on. Fort George was abandoned. The next objective was a base of Swazi renegades on the Transvaal border. They had posed as supporters of the Zulu King and raided settlements near by. Their stronghold was a mountain riddled with caves. British mounted infantry and Teteleku's troops reconnoitred the position on September 4th. The British officer commanding the reconnaissance persuaded seven of the renegades to surrender, promising their lives would be spared. They were then given over to Teteleku's men for safekeeping. The officer went up the mountain to persuade other renegades to surrender. One fired at him and Teteleku's men promptly speared every one of the prisoners. For some reason Mr. Beachcroft, their European leader, was not there to stop them. The renegades on the mountain saw this and refused to parlay. The reconnoitring party returned to camp, Teteleku's men singing of victory.

Next day, the 5th, Colonel Baker Russell brought infantry and cavalry to storm the mountain. Teteleku's troops were sent behind it to cut off any retreat. The attack was not a great success. Some homesteads were burnt and livestock captured, but most of the people had fled before the attack and those who remained could not be winkled out of the caves. The column returned to the mountain on the 8th, but again had no success. But, as in Zululand, the British presence had an attritive effect and the renegade chief surrendered on September 22nd.[2]

Clarke's column left Ulundi on September 2nd. It was directed to march to St. Paul's and then return to Natal by way of the Middle Drift of the Thukela. It was to pass through a border region where Zulu chiefs remained hostile. Clarke's mission was to force their submission, to arrest Natal renegades who had been involved in the Zulu raid into the Colony, and to recover the cattle they had taken.[3]

Jantze's Horse and the Mafunzi Corps either left the column at Ulundi or accompanied it only as far as St. Paul's before being sent to the lower Thukela. Information is wanting. They were not needed any longer, and probably both units were worn out by the king chase and no longer deemed serviceable.[4]

No. 1 Pioneer Company, which had been unhappy at being detained in service in July, was even more so at being detained now. The Special High Commissioner had complimented the company for its 'workmanlike appearance' and steadiness in the march-past at the final review on September 2nd. Four days later, on the road to St. Paul's, Captain Nolan, in command of the company, reported to Colonel Clarke that his men were saying they wanted to go home at once and would not go by the road to the Middle Drift because they would have to work on it. About forty men of the company went to the Colonel's staff officer to make representations without the knowledge or consent of the company officers.

The Colonel ordered some of the British infantry to make them prisoners. He told them they could not choose their road. They must obey the orders of the commanding general. He had Captain Nolan point out the ringleaders of the mutiny. The Captain pointed to two men, who had nothing to say for themselves. The Colonel ordered twenty-five lashes each. The two were flogged on the spot. He told Captain Nolan to punish others with fines as he thought fit. There was no further insubordination.[5]

The column arrived at St. Paul's on September 7th. The death of many of the oxen from lungsickness slowed the march. It took three days to move from St. Paul's to near Eshowe, where fourteen days' supplies were received from one of the coastal depôts. The column turned west, following a track along the watershed between the Mhlathuze and Matikulu. The country was very broken and the pioneers and detachment of engineers with the column repeatedly had to be sent ahead to improve the track.

The distance to the Middle Drift of the Thukela was about thirty-six miles. The column travelled it in seven days, with only one day's halt. The Colonel made much use of Barton's 4th Battalion. Individual companies were dispatched, often with a detachment of mounted police or mercenaries, to search for firearms and renegades at various homesteads, while the British infantry and artillery remained with the wagons on the track.

Not all the chiefs and head men were prepared to turn over the renegades and royal or captured cattle, and their men were loath to part with their firearms. Consequently fines were laid upon them for their own cattle, sheep and goats. The battalion appears to have done its work well in the difficult circumstances. By the time the column crossed the Thukela on September 18th all the chiefs, more or less willingly, had submitted. Five of the companies were sent on to Greytown on the 19th. Two others remained as cattle guards. The last company was still on a patrol in Zulu country.[6] In due course the battalion returned to the coast, while the British element of the column marched to Pietermaritzburg.[7]

At the same time the flying columns were forcing the submission of Zulu diehards, the garrisons of the various forts on the lines of communication were being withdrawn to Natal. Bengough's and Nettleton's battalions each had several companies in the forts.

Disbandment

According to the British official history of the war the four battalions of the Natal Native Contingent were disbanded in September, and the three companies of pioneers in October.[8] Bengough's 2nd Battalion marched to Greytown. It arrived on the 15th or 16th of September and remained about a week, as the men had to be paid off and to turn in their rifles before being disbanded. They were a well clothed, well fed lot, and well behaved in spite of having to wait a further while before they could go home. Cherry's 1st Battalion arrived in Greytown from Kranskop on the 28th to be disbanded.[9] Barton's 4th Battalion seems to have been disbanded about the same time.[10] Nettleton's 5th Battalion was disbanded at the lower Thukela on October 1st.[11]

The last of the mounted troops were disbanded on Thursday, August 21st. Shepstone's Horse – Zikhali's Horse of old – arrived in Pietermaritzburg. They were in good spirits. The officers, whom they had left at Ladysmith in July, went out to meet them. They rode up the main street chanting war songs and handed in their rifles at Fort Napier. They were paid off at a house near by, where one of the officers was staying.[12] Jantze's Horse and the Mafunzi Corps probably came in and were discharged early in September. Teteleku's troop apparently left Baker Russell's column shortly after the attack on the renegades' mountain and probably returned to Pietermaritzburg about the middle of the month.[13]

Nettleton's battalion made up the rearguard of the withdrawing army. It bivouacked on the hills overlooking the lower Thukela before making the final crossing. Spring rain fell. The men had no tents and slept in their blankets, but each had a little trench round his bed of earth to drain off the water. The rain continued through most of the next day. Towards evening the sun appeared and began to dry things. Mqawe, the chief of the amaQadi, sent word that he was coming to address his men and others, too, who would listen. They formed a circle three or four deep and waited.

At a signal one man, a tenor, began to sing. Other men gradually joined in. It was a war song which became louder, with a chanting bass, whistling in time, and stamping of feet. Spears were raised and glinted in the last sunlight. A passage was made for the chief. He entered the circle and walked slowly round. The singing was at its loudest. He cast aside the blanket he had wrapped about him and walked round the circle once more, inspecting the men. Then he walked to the centre. He waved and the singing ceased. Silence. Not a man moved. The sun was setting. The western sky was gold and crimson and a light mist hung over the hills across the river.

Mqawe started to speak. A murmur rose from the men. He continued:

> Let there be silence … . Who am I? I am Mqawe, the son of Mahlanyan. You are my people and we are also the children of the English. See that river [pointing to the Thukela]. There my father fell. There the children of our tribe were speared by the thousands. That river ran black with their blood. They were our brothers – they are dead – killed by Cetshwayo, but we are here. We were saved by the English, in the country of the Great Queen we were saved. We built our homesteads then amongst our friends. War came; we told the government that we were their children. We have now proved it in battle, and are going home because the war is over. To-night we dance on these Zulu hills, and none can make us afraid. Where is Cetshwayo? He is not here; he is away. Go, you have done well. I have spoken.

At intervals the men had burst out with, yes, chief. Afterwards they dispersed to their places in the bivouac and the chief returned to his hut.[14]

A short time later, Commander Nettleton bade farewell to his battalion. The last order was given on October 1st.[15]

> The Commandant before dismissing the natives of the battalion to their homes today, wishes to express to them his thorough appreciation of their many good qualities, and their cheerful performance of trying and arduous duties, during the past nine months they have served under his orders in the field.
>
> Their conduct has been most creditable, and the good and efficient work done by them has been recognised and favourably noticed by both Divisional and Brigade commanding officers.
>
> The Commandant records with considerable pleasure the fact that in his Battalion numbering at times nearly twelve hundred men not a single case of dishonesty, or other serious crime has been brought before him.
>
> Whilst the loss in action of the Battalion amounts to about thirty killed and wounded the proportion of men who have been invalided, has been very serious. The Commandant expresses his sympathy with their family and friends.
>
> In saying 'good bye' to the men and wishing them a prosperous and peaceful future the Commandant marks with great satisfaction the confidence and perfect understanding that has existed between the European officers and the Native officers, N.C.O.s, and men of the Battalion.
>
> The Commandant takes this opportunity of tendering his best thanks to Mr. Jackson and Mr. Barter [Resident Magistrates] for the cordial and able assistance they have given him in organising and maintaining the efficiency of the Battalion … .

This order, though formulaic and slightly fulsome, does bespeak a genuine regard on the part of the commandant for the men of his battalion. It is not improbable that the same sentiment was shared by commanders of other battalions. The Natal Native Contingent had performed services in the field which the British units were not capable of, and for the most part they had performed these well. The war might have been more costly and had a less timely ending without them. Its course would certainly have been different. They had contributed materially to the success of the second invasion and the British victory over the Zulu.

Duty well done

The Supreme Chief was cognizant of the contribution the people of the Colony had made to victory. He had tried to ensure that the war disrupted their lives as little as possible. He had resisted the impositions of the army which he considered injurious to them, such as 'regimental' organization and largescale drafts. There had been the fear among settlers that the people would not understand where their interests lay, with the British or with the Zulu, and that they might be inspired to take the side of the latter. The war proved this fear to be groundless. The people, with the exception of a few individuals, had demonstrated their loyalty to the British Crown. The Supreme Chief expressed his gratitude in a message which was sent to the Resident Magistrates of the divisions of the colony. It was to be read to the assembled chiefs and head men who had furnished men for service in the war.

In the message the Supreme Chief announced the end of he war and the restoration of peace between the British government and the Zulu. Her Majesty's regular troops had required assistance and nearly every tribe in the Colony had been called on to supply men for service in the war. The call, with few exceptions, had been responded to well. Delays were due rather to the men who had been ordered out than to the chiefs. He was satisfied with their performance of their duty. Some of them – he especially named Homoyi, Mgcangca and Sobuza of the amaBomvu in the Umvoti Location,

Mqawe, Hlubi, Mqundane ('Jantze'), Teteleku and Ncwadi – had taken the field with their men. All had entered the Zulu country. Most of them had participated in the battles there. 'His Excellency desires to notify to them, his sense of the services rendered by them and of the good way in which they did their duty to their Queen and Country.'

This message was read out by the Resident Magistrate of the Inanda Division to eighteen chiefs and head men at Verulam on November 7th. The magistrate personally thanked them as well for their support during the war. 'They received the message with the same quiet acquiescence which they always display on these occasions.'

The chiefs pointed out that the message contained nothing about a share of the cattle captured from the Zulu King, which, they said, the Acting Secretary for Native Affairs Mr. Shepstone and the military's representative Mr. Drummond had promised to them. Their tone was neither plaintive nor pleading. It was not so much the cattle as the lack of mention of it that exercised them. The magistrate said that he would refer the matter to the Acting Secretary. He gave the chiefs and head men food and dismissed them.

The Acting Secretary for Native Affairs asked if the men or the column to which they were attached had captured any cattle from the Zulus. The magistrate replied that they had not. He had been told that they could have captured cattle but they had not been permitted to do so. After the battle of Gingindlovu they had taken a lot of the enemy's cattle, but the cattle had been released by order of the Lieutenant General.[16]

At least one chief gave vent to his dissatisfaction. Mqawe, who had served in Nettleton's battalion, professed not to understand. A settler fluent in Zulu paraphrased his grievance:[17]

> Never more will I fight for the white man. Why should I? I was called out with my people to help in the punishment of a common and dangerous enemy. Here have I, the son of Dabeju, of royal race, been lying in ditches and in mud, ripped by frost by night, drenched by rain and scorched by noon-day marches. I have stood out in the fight with my men; I have seen my favourite councillors, my relatives, my head men and my young men drop by my side shot by men whose whole life is evil. I have accepted the dispensation of the spirits, thinking I was assisting in removing the incubus of generations and felling the tree saturated with the blood of my fathers and my people's fathers, and now I find that we have been fighting for nothing, for a shadow. We are wholly losers by the campaign; the Zulus are wholly gainers. Nothing has been done to show them they are punished or conquered; not a head of cattle taken. I come, out of the fight unrequited in any sense. Well, so be it. You are not human beings, you white men, but phenomena. Your missionaries talk platitudes about a man giving his left cheek to be smitten by the men who has already hit his right. It is all very well as a platitude, but it won't do well with us black people, Zulu or no Zulu. My heart is angry, and never again will I respond to the call of your Government.

Homecoming at Edendale

Wednesday, August 13th, was a fine winter's day. The school hall of the Wesleyan mission station at Edendale was decorated and the tables were laid out for a feast. The fathers of the men who had served in the Edendale Troop thus paid respect to their brave sons. Union Jacks flew outside. In the centre of the hall was a banner inscribed 'God Save the Queen'. Evergreen branches festooned the walls. The names of the battles in which the troop had fought were spelt in gilt letters on strips of calico; also the caveat 'Natal Native Horse, not Basutos'.

Vehicles bearing guests from Pietermaritzburg began to arrive about noon. A crowd of villagers gathered to see them. There was commotion down the road. The Edendale Troop had gone out to meet the Lieutenant Governor's carriage. In their finest attire they escorted him the mile to school building. He was accompanied by the Colonial Secretary and a retired British general. The carriage arrived in front of the building at 12.30. The escort formed in line on the other side of the street. The Reverend Allsopp received the Lieutenant Governor on the steps.

The guests entered the front door and were shown their places at a large table at one end of the hall. There were over twenty-five of them, most of them important burgesses of Pietermaritzburg, some with their wives. The members of the troop and their ladies entered through the back door of the hall. The four tables in the centre of the hall were for them. At the other end of the hall was a table for the choir.

Behind the choir was a trophy consisting of three large white shields. Above it was inscribed the name 'Ulundi'. The trophy was topped by a leopard skin circlet and two large feather head-dresses taken from Zulu chiefs killed in the battle.

On every table a folded napkin pyramid held a small bouquet. The food was already set out.

The men wore velveteen jackets. Some of these were edged in white. Many had white waistcoats. They wore red sashes. Of course, their hats had the red puggaree. Their wives and sweethearts were dressed fashionably in satins. Some of them were quite striking. Amber, blue, green, maroon were the predominant colours.

The choir sang the grace, after which everyone dined. There was an abundance of food. Tea and coffee were the beverages.

The meal finished, the Reverend Allsopp, in the chair, proposed the toast, 'To the Queen'. The absence of champagne, he remarked, need not interfere with the heartiness to which it would be responded. There were three hearty cheers. The choir sang 'God Save the Queen'. The Reverend then proposed the health of the Lieutenant Governor, which was also well received.

The Lieutenant Governor rose. He replied that he regretted he was not able to speak the language. He asked the interpreter Jacobus to translate for him. He spoke very deliberately. The audience listened attentively. He said how pleased he was to be there. He expressed his appreciation of the part Edendale had played in the war, of its sacrifices and the dangers. The number which had entered service was relatively small, but their conduct had been exemplary. They had done their duty and done it well. He thanked them in the name of the Queen. He trusted that as good citizens of Natal they would display the same energy in peace as they had in war. He complimented the mission and its work. The speech received hearty applause and three loud cheers.

The Reverend Allsopp spoke. He described how the Edendale Troop had been raised. (He mentioned the Driefontain troop as well.) He did not speak of their career at war, but referred to a book, which he said had been compiled, giving their experiences. He spoke of their return and thanksgiving, and finally of this formal welcome home. They were all loyal subjects of the Queen, ready at a moment's notice for any further service required of them. The speech was followed by applause.

The Reverend Mason, general superintendent of Wesleyan Missions, welcomed the Edendale men home. The English people were glad to see them back because they had done their duty to Colony, Queen and God. The white people were watching their work; in their homes and newspapers they spoke of it with approval. He did not want to elate them but to make then humble. He grieved that some had not come back; but they had died a death full of honour and they would be remembered. He mentioned widows and children. Above all he rejoiced they had come home to resume their work. Now that there was peace, he hoped that all (white and black) would live together peacefully. The speech was followed by cheers.

The choir sang 'Who is a Noble Man?'

The next two speeches recounted the career of the Edendale Troop in the war. Sergeant Major Simeon Kambule told of the battle at Isandlwana and the escape from the battlefield. He spoke movingly of Colonel Durnford and Captain George Shepstone who had fallen there. He said that he had been so distressed at what happened at Hlobane that he had hardly been the same since, and left the rest to John Gama to describe. After applause, Gama told of Hlobane, Khambula and Ulundi, especially the latter. He had learnt a lesson then, there was no rock on earth like the Englishmen, and he felt throughout that God had been on their soul-rock and protection. More applause.

The choir sang 'Yes or No'.

Captain Shepstone was called on to say a few words. He had no connection with the Edendale Troop, but some later Edendale volunteers and the Driefontein Troop had been in Shepstone's Horse. As he rose he was cheered loudly.

He spoke deprecatingly. He could not add to anything that had been said; but there was one thing that had particularly impressed him about the Edendale men as comrades-in-arms. Every day in camp, morning and evening, whatever the weather, they had fallen in without orders for religious service. They had sung hymns, with earnestness and without ostentation. The services just before and after the battle of Ulundi had been most impressive. British soldiers had stood by, listening in admiration to the hymns and indeed to the sermon, though they did not understand the language. He knew what had been said. The sermons were the most eloquent he had ever heard. They had behaved well in the campaign and he heartily thanked them for it.

One of the burgesses, Mr Topham, welcomed the troop back on behalf of the colonists. He presented it with a silken flag, the best England could produce, inscribed with the names of the battles in which the troop had fought. He would consider it a great honour if they would accept it from him as a fellow citizen.

Cheers.

The Reverend Allsopp had a basket passed around the tables. The donations, he said, would partly pay off mission debts and help erect some memorial for those who had fallen. This took some time. He asked the guests, who were not approached, to be patient. Another missionary said a few words about the work of the mission. The money was turned over to the Reverend Allsopp.

The final speech was given by the Colonial Secretary. On behalf of the guests, he thanked the Reverend Allsopp and the men of Edendale for a very pleasant day and the privilege of attending. He said that at the outbreak of the war very many colonists had doubted that the natives could be trusted and had felt that the white man had better do the work. Events showed that the natives could be trusted in every way. The way in which they, especially the Edendale men, had acquitted themselves demanded the highest respect. It 'entitled them to be looked upon by us as brave and honourable men, and to be considered in every way, as they were at heart, Englishmen.'

The Edendale men who knew English applauded. Many others joined in.

The Colonial Secretary referred to the personal accounts of the war just given. From them he drew out three qualities which characterized the troop: a manly and honest respect for their late commanders, a sense of discipline, and a self--effacing modesty. He spoke of Colonel Durnford and of George Shepstone. He spoke of Sir Theophilus Shepstone and the Colony's debt to him. He turned to the interpreter Jacobus, evidently to make sure of the message – what the Edendale men had done would be known not only to the colonists and to the Lieutenant Governor but also across the water by the Queen of England.

There were cheers.

The long peace had not, as feared, destroyed their warlike qualities. Rather, they showed that men who cultivate the arts of peace fight best for their country. He trusted they would pursue peaceful employments; but they and their children would not forget how they and the white subjects of the Queen had fought side-by-side at Isandlwana, Khambula and Ulundi.

The speech was followed by cheers.

There were one or two more short speeches. The Reverend Allsopp thanked the Lieutenant Governor and the other guests for attending. A handkerchief containing some money was given to the Reverend, so that he might purchase something in memory of the Edendale men 'to hand down to his children'.

The choir sang the last grace, and the company parted. The troop escorted the Lieutenant Governor and his party the mile towards Pietermaritzburg, and as they took leave of him they gave three cheers.[18]

Envoi

The war between the British and the Zulu was at an end. The Zulu kingdom was destroyed. The British established thirteen chiefdoms in place of it. The British did not wish to interfere further. The chiefs would squabble, of course, but presumably they would keep some kind of balance of power. A rough peace and stability would be preserved in the region. In time the Zulu successor chiefdoms might even develop a harmonious relationship under a British Resident and become a British protectorate. Zululand would thus resemble Natal.

For the chiefs and people of the Colony the Great Queen had vindicated herself against the ultimate enemy. They had loyally supported her in crisis and victory, and she had conquered. The Natal Native Contingent was the greatest manifestation of their loyal support. The chiefs had sent about eight thousand men to serve in the imperial forces. These men were the eyes and ears of the British army in the field. They served as scouts and skirmishers, stalkers and harriers. The British would have been hard pressed to supply units for these duties from elsewhere. Probably they could not have done so in sufficient numbers, and what men they got would have lacked knowledge of local conditions. The Native Contingent was indispensable to British victory.

It was indispensable. It also worked well, but it did not work well in every way. The contest between the military authority for 'regimental' organization and the civil authority for 'traditional' organization did not resolve the question which form of organization was superior.

It is unfair to criticize severely the regimental organization imposed on the levies at the outset of the war. There was not time enough to accustom them to and train them in the European techniques. The military authority insisted on retaining regimental organization after the Isandlwana disaster. The civil authority had to make some concession to modern warfare. Chiefs and men alike wanted firearms, whatever they thought about organization. In time the remaining battalions of the contingent became accustomed to the new organization, which was simplified in their favour, and were trained sufficiently to do what was expected of them. Probably they achieved maximum efficiency at the time of the second invasion. Morale generally was good. The men all had firearms, even if most of them did not know how to use them properly. They were still skittish under fire, and British commanders were reluctant to put them in line for battle. The maximum efficiency achieved in May and June was still not enough to make the contingent entirely self-reliant.

There are two major reasons why the Natal Native Contingent was not a better fighting organization, in spite of the regimental organization. First, the chiefs, head men, and men, while understanding what was desired by British officers, still did not understand why British officers desired it. The European way of war remained a mystery to them, and in dangerous and doubtful situations they lapsed naturally into the African way. After sufficient training this should not have happened. Probably it could not be prevented, for the second reason. That was the lack of sufficient British officers and non-commissioned officers to instill and to enforce the order and discipline required for the regimental organization. The European non-commissioned officers were a failure and after learning it the military got rid of them quickly. The European officers were better stuff, but few of them had professional military training, and after expiry of their six months' term, many of them left. The result was that, regimental organization notwithstanding, actual command fell increasingly to head men and other men of status in their communities. The civil authority would argue that this was right. Right or wrong, leaders who did not understand the regimental organization readily and were not sympathetic to it were increasingly responsible for making it work. Thus the purpose of the military's reform was correspondingly stultified.

The experience of the mounted troops was quite different. By their very nature they were an elite group. There was no traditional alternative to European mounted warfare. Yet the mounted troops, few in number and in small units, did not fit into the regimental organization. They were *sui generis*. Not surprisingly, in later South African conflicts, the government would use them again, when it would not consider using foot levies.

But even horsemen had their faults. In the heat of battle or of a pursuit they sometimes did not obey orders, although it must be noted that their failure in this respect exposed them to greater not lesser danger. They also remained rather poor and profligate marksmen.

Finally, there was never a question about the *personal* bravery of the men. Panics occurred, but this was the mob taking hold. Europeans panicked, too, on occasion. Fear and nervousness affect all soldiers who are new to battle. Some British observers disparaged the appearance of fear and nervousness among the levies, as though Africans should emulate them in their own nonchalance. Yet in hand-to-hand combat and firing at close quarters, the men of the contingent showed they were as ready to fight and die as their fellow colonists. We have glimpses of encounters in the flight from Isandlwana. We shall never know how many went down locked in combat on the battlefield itself, but the dead of the contingent lay with the rest and suggest no different fate. The coolness under fire of the horsemen at Isandlwana, at Khambula, and at Ulundi is remarkable. Equally praiseworthy is the perseverance of those contending against adversity and ambush in the Mfolozi bush. In the circumstances the veterans of the war could take pride in the discharge of their duty.

NOTES

1 *Narrative*, pp. 136–138. South African Journal of Sir Garnet Wolseley, pp. 95, 104–106. WO 32/7782: Diary and journal of Colonel Baker Russell's Column, August 25 – September 7, 1879. WO 32/7783: Journal of Clarke's Column, September 1–21, 1879. The Zulu country was divided into thirteen districts, each with its own ruler. A British Resident was appointed. The actual agreement provided for recognition of the British victory and Her Majesty's right to deal with the Zulu chiefs and people and country as she saw fit. Its terms required acceptance of the territorial division, prohibition of the traditional military system, freedom of men to marry as and when they chose, nonimportation of firearms and ammunition and confiscation of munitions found, imposition of the death penalty only after a proper trial, surrender of fugitives from British territory on demand, abstinence from war and referral of disputes to British arbitration, succession to chieftaincy according to tradition and with British approval, inalienability of land, subjection of the inhabitants of a territory to its chief, referral to the British Resident of cases involving British subjects, and government according to traditional law and custom.

2 *Narrative*, pp. 130–131. WO 32/7782: Diary of Colonel Baker Russell's Column, August 25 – September 7, 1879. Laband and Thompson, *Kingdom and Colony at War*, pp. 205–207.

3 WP 32/7785: Journal of Clarke's Column, September 1–21, 1879.

4 The last mention of these units found in the sources seems to be August 25th. It refers to the 'parties' of Captains Hay and Nourse, the unit commanders (Norris-Newman, *In Zululand with the British*, p. 246). These officers are mentioned as returning with Lord Gifford to Ulundi on the 29th, but whether they were with their units during the interval or not is questionable, for Gifford considered his force insufficient to attempt the capture of the Zulu king on the 29th (TN, September 15, 1879: 'With Sir Garnet'). WO 32/7785: Journal of Clarke's Column, September 1–21,

1879, lists the units in the column on September 2nd, and Jantze's and the Mafunzi are not included. An account of Clarke's column from the 2nd to the 7th (TN, September 15, 1879: 'The Return from Ulundi') states that the Natal Horse left the column at St. Paul's on the 7th to proceed to Ft. Pearson. The Journal of Clarke's Column makes clear this 'Natal Horse' was not Lonsdale's Horse (a mercenary unit), so the account may be referring to Natal Native Horse. There is a brief mention of an unnamed 'regiment' of the mounted contingent arriving in Pietermaritzburg on the Greytown road on August 23rd (TN, August 29, 1879: report). Possibly this unit was the Amabomvu or Amangwane Corps or both returning from Zululand, although it would seem rather late after the disbandment of the 2nd Division. (Another possibility is that the unit was Lugaju's troop of amaXamalala, from the Umgeni Division, which had been ordered to join Major Barrow at the coast on May 7th (NW, May 8, 1879: GO -); however, it is not among the units listed in *Narrative*, pp. 168–169, and evidently it did not join Barrow and nothing more appears in the sources about its assignment.)

5 WO 32/7785: Journal of Clarke's Column, September 6, 1879. *Cf.* TN, September 24, 1879: 'With No. 1 Company Natal Pioneers' and Clarke's comment on Native Levies in Précis of Information concerning Zululand, p. 131.

6 WO 32/7785: Journal of Clarke's Column, September 7–21, 1879. TN, September 24, 1879: 'With No. 1 Company Natal Pioneers.' See and cf. *Letters of Major-General FitzRoy Hart-Synnot*, pp. 171–174.

7 The 4th Battalion certainly was not with the column when it reached Pietermaritzburg. See TN, October 3, 1879: 'Arrival of Clarke's Column;' and NW, October 3. 'Return of Clarke's Column;' and October 4, 1879: 'Greytown.'

8 *Narrative*, pp. 169–170. NW, October 7, 1879: 'Native Contingent.'

9 NW, September 30: 'Greytown,' with which *cf.* SNA 1/6/16, no. 77 and TN, October 8, 1879: report. Bengough's imminent return to England is mentioned in TN, October 3, and NW, October 4, 1870. He himself describes (*Memories of a Soldier's Life*, pp. 139–140) the difficulty with which he parted from the Bomvu chief, Homoyi; however, he may be confusing this with Homoyi's earlier insubordination.

10 NW, October 16, 1879: report, which also states that Barton would proceed to England.

11 1/VLM, 3/2/1: 854I/1879.

12 Fairlie Diary, August 21, 1879. TN, August 22, 1879: 'Military Notes.'

13 No mention is made of the unit in the reports from Russell's column on September 8th and 25th in TN, September 19 and 22 and October 3, 1879, nor in one on the mercenaries' disbandment, in TN, October 13, 1879.

14 NC, November 22, 1879: 'Sketches from Nature. No. 11.' I have substituted 'homestead' for 'kraal' and modernized the spelling of 'Umqawe', 'Tugela', and 'Ketshwayo' in the quotation.

15 1/VLM, 3/2/1: 854I/1879.

16 SNA 1/1/35, no. 149.

17 NW, October 2, 1879: 'Zululand. Extraordinary statement by Umqawe'.

18 The account here represents a conflation of two accounts – NW, August 16, 1879: 'The Natal Native Horse. Festivities at Edendale,' and TN, August 15, 1879: 'Welcome to the Edendale Men.' There are shorter accounts in NM, August 16, and NA, August 19, 1879, as well as several newspaper leaders and some correspondence which add nothing further to the account.

THE AMBIGUOUS MEMORIAL

In the village of Georgetown, at the heart of Edendale, there is an obelisk. It is about twelve feet high and at the base a sixth the distance across. It stands in the Methodist church yard, eight paces off the front right corner of the hall, and overlooks Scott Street. It is made of sandstone, but it has weathered well because the vertical surfaces have shed the rain and trees and the hall have provided some shade against the sun.

On the west face the plinth is inscribed –

Isandhlwana

–

In memoriam
Ezra Tyingila
Klass Sopela
Killed in action
January 22nd 1879

On the south face, overlooking the street, it is inscribed –

Ulundi

–

Johannes Mgadi
Killed in action
July 4th 1879

There is no inscription on the north face.
The inscription on the east face is very short –

For
Queen
and
Country

For different people the memorial has different meanings. Some people would have it destroyed, as a reminder of the colonial past they despise. Others would have it preserved, out of respect for those it commemorates and the good faith with which they served. Some would have it preserved but removed to another place.

BIBLIOGRAPHICAL ESSAY

Introduction

The Natal Native Contingent is the most elusive of imperial units in terms of source material. The career of the British regulars in the Anglo-Zulu war of 1879 is well documented and published, that of the colonials adequately so. Only the African soldiers of the Queen have been slighted. Neglect owes partly to the customary portrayal of the war as a conflict between European and African, between black and white, in which Her Majesty's African forces, most notably the Natal Native Contingent, do not fit conveniently and therefore are more easily left out. Otherwise it owes to a dispersion of information, which this essay describes.

Official documents

The records of the War Office (cited by the prefix WO in the notes) concerning the Anglo-Zulu war are housed in the Public Records Office at Kew. The diaries, reports and returns of the imperial forces are concentrated in the records groups 32 and 33/34. These are invaluable, as the notes indicate; but they contain very little on the Natal Native Contingent *per se*. It is remarkable that no corpus of material seems to have survived, if, indeed, it ever existed, for what in fact was the largest imperial unit in the war.

The War Office records are concerned with military affairs. The various records in the Natal Archives Depôt, at Pietermaritzburg, which pertain to the contingent, are not concerned with military affairs but rather with the organization and mobilization of levies. Most useful are the records of the Secretary for Native Affairs (SNA), especially files 1/6/11 through 1/6/15, entitled 'Papers re War of 1879 and the calling out of the Natives'.

Intimately connected with the correspondence in this records group is that found in the records of the various magistracies, notably those of the Inanda (VLM), Umgeni (PMB), Umvoti (GTN), Upper Umkomanzi (RMD), Upper Tugela (BGV), and Weenen (Weenen-Add) divisions. Taken altogether, the correspondence and reports in these record groups reveal and filter the problems of the chiefs and head men and people involved in the war sympathetically, if not always with great understanding.

Important for matters of policy and assignment are the records of the offices of the Governor (GH) and the Colonial Secretary (CSO), also in the Natal Archives Depôt. The differences between the Supreme Chief and the Lieutenant General are clearly delineated in the records of the former. The records of the Colonial Secretary contain relatively more on officers and units, and frequently overlap matters of concern in the SNA.

Among the printed documents there is a wealth of information, but it is largely in bits and pieces. The British parliamentary papers, published contemporaneously at intervals by Her Majesty's Stationery Office at short intervals, contain much that is found in the unpublished records described and sometimes more. They are cited by their Command (C) numbers. The most important single official document is the *Narrative of the Field Operations connected with the Zulu War* (London, Her Majesty's Stationery Office, 1881), compiled by the Intelligence Branch of the Quartermaster-General's Department, the Horse Guards, War Office. This is an expanded diary of events, divided into chapters according to larger units and sectors and logical intervals. It is essential first-reading for a grasp of war. Later information, including that acquired in the war, is in the *Précis of Information concerning Zululand With a Map ... Corrected to December, 1894* (London, HMSO, 1895), also prepared by the Intelligence Division of the War Office.

There is no corresponding publication of documents on the colonial side; however, there are several reports which focus on the people of the Colony just after the war and which contain useful insights into their response to it. These are the *Report of the Natal Native Commission*, 1881–2; *Evidence taken before the Natal Native Commission, 1881;* and *Evidence taken by the Sub-Commission for Umvoti County* (Pietermaritzburg, Vause, Slatter, 1882). There is also the *Blue Book of Native Affairs*, published by order of the Legislative Council in 1884. *The Blue Book for the Colony of Natal*, published annually (and for 1879, also by Vause, Slatter), contains information and statistics primarily descriptive of the settlers' transformation of the country. *The Natal Government Gazette* (NGG), the official periodical, gives some information on the war-time period, notably on casualties.

Newspapers

Among non-official sources a great amount of information appears in the contemporary colonial newspapers – the *Natal Mercury* (NM) in Durban and the *Natal Witness* (NW) and *Times of Natal* (TN) in Pietermaritzburg, and to a lesser extent, the *Natal Advertizer* (NA) and *Natal Colonist* (NC), in Durban. The *Mercury, Witness* and *Advertizer* also carried lengthy articles, chiefly reminiscences of the war, to mark the fiftieth anniversary of the outbreak of the war and battle of Isandlwana, in January 1929. Useful compilations of the British press are *The First Six Months of the Zulu War of 1879 as reported in "The Graphic"* and *The Concluding stages of the Zulu War as reported in "The Graphic"* (compiled by S. Bourquin; Durban, the compiler, 1963 and 1965, respectively); and *The Zulu War as reported in "The Illustrated London News" during January-December 1879* (compiled by S. Bourquin and Tania M. Johnston; Durban, the compilers, 1971).

Contemporary accounts

There are several very good accounts by British participants written shortly after the war and obviously based on diaries. Incidentally they provide histories of their authors' military units. They are W.E. Montague, *Campaigning in South Africa: Reminiscences of an Officer in 1879 (London, Blackwood, 1990);* W.H. Tomasson, *With the Irregulars in the Transvaal and Zululand* (London, Remington, 1881); T. St. Lo. Malet, *Extracts from a Diary in Zululand* (Upper Norwood, Platt & Burdett, 1880); Edward D. McToy, *A Brief History of the 13th Regiment (P.A.L.I.) in South Africa during the Transvaal and Zulu Difficulties, 1877–8–9* (Devonport, Swiss, 1880); and H.F. Norbury, *The Naval Brigade in South Africa during the Years 1877–78–79* (London, Sampson Low, Marston, Searle & Rivington, 1880). There is much about the contingent and the operations in which it was involved in these works, although the information is often anecdotal.

There are several histories of the war which are of similar value. The best is Charles L. Norris-Newman, *In Zululand with the British throughout the War of 1879* (London, Allen, 1880), a revision of reports by a newspaperman 'on the spot'. It is a good companion to the official narrative. It does not pretend to be a comprehensive or balanced account of the war, as does W. Ashe and E.V. Wyatt Edgell, *The Story of the Zulu Campaign* (London, Sampson Low, Marston, Searle & Rivington, 1880), a second-hand account based upon and generously quoting first-hand contributions, some of them questionable. H.H. Parr, *A Sketch of the Kafir and Zulu Wars. Guadane to Isandhlwana* (London, Kegan Paul, 1880), a sound work by a staff officer, unfortunately is cut short. *The South African Campaign, 1879* (compiled by J.P. Mackinnon and Sydney Shadbolt; London, Hayward, 1882) is a panegyric first and compendium second; it provides information on all the British officers and units in the war. Thus it is valuable on officers seconded to the contingent. Unfortunately its histories of units do not extend beyond the regular army establishment; *ad hoc* units such as the contingent are not described.

Another history, interesting for a colonial perspective and degree of sympathy with the Zulu, is Frances E. Colenso, *History of the Zulu War and its Origin* (London, Chapman & Hall, 1880), which draws on both the published parliamentary papers and private sources. In the same vein are two works focusing on Anthony Durnford, who may be considered the father of the contingent and with whom Frances Colenso was well if not intimately acquainted. *A Soldier's Life and Work in South Africa 1872–1879. A Memoir of the Late Col. A.W. Durnford, R.E.* (edited by E. Durnford; London, Sampson Low, Marston, Searle & Rivington, 1882) and Edward Durnford, *Isandhlwana, 22nd January, 1879. A Narrative* (London, King, 1879) both contain valuable information, the former especially on the contingent. A useful composite account by Julian Whybra is 'The Cochrane Accounts of Isandlwana,' in *The Journal of the Anglo-Zulu Historical Society*, XIII (June 2003).

Three clerics have left accounts which afford glimpses of the contingent – W. Clifford Holden, *British Rule in South Africa* (London, Wesleyan Conference Office, 1879); Thomas B. Jenkinson, *Amazulu. The Zulus, Their Past History, Manners, Customs and Language* (London, Allen, 1882); and the unique *Defence of Rorke's Drift. January 22, 1879. By an Eyewitness* (Durban, Natal Mercury [1879]). Two British travellers also provide glimpses – F. Francis, *War, Waves and Wanderings* (London, Sampson Low, Marston, Searle & Rivington, 1881) and Bertram Mitford, *Through the Zulu Country* (London, Kegan Paul, Trench, 1883), the latter recording some accounts of participants in the war. Alone in its field is D. Blair Brown, *Surgical Experiences in the Zulu and Transvaal Wars* (London, Simpkin, Marshall, 1883), which gives a very close look at several members of the contingent.

Published diaries and letters

For the 2nd Regiment the *Letters of Major-General FitzRoy Hart-Synnot* (edited by B.M. Hart-Synnot; London, Arnold, 1912) is invaluable. An account of the war constructed on extracts from the letters of participants is Frank Emery, *The Red Soldier: Letters from the Zulu War* (London, Hodder & Soughton, 1977), to which may be added his 'At War with the Zulus 1879. The letters of Lieutenant C.E. Commeline RE,' in *The Royal Engineers Journal*, XCVI, No. 1 (March 1982), pp. 33–39. Useful collections are Sonia Clarke, *Zululand at War 1879. The conduct of the Anglo-Zulu War* (Houghton, Brenthurst, 1984), containing letters from the field to the deputy quartermaster-general for intelligence, and *War and Peace in South Africa 1879–1881: The writings of Philip Anstruther and Edward Essex* (edited by Paul H. Butterfield; Melville, Strydom [1986]). Observations of the contingent are sparse and chiefly incidental in these. On the other hand, *The Fannin Papers. A Pioneer's Story of the Diamond Fields and the Zulu War* (edited by Natalie Fannin; Durban, Robinson, 1932) contains much information on the battalions stationed at Fort Cherry.

In a category by themselves in terms of perspective and richness of detail are *The South African Journal of Sir Garnet Wolseley 1879–1880* (edited by Adrian Preston; Cape Town, Balkema, 1973) and *Campaigns: Zulu 1879, Egypt 1882, Suakim 1885. Being the Private Journal of Guy C. Dawnay* (privately published in 1886 and reprinted in 1989 by K. Trotman). Straddling the line between official and private documents are Gerald French, *Lord Chelmsford and the Zulu War* (London, Lane, 1939), which is part narrative, part documentary, and withal an apologia; and *Lord Chelmsford's Zululand Campaign 1878–1879* (edited by John P.C. Laband; Stroud, Army Records Service, 1994), essentially a collection of documents, official and private, far superior to the earlier work. The Natal Native Contingent is mentioned frequently, but usually in passing, in these.

Memoirs and reminiscences

There are several accounts of the war written much later by European members of the Native Contingent. Pride of place belongs to H.M. Bengough, *Memories of a Soldier's Life* (London, Arnold, 1913). The commander of the 2nd Battalion tells much that is of interest and important, but not always accurately or precisely; and there is much that he does not tell. G. Hamilton-Browne, *A Lost Legionary in South Africa* (London, Laurie [192?] is very much a racy account, a mixture of verifiable fact and imaginative embellish- ment. Since the 3rd Regiment was disbanded just after Isandlwana, Browne has nothing to say about the contingent beyond that time. There are two other accounts from the 3rd Regiment. *The Zulu War Journal of Colonel Henry Harford CB* (edited by Daphne Child; Pietermaritzburg, Shuter & Shooter, 1978) is more memoir than journal, since the original appears to have been glossed heavily with information from other sources, notably Norris-Newman. John Maxwell, *My Reminiscences of the Zulu War* (edited by Leonie Twentyman Jones; Cape Town, University of Cape Town Libraries, 1979) is an unpretentious but careful work. *Henderson Heritage* (compiled by Peter Hathorn and Amy Young; Pietermaritzburg, the authors, 1972) includes a few short letters from A.F. Henderson, the officer attached to Hlubi's mounted troop. A.N. Montgomery, 'Isandhlwana: A Visit Six Months after the Battle,' in *Leisure Hour Magazine*, XL (1892), pp. 536–540, contains a few remarks on the 1st Battalion at Kranskop.

There is useful information on the contingent at Isandlwana in H. Smith-Dorrien, *Memoirs of Forty-eight Years Service* (London, Murray, 1925) and at Gingindlovu and Ulundi in W.C.F. Molyneux, *Campaigning in South African and Egypt* (London, Macmillan, 1896). Disappointingly little is found in the *Memoirs of Field Marshall Lord Grenfell* (London, Hodder & Stoughton, 1925) and *Four Score Years and Ten: Sir Bindon Blood's Reminiscences* (London, Bell, 1933). *Eyewitness in Zululand: The Campaign Reminiscences of Colonel W.A. Dunne, CB [:] South Africa, 1877–1881* (edited by Ian H.W. Bennett; London, Greenhill, 1989) has little on the contingent at Rorke's Drift.

Bits of information are found in several articles. H.F. Fynn, 'My Recollections of a Famous Campaign and a Great Disaster,' appeared in the *Natal Witness*, January 25, 1913. (There is also a typescript in the Killie Campbell Africana Library). It seems to have had much influence on secondary literature, perhaps because of its timing as well as content. More pedestrian are Charles E. Fripp, 'Reminiscences of the Zulu War,' in *Pall Mall Magazine*, XX (1920), pp. 547–562; Edward Hutton, 'Some Recollections of the Zulu War, 1879,' in *The Army Quarterly*, XVI, April 16, 1928, pp. 65–80; and H.L. Hall, 'With Assegai and Rifle: Reminiscences of a Transport Conductor in the Zulu War,' in *Military Historical Journal*, IV, No. 5 (June 1979), pp. 196–200.

There are some unique works in this category. Most notable is *The Silver Wreath: being the 24th Regiment at Isandhlwana and Rorke's Drift, 1879* (edited by Norman Holme; London, Samson, 1979), which would seem to exhaust the subject so far as the regiment is concerned. It contains much incidental information on the contingent. *A Zulu King Speaks* (edited by C. de B. Webb and J.B. Wright; Pietermaritzburg, University of Natal Press, 1978) occasionally adds an interesting dimension to operations in which the contingent was involved. Also of interest in this respect is *Paula Dlamini: Servant of two Kings* (compiled by H. Filter and edited and translated by S. Bourquin), with a brief account of the King's efforts to dodge pursuers in the Mfolozi bush. At the other end of the social scale is George H. Swinney, 'A Zulu Boy's Recollections of the Zulu War,' in *Natalia*, No. 8 (December 1978), pp. 6–21, with an anecdote on Gabangaye and Sikhota at Isandlwana.

The most vivid account of the battle and flight from Isandlwana, is J.A. Brickhill, 'Survivor's Account,' in *Later Annals of Natal* (compiled by A.F. Hattersley; London, Longmans, 1928), pp. 150–159, and 'How I Escaped from the Fatal Field of Isandhlwana,' in *African Notes and News*, XXIX, No. 2 (June 1990), pp. 74–82. The account originally appeared in 1879 and was revised several times. It contains several observations on the placement and conduct of the contingent. *The Natal Carbineers: The History of the Regiment from its Foundation* (edited by J. Stalker; Pietermaritzburg, Davis, 1912) also contains a similarly useful account of Isandlwana by Trooper W.W. Barker.

Private Manuscripts

The variety and extent of unofficial collections is enormous. Invaluable are the Chelmsford papers, (CP) held in the National Army Museum, of which there is a microfilm in the Natal Archives Depôt; and the Diary of W.H. Fairlie, who served with Shepstone's Horse, which is also held in the National Army Museum. Also very useful are the diaries of D. Stainbank and R.W. Vause, the typescript J.P. Symons, My Reminiscences of the Zulu War, and a letter by R.J. Hall on Rorke's Drift, all in the Killie Campbell Africana Library, in Durban; and the letters of J.E. Fannin, in the Natal Archives Depôt, in Pietermaritzburg. W.H. Stafford's 'Stirring Days of Old Times. A story of Isandhlwana' is in the Killie Campbell library, and his 'Personal History' and 'Statement' on the battle are in the National Army Museum. The Bedfordshire County Record Office has 'The Story of what Col[.] Durnford, with his troops of Mounted Natives did at Isandlwana, told by Jabez [Molife], a Basuto,' a handwritten, apparently early version of the well-known document.

The Colenso, Carl Faye (CFP), Shepstone (SP) and Evelyn Wood (WC) papers in the Natal Archives Depôt have yielded a few items; and some information has been gleaned from the letters of Charles Commeline, a memorandum of H.C. Lugg on the battle of Rorke's Drift, and the microfilm Wesleyan Mission records, also held there. The Evelyn Wood papers at the Killie Campbell Library have some helpful maps of Isandlwana.

There are a few letters from R.C. Birkett, an officer of the 2nd Battalion, in the National Army Museum. Some letters of H.T. Curling, referring to Isandlwana, are in the possession of A.J. Lucking (AJLC) of London. The Diary of E.S. Newmarch, which refers to affairs in Umvoti County, is also privately held, but the Greytown museum has a copy.

Unit histories

The Edendale Horse receives unique attention in F. Reginald Statham, *Blacks, Boers & British: A Three-Cornered Problem* (London, Macmillan, 1981) and Owen Watkins, 'They Fought for the Great White Queen,' reprinted from the *Methodist Recorder* in *The Zulu War and the Colony of Natal* (edited by G.A. Chadwick and E.G. Hobson; Mandini, Qualitas, 1879).

McToy's history of the 13th Regiment and Norbury's of the Naval Brigade have been mentioned. There are four histories of the 24th Regiment which have been useful – *The Silver Wreath*, also mentioned earlier; Philip Gon, *The Road to Isandlwana: The Years of an Imperial Battalion* (Johannesburg, Donker, 1979), which focuses on the South African experience; *Historical Records of the 24th Regiment* (edited by George Paton, Farquhar Glennie, and William Penn Symons; London, Simpkin, Marshall, Hamilton, Kent, 1892); and C.T. Atkinson, *The South Wales Borders 24th Foot 1689– 1937* (Cambridge, University Press, 1937), both of which are full histories of the regiment. They are important in shedding light on the shared experience of Sandlwana and Rorke's Drift. The 1892 history is particularly important, because the author Symons is said to have used information personally obtained from survivors of the battles.

Recent histories of the war

There has been a renascence of literature on the Anglo-Zulu War since the centenary. Some works produced in this period have already been mentioned. The object here is not to describe all the works or even all the major works of this renascence, but rather to cite those which contain generally reliable information on the Natal Native Contingent.

Three works deserve special attention because they focus on the contingent. S. Bourquin, 'The N.N.C. and Associated Units during the Zulu War of 1879,' in *The Zulu War and the Colony of Natal* (1979, cited earlier), is the only attempt before this time to deal discretely with the contingent. It makes good use of some printed sources in an abbreviated manner. R.W.F. Drooglever, *The Road to Isandhlwana: Colonel Anthony Durnford in Natal and Zululand 1873–1879* (London, Greenhill, 1992) deals perforce with the contingent, but is better on Durnford than his command. Its analysis of Isandlwana is also somewhat idiosyncratic. Ingrid Machin, *Antbears and Targets for Zulu Assegais: The Levying of Forced African Labour and Military Service by the Colonial State of Natal* (Howick, Brevitas, 2002), based on a much earlier thesis, has two chapters on the contingent in the war. Several recent works on Isandlwana are notable for their attention to the contingent. Ian Knight, *Zulu: Isandlwana and Rorke's Drift 22nd – 23rd January 1879* (London, Windrow & Greene, 1992) is extensive and exhaustive of printed sources. It was the first to give sufficient attention to the contingent, although it contains a few errors. Ron Lock and Peter Quantrell, *Zulu Victory: The Epic of Isandlwana* and the Cover-Up (London, Greenhill, 2002) gives even more attention to the contingent, and especially to Durnford. F.W.D. Jackson, *Hill of the Sphinx: The Battle of Isandlwana* (London, Westerners, 2002) comprises a series of articles published in 1965 and issued as a booklet in 1999. It has much on the contingent, but it is also idiosyncratic and now much dated. All of these books on Isandlwana differ on their emphasis on the role of the contingent in the battle and no two agree in their placement of its units in the battle line.

John Laband, *The Battle of Ulundi* (Pietermaritzburg, Shuter & Shooter, 1988) is the best secondary work on the battle. The same may be said of Ian Castle and Ian Knight, *Fearful Hard Times: The Siege and Relief of Eshowe 1879* (London, Greenhill, 1994) for the operations covered. John Laband and Paul Thompson have written several books on the war: the utilitarian *Field Guide to the War in Zululand and the Defence of Natal 1879* (2nd revised edition; Pietermaritzburg, University of Natal Press, 1983); the border histories *War Comes to Umvoti: The Natal-Zululand Border 1878–1879*, and, with Sheila Henderson, *The Buffalo Border: The Anglo-Zulu War in Northern Natal* (both Durban, University of Natal Department of History, 1980 and 1983, respectively); and *Kingdom and Colony at War: Sixteen Studies on the Anglo-Zulu War 1879* (Pietermaritzburg, University of Natal Press, 1990). The last three give a great deal of attention to the Natal Native Contingent. John Laband has also written the only scholarly analysis of the Zulu polity during the war, *Kingdom in crisis: the Zulu response to the British invasion of 1879* (Manchester, University Press, 1992), to which there are some additions in his *Rope of Sand: The Rise and Fall of the Zulu Kingdom in the Nineteenth Century* (Johannesburg, Jonathan Ball, 1995).